THE ALL-AMERICAN BOYS

AN INSIDER'S LOOK AT THE U. S. SPACE PROGRAM

WALTER CUNNINGHAM

ipicturebooks

1230 Park Avenue
New York, New York 10128
Tel: 212-427-7139
bricktower@aol.com • www.BrickTowerPress.com

Library of Congress Cataloging-in-Publication Data

Cunningham, Walter
The All-American Boys, An Insider's Look at the U.S. Space Program

ISBN13: 978-1-87696-324-8
Library of Congress Control Number 2009922705
Non Fiction, Adult/General

Copyright © 2009 Walter Cunningham
Second Edition, July 2010
10 9 8 7 6 5 4 3 2 1

Contents

Preface

SOMEONE ONCE SAID, "It is better to have written a book than to be writing one,"—a statement I wholeheartedly endorse. It refers, of course, to the great amount of work involved. Having written this book once, why would I subject myself to the ordeal of updating it? That is a good question and there are a number of answers. The "space race" has evolved into international cooperation. Astronauts have also changed. They encompass a wide variety of technical disciplines and their number has increased ten-fold. They also come in all colors, many nationalities and both sexes. NASA has changed from an entrepreneurial into a bureaucratic organization with less vision, lowered goals and less willingness to knowingly accept risk. The public also seems less interested in taking risks, pushing back boundaries and embracing exploration as an inherent part of the human spirit. Finally, I am older, wiser and have gained a better perspective on both past and present.
All of these things cry out for informed comment.

Writing a book makes those being written about nervous. Before The All-American Boys was first published, some of those with whom I had shared experiences were legitimately concerned. I was known (and sometimes criticized) for "telling it like it is." They expected what I wrote to be the truth, or, at least, the truth as I saw it. Astronaut books are now old hat and I am now writing from the perspective of an informed outside observer. My observations are still as candid but there has been much less personal interaction between myself and the people and events about which I write.

In the Sixties, NASA was able to fashion its own image, but the myth of the super-hero astronaut was strictly a creation of the news media. Most of us found it flattering and easy to go along with. Some even cultivated that image, but few could measure up to it. Most of us recognized it was unliveable only slightly before we realized we were stuck with it for the rest of our lives. We were trapped in that image until the public took off its rose-colored glasses and began to see us as people. In this book, I have attempted to strip away the veneer and tell how America's most famous heroes were made; and why and what happens to them. We weren't all simon-pure nor were we all hell-raisers. Some of history's greatest deeds were accomplished, and a remarkable adventure fulfilled, by men who were all too human in their weak¬nesses as well as their strengths.

When The All-American Boys was first published in 1977, astronauts had been in the public eye for seventeen years, but how we thought and worked, acted and reacted had yet to be told. It was the inside story of NASA and America's first fifteen years in space and of the principal actors and stars of that experience—the astronauts. My objective was to share the enthusiasm and skill we brought to our work, as well as tell about the warts and moles that sometimes compromised it. "A lunar landing in this decade" was much more than the goal of a decade. This tribute to man's desire to explore will remain a permanent fixture in the history of America and the world.

This book is not a definitive account of NASA or its people, even during the "golden years" when I was there. And it is not an autobiography of Walter Cunningham, although it is bound to reveal much about me from what is both said and not said. It is but one man's perspective. It began in 1961 in the curve of a mountain road above Los Angeles.

In the 30 years since I left NASA, we should have landed on Mars or be well on our way there. Instead, we are stuck in earth orbit. What will it take to re-commit to that "chance of dangerous adventure" and satisfy once more man's longing to explore the unknown?

Dedication

This edition of The All-American Boys
would still be on a list of things "to do"
were it not for the commitment, prodding
and editing of my wife, Dot.
Thank you, my love, for making it happen.

1

"We've got a fire in the cockpit!"

FROM THE ROOF of the building where we and the other flight crews lived, slept, and maintained our offices, we could see the giant, skeletal outlines of the gantries, standing like monstrous oil derricks on a stretch of sand along the Atlantic at Cape Kennedy. Rising above the palmetto trees and slash pines, beyond the ribbon of blue water that circled Merritt Island, it was a beautiful sight.

Some days we would sit up there, peel off our shirts to catch the sun, and study the flight plan or mission rules. This was not one of those days. It was Friday of a long week and across those eight miles of Florida jungle, on Pad 34, the Apollo 1 spacecraft sat on top of a Saturn 1B rocket being tested for the first step in a series that would fulfill man's dream of walking on the moon.

Wally Schirra, Donn Eisele, and I, the Apollo 1 backup crew, had performed our own drills that day. Our presence was not required out at the pad, but we were sweating out the test and clock-watching anyway. We planned to fly home to Houston to visit our families, but it would be bad form to leave before the prime crew had finished their chores; who knows, we might be needed.

Our offices were on the third floor, just down the hall from the control room for all the spacecraft tests. Every half hour or so one of us would wander down to see how things were going.

They were going slowly and the usual, cool professionalism was now and then giving way to emotion. At one point, when the intercom between the spacecraft and the blockhouse was acting up for the umpteenth time, static drowned out all voice contact. "How the hell can we get to the moon," snapped Gus Grissom from the spacecraft, "if we can't talk between two buildings?"

Grissom and his crew, Ed White and Roger Chaffee, were performing the spacecraft's first full "plugs-out" test. Technicians had disconnected everything that could be and the Command Module was left to run on its own internal power. It was not a complicated test and was classified, at that time, as non-hazardous because there was no fuel on board. There had been some discussion about whether to run it with the hatch open or hatch closed. The hatch was a brute of a thing that took at least ninety seconds to open and required help from the outside if it was to be done without damaging it. For realism, it was decided to close it.

Only the night before, our backup crew had run the "plugs-in" version of the same test, meaning the auxiliary power cables remained connected to the spacecraft systems through the open hatch. It had been routine and we finished around 8:00 P.M. After a debriefing, we showered, changed, ate, and drove into town—Cocoa Beach—to raise a little hell.

The test that Friday—January 27, 1967, almost one month to the day before the launch—was to begin at 11:00 A.M. That would guarantee us all an early takeoff for Houston. But from the outset there were nagging delays. It was after 1:00 P.M. when Gus, Ed, and Roger, awkward in their heavy, bulky space suits, finally squeezed into the cabin. All around the area, the chores of the day came to a halt as they rode the elevator to the twenty-second level and walked across the catwalk to the sterilized "white room." At such moments, workmen often broke into applause. Every eye was on them. I was struck again by the ease with which the spotlight shifts to the crew making the next flight and the naked admiration of the technicians who followed their every step. It was once again the Hour of the Astronaut at the Cape. Show time for Apollo 1.

There's no denying a feeling of envy when you're on the backup crew. Wally, Donn and I had functioned in that role for ten weeks, since the cancellation of our own mission. In the backup role you blend into the scenery and do it willingly, even gladly, because in the recesses of your mind a voice is whispering, "My turn will come."

The crew took their places and were strapped into their couches. The countdown was stopped once when Gus complained of a sour odor in the cabin. The test conductors considered scrubbing the test but then decided to press ahead.

Wally, Donn, and I kept checking our watches. The day was wearing on. By 5:00 P.M. one of us said, "Hell, those guys could be out there all night. Let's bug out." We had to be back at the Cape in forty-eight hours. It was a simple test, a piece of cake. What could go wrong? The prime crew would probably finish late and fly to Houston the next day.

We jumped into three separate cars for the half-hour race to Patrick Air Force Base. We traveled light—flight suits and shaving kits. At Patrick we strapped on a pair of T-38s. I was at the controls of the first airplane, with Wally in the rear cockpit, while Donn flew our wing in the second. With clear skies and no headwind, we enjoyed a loose, easy flight home, touching down at Ellington Air Force Base right at dusk. We were in good humor and lighthearted, with that Friday out-of-school feeling.

Then we saw Bud Ream.

We had taxied up to the NASA hangar, where we were usually met by the lineman who begins to get the airplane ready for the next flight. That night, standing along side the lineman, was Bud Ream, the Number 2 man in flight operations. Bud was a NASA test pilot, short, solid, with a crisp manner. There was no reason for Bud to be there. He stood on the concrete apron, waiting for us to climb down. His face was grim.

He motioned for us to follow him up the stairs to his office. As we walked he spoke, his voice hoarse and tense, "There's been an accident at the Cape. The prime crew has had an accident."

An accident? How could they have an accident? They were on the pad. A fall on the gantry? A car accident? At such moments, your mind spins. Downstairs my wife, Lo, was waiting in our car with the kids. The three of them had watched us taxi in, and she would be wondering what was taking so long. All we usually did was drop off our flight gear and head out.

At first no one spoke. We just looked at each other. Then the questions began pouring out as we all talked at once. What accident? Who was hurt? How? When?

"The crew is dead," Bud said. "They're dead. All of them."

Suddenly, Lo appeared at the door. She had seen Bud walk out to meet us and soon after had heard a news bulletin on the car radio. Something had gone wrong at the Cape. No details.

Bud Ream was trying hard to keep himself under control. He had been close to Gus ever since 1959, when Project Mercury, our first manned program, began. Roger and Ed were also friends. He was shaken. We all were.

We got on the phone and dialed Mission Control at the Johnson Space Center (JSC), five miles away. Any NASA senior managers in Houston at the time had already assembled there. They were replaying the tapes of the test, trying to determine what had happened. We spoke with two of the brass, George Low and Chris Kraft. They gave us all they had: There had been a fire. It had flashed through the cabin in seconds. They were burned alive.

Whatever illusions any of us carried about our jobs were temporarily forgotten that night. Envy of the prime crew had been replaced by shock. If we ever talked about death—which we did not—none of us could have imagined it coming as it did: to three men, helpless, in maybe half a minute, only 218 feet above the ground.

And I remember one of us said, "Thank God, it happened on the pad."

That may sound like a cold and strange way to think. But in a time of crisis or tragedy or embarrassment, a convenient reflex takes hold of men who live by flying. We go on instruments; instincts take over. The crew was dead; nothing could be done for them. The important thing now was to find out how and why—to protect the living. It was that simple. Even as we felt the first dull shock at the deaths of Gus Grissom, Ed White, and Roger Chaffee, we thought, "What about the program? What about us?"

I doubt whether we were very, different from the rest of the country. We believed the effort would continue, that America still must reach for the moon. But it was obvious that there would be no more manned flights until we knew what had gone wrong with the spacecraft that had been designed to get us there.

But at least the evidence was right in front of us—on Pad 34.

That was important, not just for scientific or technical or even humane reasons, but for our own sense of order. It meant that we had a chance to uncover the cause of the fire before another spacecraft was wheeled out of the barn.

You have to understand the double-edged sword that hangs over every aviator's head. Imagine the mental conflict: your buddy has just been killed in your favorite fighter plane. You respected him as a pilot. You want to believe that he did everything possible to stay alive—that he was undone by some perverse fate that caused an obscure part to fail. But then a shadow crosses your mind. If that's the case, it could happen to you; it could be *your* body going home in a box with a flag draped across it.

So when the Accident Investigation Board brings in a finding of "pilot error," you breathe easier; it wasn't equipment failure. It's better to believe that the other fellow blew it: "Poor guy, he bought the farm. But I won't let it happen to me. I'm too smart, too good, too cool."

Of the eight astronauts who died during my time at NASA, four were in air crashes: Ted Freeman hit a goose, Elliot See and Charlie Bassett hit a building in St. Louis, and C. C. Williams hit the ground in Florida. In none of these cases did the Accident Board attribute the primary cause to pilot error, but we knew that in each case skill or judgment could have changed the outcome. Each of the deaths could have been laid to the pilot's hand. In truth, most pilots kill themselves.

But not this time. And so we thanked Providence that we could look for answers. All along our fear had *not* been that we might have an accident but that the hairy mishap, when it came, would occur in outer space, leaving no traces, offering no clues—only an eternal silence.

The truth of this is not easily understood. But the death of Gus Grissom's crew at the Cape, on the pad, made it possible to land a man on the moon on schedule. Indeed, it may have saved America's space program. So we cannot consider their deaths to have been in vain.

The fire did something else. It reminded the American public that men could and would die exploring the heavens. The tension and uncertainty associated with the early flights of Shepard, Grissom, and Glenn replaced the complacency that had set in. We had reached a point where the public was aware of space only when a crew was out in it. That environment, they knew, was strange and dangerous. With the fire on the pad, it was obvious that even the daily routine of the astronaut involved risk. The public was reminded that astronauts belonged in that category of men who roll the dice, who—like race car drivers or bullfighters or the cliff divers of Acapulco—put their hides on the line every day.

If we didn't see ourselves that way, it didn't make it any less so. It wasn't so much that we accepted the risks, but rather that we never admitted the risks existed in the first place. It was all tied up in what the writer Tom Wolfe once described as "The Brotherhood of the Right Stuff." It is part of what sets flying apart as an art, as a science, as a way of living. And dying!

Wolfe came as close to describing it as anyone ever has: "The main thing to know about an astronaut, if you want to understand his psychology, is not that he's going into space but that he is a fighter pilot and has been in that game for 15 or 20 years. It's like a huge and very complex pyramid, miles high, and the idea is to prove at every step of the way up that pyramid that you are one of the elected and anointed ones who have *the right stuff* . . . .

"The right stuff is not bravery in the simple sense; it is bravery in the most sophisticated sense. Any fool can put his hide on the line and throw his life away in the process. The idea is to be able to put your hide on the

Brother Ken and me, 1947

line—and then to have the know-how, the reflexes, the talent, the experience, to pull it back in at the last yawning moment—and then to be able to go out again the next day and do it all over again—and, in its best expression, to be able to do it in some cause, in some calling that means something."

Whatever it was that qualified us to be astronauts—whatever the chemistry that created in us the *need* to fly—also gave us a different view of life and its challenges, of the earth and its treasures. Our response at any given moment was not likely to be conventional. From the outset, the space program was related through spiritual bloodlines to the era of scarves and goggles and open cockpits, to Lindbergh and Rickenbacker and the Red Baron, and to all those old Chester Morris movies and the immortal line, "My gawd, they're not going to send the kid up in a crate like that?"

If you have been a fighter pilot for any length of time, you have seen your friends get killed—often. You build up a certain immunity. I flew with such men and knew them well, men whose faces I can no longer remember. They are frozen in time now as shadows in old group photos. My younger brother Ken will always be the twenty-nine-year-old fighter pilot.

Two weeks before I was to report with the third generation of astronauts, Ken was killed flying an F-104 in a weekend air defense exercise at Webb Air Force Base in Midland, Texas. We had grown closer as we grew older with similar interests and horizons. Ken had been the only family member to fully appreciate and share the enormity of the space program and what it meant to me. I still occasionally think of Ken with an emptiness in my heart. Yet, when I learned of his death my emotions remained intact. I was conscious of doing what was expected of me under the circumstances.

It was my regular weekend to fly with my Marine Reserve Squadron, after which I stopped by to visit my parents. I walked into the house to find everyone crying. They had just received a telephone call notifying them that Ken's plane had crashed. It was Sunday, December 15, 1963, ten days before Christmas. He left behind a pregnant wife and a young daughter.

I immediately called the base. When the Duty Officer answered, I learned that Ken had crashed while returning from an air defense exercise in very bad weather. When he had lowered his landing flaps at 800 feet on an approach, they had come down on only one side. The plane had spun, almost like a top, and corkscrewed into the ground. One of his closest buddies had been killed in a similar accident only two weeks earlier.

Ken was an excellent pilot, and as I flew to Midland that night in one of our squadron airplanes, I took some comfort in knowing he had been able to spend seven years doing what mattered most to him. In that respect, he was fortunate.

My mother, of course, felt flying had killed him. She may even have blamed me for inspiring him in that direction.

If you are one with flying, it can change you. It remakes you. Your heart beats stronger and your ego grows larger and your instincts become more sensitive. Life takes on a dimension that those whose feet are anchored to the ground can never know. I have never strapped myself into the cockpit of a jet airplane without consciously thinking of how fortunate I was.

Flying is a death-oriented business. You either accept the odds or you stay the hell out. No one had understood this any better than Gus Grissom. "If we die," Gus had once said, "we want people to accept it. We hope that if anything happens to us it will not delay the program. The conquest of space is worth the risk of life."

Prophetic? A portent of the tragedy to come? I don't think so. Gus was just expressing what we all felt. No other attitude would have been tolerable.

When a friend or even a brother dies in the crash of his jet, we tend to grieve less for him than for those who cannot understand why a man would be willing to die for something. We believe there are worse things than dying. Maybe it sounds like happy nonsense. Or an act. Or superstition. But that was the world in which we chose to live. None of us in this business comes to death unprepared. Yet it wasn't something we thought or talked about, not now, and not on the night of January 27, 1967.

Yet it was hard to accept the fire. We had performed virtually the same test the night before, with the persistent irritation of "glitches," those minor problems we had almost come to expect. We kept telling ourselves, as did the engineers, that we couldn't expect the first machine out of the factory to be bug-free. Wally had complained that the same problems kept showing up. In the push to keep on schedule, they were not being completely and finally resolved. His words to Gus were, "If you have a problem, even a comm [communications] problem, get out of the spacecraft until they've cleaned it up." Wally was more inclined than most to say, "Hey, it's not working. Call me when it's right."

We thought of that later. We thought of the weeks and months of grip-

ing about the test failures and the marginal workmanship that kept sur-
facing as the spacecraft was being built. Now it came back to bite us. We
cursed the spacecraft that killed them.

During one test the nozzle of the Service Module engine had shattered. During another, when dropped at high speed into a water tank, the
heat shield split wide open and the Command Module sank like a stone.
There had been fuel ruptures. The cooling system had failed. It had been
one damn thing after another. Now three men were dead.

I tried to imagine what it must have been like for those at the Cape
who stood helpless and listened to them die. "It was about twenty, minutes," Joe Shea, the Apollo Program Manager, said, "Before we realized
that they were not about to get out. It was pretty tough."

Wally, Donn, and I stayed in our flight suits for the next six hours. We
stopped by Mission Control at the Johnson Space Center to see what else we
might learn. What we found was shock, confusion and consternation. Then
we did what pilots usually do at such times. We fanned out to visit the wives.
My children—Brian, age seven, and Kimberly, age five—were shaken up but
not quite sure why. They had sensed this mood before. Their playmates
included the children of Ted Freeman, Elliot See, and Charlie Bassett—all of
whom had died in the preceding thirty months. They had begun to notice
that some of Daddy's friends some times didn't come home from work.

After dropping the kids at a neighbor's house, Lo and I headed for
the home of Martha Chaffee. The news media had already collected in the
front yard, but the neighbors, most of whom were involved in the space
program, had rallied around to protect the families. Lo is a pretty woman
with brown hair and bright eyes. She had spirit and an active mind. But
having married me one month before my release from active duty, she
had little experience in the rituals of a fighter pilot's wife—such as comforting a widow. Now here she was, nervous and uncomfortable, standing with me at the front door of the first astronaut family we had met,
only three years before. Inside was the usual mourning scene. Those
doing the comforting seemed more uncomfortable than the comforted.
The role of the bereaved is at least spontaneous. In this case, the look and
kitchen conversation of each wife left little doubt that they felt, "There but
for the grace of God ...." While, as husbands, we were brought face to face
with something seldom discussed and usually ignored: the fear our wives
felt about the jobs we loved. We saw a lot more of each other than our

wives did. Yet we maintained a more impersonal relationship. It was much easier for the wives to empathize with each other.

Lo was closer to Martha than to any of the other wives and knew the preceding year had not been a smooth one—for any of the widows or any of the wives. The system worked against them. Training kept their husbands not only occupied but preoccupied as well.

Martha was still glassy-eyed and had obviously not yet come to believe that Roger had really died.

With the sudden cancellation of our own flight on the second Apollo mission, in one week we had gone from testing spacecraft 014 to performing similar tests on Grissom's spacecraft 012. Our training even picked up for a while due to the higher priority we gained on use of the mission simulators. We made the best of what we accepted as a bad deal. I was pleasantly surprised to find Gus to be a decisive guy, a team leader and an independent thinker, who nevertheless encouraged input from the rest of the crew. It was a nice change to work with him.

Gus, a taciturn, grizzled fellow, was scheduled to become the first man to make three space flights. An air force cadet at eighteen, he had flown a hundred combat missions in Korea. One of the stories told about him was how, when he first got to Korea, he found that pilots who had not been shot at by a MIG weren't allowed a seat on the bus to the hangar. Gus stood only once. He had shot it out on his first mission to qualify for a seat—and the "brotherhood of the right stuff."

Gus had backed up Shepard's historic first Mercury flight. Five weeks later, aboard Liberty Bell 7, he had become the second American in space. When his spacecraft hatch exploded off after splashdown and the capsule flooded, Gus swam to safety and lived to be periodically embarrassed as the only man ever to lose his spacecraft.

He filled the bill as the prototypical test pilot. He could sit at a bar for hours, and he never failed to notice a pretty girl in the room. He was into the racecar scene with Gordon Cooper and Jim Rathman, the Indy driver. He could be cranky and tough, but he went his own way. He wasn't a hanger-on.

Betty Grissom was the only one who didn't cry. She was stoic, composed. The Schirras, their next-door neighbors, were quickly on the scene, and Wally was trying to take care of things. But Betty was a veteran. She had traveled a lot of miles with a much rougher guy than had the other wives. Having, obviously, made her own adjustment to that fact, she kept her calm and her dignity, and from that night on she fought for Gus Grissom's legacy. Gus had been a professional and believed what Betty soon forgot: if you lived by the sword, you could expect to die by the sword.

Some months later Betty was invited to the White House to accept a Distinguished Flying Cross awarded posthumously to her husband. She declined to make the trip. "Medals don't mean much to me now," she said.

Ed White was one of the second-generation astronauts. On June 8, 1965 he became the first American to walk in space, which made him feel, "red, white, and blue all over," as he described it later. He was, I think, consciously cultivating the All-American, John Glenn image. That was Ed—at least most of the time. The rest of the time Ed White was not much different from the rest of the guys. Take the way he ran the Astronaut Training Gym. It originally contained one handball court and one squash court. Ed and two or three others were the only squash players in the group; the rest of us were dedicated handball addicts. When money was budgeted for two more courts Ed began to plan for one more of each. When we were polled as to our preference for two more handball courts or one of each, the vote came out something like seven to one for the handball courts. Running into Ed at the gym one day, I asked, "Did you see the vote?"

Ed's reply was short and to the point: "Yeah, I've seen it, but as long as I have anything to do with the project, there's going to be one more of each." To this day, guys wait in line to use the two handball courts while the two squash courts generally stand empty.

Ed was a West Point graduate and the son of a retired Air Force General. He was also an athlete who barely missed qualifying for the 1952 Olympics as a 400-meter hurdler. Ed was a golden boy; meticulous, tall, clean-cut, and a fierce advocate of all the basic virtues; God, country, Mother, and religion. On Gemini 4 he took along a gold cross, a St. Christopher medal, and a Star of David.

The grief of his wife, Pat, was visible—she took it hard. But she also felt a sense of public loss; she had shared her man with the nation. Theirs had been an All-American marriage, a better one than most of those buffeted by the winds of space. Ed wasn't the kind of guy who parked at bars, drinking and flirting—the more popular fighter-pilot recreations.

Roger Chaffee was the rookie of the crew, a contemporary of mine. He was one of the younger astronauts with a short but illustrious navy career behind him. During the "eyeball-to-eyeball" 1962 missile crisis, he had flown most of the photo missions over Cuba, mapping the missile sites.

Roger was success-oriented and had his eye on the moon landing. He and Martha had had a lot going for them; now it was gone,

Out of all the despair and remorse and uncertainty, we were sure of one thing: there would be hell to pay before another spacecraft was launched. Wally, Donn and I figured it would be months before our presence would be required again at the Cape.

Saturday, the day after the accident, doctors at the Cape asked for a uniform in which to bury Gus, and Wally asked if I would fly it to Patrick Air Force Base. That afternoon I quietly pulled my Porsche into Wally's drive, slipped next door to Gus' house and took the uniform from Wally, who passed it through a partly opened door. He had sneaked it out of the bedroom closet to avoid upsetting Betty.

When I landed at Patrick, one of the doctors was waiting at the hangar for the uniform. My making the flight was somewhat unusual. Military flight surgeons usually try to keep aviators grounded after the death of close associates, believing they may be distracted and contribute to another accident. Whether it was the non-flight nature of the accident or that we were considered more stable, I was glad to have something to do that was more business as usual—anything that didn't keep me too close to the survivors' grief.

Memorial services for all three astronauts were held in the Clear Lake area that weekend. I flew the number 3 T-38 in the "missing man" flyby for the Ed White ceremony. The missing man formation is a flight of four with one spot vacant. It is the aviation equivalent of the riderless horse in an army funeral procession. A quote from Ed's pastor, the Rev. Connie Winborn, appeared in Time magazine: "Let us not expect to sing the victor's song, unless we are willing to risk the harsh notes of tragic loss and personal sacrifice."

I dread funerals. I don't like to get that personal with death. But we all flew to Washington to attend two funerals at Arlington National Cemetery the following Tuesday: Gus' in the morning and Roger's in the afternoon. Ed White was buried at West Point.

Donn and I left our wives in Washington and flew directly to the Cape in our T-38s. We intended to clean out our quarters and retrieve our clothes.

I finally made it home three weeks later. We were both put to work with the official Board of Inquiry. I was appointed to the Emergency Provisions Review Panel, one of twenty-one established to investigate every aspect of the catastrophe. Like everyone else, I was aware that if we couldn't come up with some right answers, the program might not survive. The climate was ripe for an emotional backlash against the space effort. The accident would have been even more tragic if the work the crew started had not been allowed to continue and they had died for nothing.

Donn and I were quickly caught up in the state of urgency that gripped the Kennedy Space Center. Wally remained in Houston, still smoldering over the deaths and railing against the inadequacies of a dumb machine built by contractors who should have known better. He was attending to Gus' personal affairs and adjusting his thinking to the long delay we all knew was ahead.

Some of the more ghoulish details had been completed by now. The offices of our fallen buddies at the Cape and back in Houston had been sealed to prevent the curious from stealing souvenirs. Certain effects had been removed from the spacecraft but their bodies had remained in place, in the charred cockpit, for seven hours before being brought down. No one wanted to risk disturbing the evidence. And no one really knew what the hell to do. There were simply no procedures. The United States, after all, had never had any of their space heroes die, let alone ignominiously in a fire on the ground.

The investigation was already on a twenty-four-hour-a-day crash basis. That first night back Frank Borman, Donn and I found an empty studio in one of the small control centers and began playing the last voice tapes from the spacecraft. Only a handful of people, other than the controllers in the blockhouse at the time of the accident, had actually heard them.

We listened over and over, trying to be detached yet mesmerized by the few seconds of sheer, stark terror that emerged from the tapes. It left a sick feeling at the pit of my stomach—not just because someone had died; not just because they had been friends and companions; but because of the horrifying way they had to die.

Fire! It is the most detested of a pilot's enemies, slower and more painful than any other—and sometimes not sure enough. The Apollo 1 spacecraft cabin was a bomb fused with a 100 percent oxygen environment, the most inflammable kind of atmosphere. Yet the possibility of a fire on the ground had been given precious little thought. The cabin didn't even have a fire extinguisher.

As we concentrated on the crucial last half-minute, we had two objectives: determine who was saying what and—if we could—reconstruct what the crew was doing during that time. We hoped desperately to find a clue to the problem they had encountered in the last few seconds of their lives.

It was an ordeal to listen to the tapes, starting, stopping, backward and forward, trying to isolate each split-second. In the end, a number of people came up with different versions of what was said. The engineers at North American Rockwell had their version. So did Bell Laboratories where the voices were processed by computers, analyzed, and broken down into components. There has never been total agreement on what was said or by whom.

According to the tapes, the first indication of the fire came at 4.7 seconds after 6:31 P.M. with the crew's announcement of alarm. Fourteen seconds later, the inner shell of the cabin exploded. It is unlikely that they could have lived beyond 6:31:20. As I interpreted the tapes, all the transmissions were from Chaffee. White was working to remove the hatch and Gus was probably trying to help him.

"Fire!"

"We've got a fire in the cockpit!"

"We've got a bad fire.... Let's get out. We're burning up ...."

The only other transmission was a very brief scream. Total elapsed time: twelve seconds.

We went back to the crew quarters that night and had more than one stiff belt. The end had come quickly, but what a horrible way to die!

The blackened, burned-out capsule sat in the "white room" under the tightest control. Every last bit of ash was sifted, a false floor was suspended in the cockpit and a thousand other precautions were taken to keep from disturbing any possible evidence and still the cause was never determined.

The investigation's conclusions became a virtual indictment of everyone connected with Apollo, including those of us who were to fly it. We contributed to the disaster by our willingness to tolerate questionable designs, equipment, and testing procedures; by ignoring our own good sense and accepting borderline safety margins; in short, by our eagerness to blow the bolts and get off the ground.

All of us who participated in the design and testing at North American Rockwell felt there were deficiencies in some of the systems and that crew safety had been given a lower priority than in the past. NASA program management and contractors alike were marching to a different drummer than the flight crew on this one. The birthing pains of Mercury and the just-completed Gemini program seemed like perfection alongside Apollo.

A great number of things had needed improving but changes meant delays. The Program Manager weighed the crew's demands for performance, safety and other operational improvements against the payload of the spacecraft, schedules and, not least, cost.

But while all this had alarmed us, it gave no premonition of what was to come. The closer we came to launch date, the more omnipotent we felt. In the Astronaut Office, we were already looking ahead to spacecraft 101, which would incorporate many of the improvements we had fought for but been unable to obtain for Apollo 1. All subsequent Apollo Command Modules would be designated Block II spacecraft and would be Cadillacs by comparison. Spacecraft 101 was the first of the new line.

There had been so many changes to the original design that the first two Block I spacecraft, 012 and 014, were the only two produced.

OK, we had shrugged, so spacecraft 012 was a piece of junk. Any astro worth his salt would fly the crate anyway—or die trying. This was no time for "the right stuff" to waver. The simulators and mockups were also well behind schedule. From our vantage point as the backup crew, Wally, Donn, and I seriously doubted that the prime crew would be sufficiently trained to meet the launch schedule. We certainly knew we would not be well enough trained to take their place if it became necessary. But ready or not, the program went forward. There was a lot of pressure within NASA to get off on time. In a very real sense, time was money and the annual funding battle with Congress had been getting tougher.

No one wanted to sound the alarm, to be caught holding the umbrella of delay, so to speak. North American, the prime contractor, wasn't about to say, "Whoa, we need more testing, hold the flight." And our boss, Deke Slayton, wasn't going to tell NASA, "Hey, we're not going to be trained in time"—Deke's boys were always ready. The simulators were still full of bugs but the flight crew wasn't going to raise the umbrella, either.

So many things weren't working on the Apollo simulator that one morning Gus hung a lemon outside the entrance hatch. But their attitude—and we all shared it—could be characterized as, "Blow the bolts and we'll do whatever the hell is necessary to make it a success after we get in the air."

As the fire investigation proceeded, it became clear that Washington was not going to kill the program. Our main worry was that, once the Board of Inquiry made its report, NASA would overreact and load us up with so much safety equipment we wouldn't be able to get the damn thing off the ground. We wanted a better spacecraft, but we wanted it while we were still young enough to enjoy it. We didn't want one so safe that it wouldn't fly. We couldn't reach the moon in an armored tank.

Frank Borman had been assigned to the Board of Inquiry and represented the flight crew—and himself—admirably. He handled himself with professional assurance, providing credibility to an investigation that many feared would be a whitewash. Frank is a practical and extremely able guy. Reading the names on the astronaut offices, we had so many Colonels and Navy Captains that it looked like the Mexican army. Frank Borman is one of those who would have reached that elevated status regardless of what career path he chose. The same couldn't be said of all the others.

My involvement in the investigation was finished in a matter of weeks, but the inquiry itself lasted for nearly a year, with the first reports submitted in April, three months after the fire. Experts had microscopically examined the cockpit, the blobs of melted wires and the scorched dials and toggle switches of the instrument panel. A partially completed Apollo spacecraft—the very one Wally, Donn, and I had trained to fly—was flown to the Cape and cannibalized so that its components could be compared piece by piece to the blackened debris scattered about the ruined, burned out command module.

The board was never clearly able to establish the cause of the fire but indications pointed to a short circuit in the insulated wiring beneath the left-hand couch, which Grissom occupied, as the most probable cause.

The wiring itself was found to be defective.

The exit hatch, of course, was a monster; heavy as hell, awkwardly placed above and behind the middle seat. It had to be hand cranked to get it open. A fellow like Ed White, strong as a young bull, had to reach back over his head and strain for several minutes to release it. It was apparent from the position in which he was found on the couch that he had made a desperate stab at just that.

Escape provisions, rescue and medical assistance plans, wiring, and plumbing were all found to be inadequate. There were deficiencies in design, manufacture, quality control, and testing.

Too little attention had been given to crew safety. The pure oxygen atmosphere, an unwarranted amount of combustible materials in the cabin, careless workmanship, and poor judgment—all had contributed to the tragedy. Proper emergency procedures had not been established. Fire, rescue, and medical teams had not been present since the test had not been labeled hazardous.

In short, Gus, Ed, and Roger never had a chance. The fact that they found no pilot error left us all with some concern about the hardware.

The indictments went on and on. The investigation also established that they died of asphyxiation. The inside temperature reached more than 1,000° Fahrenheit.

Step by painful step we began putting the pieces together.

NASA shifted personnel, clamped down hard on test procedures, and put a foot to the neck of North American. At a cost of $500 million, the Command Module was re-designed. Among the changes was a new one-piece hatch that swung outward and could be opened in ten seconds.

To snuff out any fire that might develop, an emergency venting system was added that could reduce cabin pressure in seconds. While the spacecraft was on the pad and during launch, a mixture of 60 percent oxygen and 40 percent nitrogen was substituted for the 100 percent oxygen formerly used.

From the astronauts' point of view, the changes encouraged us to believe that a spacecraft would be built that could, at last, perform its intended mission. The relentless pressure to meet a schedule was gone for the first time since the program's inception. With the federal purse loosened a bit to make the spaceship safe for "our boys," many of our earlier rejected changes suddenly had new life. A rapid re-pressurization system, an emergency oxygen breathing system, electric power system changes— from brand-new crew couches to an additional urine dump nozzle, there was scarcely a system that didn't benefit from the exercise. All told, over 1,300 modifications were made to the command module following the Apollo 1 fire.

And out of the whole mess, North American was to bring forth one of the greatest machines ever built by man. I am convinced that we would never have reached the moon in only five missions had we not gone through this rebuilding process—the inevitable result of the fire on Pad 34.

Within days of the tragedy, the guarded, solemn attitude around the astronaut office was already dissipating and speculation on who would get the next flight was beginning. That might strike some as dancing on the coffin. Here we were, still sorting out the facts of a nightmarish accident, and we're wondering who will go next. It was an echo of the days of the old Roman gladiators, when the crowds would hail the new champion even as the old champion, now dead, was being dragged from the arena.

But the program was going to survive. Someone would fly the next mission. Some crew still had to test the Apollo spacecraft in the environment for which it was designed. By God, I wanted to be there. My closeness to the crew of Apollo 1 only strengthened that resolve. I felt it would be a gratuitous low blow if our crew *did not* fly the next mission.

It was five weeks after the fire when Wally, Donn, and I flew into the Cape for some meetings with the checkout crew. We had finished dinner one evening and were sitting in the living room of the crew quarters, when in walked Deke Slayton. We passed a few amenities before Deke casually said, "I want to let you guys know that you have the next flight."

I looked quickly at Donn and Wally. We nodded. There was no show of emotion. Decorum required that a certain amount of regret be shown for the manner in which the assignment was inherited.

By the time I completed my work on the inquiry and finally left the Cape to return to Houston, it was impossible to contain my feelings. As I drove toward Cocoa Beach, crossing the Banana River, I Instinctively looked toward Pad 34. Here at Moon Base, USA, with all those gantries and launch towers lined up along the beach like toys in a giant Erector set, Pad 34 was now empty again, the charred spaceship removed at last.

And I thought, "By God, the next time a man lifts-off from here, it will be me."

The hair on my arms stood up. I was a step closer to flying in space and I luxuriated in that feeling all the way home.

You Lucky Sonofabitch

I SWUNG MY Porsche Speedster off the road and parked it in a bend on Mulholland Drive at the top of the Santa Monica Mountains. The city of Los Angeles sprawled far below, a hazy, sweeping panorama. Beyond it stretched the California coastline, miles of sand and surf and taco burger huts.

It was a picture-postcard view, but at that moment I didn't see it. I was concentrating on my car radio, oblivious to everything else. My hair could have been on fire and I wouldn't have noticed.

My trance was broken by a rush of words exploding in my ears, shrill and profane: "You lucky sonofabitch!" It took a moment to realize that the voice I heard was my own. I was screaming at an American pilot, 2,500 miles away, who was a hundred feet above the earth and on his way out of the atmosphere. I shared that moment with Alan Shepard two years before we ever met.

Sheepishly, I looked around, half-expecting to find a curious crowd staring back at me. Or maybe a deputy sheriff, wondering why a guy would be parked in a car, alone, in the middle of nowhere, lips moving, yelling at demons. No one was in sight; no one saw me. I turned back to the radio.

A little before 7:00 A.M. on that morning of May 5, 1961, while I was driving to work at the RAND Corporation, Alan Shepard sat in a tiny Mercury capsule called Freedom 7 atop a Redstone Rocket. He had just growled impatiently at his ground crew, "Why don't you guys fix your problems and light this candle?"

It was that time in my graduate student life when I supported my family by simultaneously holding down five different jobs, including flying with the Marine Corps Reserve. The Porsche's top was down and the car radio was tuned to the final countdown for MR-3.

Driving along those quiet mountain roads, I was conscious of how damn little I knew about the space program. It was very much in its infancy. The Russian Sputnik still circled above us, giving off those strange electronic beeps that resembled the sound track of an early Mickey Mouse movie. Sputnik had changed the direction of American science, had touched all our lives, and had brought Alan Shepard to that moment and that place—Launch Complex 5—at Cape Canaveral.

Of course, I had read about the seven Mercury astronauts in *Life* magazine when they were selected, an American dream team. Instant celebrities. Lower-case gods. Not so much selected, I had thought, as ordained. At twenty-nine, I was a Marine Corps fighter pilot in danger of becoming a career student at UCLA and a physicist at the RAND Corporation, the famed think-tank. But nothing in my life had prepared me for the vicarious thrill of that incredible moment when Alan Shepard became America's first man in space.

It was one of those rare moments that, with just a tug of the memory, you can recall exactly where you were and what you were doing. The successful launching of Sputnik had caused a national trauma. Shepard's flight was to be the start of our comeback, and no one knew quite what to expect. Our unmanned rockets had been blowing up, keeling over, or cart-wheeling into the ocean with appalling frequency. Millions hugged their radios and TV sets to share the exquisite suspense of that morning. Would Al Shepard be our first space hero or would they be picking up pieces of him over the entire length of the Eastern Seaboard?

At five minutes to lift-off, the excitement became too much and I stopped my Porsche at the side of the road to just soak it all in. The damn announcer kept injecting his thoughts into the action when all I wanted were the lean, bare bones of what was happening. I wanted downs and yardage, not crowd color.

The count continued ...three, two, one, Lift Off! And before that Redstone rocket cleared the launch tower, I heard myself screaming at the top of my lungs, that involuntary announcement of envy.

The announcer seemed embarrassed to be so excited. "Just think, an American is going into space on that rocket. I don't want to sound like a super-patriot, but doesn't that *almost* make you proud just to be an American?" What was wrong with him? Hell, yes it did!

At the instant of lift-off, I luxuriated in the feeling of the moment. Alan

Shepard was off on the most beautiful fifteen-minute ride that any American had ever known. I wouldn't have recognized him had he tapped on my car window, but I was thrilled by his adventure and envied him as I had envied no man. Only later would I realize how that moment of lift-off had transformed my envy of the Mercury astronauts into the concrete goal of sharing their experience. Two short years later, Al Shepard was my boss and we were sharing an office. I quickly learned he was not so much a lucky SOB as he was a tough SOB. He was also capable, tenacious and just plain good at whatever he tackled.

My opinion of Al Shepard has always been shaped by that first awareness of him. While each of his Mercury classmates had their strong points, Al always seemed the most competent. I understood why he was selected to be the first American to ride a rocket into space. That's what the competition was all about—to be the first to accept the challenge, to meet the test, to take the honors.

I recalled that spring morning on the Santa Monica mountain top when, two years later, I made application for selection as a United States Astronaut. To most Americans the space program was not quite real and astronauts were a cross between Buck Rogers and James Bond. The two years since Freedom 7 had been filled with immediate goals, such as education and making a living, leaving precious little time to think of the space program. But the envy returned with each lift-off.

One sunny weekday afternoon in June 1963, I confessed my desires to Gerhard Schilling, an associate at the RAND Corporation. Gerhard had just returned from a year's loan to the National Aeronautics and Space Administration working for one of their top administrators, George Low. Gerhard wrote George of my relatively unique qualifications and a few days later a phone call from Washington got me started. Screening was already underway for the third group of astronauts; the deadline for application was only two weeks away. I was pleasantly surprised to learn I met *all* the qualifications for applicants: United States citizen, less than thirty-four years of age, six feet or less in height, a degree in engineering or the physical sciences, and fifteen hundred hours of jet pilot time.

Hell, if they had added hazel eyes and crew cut, the description couldn't have fit any better. There were 770 applicants who met the qualifications, including two women, and hundreds more who did not.

My superiors at RAND were delighted to recommend me (another

The 14 Group 3 Astronauts, selected 14 October 1963

qualification). On the other hand my mother must have thought I was out of my mind. "What makes you think you can do something like that?" she asked.

I was a Marine Corps Fighter Pilot and within a year of finishing my thesis for a doctorate in physics; two tasks I had tackled in spite of the fact they were difficult and challenging. Becoming an astronaut was only reaching for one more star.

The summer of 1963 became a blur of forms, questionnaires, medical exams, screenings, briefings, technical interviews, and intermittently clinging to straws of gossip. From the hundreds of qualified applicants, thirty-two of us made it to the August semi-finals: the physical examination at Brooks Air Force Base in San Antonio, Texas.

There we began to shape the curious, friends-and-rivals relationships that would be an essential part of the astronaut years.

The forty-five hours of screening at Brooks fell into three broad categories: health, physical fitness, and psychological. The breakdown is mine. It is possible to be in good health but poor physical condition through lack of exercise. Mental state can be another matter entirely.

If a general observation can be made of thirty-two candidates from varied backgrounds, I would say that we were, with rare exception, excellent in health, from good to excellent in physical condition, well above average in intelligence, and with good flying credentials. We shared a strong feeling of self-identity, self-confidence, and awareness of where we were going and how we would get there. Some might call it ego. The competitive instinct surfaced quickly. There was very little interaction among the candidates except in the evenings—and then generally limited to one's three roommates. Whatever any of us lacked, it wasn't motivation. C. C. Williams stayed awake all night, bouncing up and down in order to insure he would be under the six-foot maximum height in the morning. He made it.

Some of the candidates weren't above trying to psych out the shrinks. One of my roommates checked out a textbook on Rorschach ink blot tests from the base library to determine the "correct" responses for the psychiatrists (he didn't make it). Others engaged the good doctor in stare-down contests.

My appointment with the shrink came several hours after having my eyes dilated, and I harassed him by wearing sunglasses for the first hour of the meeting until he finally asked me to remove them. We sat there discussing subjects like *The Love and Fear of Flying,* a book written by another psychiatrist. It seemed my analyst endorsed such a love-fear relationship in all aviators. I left just a little curious about how many, like myself, didn't fit his model.

All in all, the sessions with the shrink were interesting but a farce to most of us. I never met an aviator who had a lot of time for either psychiatrists or psychologists.

My self-evaluation going in was: excellent health, for which I really couldn't take much credit; good physical condition, in spite of the mostly sedentary college life I had led for the preceding eight years; and excellent mental and psychological form, which I had consciously worked at all my life.

But this was one time when the admonition "Know thyself" didn't take priority. You also had to know the competition. We were constantly measuring and comparing. They all looked good, and some (like Charlie Bassett) looked like shoo-ins. I might slip into the snack bar between tests to wolf down a bite of something—at lunchtime we were usually involved in a test—and find Rusty Schweickart or Mike Collins enjoying a diet of coffee and Boston cream pie.

What followed would not be a conversation in the usual sense; that is, an exchange of views. One might make a leading statement, tentatively, and hope that someone else would commit himself to an evaluation: "Man, that tilt table was interesting," or, "I hear some of the guys had trouble on the treadmill," or, "Some of the shrink's questions are real beauts!" It was not unlike one fighter pilot trying to entice another airplane to "jump him" so he could engage in a "dog fight." Initiating a "dog fight" might be against regulations but defending oneself was simply a matter of honor.

One of my roommates at the Brooks Medical Center during the selection process was a handsome, young Navy lieutenant named Robert Shumaker. Bob was your typical All-American boy with an excellent flying background, and I conceded him better odds than myself of being selected. Surprisingly, he was one of four eliminated by the doctors at Brooks. Worse than that, it was a personal catastrophe, since he departed Brooks grounded from flying. The doctors had detected (or thought they had) a rare condition for Naval Aviators, mononucleosis. It violated their standards and, taking a conservative stance, they grounded Bob.

Bob returned to Navy Postgraduate School at Monterey, California, where he spent time fighting to get his wings back. He was successful. In 1965, he returned to a fighter squadron just in time to be deployed to the Far East on an aircraft carrier. Bob was the second American pilot shot down over Vietnam, which I learned about in 1966 sitting in my living room in Houston, Texas. There, on the evening news, was a North Vietnamese film showing captured U.S. airmen being paraded through the villages. At the front of the line, with his arms tied behind his back around a piece of bamboo, walked Bob Shumaker. It struck me then and a hundred times more in the next eight years how fateful are the rare opportunities we have to significantly change our lives. While I was enjoying the fruits of the good life, Bob was rotting in Vietnamese prisons. He was also on my mind as we orbited high above Vietnam in October 1968.

Bob would not have been grounded had he never tried to become an astronaut, and he didn't make it only because of a complicated mistake. He returned home with the rest of the POWs in 1973 and made a good adjustment. But who knows what might have been?

Two days after completing the weeklong physical, twenty-eight of us were directed to report to Houston for the final interviews. I had just passed Go!

The first week of September we were all in Houston for further evaluation. By then I was more familiar with the qualifications and backgrounds of the others and was consciously giving some candidates an edge. Dick Gordon had recently set a transcontinental speed record and was a retread on the selection process. Half a dozen of the group had been considered a year earlier for the second group—the Gemini astronauts—had missed the cut, and were recycled to compete with our bunch. Another half dozen were big-time civilian test pilots. Buzz Aldrin had shot down MIG's over Korea and written a Doctoral thesis on space rendezvous.

It was easy to be impressed with the inside drag of a guy like Gordon. At a cocktail reception one evening Dick walked right up to and spoke with Wally Schirra and Deke Slayton and Al Shepard. He *knew* them! *Personally!* My God, what chance did I have—these guys already knew each other! I not only did not know anyone inside the program, I did not even know any of the candidates trying to get in.

We were constantly calculating our chances of being cut. Wondering how much of the process we could control and how much was left to fate or blind luck.

Between the physicals at Brooks and the final interviews in Houston, two of the candidates, Mike Adams and Dave Scott, narrowly escaped death when the F-104 they were flying suffered a flameout during final landing approach. Each made diametrically opposed decisions and each got away with it. Mike, in the rear seat, ejected at the instant the plane hit the ground. Had he chosen not to eject, he would have been killed a few moments later when the engine of the F-104 slammed through the rear cockpit. Dave stayed with the plane and rode it out. He learned later that his ejection mechanism had been damaged in the crash, and he would have been killed had he fired the rocket cartridge. Each had considered just such a situation in advance and each carried out his pre-planned decision.

Dave Scott was one of the fourteen selected, and had an eventful career as an astronaut. A back injury forced Adams out of the competition, but he was later selected as one of the first Manned Orbiting Laboratory (MOL) pilots for the Air Force. As the MOL program dragged on with no one getting into space, Mike resigned and went back to flying the

X-15. He was killed in a high-altitude test of that winged rocket.

Nothing discouraged us. It was grand! It was glorious! It was patriotic! It was a challenge! It was man's greatest adventure and, by God, it meant a chance to be the first man on the moon.

Now there was nothing to do but wait—and worry. Slowly, not unlike college freshmen hoping to be pledged by the most snobbish fraternity, we formed our small alliances, sought out one another, pooled our insecurities, and—up to a point—lent each other support. I had a soul mate in Vance Brand. Vance was a civilian test pilot for Lockheed Aircraft Corporation in Palmdale, California, who seemed to have no better connections than I—that is, none. We roomed together during the Houston phase and vowed to keep each other informed if any gossip came our way. I emerged from the three days in Houston feeling I was strongly in the running.

Flying back to Los Angeles, I found myself on the same flight with Dick Gordon and Ron Evans, who were returning to the Naval Post Graduate School in Monterey, California. They had a few hours layover in Los Angeles and, hungry to keep the talk going on what we had experienced or what might be ahead, I invited them out to the house to kill the spare time. Lo met us at the airport and we drove home.

Gordon did most of the talking. He is a good-looking, compact fellow with a breezy, James Cagney self-assurance, and he completely captivated Lo. There seemed to be no doubt in *his* mind that Dick Gordon, in a matter of weeks, would be a living, breathing spaceman. My own confidence began to wilt a little as I inhaled some of Gordon's exhaust. (Dick made it, of course, was twice in space and, in that unpredictable post-orbital scramble, wound up as the General Manager of the pro football New Orleans Saints.)

We tipped a few frozen daiquiris and talked for two hours of how our lives might be changed by admission to the space program. That week an item had appeared in the newspapers announcing the signing of a publishing contract between the astronauts and Time-Life and Field Enterprises. It was worth a half-million dollars annually to be shared equally among the astronauts (then sixteen in number, soon to be thirty). We were aware, for the first time that more than just glory was at stake. From our standpoint it meant, at a minimum, financial comfort.

We agreed to share any early news on selection with each other, knowing full well that if NASA asked us to keep any news quiet, we damned sure would. At the airport we shook hands and I wished them luck, but only their fair share of it.

With the cooperation of the RAND Corporation I made one more trip to Houston. This time as one of RAND's two representatives at the Summary Conference for the Mercury Program, only recently concluded, which had demonstrated that man could survive in space.

I stayed at the Rice Hotel, one of Houston's landmarks. One afternoon I wandered into the Old Capitol Club with Wes Hooper, the sales director at the Rice. There we found Grissom, Shepard, and Paul Haney, who had succeeded Shorty Powers as the "voice of the astronauts." They invited us to join them for a drink. In my search for positive signs, I took that purely social gesture as a favorable omen. I felt spacey.

But my first real burst of optimism came as the result of a phone call to Jack Cairl, in the personnel office at NASA. I wanted to know how soon we might get the word. "Soon," Jack answered. "Maybe a week. They'll notify those who haven't made it first."

Then, almost as an afterthought, Jack said that no decision had been made yet on what salaries would be offered any of the candidates who came in as civilians. "We're thinking in the thirteen-to-fifteen-thousand-dollar range," he said. "How does that sound to you? What's the least you'd come in for?"

What a question to ask someone who had never made more than $10,000 a year, and then only by pursuing three or four jobs simultaneously. I felt I would pay for the privilege, if I could afford it, and tried to sound casual. "Oh, thirteen-to-fifteen sounds OK to me," I mumbled. But even in that first inkling that I might be chosen for man's greatest adventure, I dared to think that I was being squeezed. "Hell," I thought, "I *know* being an astronaut is worth more than thirteen grand a year. Haven't they filtered the cream of American manhood? . . . for a twenty-five-billion-dollar program?"

Returning to Santa Monica, I was still in the dark but more optimistic. That night I called Vance with my scuttlebutt.

A little over a week later, on the night of October 13, Vance called me. He was really down. "Walt? I just heard from Jack Cairl . . . I didn't make it. What have you heard?"

I remembered what Cairl had said. Vance's disappointment, his sense of loss, came through clearly on the phone. I didn't know what to say and hoped I wouldn't have to share his hurt. My own odds were getting better.

The next day I sat in my office at the RAND Corporation, doing what I had done for the past ten days: waiting for the phone to ring and putting off work on my Ph.D. dissertation: *The Design And Development Of a Tri-axial Search Coil Magnetometer To Measure Fluctuations In The Earth's Magnetosphere.* (Don't ask!)

And that day, October 14, 1963, the phone did ring. It was Deke Slayton, the Director of Flight Crew Operations. Deke was the Mercury astronaut grounded by a heart murmur, the only one who hadn't flown in space. It was an odd sensation to be able to say, with practiced familiarity, "Hello, Deke." (I've never been one to stand on ceremony, coming or going.)

Deke doesn't believe in dragging out the drama of a situation. He got right to the point. "Walt, we'd like to have you come to Houston and join us, if you're still interested."

I hesitated for, oh, maybe a tenth of a second—I had hoped to complete work on my doctorate. "Yes, sir, when do I report?"

I would learn many years later, and quite by accident, that I had just barely made the cut.

In anticipation of a press release on the newly selected "Apollo Astronauts," Deke Slayton made a presentation to NASA management. In that meeting, Deke identified each of thirteen selectees, followed by a brief description of the pilot's qualifications. Max Faget, NASA's Director of Engineering, pointed out that thirteen was not a good number, and Deke should probably go with twelve or fourteen.

Deke said he really wanted number thirteen. He pulled out one more viewgraph, flashed my picture and background on the screen, and said, "If I have to take fourteen, the last one will be Cunningham."

Deke told me to be in Houston on October 17. It was to be very hush-hush until the announcement press conference. I was to register at the Rice under the name of Max Peck. Years later I learned that all fourteen of us had been registered under the same name. Max Peck was the general manager of the hotel. I was to tell no one, other than my wife, that I had been selected. For a brief time, it looked like I wouldn't be telling her, either.

The phone at home was busy. And busy. And busy. I was bursting with the need to tell someone and I couldn't get through to Lo. It was frustrating. After more than an hour, she answered.

"Who have you been talking to all this time?" I snapped. (The biggest moment of my life, and I'm picking an argument.)

"I was taking a nap," she replied, sleepily, "and I took the phone off the hook. Why? What's the matter?"

"I made it, that's the matter," I shouted, my spirits up again. "Lo, I got the call from Deke Slayton. We're in. We're going to Houston."

Lo was awake now. She caught my excitement. Soon we were giggling over the phone like school kids.

"I'm not supposed to say anything," I said, lowering my voice, "but if anyone walks in and sees the look on my face, they'll sure as hell know."

We had two days to savor the news, to think about the implications and mentally rearrange our lives. A new career. New city. New friends. A new environment for our kids: Brian, then two, and Kimberly, still in diapers. We both recognized going in that it was a fantastic opportunity. Not just being an astronaut, but for what it offered in the way of a career path. I wasn't joining the space program to make it a career, but with the expectation of devoting a reasonable period of my life to it and then stepping out and going on to other things.

Flying alone to Houston on October 17, I gave myself a pep talk all the way down. I thought about my credentials: six years of active military service, eight more of schooling and research. Twelve years a fighter pilot, I considered myself a skilled aviator—the best. But I'd be competing now with thirteen other pros, half of them test pilots. "This is the big leagues," I told myself. "You can't let up. You've got to keep charging." For a goal-oriented man it was one more mountain to climb.

The Apollo astronauts were introduced to each other and to the world on October 18, 1963, exactly five years before traveling into space. We were an interesting mix: seven from the air force (Edwin E. "Buzz" Aldrin, Bill Anders, Donn Eisele, Charlie Bassett, Ted Freeman, Dave Scott, and Mike Collins); four from the navy (Dick Gordon, Gene Cernan, Alan Bean, and Roger Chaffee); one marine (C. C. Williams); and two civilians (Rusty Schweickart, a research scientist from MIT, and myself). Rusty had just resigned from the Massachusetts Air National Guard, but I intended to continue flying with the Marine Corps.

Our group was to represent a cross-section of the Apollo Program itself, with all the highs and lows of astronaut careers. Bassett, Freeman, and Williams would be killed in jet crashes. Chaffee would die in the fire on the pad. Aldrin and Collins would fly the first lunar landing mission. Eisele would become the first divorced astro. Scott would be at the center of a scandal for taking envelopes to the moon.

We were entertained at a cocktail party the night we arrived, and some of the older hands dropped by to welcome us. I learned later that they did not attend such affairs happily. They were busy traveling, working on the Gemini Program, and it was an imposition to intrude on one of their rare free nights at home. Still, we visited with Deke Slayton and Al Shepard. Wally Schirra and John Glenn, the reigning hero, showed up along with Pete Conrad, Jim Lovell, Jim McDivitt, and a few others from the second group. Their poise and sharpness were dazzling. Under the circumstances it was easy to overrate them. I wasn't familiar enough yet to know their weaknesses. They were all impressive. The Gemini astronauts seemed better equipped and more well-rounded, though they lacked the charisma of the Original Seven. They hadn't tasted the glory of space flight and were still unknown quantities.

Dr. Robert Voas, a psychologist who was the Mercury astronauts' training director, detailed the required characteristics as he saw them: intelligence without genius, knowledge without inflexibility, a high degree of skill without over-training, fear but not cowardice, bravery without foolhardiness, self-confidence without egotism, physical fitness without being muscle-bound, a preference for participatory over spectator sports, frankness without blabber mouthing, enjoyment of life without excess, humor without disproportion, and fast reflexes without panic in a crisis.

Against that backdrop, I could understand how a rookie football player out of, say, Bethune-Cookman College might feel at his first training camp with the Green Bay Packers. We were grateful just to be there and in some ways awed by it. We flat bathed ourselves in the feeling of being on the team. We were a little nervous, and, at the same time, a little cocky.

We were in, and there was just one public hurdle to face—our first press conference. Paul Haney briefed us before we met the newsmen and fed us sample questions. We were assured that the questions would be simple and friendly: "Were you a Boy Scout? What is your religion?" Paul added, "The only problem might come from questions about the personal-stories publishing contract. You can honestly answer you don't know much about it yet."

After the briefing, Rusty Schweickart and I hung back. We cornered Paul and, as it quickly developed, we both shared some concern for the same potential question. "Paul," Rusty blurted out, "I don't know how you'll react to this, but I'm not what you'd call a religious person. I can't claim any religion."

It was my turn to chime in and add to Paul's problems. I had abandoned organized religion fifteen years before, and was at best an agnostic in most people's eyes. Rusty, and I weren't amused by our mutual dilemma. We weren't taking it lightly. The American public (and NASA) might not look with favor on sending astros without a firm belief in God on a mission deep into the heavens—that close to the home office, so to speak.

And it was no frivolous point. When Yuri Gagarin returned from his first orbital flight, he made a point of sniping at the spiritual attitude that has been so much a part of the American ethic. "I didn't see God up there," he cracked. "I looked and looked and looked and I didn't see God." The American public was shocked and repelled by Gagarin's blasphemy, and cited it as one more example of "godless Communism."

We only had a few moments, but Haney betrayed no real concern and responded matter-of-factly. "If they ask, just hedge. Tell them your family's faith, or something." Although a devout Catholic, Paul didn't presume to judge us, nor did the disclosure seem to disturb him.

The reporters' questions were trivial enough. Then, addressing all of us, one of the reporters asked, "What is your religious preference?"

We responded one by one, starting at the tail end of our alphabetical seating. When they reached Rusty, he replied calmly, "I have no preference," and the questioning continued down the line. No one thought anything about it.

When my turn came I copped out. I couldn't bite the bullet, and Rusty's answer was too perfectly conceived to copy. Being candid isn't always a virtue, and I said, "My mother and sisters are Lutheran, but I've attended many different churches."

The press conference ended without incident. The next day's Houston papers ran our photographs on the front page with long strings of words under them. It was official. We were the third generation of astronauts. We were the men of Apollo.

I thought I knew what NASA had to offer me. But even with all the background checking—questioning of neighbors, friends, classmates, and co-workers—I wondered if they really knew what they were getting in Ronnie Walter Cunningham.

Mine wasn't a remarkable story. Up from poor; the oldest of five kids; an egghead in school who struggled to be recognized for his athletic endeavors; I began delivering newspapers at the age of eleven and have paid my own way ever since.

My ticket to upward mobility was ambition; the vehicle was the airplane. At ten, brainwashed by a World War II movie, *Navy Hell Divers*, I resolved on the spot to become a Lieutenant Commander in the Navy Air Corps. In grammar school, my claim to fame was being able to identify aircraft flying overhead simply by the sound of their engines. At the first distant hum of an engine, the teacher would look at me. I'd cock an ear and announce, "P-38 out of Lockheed," or "an A-20 just taking off from the Douglas plant." In 1941 and 1942 southern California had a lot of aircraft in the air.

Sisters Carol, Char and Cathy, with Mom, brother Ken and me in 1942 after moving to California.

It was the era of radio and *The Quiz Kids* was a hit. I was nominated but unsuccessful in competitions to qualify for that precocious panel. The reputation of being a brain haunted me all through school. From accelerated classes in grammar school through high school, I carried what seemed the double burdens of being both an intellect and a shrimp. My full growth didn't come till after high school.

I was athletic and earned varsity letters in gymnastics. In one of the team pictures I was the only guy standing and was still the shortest one in the picture, five foot four and wiry—or "lean and mean," as I characterized it in later years.

I was a smart punk who made A's without effort and generally had my nose in Mickey Spillane's latest thriller. I could knock off one of his paperbacks in two days just reading as I walked between classes.

My school years seemed a constant struggle to become one of the guys, to hang around with the school toughs, and in general to make a conspicuous effort to be something I wasn't.

Mother was ambitious for her children and encouraged my studies. Dad had a small cement contracting business, but he liked being on his own primarily for the freedom it gave him. He dearly loved to fish and hunt with his cronies. That was his declaration of independence.

From out of all this, I somehow was motivated to set high goals and achieve them. I grew up with the notion that with hard work I could do better than the next guy.

Following high school, I enlisted in the U.S. Navy, becoming the first Cunningham to ever join the service. I began to grow up and, more importantly, to learn a few lessons of life. On the first day in "boot camp," we were told that the first four recruits to learn the semaphore code would be made squad leaders. A half hour later, after demonstrating to my drill instructor my mastery of the system, his response was, "That's fine, Cunningham, but you're just too small to be a squad leader."

The first one to the finish line is not always the winner.

Boot camp was followed by a couple of Navy schools. While learning to be an electronics technician at Memphis Naval Air Station, my bunkmate was a gifted halfback who was ineligible to play. While the football team was practicing, Aronno was in night school trying to pass a Morse code test at eight words per minute. Some of the team convinced me it was practically my patriotic duty to take the test for my friend so he could

play. The scheme was uncovered when I tried too hard and accidentally—
I do mean accidentally—got a perfect score. The Chief in charge just
couldn't believe Aronno could have no errors on a test after eight weeks
of night school. The only thing that kept the two of us from court martials
was that Aronno had donated blood the week before to the Commanding Officer's wife when she was dying in childbirth. It cost me an automatic promotion to the next higher rating but it could just as easily have
nipped a promising career before it even got started.

The cynical might say, "No good deed goes unpunished!" but the real
lesson was "Think carefully before you compromise your principals—
even for a friend."

All of this became academic when I passed a two-year college equiv-
alency test and was accepted for Pre-flight School at Pensacola, Florida.
Noting that my classmates all had two to six years of college behind them,
I gave myself the old nose-to-the-grindstone speech, and it took—for
about six weeks. The posting of our first "grades" showed me second in
our class of fifty-six and, characteristically, I coasted and held that position for the rest of Pre-flight.

When we moved into the flying phase of our instruction, my tendency to get by on less than 100 percent effort was shed immediately. Nothing had ever come to me more easily or naturally than flying. It was as if
Walter Cunningham had been re-born. I felt like Van Gogh picking up his
first paintbrush. From the beginning, I lived, grew, belonged in an airplane. I loved it for reasons I only began to understand years later.

Mechanical skills are only a small part of what makes an aviator. It's
what's in the head and heart that makes a great pilot. Flying single-seat,
high-performance airplanes is the pinnacle for those who *know* they
belong above the clouds. From the beginning, I viewed flying as a joyous,
liberating experience. I was ecstatic when I whipped my instructor in
mock combat—but it seemed a natural thing to do.

What I didn't realize was how this phase of my life was shaping me
for the future. In time, I came to know that the magic for me was in the
control or mastery one has over one's destiny when flying an airplane. It
hit me first on a night formation flight, during advanced training, in an
F6F Hellcat. In 1953, in South Texas, the nights were dark and there
weren't many lights on the ground. In fact, it looked a lot like the sky
above it. While flying in the number two position in a flight of four, we

began making gentle turns, which seemed to gradually get steeper until we were maneuvering at ninety degrees of bank. At this point, my instructor in the lead F6F blinked his navigation lights, signaling me to slide over between his aircraft and the Number 3 man to form an echelon (all four aircraft in a single line). In the few seconds it took to move across, I thought, "My God, he trusts me—giving me a crossover in a ninety-degree bank. The slightest mistake on my part and we'll both be dead!"

There was *no* way I'd make that error. I'll just relax a little of this pressure I'm holding on the top rudder and … zap, there I was in position. It wasn't a good crossover—too fast, even dangerous—but it shook me out of the vertigo I had been experiencing. Suddenly, there we were, <u>as we had been all along</u>, flying straight and level. Without realizing it, I had developed a rock-solid case of vertigo. My senses misled me to believe we had been flying formation in a near-ninety-degree bank for the preceding ten minutes. The realization that came that night—that I was carrying my life in my own hands—has stayed with me to this day. In fact, the entire pattern of my life was established by my pilot training. I learned to embrace the chance of dangerous adventure—not avoid it; to confidently accept a challenge when it's encountered; to charge ahead and to never look back. The opportunity to achieve a feeling of mastery and control over oneself, a certain feeling of omnipotence, is worth all the effort (and the risk) it takes to get there.

In another sense, flying was a maturing, exciting way to move from a rather humble childhood toward the good life. It was a profession that left survivors with a competitive advantage. In retrospect, it was also the first step of a screening process toward becoming an astronaut and flying in space.

Following a tour in Korea as a Marine Corps pilot, I got married, transferred to the Marine Corps Reserve and enrolled in college—all within a period of two months. That first year, we lived on the G.I. Bill and Lo's salary as a secretary. I was strongly motivated to produce and, if anything, I overcompensated, finishing the first several years with straight A's. After taking a job and adjusting my priorities, an old characteristic took over: laziness. I concentrated hard on math and physics and settled for Bs in everything else.

That strategy had carried me through my military and college careers. Now I looked upon the space program as the ultimate testing ground.

Whatever my talents, whatever my capacities, they would surely be tested and found out here.

We Plebes had reporting dates to Houston of around 1 January 1964. Rusty Schweickart showed up before Christmas, which made him an old hand when I arrived at the beginning of January. The two of us shared an office in a reconditioned building—formerly condemned—at Ellington Air Force Base, eighteen miles southeast of Houston.

First tour of duty as a Marine Corps fighter pilot flying F3D-2
night fighters in Korea.

Our indoctrination, education, and some disillusionment were still ahead of us. Soon after the group assembled, we were treated to a memorable lecture by Wally Schirra, introducing such subjects as Astronaut Deportment, Fringe Benefits, and How to Handle Per Diem Checks and Travel Expenses. Wally offered such pearls of wisdom as suggesting each of us open a separate travel account into which our per diem checks would be deposited. This would allow us to keep track of expenses and simplify the handling of business deductions at income tax time. It was also the first indication we had that being an astro would involve interminable travel and that our finances were apt to get complicated, and—for some—best kept private.

Wally's lecture also contained smiling references to something that was already becoming obvious to us. The ladies just loved astronauts. It was wild, the lengths to which they would go to be, well, friendly. We were expected to tolerate a certain amount of freewheeling behavior on the part of our compadres.

With the astros the biggest problem was loose women. The opportunities and the temptations were fantastic. C. C. Williams, the first bachelor astronaut, already had someone from Lubbock, Texas, chasing him with a paternity suit by the time he reported to NASA. It wasn't too surprising, in light of later stories that had no truth, to learn that C. C. had never been in Lubbock. Some dude had passed through town saying he was C. C. Williams, famous birdman, and left a girl pregnant.

The sense of what Wally told us was to cool it around the flagpole. There were going to be goodies we never dreamed of—good deals on Corvettes, four percent home loans—and we, the weenie astronauts, would be cut in by the old hands. In return we were expected not to rock the boat and not to make waves by repeating indiscreet remarks to the press, neighbors, or to our wives.

Of the thirty astros then in the program, twenty-six were career military men. (The four civilians, all military trained fighter pilots, were Neil Armstrong, Elliot See, Rusty Schweickart, and myself.) So even though NASA was a civilian government agency, the Astronaut Office had a decided military cast. I felt as though I had been recalled to active duty with a fighter squadron and that was a good feeling. The Astronaut Office, which was headed throughout the sixties by Al Shepard, operated on an obvious "Rank Has Its Privilege" basis.

Yet, as in most things involving the astros, a paradox existed. Few wore uniforms even once a year (flying weekends with the Marine Corps Reserve, I was in uniform a helluva lot more than the career military men). After years at NASA, most would feel out of place and at some disadvantage when called back to their parent service. Col. Buzz Aldrin returned to the Air Force and lasted only a year; Gen. Tom Stafford did somewhat better.

More important than service rank was the pecking order: whether you were first-, second-, or third-generation astro. We were the new guys, the rookies, the bottom of the pecking order.

I had reported with an open mind toward the experience but a little defensive about my flying background—not having any test flying experience, although half of our group were in the same boat. I was a civilian Marine Reserve officer at whom regular career officers tended to look down their noses. Reporting directly from a campus, academic background did little to enhance the picture. So I bent over backwards to show I was a tiger, aggressive, competitive and the best qualified of the bunch— not without creating some problems for myself.

From the beginning, Rusty and I suspected we had been selected as sops to the scientific community, but it took that august group, the National Academy of Sciences, only a little while to find out that we were just like the rest of the "dumb fighter jocks." Flying was a much more desirable way to spend your days than working out a problem in physics.

The Astronaut Office was one of three divisions (the others being Flight Operations and Flight Crew Support) in the Directorate headed by Deke Slayton. Deke's appointment as Deputy Director had been (at least partially) a consolation prize bestowed on him by the other Mercury astros when the medics had grounded him. Expecting that Deke would never make a space flight, the Mercury astros relinquished a certain amount of individual autonomy by "allowing" him to be in charge. He lacked management experience, but started right off running the show. He was successful because he had their respect. He was one of them; he had gone through the same selection process, the same trials. This was no outsider trying to issue orders.

Many times his authority required a delicate hand. It was never exactly a jellyroll to be "in charge of" Gordon Cooper, Scott Carpenter, Alan Shepard, Wally Schirra, and Gus Grissom. John Glenn, of course, was soon to be leaving the program. In some respects, his buddies gave the impression that it was "Deke Slayton, Director of Flight Crew Operations, by the authority of the National Aeronautics And Space Administration and the grace of the Mercury astronauts."

Within days of our arrival we were on a full schedule of orientation, classes, flying and training. It was a demanding, all-consuming job. Waking up in the morning, my first thought was always on that day's activities.

The general training was also invaluable as an exposure to each other's strengths and weaknesses. Flying around the country with different astros provided an opportunity to differentiate between those who felt there was only one way to do things— their way, and those who were more flexible and tolerant of different points of view.

The routine, the training, in a sense, our careers were loaded with ironies. After several flights with Ted Freeman, I was convinced he was one of the better pilots I had ever flown with. Only a few weeks later, Ted became the first astronaut to die . . . in a jet crash.

Scott Carpenter and Gordon Cooper gave us the warmest and most sincere receptions of any of the Mercury astros. They were the only ones eventually frozen out by their contemporaries.

From the outset there were signs of the frustration to come. We had no clue as to when flights would be projected for our group or who would be selected to make them. In a corner of my mind was the nagging thought that maybe all this early activity was simply to keep us busy while the Mercury and Gemini guys got ready and flew their missions.

Our uncertainty was aggravated by the fact that we were attending "gentlemen's classes"—no grading. I had looked forward to, even craved, the intense competition that the public suspected was encountered on every level. If I was going up against twenty-nine other aces, I wanted it objectively measured, taped, recorded—and wanted to see it affect each man's progress. The reason for "gentlemen's classes" was simply that the old heads wanted it that way. In the absence of objective criteria, politics could rule the day. The Mercury astros refused to be graded on anything they ever did. They were reluctant to leave a record showing that Wally Schirra was better (or worse) than Scott Carpenter or Gordon Cooper, let alone the Gemini or Apollo guys. They sat at the top of the hierarchy and could only lose by laying it on the line to be measured.

In the end it didn't make a nickel's worth of difference how we performed in class. Take geology, which not all of the fellows could. We had lectures and lab work, at first two or three times a week, later two or three afternoons a month. We showed up if we wanted to, and the new guys always did—at least until we got a bit salty or grew tired of looking at rocks. Out of the Mercury group, only Carpenter and Cooper made a consistent effort to attend. Deke Slayton was up to his armpits in paperwork, but he made a point of showing up when he could. Deke was trying to set an example as well as hoping that he would be returned to flight status.

We weenie astros attended faithfully for one good reason: we were looking desperately for an edge. In terms of making an impression, we had precious few options. We didn't get to fly around the country with Deke, selling ourselves. We were spending most of our time in classes—staring at a blackboard or attempting to sort out a box of rocks. Our professors had zero influence on assignments, and there weren't many dramatic possibilities in a box of rocks: no safely bringing down a burning aircraft, no untying little Nell from the railroad tracks.

It quickly became apparent that in order to make out in the program—to get in line for a flight crew—you needed the right game plan. Bill Anders and I shared one based on the hard-work ethic: bust your ass, do your best, don't let up, and the boss will eventually notice and reward you accordingly. We stuck to that for the first two or three years. It wasn't the best plan.

Everywhere we went, flight crew assignment was the major topic of conversation. In late 1965, most of us traveled up to Boston for an introductory course at Massachusetts Institute of Technology on the Apollo Computer and Inertial Guidance System. One night Anders, Schweickart, Bean, and I—we usually ran around together—went to the famed Concord Bridge, where the Minutemen of the American Revolution fired "the shot heard round the world." But instead of being inspired by the history of the place, instead of talking about American history, we stood there talking about space and our chances of getting into it. Another night we drove over to Harvard to poke around the famed Harvard Yard. While sitting in a small cafe on campus, we talked some more about how to get on a flight crew.

Some of our guys (Mike Collins, Dave Scott, and Dick Gordon) were already assigned to Gemini backup crews, and we quickly began to discuss the mysteries of crew selection. By what process did the magic wand reach out and tap you? Who would get the first Apollo flight? Who would fly to the moon? What could one do to enhance his chances of being chosen?

"It doesn't work; it's not enough," Anders finally decided.

"What isn't?" I asked.

"Hard work and doing a good job. No one really notices."

We were constantly analyzing the system and playing the name-the-crew game, over coffee or a drink or when we were rooming together on the road and the lights were out and we couldn't sleep.

We were slowly waking up to the fact that politics and favoritism were very important. It wasn't that much different from any other job where personalities play a big part, where it helps to be in the right place at the right time, and where certain factors—service relationships, first impressions, and pressure from friends (pro and con) created fair-haired boys.

It wasn't even necessarily a power play. It might work like this: Deke Slayton had worked with Frank Borman in the Air Force, and Borman had worked with Mike Collins. When it came time to move the first Apollo astronauts into flight positions, Mike Collins would be selected to back up Gemini 7—which happened to be Frank Borman's mission. Later, Collins would move on to Borman's Apollo 8 crew.

Another example: Dick Gordon (who had been friends and room-mates with Pete Conrad since Navy test-pilot days) was paired with Pete as backup on Gemini 8. From there the two of them flew Gemini 11, backed up Apollo 9, and flew Apollo 12. Al Bean, who also knew Pete and Dick from Naval Test Pilot School, joined them as the third member of their crew after the Gemini program.

It really paid to have a champion in the hierarchy above you. Once in the rotation, the chances were strong of being recycled on still other missions, leading, one hoped, to that great pyramid in the sky: the lunar landing.

The days flew by and frustrations mounted. There was seldom, if ever, any feedback on how we were faring: good, bad, or indifferent. We slowly got fed into the paper mill, with directives and memoranda and meeting notices constantly coming across our desks. We worked our butts off on the Gemini program even if we were quite certain we'd never make a Gemini flight. We never knew who was watching and making what kind of decision based on what information. It was an open-loop competition at all times—no feedback to the contestants.

We went to class and scrambled to get a few minutes in the Mercury simulator. We hustled to get an early checkout in helicopters. In our ignorance or naiveté, everything or anything could have some importance, even the dullest classroom lectures. It wasn't just that someday our lives might depend on some piece of casual information. We paid attention because someday, somewhere, someone in a meeting might ask a question. If we could summon forth that one jewel of an answer, retained from hours of drudgery, then bingo, our lives would move out of the shadows and into the center arena.

All the time we were competing with some real masters in the art of gamesmanship. One never admitted that a drill had been difficult, that he was encountering problems, or that he *ever* felt insecure. We were always doing "great, just great."

One of our early brushes with "playing" astronaut was the Mercury simulator. (The Gemini model barely arrived in time for the first Gemini mission and simply wasn't available for practice licks by guys who weren't even in line.) The challenge in the Mercury simulator was to fire the retro rockets to bring the spacecraft out of orbit with bad misalignments in all three rockets. (There could be serious consequences to this exercise. Scott Carpenter landed his Mercury capsule 350 miles off-target, down-range as a result of not adequately controlling the vehicle attitude during retro fire.)

Three rockets were fired, one after the other, and the object was to hold the spacecraft precisely on attitude during the burn, regardless of misalignments—a process at which I became quite good. But unless somebody came and looked over our shoulders, which we resented, or unless the technician at the training desk told someone, no one would ever know how well or how poorly we did. I might discuss the task in general terms with Charlie Bassett, but if he got curious as to how I was doing, "It was a piece of cake."

3

Taking the Bad With the Good

I DON'T BElIEVE it would be an overstatement to say that we were in endless conflict with our own egos. No matter how hard we might try to *not* take ourselves seriously—and some tried harder than others—we were constantly reminded of our special role as men being trained to leave this planet.

There were many models for us to choose from: John Glenn, with his sense of obligation and higher purpose. Tough, intense, cocky Gus Grissom, the kind of guy who didn't care if the sun came out or not. Scott Carpenter and Gordon Cooper were independent and adventuresome and seemed willing to pay the price. They both did.

Then there was Al Shepard. I suspect that even the most cynical of us admired the sophistication, the social poise he brought to the job. Al was acquainted with everybody. Governors knew him. Millionaire oilmen knew him. Kings-in-exile knew him. His technique was flawless.

Our own situation—so near and yet so far—was apparent to us even on such exercises as our jungle training expedition to Panama in July 1964. We hacked our way through the jungles for nearly a week, in groups of two, enduring the humid heat and underbrush and mosquitoes that could carry off a small dog. After joining up and another half day's walking, we were paddling our way down a river in two dugout canoes when Pete Conrad glanced up and spotted a lean-to hut squatting on a hilltop.

"Hey, how about that," yelped Pete, pointing. "Way out here in the middle of nowhere, in the middle of the jungle, a little old hut up there with a family living in it."

"Yeah," said Jim Lovell, dryly, "and hanging on a wall in there someplace is a photograph signed, 'Warmest Personal Regards, Al.'"

That broke us up, even as we glided along the backwaters of the Panama jungle. Shepard, of course, was famous for his photos with that stock phrase. I have one on my own office wall with the same inscription. When you have to sign them by the thousands, a fellow can't be blamed for using little imagination.

In an entirely different spirit, another astronaut trait became evident early in our training: knocking the other guy. In eight years at NASA, I rarely heard one astro volunteer anything complimentary about another or admit to his own problems. The one consistent exception was a post flight acknowledgment of a mission professionally conducted—if it was truly warranted.

It was disturbing to know that your friends and co-workers thought nothing of putting you down in the eyes of the NASA brass, most notably Al Shepard and Deke Slayton, who could tap your shoulder and say, "You're gonna make a space flight."

The putdowns might deal with behavior or office style ("Cunningham? He can't get much done with that phone stuck in his ear"). Or might plant a seed of doubt about a buddy's flying competence ("Have you noticed Al Bean rarely flies at night anymore?" Or, "I wonder why Bruce McCandless never flies in formation?").

Under the circumstances it wasn't always easy to remain friendly. The more open you were, the more exposed you became to snipers.

It wasn't so much out-and-out cutthroat as it was a spirit of laissez-faire, free enterprise, anything goes, win-at-any-cost competition—all accepted values in the fields of sport, commerce, and politics. It left me occasionally confused, sometimes isolated, but rarely bitter. There was no handle to be found, no real understanding of how the machine operated and how to deal with it.

With good contacts in the first or second groups one might pick up a fragment of useful information now and then. But I hadn't known any of the other twenty-nine astronauts before joining NASA and none of them had any reason to know me. So my intelligence loop revolved around the likes of Anders and Bean and Schweickart. We were terrific at gossiping and forming opinions, but we had few facts to exchange. We were, even collectively, a fairly useless intelligence network.

There was one respect in which the program was eminently fair. Undesirable assignments seemed to be distributed, without prejudice, to all.

A notable example of what we considered undesirable was what we called our "Week In The Barrel." The inspiration for the name came from the old story about the sourdough who staggers into an Alaskan mining camp, looking for a woman—any woman. He has rather serious biological needs. And they refer him to a back room that features a large barrel with a hole in the side.

The week in the barrel was the result of an arrangement between the Astronaut Office in Houston and NASA Headquarters in Washington, D.C.. Every other week our office would deliver one warm, astronaut body to NASA Headquarters to brief, schedule, and use as they wished. It was a public relations ploy designed to help NASA sell the program to the taxpayers and congressmen of the United States. The agency had literally thousands of requests a year for us to speak to everything from kindergarten classes to Congress (Congress got priority). On a rotating basis, starting with the A's (for Armstrong), each astronaut was expected to spend one week on what amounted to a whirlwind speaking tour.

For those of us who had yet to get a taste of space—who were, in fact, still years away from going up—-the week in the barrel was somewhat of an embarrassment. I never got used to the idea of a roomful of citizens giving me a standing ovation, when all I had done was fly my T-38 in from Houston. The most exciting thing to talk about firsthand was the trip to Panama and the week of jungle survival training. We looked forward eagerly to the arrival of a newly selected group of astros, simply because it meant more time between repeating your week in the barrel.

My first such week began with a briefing in Washington, where James Webb, the NASA Administrator, Julian Scheer, then the Director of Public Affairs, and other big guns helped me bone up on the political aspects of the program. Then, starting with an audience of four hundred engineers in Schenectady, New York, I went on to make thirty appearances—-or, more correctly, the same speech thirty times—in five days.

After Schenectady I made a swing through Alaska, hitting every high school and service club in Anchorage and Fairbanks. The week was an education, starting with the VIP treatment; NASA assigned a protocol officer—in those days the agency could still afford it—to keep me on schedule and out of trouble. Mine was a cool twenty-four-year-old named Fred Asselin who had a splendid instinct for knowing when and how to get you out of a crowd and away from autograph seekers without making you the bad guy. He had moxie and knew how to play the game. The

mayor of Philadelphia listened meekly as Fred assigned automobile priorities to the dignitaries when the city honored Al Shepard with a parade.

These speaking tours provided most of us with our first real glimpse
of the adulation lavished upon anyone with "astronaut" in front of his
name. It was late November 1964 and $0°$ Fahrenheit outside when we
landed in Anchorage. The coldest weather I had ever experienced previously was $12°$ *above* zero during a bleak Korean winter. Being from southern California, I freeze my tassels when the thermometer drops below $70°$·

After a full day of listening to myself orate—I had a ten-minute film
and a stock spiel about the training grind, the only thing I really knew
about—-there was a midnight flight to Fairbanks. When we climbed out
of the plane, it was *thirty below zero.* I thought I was going to faint. And
there's a crowd at the airport to meet me, as though I had just flown the
Atlantic in a bathtub or something.

Someone loaned me a fancy wolverine parka, and it sure came in
handy the next day. The local school kids were excused from class in the
morning for my appearance at the air force base. I stood in an open Jeep
and waved at the kids in a kind of three-block mini-parade. It was so cold!
Even today, I shiver when I think about it.

But the incident that made my week in the barrel memorable was a
classic case of astronaut over-extension. That's a combination of what
other people *think* we can do, and our willingness to try it anyway.

To keep our appointments, the commanding general of the Alaska
Frontier had made available his personal helicopter: an HU-1A, or Huey,
made famous in Vietnam rescue and support missions. It was a turbine
chopper with a deluxe interior, all dolled up for the big brass. The pilot
was a bright, friendly, obliging army captain by the name of Toso.

Having bootlegged four or five hours of stick time in helicopters over
the years, I was looking forward to checking out in them. Over the noisy
clatter of the chopper I yelled at him, "I'm going to helicopter training in
February," and again, louder, "I'm going to helicopter training."

He smiled and nodded. After a bit he asked if I'd like to take the controls. I accepted with alacrity. After all, I was an astronaut; I could do anything. A moment later I was flying the general's helicopter. I was lifting
off, hovering, flying to the next speech, and we're both having a damn
good time.

Later, we had ten minutes between speeches, and the captain offered to let me practice on their training course nestled between the trees on an old airport. I leapt at the chance. We had Fred and another passenger in the back seat and I wasn't doing badly for a guy with maybe five hours of chopper time, eight years ago.

The ground was blanketed with snow and I was threading my way around the course, with trees on either side of me. Just as my confidence was soaring, I spotted a telephone line immediately in front of me. With that fabled reaction and quick wits of the trained aviator, I realized there were two choices: I could go up and hit the wire with the canopy or go down and cut it with the rotor blade.

With unfailing judgment, I took a third choice, turned to the captain, and said, "You've got it!" He went straight through it, cutting the lines and wrapping them neatly around the mast. We were only about five feet off the ground and he sat the chopper down smoothly.

I sat there, feeling stupid. He looked at me, hesitated, and asked, "When did you say you went through helicopter training?

"Next February," I said.

"My God," he said. "I thought you had already completed it."

We were unable to untangle the telephone wire from the rotor blades and it was 4:30 P.M., getting dark and growing colder. We were unable to raise anyone on the radio and it was starting to look grim. Finally, an army observation plane spotted us and called in a spare helicopter. I ended up missing one speech and getting a lesson in the folly of believing your own press clippings.

I really felt bad about it—not only because of my own embarrassment, but because my new friend, the captain, was responsible for the general's personal helicopter. I wrote letters to the general and to everyone else connected with the trip and, fortunately, there were no repercussions. I learned another lesson: no one was anxious to take potshots at a working astronaut.

During this early training period, we welcomed any kind of individual assignment. We existed for those moments when we, for whatever reason, were singled out from the pack. One such assignment was a capsule communicator (CapCom) at Mission Control—at least you got to talk to the *real* astronauts—or in a mission support role at the Cape. My first such opportunity came when I was assigned to test the new Apollo spacesuit on a field trip to the McKenzie Lava Flows in Oregon. It was no big deal. I might even have been chosen because the only suit available was in my size or because everyone else was busy. But at least it was something I wouldn't be doing in a group.

The test turned out to be difficult, tedious, and tiring. I struggled and scrambled to climb a mountain the likes of which no one would ever encounter, much less climb, on the moon. In the process one day I slipped and fell against a sharp rock, punching a tiny hole in one glove of my pressurized suit. It caused a small leak and the suit wouldn't hold pressure, so we had to send for a spare glove.

While all this was going on, photographers with telescopic lenses were zeroing in from fifty yards away. The next day all the papers were full of Cunningham falling on the lava bed and ripping a glove.

The test was quite successful, and we accomplished what we had set out to with the suit. It had been hard work, but I was satisfied. On returning to Houston the only thing Deke said to me was, "Walt, you shouldn't have fallen down like that in front of the news media."

The trip did produce one nice surprise, though. While I was out there on the lava beds, a string of cars pulled up. Out of one of them stepped Mark Hatfield, then the governor of Oregon. He introduced himself and we shook hands, posed for pictures, and quickly finished the political amenities. While we were making small talk, he mentioned that the local pilot who had flown me in from Klamath Falls had reported I was planning to put a lava rock wall, symbolic of the lunar surface, in the home I had under construction. The upshot was that a few days later the governor had some lava rock crated up and shipped to me, enough to finish the end wall in my living room. It made a nice conversation piece for many years.

It was a period in our lives when, every time we went on a trip and shared a room with a close friend, we'd lie in bed at night and let out whatever was inside us. Unless one was on a flight crew, he was predictably mad as hell about the system, and we bitched about crew selections and complained of the trapped feeling. We were victims of the judgment of some nebulous higher authority, and it was frustrating. No one ever expressed concern about failing, only about not getting an opportunity.

Our lives resembled the famous line by Henry Jordan, the Green Bay Packers tackle, about Vince Lombardi: "Coach is fair. He treats us all alike.

He treats us all like dogs." The system was fair in that respect. Nobody told you anything, nobody promised you a damn thing.

We all went through those emotional bends at one point or another. I rode home from Ellington Air Force Base one day with Pete Conrad, then training for his Gemini 5 "eight-days-or-bust" flight with Gordon Cooper. Pete was tooling his Corvette down the Galveston highway, batting along at 100-plus and blowing off steam. He had decided that the space program wasn't all that neat, after all. He was going to hang up his jock. He had it all figured out.

"You can't quit this damn business," he said, dead serious, "until after your second flight. If you quit after the first one, they'll say it scared you to death and you didn't want to go back. So you have to make a second flight. But after that, they can have it. There are other things a guy can do besides taking all this bullshit."

I was sitting there agreeing with him—but on an entirely different level.

The kicker, of course, is that in June 1973, eight years later, Pete Conrad commanded the first Skylab mission, his fourth space flight. When it came to leaving NASA, there was a wide disparity between promise and performance.

At least 75 percent of our time during that first two years was spent in an organized training regimen. When we weren't in classes, on field trips, or in the simulators, we were flying, often in pairs with other astros. It was natural to begin calibrating them. My second flight in a T-38 was my first with Elliot See. It destroyed any visions I might have harbored about the super-engineer-test-pilot types. I don't think I ever flew with him again.

Elliot had flown the T-38 as a test pilot for General Electric long before he came to NASA. On this particular flight he was up front, with me in the rear. Immediately after takeoff—while we were still heavy with fuel— he indicated he wanted to fly over Taylor Lake and buzz his house, a not uncommon astronaut practice. Elliot had told his wife, Marilyn, when to expect him.

I didn't object. A buzz job to me was fun; it meant coming down faster than a bat out of hell and saying, "Adios" before anyone gets your tail number. I have flown landing gear checks faster than this particular low pass. Elliot dropped down slow and got set up to cross Taylor Lake at fifty feet with a full load of fuel, at 170 knots and no flaps down. (Apparently, Elliot had never heard of that old pilot axiom: "If you're gonna fly low, don't fly slow!") For the uninitiated, let me inject here that the T-38 with a full load of fuel won't fly a whole lot slower than 165 knots, even with the flaps down. I was in the rear cockpit, rationalizing that he was a good aviator; he had to know what he was doing, didn't he? After all, he was an astronaut, one of the big boys. The fact that he was flying way too slow troubled me only to the extent that it could get me killed.

In ninety-nine out of a hundred such situations, the second pilot does nothing but try to anticipate where the boundary is when you both must suffer the consequences. Deciding we had passed that boundary, I finally piped up and said, as casually as I could, "Hey, how about half flaps?" He dropped half flaps, waved to Marilyn, and we flew away. Unfortunately, that was the first thing I thought of when Elliot and his seat-mate, Charlie Bassett, were killed the following year in a low, slow landing approach at St. Louis that ended in a stall and crash.

Elliot was a great guy, a friend of mine, but a weak pilot. When judging another pilot's capabilities, someone on whom your own life might someday depend, you can't afford to be sentimental.

In late 1964, as we neared the end of our formal training, Deke dropped an overnight assignment on us called a "peer rating." It was a procedure that had been followed by the Mercury and Gemini groups before us. The peer rating process was familiar to the fellows who had been through Annapolis and West Point, but to the rest of us it inspired only a blank stare.

Said Deke, patiently, "You simply eliminate yourself and then consider in what order you think the other guys in your group ought to be flying a space mission."

Deke advised us to think about it overnight. In effect, we were being asked to speculate about each other's performance. I went home that evening and thought about it. I suspected there were various bits of gamesmanship that could be played with such a list. Some might have been tempted to put the softest competition at the top on the chance that Deke would allow so many points per vote, like football ratings. But even that theory, required a double-think. A guy who turned in a stupid rating sheet might himself be faulted, for poor judgment.

Having little political acumen, I quickly concluded that the best course was to play it straight. Shedding my personal likes, dislikes, and biases, I tried to rank my classmates based on their capabilities and potential as I saw them at that time. Was he a hard worker? Did he plan ahead? Was he cool under pressure? Did he know the spacecraft? How would he handle the overall responsibility?

After agonizing over the list for much of the night, I felt reasonably confident that I had been able to suppress my personal feelings. For example, I was able to rate Dave Scott next to the top even though there had been continuing friction between us. There was an edge to his needling that reflected, I thought, the disparity in our backgrounds. (Dave fit the classic mold: son of a general, in the top five of his West Point graduating class, test pilot. Dave probably saw me as a smartass with the wrong pedigree: reservist, civilian, irreverent.) But his performance had pretty much resisted criticism and I gave him that.

At the same time, I found myself writing in last the name of C. C. Williams, a fellow Marine whose company I enjoyed very much. But C. C. lacked the academic background of some of the others and, to keep pace, he struggled, cheerfully.

As I reread the list years later, I wondered how my judgment and that of the NASA brass (and the fickle finger of fate) could have been so different about Al Bean. I had placed him at the top in my peer rating. I thought he had it all: smart enough, the technical skills—he was a graduate engineer from the University of Texas—the experience, and the attitude. Yet he was the last in our group to fly in space. It's possible my personal feelings showed here.

To the outside world, it may have seemed like we all came out of the same factory. With a few exceptions, we were compact, short-haired, jut-jawed. And yet, we were a fairly diverse cast of characters. The list below is in the same order as on the day I handed it to Deke Slayton. The capsule impressions were added later and some of those have changed considerably over the years.

1. Alan Bean. Friendly, the prototypically cool naval aviator whose coolness, I learned later, was the result not so much of being on top of things, as of a refusal to let himself be ruffled. Both gymnasts by training, Alan and I hit it off from the beginning. Our birthdays were one day apart, March 15 (his) and March 16 (mine). We invited the Beans over for

a joint celebration early on and discovered that before he ate out Al always checked to see what his hosts were serving. He was the only astronaut whom Lo considered a more finicky eater than me. Al had a mania for spaghetti. There wasn't a city in the United States where we traveled that he couldn't tell you how to find a half-dozen Italian restaurants. With Al, it was a practical matter: a spaghetti dinner was one way of beating the expense-money pinch.

2. Dave Scott. Despite our occasional personal friction, I recognized in Dave the controlled arrogance of those who are born to lead. He was made-in-America, big, strong, clean-cut, and intelligent. He gave the impression that, though he might be wrong, he was never in doubt. Once, on a flight from Las Vegas to Prescott, Arizona, with me in the rear seat, Dave mistakenly read the mileage figure instead of the heading on his map and headed off in the wrong direction. We were 50 miles off course when the Flight Control Center called to suggest to Dave that he ought to be correcting his flight path. It was characteristic of Scott that it didn't faze him and he never even let on that it embarrassed him.

3. Charlie Bassett. Another fair-haired, good-looking, All-American type. What most impressed you about Charlie was his self-discipline. On field trips he seldom packed a lunch, taking the position that it was good discipline to do without. While the rest of us were feeding our faces, he would use the time to make notes. He was wound tight, dedicated, had fine mechanical skills, and undoubtedly would have made an excellent space pilot—if he had lived.

4. Mike Collins. From a military family, he was the only foreign-born (Italy) in our group, a quiet, unassuming guy with a dogged disposition. Mike may have been the best-conditioned of the Apollo group. He was our handball champ from the first day we opened our new gym. Hard as nails, his physical fitness accounted, I suspect, for the success of his EVA mission on Gemini 10, where so many others failed. Mike and his wife, Pat, were our across-the-alley neighbors when we first arrived in Texas.

5. Bill Anders. A strong believer in the basic American ethic: hard work, fair play, clean living. Bill was among the more serious of our group, a quietly capable guy with a good academic background in nuclear engineering. He was one of the people with whom you could share a private thought. *In retrospect, I may have rated Bill lower than his credentials deserved, bending over backward not to favor a close friend.*

6. Rusty Schweickart. The others probably judged Rusty and me on the same yardstick. We were considered the most natural competitors considering our similar backgrounds. The two civilians, the two research scholars, had automatically been assigned to share an office. In truth, we probably represented the opposite extremes of our small group. Rusty's very liberal views clashed often with my conservative ones. It led to interesting discussions, but neither was going to convert the other. We were intellectual friends more than emotional friends. A very open guy, Rusty was the one who could relate to the hippie, arty crowd and had friends who could admit, unblushingly, they had smoked pot. His wife Claire was an active campaigner for all liberal causes. At one time it was rumored she was the leader of a movement to blockbust the then lily-white neighborhood in which most of us lived, feeling with some passion that our kids were being denied the advantages of growing up in a racially mixed environment. Rusty was easily aroused by what he perceived to be social injustice. Of all of us in the program, he had the highest tolerance and greatest respect for his wife's independent activities.

7. Buzz Aldrin. From the outset, Buzz was referred to as "Dr. Rendezvous" because of his obsession with rendezvous in space, the subject of his Ph.D. thesis at MIT. In fact, he looked more like a college professor than the fighter pilot he actually was. He smoked a pipe, eagerly engaged in "deep" discussions, and should have had leather patches on the elbows of his jacket. He was always intense and could talk for hours with anyone—as long as the subject was rendezvous. Once, when his wife Joan was out of town, we invited Buzz to dinner. Then I, too, was called away and Lo just naturally assumed that Buzz would take a rain check. Instead, at the appointed hour Buzz showed up, had a couple of cocktails and dinner for two, and then drank scotch until the wee hours, all the time delivering a monologue on the intricacies of rendezvous in space. Even at this early stage in our careers, Buzz struck some of the fellows as a bit odd.

8. Dick Gordon. There was a touch of devil-may-care in Gordon's bearing. Compact, tough, he had been an athlete of some renown at the University of Washington. He had test-flown the F-4, at the time the hottest thing in the sky, long before any of the others had. His inside drag impressed the rest of us in the beginning. He knew half the guys in the space program by their first names, was sociable, well liked, and appealing to women. Our houses were a block apart, cost the same, were the

same size and differed only in that the Gordons had three more bedrooms. They had six kids.

9. Gene Cernan. Another without a test-flying background. Gene's only real strong points were his ability to get along with people, especially the right people, and his willingness to do what he was told. On the social circuit he was a charmer and would eventually surpass even Wally Schirra in this art. At the time of the ratings, none of us, including Gene, could have guessed that he would enjoy the most complete and successful space career in our group.

10. Roger Chaffee. In the early days, some tended to underestimate Roger, perhaps because of his small stature. But he had the capacity to fill a room—any room. It was impossible to attend a meeting with Roger and not be aware of his presence. He had a fighter pilot attitude, even though his brief career was in multi-engine photo-reconnaissance aircraft. When confronted with a problem, Roger would bore right in—even if it was totally outside his expertise. One of the youngest of the third group, he was fearless, confident, bright, with the All-American-boy look, and a beautiful wife to boot.

11. Donn Eisele. A hard one to figure. Donn had the proper test pilot background and knew several of the guys before he came into the program, most usefully Tom Stafford. He seemed to enjoy the hard-partying and hard-driving aspects of our business as much as anyone, but I always had the feeling that he was pretending a lot. He once confided that back in his old fighter squadron he was considered a real tiger, but among the astros he didn't feel like much of a charger at all. As a teenager in Columbus, Ohio, Donn had worked as a zoo-keeper. Both his parents died soon after he joined NASA, and one of his children, a focus of much love, died of leukemia. Donn had more than his share of hardship to live with during our astro years.

12. C. C. Williams. I felt a twinge of guilt placing him so low, but long odds never bothered C. C. Marines were accustomed to getting by with less. He was an unspectacular guy, but his flying skills couldn't be faulted. He had performed all the carrier landing, automatic throttle tests for the F-8 Crusader. He was a big, strapping six-footer who wouldn't let you dislike him. He had one other thing going for him: no family—or wife— to hamper his pursuit of the All-American fighter pilot image.

Ted Freeman is missing from the list because he had been killed in a

T-38 crash only a short time before. I would have placed Ted near the top.

To this day, I have no idea where Walter Cunningham stood on the others' peer ratings. Certainly not in the upper bracket. I didn't figure to win the Personality Award. I had excellent credentials but had to concede there wasn't much evidence on the record yet of what I could or could not do.

With some irony, a short time later, it looked as though it was all academic, anyway. I couldn't be concerned with where or how I rated because I was trying to keep the NASA doctors from washing me out of the program.

A really silly thing happened to me in February 1965: I broke my neck on a trampoline at the official opening of the new Astronaut Gym.

Five minutes after the gym was dedicated I was working out on a trampoline, under the watchful eye of a nineteen-year-old college gymnast. Along with Aldrin, Bean, and Carpenter, I was one of a handful of former gymnasts in the program who subscribed to the theory that trampoline exercises would enhance a person's adaptability to zero gravity in space.

After about ten minutes of working out, I decided to attempt what for me was a new trick, a "cody"—a front flip to a stomach drop followed by a back flip. At least, I think that's how you do it. If I had been able to get through it safely I suppose I'd remember.

The young fellow assigned to spot me (a spotter's job is to help you and see that you're not hurt) watched as I succeeded on my first attempt at a cody, albeit not very gracefully. Characteristically I bounced back up and told him I was sure I could do better. Well, the re-try was a bust right from the beginning. I stalled out on the back flip finish and came down right on my neck—fortunately, still on the canvas. I heard a strange crunching sound and a knifelike pain shot through my neck. My first reaction was that I'd have to spend the next day or so working the soreness out.

I asked the college champ why he hadn't spotted me and he replied, with some embarrassment, "I thought you could do it."

That was another early encounter with the "omnipotent astronaut" syndrome. In those days, astronauts seemed to stand about ten feet tall and people believed we could do almost anything. No doubt some of us agreed with them. When I said I could do another cody, and a better one, he not only believed me, he stood back to get a clearer view.

He felt terrible when he saw I was hurt, and to save face—his and mine—I quickly attempted to shake it off. I moved over to another trampoline and spent about ten minutes on another piece of equipment but the pain was intense and I finally gave up and headed for the shower. Our gym, our brand-new gym, had been opened and dedicated at noon and a half hour later I was literally headed for the showers.

That afternoon, as I sat in class, it began to dawn on me that something was radically wrong. I could not turn my head. To look to either side it was necessary to rotate my entire body, using both hands to hold my head still against the pain. So long dumb and so quick smart, I now wasted little time getting to the doctor's office. From there I was sent to the hospital, where the diagnosis was made: a broken neck, compression fractures of the C-5 and C-6 vertebrae.

The doctors assured me I had been lucky and would suffer no paralysis. From that point on, I was less concerned about the road to recovery than I was that the NASA flight surgeons and Deke Slayton might leap to premature conclusions and write me off as physically unfit. As it was, I'm sure some of my buddies were yielding to our customary schizo reaction: "Poor Walt, tough break, but that's one less to worry about for a flight."

There was only one way to fight back against the inevitable doubts and suspicions and that was to prove from the outset that the injury wouldn't handicap me. The moment my neck brace was fitted, I resolved not to miss a day of training, at the same time realizing I would be grounded from flying for an indefinite period.

Two days later I was in the front of the pack, hiking up the side of Meteor Crater in Arizona during a geology field trip. I made damn sure I was up front, more for the psychological effect on my friends (and myself) than anything else.

The only real problem during the four months of living with a neck brace was flying—or, rather, not flying. Flying is a lot like sex; when you're getting a lot you always want more; if you're not getting very much, you gradually get used to doing without.

Returning to flying status came in easy stages. At first, I was limited to flying co-pilot on the Grumman Gulfstream, a twelve-passenger executive aircraft. Ed White and Jim McDivitt were starting their Gemini 4 post flight activities and I became their chauffeur on trips to Washington, D.C., and their hometowns.

The flight surgeons were reluctant to let me fly even as a passenger in the T-38, because of the ever-present possibility of ejection. They thought my already damaged back could suffer permanent disability if it had to endure the rigors of a rocket-seat ejection. During the third month my brace and I were approved for helicopter flying. Only after I had shed the neck brace—a month later—was I allowed to climb back into a T-38.

I never dwelt on the thought that the injury could have crippled me. I came through with no ill effects, although I shudder now at how close it came to wiping out so much work and so many hopes. It left me stronger and more determined for having overcome adversity.

4

Getting in Line

BY JUNE 1965, even as we awaited the launch of Gemini 4 and America's first space walk, the old order was changing.

John Glenn had retired, explaining—with John's usual perception—that he did not wish to become the oldest, permanent training, *used* astronaut. Scott Carpenter and Gordon Cooper were losing favor. Al Shepard was grounded by an inner ear disorder, his future uncertain, and Deke Slayton was buried under administrative paperwork. It was the hour of Gemini, with exotic promises of space rendezvous and docking and the sight of men outside the capsule, swimming in space. All of us Apollo jockeys were itching for a piece of the action.

Subtle changes were taking place and we were carried along as if on a moving sidewalk. Tensions were rising within management ranks and the old NASA team spirit was showing signs of strain. Strain, hell, it was a full blown power struggle.

Prior to Gemini 4, an astronaut would breeze into each of the critical tracking stations around the globe prior to each mission. They were always the last to arrive and quick to assume command. But now the star of Chris Kraft, the Director of Flight Operations, was ascending, and he had different ideas on the relative roles of his flight controllers and Deke's astronauts. Chris was emerging as a better organized and stronger administrator than Deke, whose astronaut office had the glamour but was far harder to regulate—or should we say control?

In Deke's shop no one wanted a job perfecting their paper pushing. Not even Deke.

Chris Kraft had always wanted a flight controller in charge of each tracking site, and he eventually won his point. Our training schedule really no longer left us time to assume primary responsibility for a month at some remote site. In our office the reaction was typical: if we couldn't be captain, we wouldn't play. We did, however, make one last evaluation of the new system during the Gemini 4 mission.

Bill Anders, Dave Scott, and I were assigned to man three of the stations. Scott won a coin toss for Carnarvon, Australia, which meant running the gauntlet of the Sydney social attractions both coming and going. I drew the tracking site on the island of Kauai, Hawaii, and Bill got the short straw and Guaymas, Mexico. We understood that this was possibly the last time astronauts would be used on such assignments.

That decision, it turned out, would depend in part on how we evaluated our roles. We were in the odd position of being able to cut our own throats on what was really choice duty by reporting that the tracking stations could get along nicely without us. They could and subsequently did.

But the three of us were cheered by the fact that someone had enough confidence to send us. I relished the opportunity to be on my own—away from the other twenty-eight, the only astronaut in town—and on the beach. It was a chance to flap my wings.

I flew to Hawaii with Ed Fendell, a big, strapping bachelor flight controller, on his way to Carnarvon to join Scott. There was a sort of gentlemen's agreement among those who manned Carnarvon that it would take at least four or five days—after the mission—to close up shop. The boys never found it easy to tear themselves away. The final reports were always late arriving from Australia, and for some unaccountable reason some of the fellows would get lost in Sydney and miss their airplane connections home. After John Glenn's historic flight, they had to send a telegram to the American Embassy to locate Gordon Cooper—apparently lost in the wilds of Sydney.

Needless to say, Ed Fendell and another flight controller were in high spirits as our PanAm flight droned over the Pacific Ocean. The three of us were partying it up, flirting with the stewardesses, and having a great time. The other guy was playing his guitar when Ed reached into his briefcase and fished out a stack of eight-by-ten photos, mostly of John Glenn.

"What's all that for?" I asked.

"Trading material," Ed answered. "You'd be amazed at what I can get in Australia for one of these pictures. How about signing a few of yourself?"

He studied one of the prints and said gratefully, "John Glenn has no idea how many times his picture has gotten me laid."

I laughed out loud. "Hell, Ed, I'm not John Glenn. Nobody knows me."

"Doesn't matter," he assured me. "You're an astronaut. Won't make a lick of difference." I had yet to learn the facts of life as Ed took them for granted.

I checked into the Kauai Surf Hotel on the beach, and Lo flew over a week later—at our expense—to spend ten days. It was her first chance to travel with me and experience some of the astronaut mystique. Kauai was the perfect spot, all sunshine and moonlight, orchids on your breakfast tray, swaying palms and the scent of fresh pineapple, and falling asleep at night to the rhythm of the surf against the shore.

The Kauai Surf was a favorite retreat for movie figures and assorted celebrities. Raymond Massey, the movie star, and his wife moved in a few days after we arrived and checked out the following morning, complaining that the surf kept him awake.

But those with a little romance in their souls found no fault with it. For most of the astronauts those rare excursions were a blessing and a tonic to marriages that were under constant strain.

From where we sat, Gemini 4, commanded by Jim McDivitt, went off smoothly. It was from our tracking station that the word went out that Ed White was "Go for EVA," the first American space walk. After twenty minutes, we had a helluva time getting him to go back in.

Chris' man was in command. I went along, avoided rocking the boat, and operated the retro-fire and computer clocks. Later, with great reluctance and a sense of loss for astronauts yet to come, Dave, Bill, and I reported to Deke that the tracking stations could manage just fine without us.

Several months passed and we were on a geology field trip in Oregon when Deke called a meeting of our Apollo group. We slouched into chairs and took up key positions on the floor of Deke's motel room, waiting for what we sensed would be important news. It was not unlike the scene in which the colonel gives the old window-shade yank to the wall map and announces to a breathless squadron that the long wait is over.

In his no-nonsense, to-the-point way, Deke opened by saying that some of us were going to be moved into the Gemini flight rotation. Initially, NASA had thought that the first two groups would be able to handle the flights through the Gemini program. But the flight schedule was becoming increasingly hectic, with launches every ten weeks, sometimes closer, and the Apollo program would soon require the assignment of three-man flight crews.

I guess the last point was the critical factor. The Apollo development schedule was being maintained while the Gemini program was nearly a year late.

In a matter-of-fact way, Deke announced that Mike Collins would be backing up Gemini 7 (with John Young), Dave Scott would be flying Gemini 8 (with Neil Armstrong) and Dick Gordon would be backing Dave up (with Pete Conrad). The significance of this did not go unfelt. Dave was flying and Dick and Mike were *in line.* At the same time, Mike's future had been hitched to Frank Borman's star and Dick was set for a long ride on Pete Conrad's coattails. They had clear shots at the downstream flights.

In the next few days they almost magically disappeared from our routine. We wouldn't see them for weeks at a time. They were playing off-Broadway, while we were still in Bridgeport.

We would try to catch one of them in the office halls for a moment, long enough for a quick question about what the big boys were doing. Their lives had changed, and the rest of us marveled at how easily and abruptly it happened.

Among those of us still waiting, the attitude was, "Well, if they're in line, I can't be far behind." There really wasn't time to feel any pangs of envy. Much.

As the weeks passed with more training and more classes but no new assignments, our frustration began to build. In October 1965 the second anniversary of my selection as an astronaut came and went. I felt as though I were trapped in zero gravity in the middle of a large tank and couldn't touch the sides. I wondered when someone would throw me a rope. No one had yet said a word to me about when, or if, I'd ever make a flight.

There was a brief respite in November as I returned to Kauai for four days. The occasion was the first Conference on Oceanography and Astronautics. Oceanography, the new rage, was receiving more and more government funding, much as the environment and ecology would a few years later. Governor John Burns of Hawaii was trying to attract private

Geology training with Neil Armstrong at
Philmont Ranch, New Mexico, 1964.

and government investment in oceanography and aerospace to his state. Dr. Hugh Dryden, Deputy Administrator of NASA, had been invited to give a luncheon address and to bring along an astronaut who would present one of the papers and be a potted-palm embellishment.

Normally we stayed in one place only long enough to finish our business before it was on to the next commitment. This, however, would be a four-day visit with my only obligation a one-hour paper to be presented on the second day. This left me with plenty of time to lie on the beach and study Gemini engineering documents.

Very little studying was actually accomplished because of the interesting distractions on the beach. The first person I ran into was Clare Boothe Luce. She was then sixty-two years old and well deserving of the reputation for charm and intellect that she had gained over the years. She had already enjoyed successful careers as an actress, writer, editor, war correspondent, playwright, congresswoman, and ambassador and, at the time, was one of the leading advocates of the relatively new science of oceanography. We spent the next couple of days lying on the beach discussing the problems of government funding for this emerging science.

From time to time, we would take a dip in the bay but never let that interfere with the conversation. That nearly got us into trouble.

On one occasion we were idly swimming toward the mouth of the bay, chatting as usual, and completely forgot about the time. She swam along very slowly in an easy little breaststroke, while I did a backstroke alongside. When we finally remembered to take our bearings, we were at the mouth of the bay and the open sea. It was definitely time to start back. The three-quarters of a mile outbound had gone fairly quickly because we had been swimming with the tide. The way back looked like forty-five minutes to an hour against the tide. I was sticking close and trying not to show my concern for her, but she just kept chugging along.

After another fifteen minutes we noticed an outrigger canoe coming toward us from the beach, and when we finally rendezvoused, it was apparent the lifeguard on board was also concerned for our safety. Explaining they had lost many swimmers in just this fashion, he began to escort us back to the beach. I expected Mrs. Luce to get into the canoe, but that just wasn't her nature and she insisted on swimming all the way to the beach. She may have finished fresher than I, even though I was spotting her nearly thirty years. With all her other accomplishments, Clare Boothe Luce was one hell of a swimmer.

It isn't in my nature to sit by passively and let the fates play on. By early December 1965, I could no longer contain myself. As I look back now, it was certainly premature impatience, when some would wait as long as eighteen and nineteen years for a flight.

The office I shared with Rusty was next door to the one occupied by Schirra, then in charge of our training group. One day I just walked in and unloaded.

"Wally," I blurted, "what's the story? I've worked my tail off for two years and here I am still sitting on the bench. Is that what I can expect? Warming the bench? In the dark?"

Wally hesitated a moment. "Take it easy, Walt, you're on the first team. I wish I was free to tell you more right now, but I can't. But don't worry about it. They'll let you know before long." If Wally wasn't part of "they," who in the hell was?

He had really told me nothing, but I walked out of his office feeling elated. In my anxiety I interpreted Wally's mild reassurance to mean my turn was coming.

In January 1966, the word came down that Gus Grissom, Ed White, and Roger Chaffee had drawn the first Apollo flight. It was a nice plum for Gus, the second American in space and the first to command a Gemini mission. Among the milestones of a test pilot's career are those rare first flights of a brand-new aircraft (or spacecraft), and now Gus would be logging two in a little over two years.

A few days later I was called into Schirra's office along with Donn Eisele. With a benevolent grin Wally announced that the three of us were to be the prime crew for the second manned Apollo mission. I was excited and, at the same time, a little disappointed. Our mission would be a virtual repeat of the first Apollo mission in an identical spacecraft. We had begun to question the capability of the early version of the command module to perform any of the design missions. So many changes had piled up that, beginning with the third spacecraft, the command modules had been re-designated Block II. The Block II vehicle was so much improved that office gossip had it that the Block I missions were just to keep the program moving while we waited for Block II to come down the pike. That gossip would prove to be well founded. No Block I spacecraft would ever get off the pad.

Flying virtually identical missions in outmoded command modules, when the Block II vehicle was so much better for the program, was not my idea of the planning and efficiency for which NASA was noted. Consequently, Donn and I never really felt comfortable about the permanence of our mission in the flight schedule. But our assessment of the situation was swept aside by the elation we felt and we went out to celebrate. We were glad to have any mission. The answer to why it was there at all wouldn't be known to me for another eighteen months.

There has always been a general impression—not just outside the program but among some of the NASA people as well—that flight crew selection involved a painstaking, almost scientific, process. It was pictured as not unlike a computer dating service where they fed data into a box and, after a lot of buzzing and whirring and blinking of lights, out pop the names of two or three people with complementary strengths and personalities—a marriage made in heaven.

The selection of Wally, Donn, and myself, if you listened to the news media, reinforced this theory. On the surface we were compatible: Schirra was the old master, experienced, with an easygoing, gregarious personality; I was depicted as the outspoken, intense, hard-charging, self-made young guy; and Eisele registered about halfway in between.

(A year later, Donn confided that he had originally been part of Gus Grissom's crew but had been dropped when he sustained a shoulder separation that required an operation. Roger Chaffee replaced him and Donn was reassigned to the next flight—our flight. I also learned later that Wally was originally a stand-in on Apollo 2. God only knows if I was originally ticketed for Apollo 2.)

At that moment, life was too sweet to nag about the system. My future seemed to stretch ahead of me like a drag strip to the stars. I was on the flight schedule ahead of most of the fellows in my group and had completely skipped toiling in the wilderness on a backup-crew. With launches scheduled every eight weeks, it looked like a fat space career was ahead.

The down side was the strong suspicion that I was out of the running for the first lunar landing. In the natural order of things, flying the second Apollo mission would keep one off another prime crew until at least the eighth launch. And we planned to land on the moon well before then.

My personal goals were threefold. The first lunar landing would have been icing on the cake—too much to really hope for. First, I wanted to get into space, which now seemed imminent. Second, I wanted to make a lunar landing. There figured to be as many as eight or ten, meaning that at least sixteen of us—out of the thirty in training—might walk on the surface of the moon. I calculated the odds at 50-50 and that didn't seem all that bad. Third, I wanted to command my own mission.

To fly in space, to reach the moon, and to command a mission would mean maturing as a man, would satisfy a need to test myself fully and— overlooked by none of us—would not exactly be a handicap in the commercial marketplace.

Unlike some, I had not joined the program expecting to stay forever. These goals, if I could achieve them, would be good stepping-off points to further accomplishments. By now we had before us the example of John Glenn, who had been hired as a vice-president of Royal Crown Cola for $50,000 a year and stock options. While we all looked on John as the first great space age hero and knew we couldn't count on doing as well ourselves, we reasoned that the technical achievements still to come in Apollo would lead to similar opportunities. Standing at the gateway to the moon, Glenn's three orbits in that simple Mercury capsule no longer seemed awesome.

Before long, the assignments were complete for the first two Apollo missions. Grissom's crew would be backed up by Jim McDivitt, Dave Scott, and Rusty Schweickart. Our backup crew consisted of Frank Borman, Tom Stafford, who showed up in May, and Mike Collins, who joined us starting in August. Tom and Mike had been tied up with the tail end of the Gemini program.

The twelve of us were now joined like lab mice to get the Apollo program off the ground. Overnight we found ourselves working on a more personal and specific basis with the prime contractor for the command and service modules, North American Rockwell. In the role of engineering and operational consultants, we would spend most of 1966 in design reviews, checking out hardware and developing test procedures.

Our relationship with North American Rockwell (NAR) was, from the beginning, a curious one. It was their first effort in manned spacecraft at a time when most of the knowledge and actual experience in spacecraft design and fabrication was residing at the McDonnell Aircraft Company in St. Louis, Missouri. MAC was where they wrote the book. MAC had created both the Mercury and Gemini spacecrafts. North American Rockwell would now build the next spacecraft with little, if any, experience but a whole new generation of technology.

Putting their best engineers and scientists on the proposal for a vehicle to carry men to the moon, North American Rockwell won out over tough competition. The Space Division was headed by Harrison (Stormy) Storms, who had previously ramrodded the X-15 rocket research plane program.

NAR was moving into a strange new world of manned spacecraft. Their engineering and technology was a step more advanced than McDonnell's on Mercury and Gemini, but also more troublesome. One development problem surfaced after another. They were continually fighting costs and schedules as they seemed to be trapped in that infamous cycle, "The hurrieder I go, the behinder I get."

In their eyes the astronauts must have seemed like spoiled brats whose whims had to be tolerated. We were into everything, not just the controls and displays and the crew couches. Was the environmental control system engineered to do what we might demand of it? Were the records for test and checkout procedures adequate for the error tracking that would be inevitable? Even: were the technicians dressed appropriately for the job?

Those astros who had worked with McDonnell were quick to observe that North American Rockwell was stumped by procedural and development problems that McDonnell's experienced crew would have handled routinely. It took the rest of us somewhat longer to reach the conclusion that North American Rockwell was pretty screwed up, and that the spacecraft they were building was sadly deficient.

We debated the potential changes amongst ourselves and usually agreed on which ones should be pursued. But no doubt about it, individual instincts—and hang-ups—did enter into it.

Roger Chaffee, for example, had what we referred to as a microdesign craze. Roger was never content with just noting that the communication system did not meet such-and-such a design requirement and, therefore, had to be changed. If he thought there was a deficiency he would sit down and, in four or five minutes, sketch out a preliminary design for his "solution." The danger in this was the perfect "out" it provided the contractor when this "back of the envelope" solution did not work and more money was required to fix "the fix." "Well, we did it just like Roger said," was an excuse heard more than once in the last six months of 1966.

Wally rarely argued at the theory or design level, but would involve himself *after* the system was turned into solid hardware. It was at that point, when the impacts were much greater and the costs much higher, that he would suggest those changes he felt were necessary. He was often reduced to trading Brownie points or a power play to accomplish things. Wally was the kind of guy who felt, intuitively, how he wanted a system changed and, if necessary, he would turn the issue into an emotional vendetta. Fortunately, Wally's intuitions were often the right ones.

But between NASA's demands and Rockwell's learning curve, the pressure was growing on both engineers and managers. As astronauts, we had no legitimate program authority. We were engineers and managers without portfolio, so to speak. We had the glamour and the glory on our side because we were the ultimate users. In effect, it was our parachute they were packing. Our de facto authority came from this role as the end-user.

Even when the contractor disagreed with an astronaut about changing a bolt, he was aware he was talking to the man whose life might hang on that bolt. If he forgot, some of our guys weren't bashful about reminding him. We were concerned with just two questions: was it safe and would the spacecraft do the job it was intended to do? The contractors had these plus other monkeys on their backs. Such as cost—and schedules.

At one point, Wally insisted that the Service Module engine installed in the flight vehicle be test-fired on the ground. But once the engine was fired it would have to be completely rebuilt, meaning that no matter how many times we tested it, the subsequent rebuild would leave it a virgin. But Wally wanted to be shown that the engine worked. He pursued his case at the executive offices of North American Rockwell, at several levels of NASA, and—most effectively—at parties and other social functions. Sure enough, we test-fired the engine. At the cost of several million tax dollars Wally felt vindicated, the contractors were relieved to get him off their backs, and to this day no one can say that the test proved a thing. When Wally got involved in emotional causes it was usually late in the game and without wasting a whole lot of time on his homework.

Over the years, astronauts acquired a mixed reputation among the contractors. Our individual engineering and technical capabilities ran the gamut from good to don't-ask. The Mercury guys were basically test pilots, not exactly enthralled with engineering design details. The Gemini group not only had solid test-pilot credentials, but also averaged five years of college. Some of them were fine engineers, and they made significant contributions to the spacecraft design. Our Apollo group stood slightly lower than the first two in flying credits but was easily the strongest in technical credentials.

When our flight crews arrived on the scene, we crawled over everything like a pride of lion cubs. It soon became obvious we could do great good or, without really trying, cause serious harm. Some of the engineers at Rockwell were so eager to please that the slightest hint from an astronaut would be picked up and quickly run through an entire design concept.

On the other hand, an astro with a valid suggestion might have to throw a tantrum at upper management levels to get his idea into the spacecraft. Many times we would have to overcome the resistance created by earlier astro changes—some of which were unwise, some even capricious.

At a two-day meeting in Houston attended by the top brass of both NASA and North American Rockwell, the enthusiasm and credibility problem broke into the open. It was beginning to appear that cost and schedule overruns on the command module were going to be, pardon the expression, astronomical. The meeting was chaired by Dr. Robert Gilruth, Director of the Johnson Space Center. Dr. Gilruth, an aeronautical and aerospace pioneer, formed the original Space Task Group at Langley Field, Virginia, in November of 1958 and is generally considered the father of America's manned-spaceflight program.

At one point a manager from Rockwell stood up and said, "Look, we do have one problem after another, but we could still be doing all right. We were on schedule and moving along just fine until the astronauts began working with us full-time at the plant. Now it's going slower and slower and slower."

Dr. Gilruth did not take kindly to outside criticism of America's space idols. His experience led him to trust our judgment. He fixed the old boy with a cool stare and said, "That's OK. We're not charging you for their time."

All joking aside, our input was really needed, and much of the work we did there was crucial. If anything, we had too little impact, not too much. The problems eventually were corrected, but it took a fire and an additional two years to do it.

Those were strange and overlapping days. We were living with brand-new machines, the only two Block I spacecraft in existence. Gus's crew was running several weeks ahead of us on the checkout, and they bore the brunt of creating and revising test procedures. Testing went on around the clock and yet we kept falling further behind. In addition to our work the social temptations were murder. The prettiest girls in the plant seemed to have large, admiring eyes, and the big-stud-astro image required that we stare back. Everyone wanted to wine and dine us. There was no end of party invitations if we chose to do a little socializing.

We literally lived at the Rockwell plant from Monday morning on through the week, usually flying back to Houston on Friday night or Saturday morning. As much as we might have been tempted, it was impossible to keep up the work pace and still play the bon vivant. Anyone who really tried would have ended up in a jar in the Harvard Medical Laboratory within six weeks.

Frank Borman and I pulled checkout duty on the midnight shift about 75 percent of the time, with Mike Collins doing his share after joining our crew. You learn a good deal about the thresholds of men in tedious, demanding situations. Gus Grissom, for example, took his regular turn at both the good and the bad right along with everyone else. He was a hard liver and loved to party, but if Roger Chaffee, the youngest astronaut in the program, was pulling some notably boring duty, you were likely to find Gus sharing it with him.

Although our presence made some of the Rockwell engineers nervous, their customer relations department looked at us more like a kind of tourist attraction. Our crews included some of the early glamour boys—Gus, Wally, Borman, Stafford, White, and McDivitt—who had been in space and whose names were known to the world. Also, our crews would be the *first* to fly the *first* Rockwell spacecraft.

We were welcomed into the executive dining room, which provided the perfect forum: it was a free lunch and a chance to sell our ideas at the same time. Here, over lunch, we would socialize with the top executives, lobbying for whatever changes seemed urgent and undercutting some engineer who might be trying to put the brakes on what we wanted done. By the time the engineer got to the meeting where the problem was discussed, his boss would already be convinced that it should be done our way. That may not have been in the spirit of fair play, but it was effective.

Since the dining room seated only thirty people, our force of twelve could practically flood the place. Sensing a crisis, we got together and decided that we would restrict ourselves to no more than five astros at one time. Even then we had to exercise discretion on which five. Ed White and Dave Scott, for example, could eat their own weight in shrimp cocktail. Either of them could put away a dessert that any self-respecting horse would choke on. And Jim McDivitt could wolf it down with the best of them.

In the process of all this work at Rockwell we became a whole team.

Behind our prime and backup crews we had a support crew (nine astros in all) and a dozen NASA engineers to work with us on the systems, the procedures, the on-board data and our training schedule. They were part of the Spacecraft 014 team. It was *our* spacecraft.

Manned space missions have always had prime and backup crews assigned. Because of the increased complexity of Apollo, a third crew was added. Deke's intention for the support crew was precisely that: support, not training. Their real responsibility was to free up the prime and back-up crews to spend more time on productive training. There were only so many meetings, reviews, tests, and simulations in which we could partic-ipate. In addition, many of the scheduled activities had a tendency to be inconclusive or leave the impression that the exercise was unimportant if an astronaut was not in attendance. Support crewmembers provided that presence. Sometimes one of them became the crew expert in some essen-tial aspect of the mission. Predictably, they also inherited any shit details that might come our way. In a world where the newest astros, at the bot-tom of the pecking order, were looking for any handhold to climb up, or any opportunity to come to Deke's attention, a support crew assignment was looked upon as a real plum.

In eight years I spent a total of ten weeks on a backup crew between prime assignments. But few got off so lightly. A more typical pattern was to progress through support team, backup crew, and then prime crew. That process could take a couple of years. This third crew was invaluable during the test and checkout phases, and in time, that assignment became a de facto prerequisite for crew assignment. Deke just naturally gave more consideration to those who came to his attention by doing a good job in this rather thankless assignment. There was no rookie crew member, from Apollo 13 on, who had not spent at least one cycle on a support crew.

In time, most of the capsule communicators (CapComs) would be drawn from the support crew ranks. The CapCom does all the communi-cating with the spacecraft and is a key control over the quality and accu-racy of information transmitted to the crew in orbit. Not so subtly, it also helped maintain the fiction that *no one* tells the flight crew what to do except another astronaut. There were astronaut support crew members in Moscow during the joint U.S./Russian mission in 1975, in the event direct communication was required with our spacecraft.

Slayton or Shepard would normally represent us at upper management meetings. They defended the flight crew's position at the many review boards at Rockwell and NASA. For major, weeklong reviews there might be several hundred participants divided into teams addressing the various subsystems and operations of the spacecraft (the guidance and navigation system, the electrical system, quality control documentation, test procedures, etc.). The Astronaut Office had primary accountability for the crew station and representation on most of the other review teams. Deficiencies or problems in any area were pursued from our role as end-user and pilot of the vehicle.

On Wednesday night, after three days of grinding it out on separate teams, the flight crew would caucus to get consensus and establish priority on those points we wished to pursue. Our lists in the early days of Apollo ran into the hundreds. On Thursday a screening board with contractor and NASA representatives disposed of all those items on which they could agree. On Friday the formal Review Board convened to endorse the activities of the preceding four days and to disposition those items, which were irreconcilable except at the highest levels of management. This board would be co-chaired by Dr. Gilruth and the contractor's Program Manager. Chris Kraft would represent flight operations and Deke Slayton would represent the flight crew.

Review weeks were tough with long hours, but it was the formal way of shaping the spacecraft to eventually fly the missions for which they were intended.

Wally was not only our spacecraft commander, but also the captain of our training team. We each had a rather free hand when it came to scheduling our activities, but if Wally said, "Get your fanny to the Cape," that's where we got our fannies.

We laughed at the so-called Jet Set and traveled so frequently and easily that we never had reason to become bored by the immediate scenery. It was easy, if we began to feel frustrated, to pick up and fly off to a different duty. We had so many legitimate reasons to move around the country, that a "business trip" to some particular location could be arranged very quickly if we felt some personal urgency to be there. It was just as easy for official business commitments to be delayed or to vanish completely if there was no T-38 available. Who needed a trip by commercial airliner? Talk about prima donnas; trips were sometimes put off simply because airplane availability made it necessary for us to fly with another pilot. Who wanted to be a back seat passenger half of the time? We were literally spread to the winds—but, I should add, generally in the interest of the mission.

Take the morning Lo and I rose, as usual, at 7:00 A.M. Almost immediately, she took a call from Al Shepard. Handing me the phone, she commented, "You've got to go to Michoud this morning."

Al had received a call only a few minutes earlier and was passing on the details of a command performance. "Walt, President Johnson is going to be in Louisiana this morning, touring the Chrysler plant at Michoud. James Webb wants the Apollo VII crew to walk around with him." Webb, the NASA Administrator, was a master politician and a respected associate of the President. He recognized and fully exploited the value of publicity to the space program as well as the glamorous effect of having "his boys" escort the President.

"The President," Al was saying, "and James Webb and Governor John McKiethan are scheduled to be at the plant at ten fifteen this morning. We may not be able to get Donn there in time (Eisele was at MIT studying the Apollo computer), but I'm calling Wally at the Cape now and he'll meet you there."

Such short notice was not unusual, but the reason was rarely as auspicious as an appointment with the President—my first with any president. I scheduled a T-38, gulped breakfast, grabbed a good suit, and headed for New Orleans. It's a short flight to the New Orleans Naval Air Station but nearly an hour's drive from there to Michoud, over by the Mississippi border, so there wasn't much time. Enroute, I arranged for a navy sedan to pick me up on arrival and tried to determine Wally's expected arrival time. After landing and changing, I delayed as long as I dared before heading for the Michoud Plant. You just don't keep the President waiting. I arranged for a second car to pick up Wally, but just as I was pulling away he breezed into a landing and we drove over together.

The tour was meant to inform the president about the Saturn boosters which were stored at Michoud, and, at the same time, to be a morale booster and publicity trip for the working troops. We were in a recovery phase after the Apollo 1 fire and the program needed a shot in the arm. It was a routine space industry tour, but three things stand out in my mind. One was the briefing to Wally and me from Jim Webb: "OK now, you two get right in there every time he stops, you get right up by the President and see to it that you're in all the pictures. Don't be bashful and don't wait for someone to tell you to get there—you just be there." Jim meant what he said, to the point of hanging back himself whenever possible and continually urging Wally and me to "move in among them."

At Webb's insistence, Wally and I joined the President in his limousine for the short drive back to the front of the plant. President Johnson relaxed and made casual conversation.

"Jim Webb is the only man working for me," LBJ declared, "who told me what he was going to do, when he was going to do it, and what it was going to cost, and he is accomplishing all three." He was referring, of course, to the lunar landing program.

A few minutes later, just before the short trip was over, the President observed, "It's unfortunate, but the way the American people are, now that they have developed all of this capability, instead of taking advantage of it, they'll probably just piss it all away." That 1967 statement has proved to be quite prophetic over the years.

This interlude lasted but a few hours—Wally headed back to the Cape and I spent the afternoon working in Houston. Late that night, I flew on to the Cape and the next morning had breakfast with Wally. We both commented on how casually we adapted to a fantasy-like existence: our business day had been interrupted by a two-hour interlude with the president of the United States, with no warning, little impression and essentially no afterthoughts, and we were back on our old routine doing what was really important to us.

As if to assure that we would get plenty of flight time, the various simulators connected with the mission were scattered all over the country. These were machines or instruments designed to simulate the functions of the hardware or operational aspects of the mission. The simulators were being modified and updated on a continuing basis, so of necessity, many were kept close to the contractor.

Some were fairly simple in concept. At Chapel Hill, North Carolina, and at the Griffith Park Observatory, in Los Angeles, California, we did our planetarium work. We simulated looking at the stars either through the onboard guidance and navigation system telescope, or through the sextant eyepiece. The object was to become expert at identifying the thirty-seven Apollo navigation stars as well as the hundreds of other twinkling signposts used for finding them. The trick was in doing it while looking at only one twentieth of the night sky, the view we got through the Apollo telescope.

You can get the same effect by looking through a toilet paper roll, shortened to approximately three inches, which is what we used to simulate it as we flew from coast to coast, mostly at night.

When performing navigation tasks, or "taking a fix in space," one identified an "Apollo star" through the telescope, placed the cross hairs of the on-board sextant on it, and pushed a button, which fed the information to a computer. Marking on three Apollo stars enabled the computer to determine one's position and attitude in space.

It had become obvious early in the astronaut game that it would be impossible to meet our schedules without our own fleet of jets. When I reported to NASA in 1963, four F-102's were available along with eight T-33's—the oldest operating jet in service. At that time, NASA had just finished evaluating other aircraft for "astronaut flight proficiency training." The Flight Operations Division selected the T-38, a two-place supersonic training aircraft, which was just coming into widespread use in the air force.

There were few hotter airplanes going at that time. The T-38 had the best high-altitude cruise speed and, when it was light on fuel, it was possible to climb from the ground to 40,000 feet in less than two minutes. It was safe, reliable, and enabled us to maintain the man-killing schedules that would otherwise have been intolerable.

With a T-38, any day in the life of an astronaut could be slightly supersonic. Many mornings I would get up at 6:00 A.M., have a quick bite with Lo, drive eight miles to Ellington Air Force Base, and be airborne by 7:00 A.M. The flight to Los Angeles required a fueling stop at El Paso, Texas, but because of the enthusiastic support of the ground crew there and the two-hour time change heading west, it was possible to land at Los Angeles International Airport shortly after 8:00 A.M. As I parked the plane, a Rockwell helicopter I had scheduled the day before would be dropping out of the sky to pick me up. It was only a ten-minute chopper ride to the space division plant at Downey, and with time to spare, I'd breeze into an 8:30 meeting with James Bond coolness.

After eight hours of technical talk and a business lunch at the Golden Trough (our nickname for the executive dining room—it never ran out of food), I'd catch the last helicopter back to the airport and ten minutes later be airborne in the T-38. An afterburner climb and by 5:30 P.M. I would be relaxing at 41,000 feet and pulling paperwork out of my brief-case to get as much work done as possible before the sun set. Since the T-38 had no autopilot, it took both experience and clever work with your knees to keep the plane on an even keel at that altitude. Even allowing for the two hours we lost heading east, with any luck and a good jet stream, I'd walk in the front door at 10:15 P.M., have a nightcap with Lo, and hit the sack—maybe to do it all over again the next day.

Without those expensive toys—in some ways they served as airborne pacifiers—many of us would have gone bananas trying to maintain our schedules. After a day with slide rules and hardware, we looked forward to the peace and quiet of a night flight between Los Angeles and Hous-ton. The T-38 is the finest airplane I have ever flown and I never tired of it. After seven years, I would still taxi out, take off with both afterburners lit, pull the nose up to watch the ground fade away and exclaim, quite involuntarily, "Jesus Christ, what an airplane."

5

Fun and Games

IT WAS a dizzying pace, but we thrived on it. It was a living demonstration, at least to ourselves, that we led glamorous and exciting lives that few others would be able to handle. Naturally, the price for this exaggerated life style had to be paid by the other half of the family.

We were busy tempting the Fates and playing hero, and our absences grew so frequent that our families came to expect them. Almost routinely, family responsibilities were being passed on to our wives: balancing the checkbook, seeing that the lawn was mowed regularly in the summer, renewing a bank loan, overseeing house construction.

Many of the domestic problems some astronauts faced later were due to this abdication of our responsibilities for so many years. Our family tried to cope with it by carrying on as though we hadn't been gone at all. The kids learned to accept it. If they misbehaved and needed disciplining they got it when I returned—if Lo hadn't already punished them.

In our family the problem was never acute. The adjustment the kids made to the demands of my job often amazed me. Once, while I was gone, Lo overheard them playing house.

Kimberly said, "I'll be Mommy," and of course Brian was Daddy.

After a few preliminaries it was time for Brian to leave the house for his office—as Daddies do. "OK," he said, "I'm going to work now. See you in a week."

Lo almost dropped the dishes when she heard that.

One effect of our constant travel was that our secretaries wound up acting as liaison with our wives. We were gone so much we couldn't afford to call home on any regular basis, and we weren't allowed to use our government credit card for personal matters. So we learned to relay and receive messages through the office. Once my secretary, Charlotte, called me at the McDonnell plant in St. Louis to pass on a message from Lo saying the refrigerator was broken and it would cost $125 to repair. The unit was eight years old and, according to the repairman, wasn't worth fixing.

I thought a moment and said, "Tell Lo to call Charlie at General Electric and see what kind of a deal he can get us on a new one." Now Charlie was not an appliance salesman; he was the General Electric representative to NASA, a space guy. But in a pinch we seldom hesitated to call on our contacts.

The next day I called the office. Toward the end of the conversation I asked Charlotte how Lo had made out with the refrigerator. She said she'd check and call me back.

Brian and Kimberly ready for Mach 25.

That afternoon I got another call from the office: "Lo says the new refrigerator arrived."

As for our neighbors, we might as well have been in the CIA. They came to think of each of us as the Shadow, so seldom were we caught at home. Slowly we drifted apart from all but our closest friends. Those friendships we did form were not cemented the way friendships are when people share their social and domestic pleasures. When home we tended to hibernate, to stay close to the hearth and breathe in some normalcy.

We had grown jealous of our privacy, so we clung to our families as an escape from the limelight and the exotic life we led on the road. Having established, while traveling, lifestyles that included dinner parties, celebrities, the rich and the famous, and people seeking our autographs, we became aware of the sharp contrast to the lifestyles of our wives at home: no social life, the washing machine on the fritz, the kids misbehaving, the loneliness. When the space hero came home, all he wanted was to sink into an easy chair and watch television. After being exposed to a wide variety of the human species, including the female half, we were able to appreciate even more the strengths, the abilities, the known qualities of the women who kept our homes and raised our kids. The irony of it, though, was being unable to convince them of it. Our wives grew more and more insecure.

Through the same media treatment we were getting, our wives came across as grown-up drum majorettes whose ambitions in life had been to play the piano and bake cookies. The size of our egos was exceeded only by their sense of insecurity.

While a dozen of us were struggling to get the Apollo program out of the starting blocks, the Gemini program was finishing up a two-year, action-packed flight program. It was the proving ground for nearly every critical step of the manned space program for the next ten years. Although we were still feeling our way, the Gemini spacecraft was not the experimental laboratory model of the Mercury program. It was produced on the nearest thing to an assembly line for space hardware we had seen so far, lifting off from Cape Kennedy at regular two-month intervals, and performing just fine. The program had been originally conceived as a gap filler between Mercury and Apollo, but it is now hard to imagine going to the moon without it. Gemini's contribution was purchased at the bargain-basement price of $1.5 billion.

The entire system, from the checkout crews to the flight controllers and the worldwide tracking network, learned how to gear up routinely for an operation that would never quite be routine. Gemini made three essential contributions to the development of manned space flight and the eventual success of Apollo.

The first was in June 1965, when Ed White stepped out of his tight but secure little cabin on Gemini 4 and into the cold vacuum of space for the U.S.'s first extra-vehicular activity (EVA). Ed's "walk in space" came nearly three months after Aleksey Leonov, the Russian cosmonaut, had become the first man to venture outside a spacecraft cabin into the airless void of space. Leonov's brief venture outside was little more than a feasibility demonstration or, more accurately, a dramatic stunt. But the same thing could be said of Ed's fifteen-minute walk. In the subsequent ten years the Russians failed to develop their capability much beyond the stunt stage, while EVA was utilized and improved upon in half the Gemini missions. It was here where we cut our teeth on a capability that has been an integral part of all U.S. space operations since 1966.

Neither Apollo, nor the Apollo-Soyuz mission, nor the Skylab program would have been possible if we had not learned how to routinely rendezvous with orbiting spacecraft—the second essential contribution of Gemini. We would not have attempted a single lunar landing without certain knowledge that the Lunar Module with two crewmen on board could rendezvous with the orbiting Command Module for return to earth. The technique may have been improved a bit on the early Apollo missions, but all phases of rendezvous were developed, tried, tried again, and perfected on the last six Gemini missions. It was on those everyday missions, with launches every two months for two years, that the studies and trade-offs were made with navigation schemes, tracking techniques, spacecraft control modes, and so on. Rendezvous became a routine operational technique that now enables us to join up with just about anything only hours after lift-off.

The Gemini spacecraft cabin contained seventy-five cubic feet of what was inappropriately described as "free volume." That is roughly equivalent to the front seat of a small foreign sports car. It was anything but "free," after filling it with essential equipment and two human bodies dressed in spacesuits. Even the Mercury spacecraft had fifty cubic feet of free volume for its one warm-body intruder.

It is difficult for me to imagine myself cooped up in such tight confinement for even forty-eight hours. And that may account for my admiration for the premier human accomplishment of the entire Gemini series. Time is relative, but I think most would agree that the first "long duration" mission was that of Gordon Cooper and Pete Conrad on Gemini 5. Their motto was "eight days or bust." Doctors, both inside and outside NASA, had expressed doubt that man could adjust to life in zero gravity. Some went so far as to predict that exposure for a long period would probably be fatal. We viewed such pessimism as a "straw man," created to enlarge the role of medical doctors. The opposing views would soon be put to the test.

In December 1965, Frank Borman and Jim Lovell climbed out of their Gemini 7 spacecraft on to the deck of the aircraft carrier *Wasp* after fourteen miserable days in those unbelievably cramped quarters. That was longer than any of the planned Apollo missions and would hold the U.S. duration record for the next eight years. It was a very human triumph. Of course, the equipment had to work to sustain them, but machinery can be designed to operate continuously for a long time, and its performance is not complicated by feelings and emotions. Yet at the end, the hardware was in much poorer shape than the passengers. The crew suffered little deterioration and regained preflight physical condition shortly after their return. But in the spacecraft two of the three fuel cells had failed and the spacecraft was drawing power from its last source when the mission concluded. Lovell would later describe the experience as "like spending two weeks inside a port-a-can."

Dr. Chuck Berry, the NASA Chief Flight Surgeon until 1974, has a picture hanging in his Houston home that captures the significance of Gemini 7. It shows a bearded Borman and Lovell walking on a red carpet from their spacecraft on the deck of the recovery carrier. The inscription by Jim and Frank reads, *"The day the straw man fell down."*

From the beginning of our astro careers we were deluged with fan mail from the curious, the well meaning, and career autograph collectors. One of the first things we did after reporting to NASA was to sit for an official photograph. Tens of thousands were printed, and the mailroom staff was kept busy filling photo requests.

Our egos were constantly being massaged, fed, pampered, and pumped up. This was especially true after being nominated for a space flight. *You were going up.* You were anointed. It was as though you had just been chosen the next Miss America.

In the phase that preceded this we were little more than a number. Alan Shepard, Scott Carpenter, Wally Schirra, all the Mercury types would be receiving invitations to various functions because they were Shepard, Carpenter, and Schirra. The rest of us might as well have been invited by our gym locker numbers (mine was 24). It was sometimes awkward as hell attending some high-powered society function to be received as celebrities except that no one knew us.

We could be shaking hands with a line of people and I would say, "Hi, I'm Walt Cunningham, this is my wife, Lo." But the listeners had already turned off their memory devices. We had been logged as "Astronauts," and by a name just didn't matter. Behind us came another astronaut, and behind him another, and another, like so many skeet at a gun club. We were looked at as a title and an image. It was a strange and sometimes unsettling feeling

From the moment the headlines appeared in the Santa Monica papers—"RAND Scientist Selected As Astronaut"—I was aware of the impact the news was having. It was amazing how many old friends wished to renew acquaintance, how many acquaintances became old friends, and how many strangers offered free advice.

I also received my first crank letter, a paste-up of words cut out of a magazine. It carried a hostile reference to my going into space and working for a war machine like RAND. I turned it over to the security people and thought no more of it.

A small percentage of the mail came from the kind of kook who is constantly solving the problems of the universe. I got one letter that went on and on, for twelve pages, dealing with the discovery (actually, his invention) of a single unit that unified all fields of physics. I never cease to be amazed that some crackpot, in blissful ignorance of the laws of physics, can sit in his home or office and dream up a tiny unit, which is supposed to open up all the secrets of mankind.

Overnight we all became collectible items. Soon after we settled in Texas we were invited to a fund-raising reception for Dallas Planned Parenthood. It was at the ranch of Gordon McLendon, a flamboyant Texas

millionaire who owned several radio stations and had run unsuccessfully for governor. There were several of us token astronauts (the old hands
had all ducked) at the party, which also included several Hollywood
types to help the fund raising. John Barrymore, Jr., was there. So was
George Hamilton, whose romance with Lynda Bird Johnson was not yet
making the gossip pages. Actor Robert Cummings was the guest contributor of short plane rides around the ranch, all in the interest of sweet
charity. Lo, so help me, was thrilled to death at the prospect of flying with
Robert Cummings as the pilot.

I guess that was fair. After all, her husband and his friends got their
kicks turning the Los Angeles-Houston airway into a jet age raceway.

It was inevitable that any time two or more astros engaged in the
same activity a contest would result. We would compete to see which
plane got airborne first, who refueled the fastest, and who arrived first at
the ultimate destination.

Once Wally and I were headed for Los Angeles and I was flying the
first leg to El Paso. As I taxied in for refueling, Jim McDivitt and Rusty
Schweickart taxied out, taking off for Los Angeles, and we waved at each
other. As juvenile as it may seem, that's all it took to start a race. We refueled and, with Wally now in the front seat, took off in hot pursuit, seven
minutes behind Jim and Rusty. We were off and running on a 700-mile leg,
hell-bent to make up those seven minutes and beat them into the parking
ramp at Los Angeles International Airport. With less than ninety minutes
to work with and pushing the plane as we'd have to, it was a cinch there'd
be little fuel to spare.

Well, Wally gave it the old wild-blue try. It was a two-burner climb to
43,000 feet and then a level cruise at Mach .98 (98 percent of the speed of
sound). Over the radio frequencies used by the Flight Service Stations, we
could hear Jim and Rusty reporting in along the route, just as they could
hear us. We tracked our progress by the time of their position reports.
Hoping not to provoke them into any special efforts, we did our best to
lead them to believe that we were not gaining on them by reporting in
late. Keep in mind, no one had explicitly issued a challenge or even mentioned the prospect of any kind of a race to Los Angeles.

But that didn't matter. We just assumed that Jim and Rusty were
doing their best to mislead us into thinking they were making progress

no faster than usual.

Just past Phoenix we played our hole card, lighting up both afterburn-ers and boosting our speed to Mach 1.2. We stayed supersonic for the next twelve minutes, as long as we dared and still have enough fuel for an idle descent down the ILS (instrument landing) glide slope and the landing—if we had calculated correctly.

By now we realized that even our supersonic fuel-gulping tactic and a high-speed letdown wouldn't enable us to land ahead of them. Our strategy turned to landing as short as possible on the runway, making the first turnoff, and possibly beating them to the parking spot. For all our efforts, we had gained only two minutes in the flight from El Paso and touched down five minutes behind them, beaten cleanly.

We got high on such encounters. That undeclared contest occupied both crews throughout the flight and it dominated the conversation between the four of us all the way to the hotel that night. Such shenani-gans wouldn't be possible today with complete radar tracking on the air-ways.

The lengths to which we went to beat each other were epitomized in what came to be called the Tire Biter's Award.

To begin with, one must understand that trying to make an early turnoff on a landing runway—as a means of beating your buddy to the parking ramp—was no small matter. It was a comic-serious business to win at anything, even if it was just parking the airplane.

The T-38 could be stopped in a relatively short distance, but it required heavy and precise feet on both brakes. The most competitive were always willing to risk a blown tire for the pure joy of beating the other guy. This led to many blown tires and the creation of a special award for excellence in the art of tire biting.

The Tire Biter's Award was born as a result of a little gamesmanship at Los Angeles International Airport. Dick Truly and Bob Crippen land-ed one day just behind Joe Kerwin and me, and tried desperately to beat us to the parking ramp. After landing Joe and I rolled to the end of the runway for a normal turnoff before we realized that Dick and Bob were trying to beat us to the parking ramp. As I turned to head back for the parking spot, really balling along the taxiway, I noticed that Dick had come to a complete stop back toward the landing end of the runway. His problem became clear when we heard the call that is not uncommon around a military airfield: "Say, tower, could you have them send out a tow vehicle and a tow bar, I'm shutting down on this taxiway. I 'think' I have blown a tire."

Sure enough, Dick had made the very first turnoff at Los Angeles International, which is no mean trick. In order to accomplish it, he had worn down both main tires almost to the rim, naturally blowing them in the process. It was fortunate he was able to turn the airplane off the runway or it would have caused havoc and delays with the commercial traffic landing behind him.

Without telling Dick, I quietly made a deal with a ground crewman to save the worst of the two tires. Believe me, they both looked like something you'd step over at a garbage dump.

We gleefully took our trophy back to Houston, mounted it on a plaque, designated it the Tire Biter's Award, and voted unanimously to make Dick Truly the first recipient. At the next pilots' meeting we had a formal presentation where Dick sheepishly accepted that creative example of one of the prices of competition. Over the years, the award would pass through the hands of many deserving tire biters.

Of course, it made no impression that we were risking our necks as well as wasting the taxpayers' dollars in pursuit of our own muse. This was how we relaxed, let off steam, and exorcised our demons.

El Paso was the scene of yet another of our private test matches. This one was for the fastest refueling and turnaround, as measured by time spent on the ground at El Paso International Airport. The service crew for transient was almost all Chicano, and I would usually chat with them in Spanish. They had a great esprit de corps and enjoyed our flying stops as much as we did. We were always given a preferred parking spot, directly in front of the Operations Building, and more often than not they had a refueling truck standing by as we pulled up out front.

The boys in El Paso prided themselves on providing the best service in the country in refueling transient aircraft. Their efficiency encouraged us to think in terms of new Olympic refueling records. I was no stranger to El Paso, having refueled there since my first cross-country flight in 1954. We would occasionally grab a bite at one of the local Mexican restaurants with the ground crew. On one occasion, knowing my taste for Mexican food, a lineman took me home for his wife's home cooking.

A normal T-38 refueling stop went something like this: park in front of the building where the refueling truck was waiting, come leaping out of the aircraft while they were connecting the hose, sign the credit slip, drop a dime in the coffee machine, duck into the john to deposit the last cup of coffee, pick up your fuel receipt, try, to swallow a half cup of coffee, take a quick check around the aircraft, and climb in as the fuel truck pulls away. By that time they had connected a starter and we could crank up and taxi out. Total elapsed time: ten minutes.

When this particular competition was in full sway, corners were cut wherever we could. Gus Grissom and Frank Borman, among others, achieved notoriety for "hot refueling"—attaching the hose and refueling the aircraft while keeping the engines running. While this is standard practice aboard aircraft carriers and on certain Naval bases where they are prepared for it, it is clearly frowned upon at all other aircraft establishments. To this day, I think Gus Grissom holds the record for an El Paso turnaround using this technique: a flat five minutes.

The race that best reflected the true competitive instinct of the astronauts, however, didn't match us against each other but against ourselves. It was the nonstop flight between Los Angeles and Houston. That might not seem a very stimulating contest until you understand that success depends not only on your own skill, but also on many factors over which you have no control, such as the tail-winds you must pick up along the way and the weather at the destination. Failure, needless to say, could cost an airplane and ruin your whole day.

You can find a lot of Air Force jocks who will argue that a T-38 can't fly 1,380 miles without refueling or remain airborne for more than two and a half hours. We demonstrated otherwise, time and again, in a contest that matched man against machine and man against the elements.

The game was usually played in late fall and early winter, when the jet stream had dipped far enough South to give us the kind of help we needed along the route. Of course, that time of year also marked the beginning of the night ground fog season at Houston's Ellington Air Force Base, an added hazard to sweeten the test.

For this trip, the important part was *not* in seeing how fast you could depart from the Los Angeles airport, but in minimizing the time spent on the ground and the fuel used for taxi, take-off and climb-out. Since the distance was beyond that which could be filed for legally under the federal air regulations, a flight plan would be filed for El Paso. Careful fuel and ground speed checks would be a continuous activity during the flight. After passing Tucson, Arizona, *if* the necessary tailwinds had developed and *if* the weather was forecast to be good enough for a visual descent, it was possible to legally (almost) re-file for Ellington, our home field.

The fuel-saving techniques we practiced were those that any good aviator acquires over a flying career. If it still seemed prudent to hedge the bet after passing Tucson, we would re-file for Austin, allowing the final decision to be postponed for one more hour. The game had a way of fully testing one's nerve and judgment because landing under your own power depended on your ability to project fuel, winds and weather conditions one hour and 700 miles farther East.

I don't recall who started this madness by making the first nonstop run, but I suspect it was John Young or Gus Grissom. I do recall that Gus and Roger Chaffee came closer than anyone else to *not* making it. One of their engines flamed out on landing roll-out, and the tanks took more fuel than the book says a T-38 will hold. Deke Slayton and the NASA flight operations people raised unshirted hell over that episode. But far from discouraging the rest of us, it merely stimulated our glands.

In eight years of flying the T-38, I made this non-stopper more than two dozen times, and it was never a boring flight. Usually it was quite the opposite, a continuing series of *go, no-go* decisions. One trip that still stands out was a flight with Wally on a clear summer night; Wally was at the controls and I was in the back seat doing the navigation and fuel calculations. We operated on a rule of thumb that if we had an average tailwind of 70 mph for the duration of the flight, then we could make it to Houston—assuming, of course, we hadn't wasted fuel on take-off and climb-out.

On that night as we crossed the Colorado River heading east at 41,000 feet, we had about 30 mph of tailwind with an increase forecast as we approached Texas. We were pulling down 40 mph as we passed abeam Phoenix, and at Tucson the tailwind had picked up to 50 mph. Over El Paso, our ground speed was 670 mph, indicating that we were finally getting our 70 mph of tailwind. We knew we had to average at least 90 the rest of the way in order to make it home with enough fuel for an idle descent and landing.

Well, faint heart ne'er won fair lady—nor a race against the clock. I re-filed for Austin and we discussed the fuel situation for the next forty-five minutes. The first low fuel warning light came on while we were still 250 miles west of Houston, indicating we had twenty to twenty-five minutes' worth of fuel remaining before the tanks were dry. I made one more calculation, re-filed for Houston, told Wally we could make it if we had no problems, and put away the calculator.

We started our letdown 100 miles out with both engines in idle and a few minutes later agreed that we'd be better off to shut down one of the engines completely. (It would save 30-40 pounds of fuel, you know.) Nearing the field on a straight-in, idle approach, Wally, not wanting to get too low too soon, was still 5,000 feet in the air as we approached the runway. That conservatism meant we had to make an overhead circle to lose the altitude, burning up more fuel.

The tower operators at Ellington were aware of our little gambits and generally had a good idea that we were low on fuel. That was a good thing for us. It would be a hollow victory if we had to declare an emergency and obtain priority for landing. We started up the second engine while Wally was banking around for the approach. With both engines in idle, Wally was still high and diving for the ground in an attempt to avoid another go-around, a somewhat precarious situation in a T-38.

At this point I was sitting in the back seat telling myself that if he had to take it around again we just might have enough fuel for a very tight 360. At the same time, though, I sat with my back rigid, my head against the headrest, and both hands gripped firmly around the ejection handles——the prescribed posture for an ejection.

When it came to stick-and-rudder work, Wally was one of the best. He made a beautiful landing. As we taxied in, patting ourselves on the back for making it in one piece, I calculated we still had a couple of minutes of fuel remaining.

Those were the hours and the personal contests we liked best. We knew NASA frowned on it and did their best to stop such mischief. But hanging our fannies over the gaping precipice and pulling them back in safely reinforced that feeling of invincibility residing in any good fighter pilot. It further increased self-confidence and, in doing so, added to that arrogance which is born of confidence. Climbing out of the cockpit after a trip like that, we felt we had squeezed something out of the machine the engineers hadn't designed it to do. A contest had been won not just over the machine but over ourselves as well. The greatest obstacles to performance are those hurdles we build in our own minds.

We were also learning things about each other—important things.

One problem with our T-38's was the complete absence of provisions for baggage of any type—for one let alone two of us, which was often the case.

It wasn't unusual for two astros to be on the road for a week or more, complete with luggage and a full load of paperwork. As soon as the T-38's began arriving at NASA, we began devising ingenious solutions to the cargo problem. The most obvious was to empty the parachute seat pack—containing such survival trivia as radio, food, water, and medical dressings—and replace it with such essentials as shorts, shirts, and shaving kit. The survival gear we simply left at home. Al Shepard caused a minor stir one day when he walked out to his airplane carrying a new attaché case that almost perfectly filled the seat pack. It was practically custom-made. Al only had to jump on one corner of the seat pack to get it closed. That was class. It took me a month to track down the source and acquire a similar case.

Since most of us traveled with some form of small suitcase—preferably soft, a suit bag, and a briefcase for paperwork, other places clearly had to be found to stow the gear. The suit bags were generally rolled up and placed above the election seat just behind the pilot's head in either cockpit. It was adequate if you didn't mind only three feet forward visibility from the rear cockpit and you liked the slept-in look.

But the really unique look came from using the seat pack itself as a suitcase. Since it was designed to carry survival equipment, and to take the shock of an ejection, it attracted many an interested stare when an astro appeared in a hotel lobby in a blue flight suit and a seat-pack suitcase at his side. And, since it also served as the ejection seat pad, taking it with you was a good way to ensure none of your buddies would go flying off in your airplane before you were ready to head home.

Eventually, NASA bought a half-dozen centerline fuel tanks, modified to serve as luggage carriers. It signaled an end to wrinkled clothes but also cost us ten minutes of fuel duration (that ruled out the non-stops), and we were never completely confident of them. Such tanks had been known to rip away at odd times, and we didn't relish arriving at our destinations without clothes and shaving kit. In the cockpit, at least, we were secure in the knowledge that if our wardrobe was lost, we were too. We did occasionally have visions of having to ditch our T-38, and a search party finding the cockpit absolutely awash with shirts, underwear, shaving cream, and reams and reams of paperwork.

In the face of all this—the social ramble, the home tensions, the instant hero worship—we never lost sight of one thing: *the mission always came first.* Where it counted, deep in our guts, nothing else existed. Everything else was parsley.

As the months and seasons of 1966 flew by, an ugly realization was sinking in. The spacecraft, as far as we could judge, left a lot to be desired. As the launch date for Apollo 1 drew nearer, we got into one wrangle after another.

The engineers at North American Rockwell had never before been in the position of dealing directly with the user. Now here we were, messing not only with their systems, which were being tested for the first time, but also with their designs.

There was a continuous process of redesign going on, and parts being retrofitted. If a test revealed a weakness that couldn't be fixed before the spacecraft was to be shipped, the equivalent of a repair kit would be sent along later to the Cape to make the necessary replacement. Staring us in the face was the fact that we were never going to have a complete spacecraft with all the right parts operating at one time until maybe right before lift-off.

Scraping nerves even more raw were the Apollo crewmen who had flown on Gemini. They kept comparing North American Rockwell's efforts unfavorably to the equipment, controls, and procedures in vogue at the McDonnell plant. And before long every office in Houston and at the Cape was getting into it. Dr. Joe Shea's program office, Chris Kraft's flight controller shop, the flight crews, the contractors and designers—all went through a crash series of meetings and conferences. The astronauts carried the least official authority but were the most vocal in their reservations. We argued for safer procedures and better margins of error.

The changes we argued for often wound up on the desk of Joe Shea, who, as NASA Program Manager, had to make decisions on how much to stretch the budget and how far to push the schedule. I suppose it was natural that on many of these exchanges we felt Joe was on the other side of the issue—lined up with the contractors.

Joe was a bright young man, a contemporary of the astronauts, and he affected many of their habits, including the casual Ban-Lon sportswear and their competitive attitudes. He was an incurable punster whose raised trouser legs—when he rested his feet on his desk—always exposed red socks. On a handball or squash court he would scrap with the best we had: Mike Collins or Rusty Schweickart. He was tough and active and ran his operation as jealously as we expected to run our spacecraft. He seemed driven to stay ahead of every astronaut.

We respected Joe and liked him, and it was ironic and sad that our efforts so rarely received his endorsement. Where many of the other program managers caved in when the astronauts insisted on a change, Joe held firm. We failed to get through many crucial changes simply because we couldn't sell Joe when the cost or (especially) the schedule were affected. Somewhere along the way we began to accept the fact that the spacecraft was going to be less than we wanted. What the hell, we'd make it work anyway. Anything to get off the ground.

Through all this, one thought continued to trouble me. Our Apollo 2 mission was clearly redundant, Gus and his crew would prove that the spacecraft could fly and support man in space. If Gus accomplished what was expected, our flight would be as useless as windshield wipers on a submarine. The only thing Apollo 2 had going for it was the fact that Gus kept throwing scientific experiments off Apollo 1 and they would be rescheduled for our mission. Gus really wanted to make a pure engineering test flight and the Apollo 2 mission was being loaded down with what both Gus and Wally considered "junk." Translation: "anything scientific."

Wally, for the first time in his life, was faced with flying a mission overrun with science and "dumb shmuck" scientists looking over his shoulder. We had a scientific airlock on board, the same one that would eventually be flown seven years later on Skylab. And there were biological tests, medical experiments, and all the laboratory jazz that over the years had bored Wally to tears. Now he was inheriting it all and taking it with a smile. I didn't learn why until a year later, when Deke confirmed he had planned for Apollo 2 to be his mission. All he needed was medical clearance.

It was the one way our redundant mission made any sense. We figured to establish little that couldn't be learned from Grissom's flight. That made it low profile with little risk to the program if it didn't succeed. It was an ideal spot for a pilot trying to get ungrounded from a questionable heart condition.

Slayton was the sentimental favorite of the original seven astronauts and the only one never to have ridden a rocket. In 1961, two months before he was scheduled to become America's second man in orbit, Deke's world collapsed. He was grounded! It was a setback, which at the time, held out some hope of being reversed. Deke fought being grounded tooth and nail and was still fighting it in January 1966 when Schirra was named Commander of a flight in which he never seemed to have his heart. At the same time, Deke took renewed interest in training activities. The explanation was simple; Wally didn't expect to fly it. He was to be the caretaker commander, standing in only until Deke was approved for the mission.

How different would have been the careers of Eisele and Cunningham if Deke had pulled it off. When he got the final turndown in the early fall of 1966 the reaction was all Deke. He headed for Alaska and a couple of weeks of hunting.

Wally, who had never been up longer than a day, was now stuck with a mission scheduled for eleven days in orbit. And he was nurse-maiding two rookies who could not care less how unimportant the flight might be. We just wanted to get off the ground.

On top of this, the hardware was bad, the testing was slow, the procedures were new and incomplete and crew training was woefully behind schedule. It just didn't seem like we could get there from here. With all the problems and work we were wrapped up in, we decided to spend some valuable time away from the office and telephones to hold one of Wally's famous seances—actually a conference or retreat—and discuss the more critical items. With all of our training obligations it was virtually impossible to get the nine members of our prime, backup, and support crews all at the same place at the same time, unless it was explicitly scheduled. We hadn't all been together away from our offices, contractors, etc., for six months, and we were overdue. The idea was not only to have a place where we could get some quiet concentration during the day, but one where we could relax, lift our glasses at night, and have a good time together as a crew.

Mid-September 1966 found all of us flying into Miami for two days of work and play. A friend offered us the use of a house with a swimming pool. It was ideal. We could work around the pool in the daytime, and at night we were right across the street from some swinging spots. This was the kind of "even strain" that Wally believed in—all nine of us in a fun city working and playing together.

We had a good time at night all right but, whatever the original intent of our daytime sessions, it got lost in what was produced at the end: a two-page list of ultimatums to the Apollo Program Office. Many were legitimate concerns already shared by the program office; some were "motherhood;" all were ultimatums ("If this doesn't happen—we won't fly"). Joe Shea wasn't the kind of man to listen to ultimatums, especially from a flight crew with a vested interest. There were legitimate reasons for some neat little thoughts like:

1. Delete the planned rendezvous exercise,
2. Delete certain major scientific experiments,
    No more assigned extra duties,
    and thirteen other items of lesser significance.

It was titled a "crew list" but, in truth, it strongly reflected Wally's personal preference in its tone and approach to problems. He possibly expected to improve our position from flying a redundant mission with an older model spacecraft. If it was related in any way to Deke's turndown for the flight, Wally never mentioned it to us. Donn and I were quite concerned and nervous as hell about possible repercussions from the moment it was drafted. We knew the manifesto overstepped the bounds of propriety and proper procedure and were waiting for the other shoe to drop. (Which it did.)

Wally saw it as a test of who was in charge, the same syndrome which would raise its ugly head during the mission. He was prepared to defend every single item on the list to a far greater degree than he actually believed in it.

Weeks passed and we heard no direct reaction to our Miami manifesto—and no action either. I had begun to think that we were in smooth waters.

On November 11, Jim Lovell and Buzz Aldrin lifted off on Gemini 12. Four days later Wally, Donn, and I sat in the third row of theater seats at

Mission Control watching the final splashdown of the Gemini program. Sitting directly in front of us were Paul Haney, the Public Affairs Officer, and some of the program managers from NASA headquarters. Paul half-turned toward Wally and handed him a memo.

"Say, Wally," he said. "Do you want to put your initials on this before we release it?" Paul explained later that he had wanted to cut us in before we read it in the paper.

I watched Wally as he read it quickly. His face flamed. The memo was a press release explaining how the Apollo flights were to be rearranged. It included the news that the second manned Apollo mission had been canceled. Even though Wally hadn't exactly been thrilled over making the flight, he wasn't prepared to have it taken away from him in this manner—being asked, after the fact, to initial a press release.

Wally motioned Donn and me out to the hall. Wordlessly, he handed us the release. He was furious. We were stunned, speechless. I couldn't help but wonder how much Wally's ultimatums—justified or not—had painted us into that corner.

That night, in the only instance I can remember in all the time we were together as a crew, we went across the street to Nassau Bay Inn and drowned our sorrows together. If we didn't get completely pie-eyed, it wasn't for lack of trying.

In the shake-up the McDivitt crew was assigned to the second Apollo flight, which would now include a Lunar Module. It would also be the first Apollo rendezvous and Wally could really have gone for that. He had his sights set on it, in fact, when we prepared our ultimatum. What happened instead was the first break in the pecking order between the Mercury and Gemini astronauts with McDivitt coming out on top.

In a few days word came down that we were to replace McDivitt's bunch as the backup for Apollo 1. This was a perfectly logical assignment since we had lived with the only other spacecraft identical to Grissom's. There was only one hang-up. As a Mercury astronaut, Wally felt he should not have to back up anyone, ever again. He was adamant about it. Donn and I were just glad to still be in the flight rotation.

So Gus, and NASA, had a problem. It was now mid-November, and Apollo 1 was to fly in February. A backup crew was essential. Given the short fuse, an experienced backup crew was highly desirable. An appeal, a very personal appeal, from both Gus and Deke was made to Wally. I mean, they damn near got down on their knees and begged him. Reluctantly he gave in.

It was clearly a letdown for us. We were faced with three months in a backup role, and then what? We were in limbo. I alternated between feeling betrayed, by fate and by Wally, and feeling angry.

Wally probably could not have prevented the cancellation. But we would have preferred not to have him pounding nails in the coffin.

6

Astropolitics

NOT GIVEN LIGHTLY to introspection, we tended to accept the judgment of the press that astronauts were "mission-oriented." The mission: to be up front when the line began to form, to haul ourselves into space and to get there before the next fellow. Oh, we were mission-oriented all right.

But we really operated on two separate emotional levels. Sure, we were swept up in the grand spirit of the moon race. But back at the office we were grubbing around in the pits, doing our damnedest to keep everyone else's footprints off the backs of our necks. Each of us was learning how to play the space game. It was brand-new and the rules were made up as we went along.

When a man was selected as an astronaut people thought of him, if they thought at all, as having arrived at the very crest of his chosen profession. In one sense, we had. But at the same time we found ourselves standing on the first rung of an entirely new profession. All of a sudden we were back at the starting blocks, surrounded by others who had been screened, selected, almost bred for their motivation and competitive spirit.

Keep in mind that astronauts were drawn from an environment where, by natural selection, they had been or were bent on becoming leaders in their activities. Whatever the crowd, we had usually stood out. Past performance had made recognition commonplace. Now we were in the Space League, Astronaut Division, where there was only room for two or three chiefs. All the rest of us had to be Indians.

Combine this with the fact that the stakes were high—glory, respect, admiration, fame and fortune—even a place in the history books—and the place could, and did, turn into a pressure cooker.

Each of us in measuring our careers understood and accepted these conditions. We weren't naive because none of us had time to be naive. We all recognized the significance of making the first lunar landing long before the Apollo program got off the ground. If it wasn't our first conscious thought after being selected, it hit you soon after reporting to the Astronaut Office. This was the boldest adventure in history; the biggest plum since Columbus and we all knew it.

If someone takes a gang like this—screened and selected from the cream of America's manhood—and sits on them, smoothes them out and presses them, attempts to make them indistinguishable from each other, what happens? They accept the obvious challenge and do what comes naturally: attempt to stand out from those around them.

Crew assignments were all the incentive we needed. Once they came within our reach it was like waving a piece of raw meat in front of a cage of hungry lions.

Jockeying for position became a constant activity. The game was to move ahead or—just as effective and often easier to accomplish—move the other guy back. It was a competition guaranteed to bring out the worst in a guy. I know of no astro who, upon leaving the program, didn't breathe a sigh of relief at dealing himself out of that part of the game. We may have loved the job, the competition, and some of the men with whom we competed, but the dog-eat-dog atmosphere that was part of the daily existence caused even the best of gamesmen to be glad when they were rid of it.

Some of the rules were similar to office politics in any corporate structure. But others were unique to the life, times, and men in the astronaut program.

Wherever two or more ambitious people come together, competitive situations are the result. That's business. That's sports. That's politics. That's life. In our circumstances it was compounded not only by our military backgrounds, but also by the complicated caste system that had come into being.

Opportunities in the Astronaut Office were influenced by seniority, a combination of military rank and the pecking order. When I joined the program there were twenty-seven of us playing this game, not including Deke Slayton, who as Director Of Flight Crew Operations floated above the sea of politics, or Al Shepard, whose inner ear problem had grounded him, or John Glenn, soon to retire. Of the twenty-seven, four of us were civilians. And of those four, there were two—Elliot See and Neil Armstrong—whose civil service rank actually exceeded the highest equivalent rank of any of the military astros. At the other end of the spectrum were the other two civilians, Rusty Schweickart and Walter Cunningham. In between were strung out all the active duty military people with their own brand of pedigree: rank, date of rank, and a lineal list by which they could even compare themselves according to their graduation date from West Point or Annapolis.

As the senior military officer in our third group, Dick Gordon was automatically singled out by Deke to be our spokesman. Actually, in terms of military seniority, Gordon had numbers on some of the earlier selected astros. That circumstance was in conflict with the most important fact of astronaut life: pecking order was more important than seniority.

The pecking order was derived from several factors but was primarily related to the hierarchy of selection. If one were a Mercury astronaut presumably only God and James Webb enjoyed higher standing—and that might be subject to some discussion. Then came the Gemini group, whose members outranked and overruled all the weenies and plebes behind them; meaning us, the Apollo astronauts. That pecking order prevailed throughout the system. In fact, it *was* the system. The only official acknowledgment of this system came in an April 1964 memo from Slayton classifying the thirty of us, according to group, as Command Astronauts, Senior Astronauts and Astronauts.

Later there would be de facto subdivisions to cover those who had been in space and those who had not; those who had been to the moon and those who had not; and finally, those who had walked on the lunar surface and those who had not.

In the beginning, though, it had been a clean and simple world. There were seven, "We Seven," all-for-one-and-one-for-all. They paraded together, went to the White House together, and lunched with the Shah of Iran together. They were a package.

Then the ranks grew. There were sixteen, and it became necessary to find a way of dividing the good deals, as well as the bad ones. The addition of the Gemini boys created a logistics problem. There wasn't always room for sixteen. The whole crowd could no longer go to the Kennedy compound.

Within the Gemini group, leadership positions were quickly assumed by Frank Borman, Tom Stafford, and Jim McDivitt. While this wasn't without some merit, it was partly based on the first impressions of Deke and the original astros. As time passed, it became more and more evident that first impressions were almost impossible to live down. Deke's first assessment of each man—even as early as the selection process—dictated what happened to him for a long time to come.

By the time the Apollo gang of fourteen was initiated, the die was cast. Not long after we arrived Gus Grissom and John Young flew the first Gemini mission. John, on his return to earth, publicly announced what we had already assumed: "You're not an astronaut until you've flown in space."

It worked this way: If an astronaut had been in space, he was a star. If he was on a crew, he was a prospect. If he was not yet in line, he was simply a suspect. He hadn't really made the team.

In the case of Rusty and myself, as civilians (along with Neil Armstrong and Elliot See), we weren't even called astronauts when we checked in. Our civil service records listed our job title as "Aerospace Engineer and Pilot." But rest assured we never filled out a form or signed a letter or completed a questionnaire without writing *Astronaut* in the space reserved for "occupation."

In those early months we were divided into four "flights," each with one of the active Mercury astros as chief: Gus Grissom, Wally Schirra, Scott Carpenter, and Gordon Cooper. Not only did they have the name and the game, they had considerable political clout upon which, to a large extent, the Astronaut Office depended to get its way.

As time passed I noticed certain forces at work that would change this order of things. For one, Scott Carpenter was being eased out. He still had his place in the pecking order, but he had inspired some disaffection among his fellows and, more to the point, among the upper management at NASA. I had been rather surprised at the sniping that went on when John Glenn resigned. Now I saw the isolation that began to surround Scott Carpenter, triggered by the fact that his peers felt he had done a less than professional job in his first—and only—space flight.

Scott's was an unusual case, the one Mercury astro who really marched to a different drummer. He was independent, with a bit of the poet in him. On his flight in Aurora 7, Scott had become absorbed in observing the beauty below and in photographing the "firefly" particles flying off the spacecraft. He was on a kind of natural high—and he didn't acquire and maintain the proper attitude for firing the retro rockets prior to his de-orbit burn. He missed the recovery area by 250 miles and, for a few suspenseful moments, there was a very real fear that he would be America's first space fatality.

Gordon Cooper, at the tracking station in Guaymas, Mexico, was monitoring Scott on a repeating set of instruments. As Scott came over the horizon from Hawaii on his last pass he was well behind the retro-fire timeline. Gordo watched his friend fire the retro rockets late and in the wrong attitude. Scott was controlling his attitude poorly, rapidly using up his re-entry fuel, and swinging so erratically no one could predict where he'd land.

At one point Gordo pushed his chair back from the console. Tears came to his eyes and he buried his head in his hands. He was certain his pal was going to be burned alive on re-entry.

But Scott made it down, and an hour later the first aircraft on the scene found him blissfully at ease in his raft, enjoying the sea breeze, his mind years away. He was a lot less concerned about himself than Gordon Cooper had been a few hours before, watching him wobble over the horizon.

None of this was discussed outside the family, and not a great deal of it on the inside. It was part of the code that astros did not ask each other point-blank about professional screw-ups. Scott received the usual medals and public back-pats, but within the group it was gradually understood that he had made his last flight. The word got around that Walt Williams, Bob Gillruth's operations director, had told him flat out, "You're never going to fly for me again."

What followed for Scott Carpenter had to be a living hell. It had taken him fifteen years of preparation to reach that moment on May 24, 1962, when he was literally on top of the world. Then it was gone. There was nothing left.

Scott was a fine, attractive fellow, one of the easiest of the Mercury bunch to get to know. Perhaps a little too much like John Glenn for some of his contemporaries, but always an interesting character. He looked like the athlete he was. He had been a gymnast and ran track, had good reactions and was in the best physical shape of any of the Mercury guys. But he wouldn't compete. When the others took up handball, Scott went for something more esoteric. When we opened our new gym, he took up fencing and invited his instructor out to join him. Seeing them uncasing their foils and putting on their wire masks, Scott could have been Captain Blood. Watching him through the years, letting his hair grow long, involving himself in deep-sea diving or ballooning or music, Scott always did his own thing. I respected him for it, but it didn't endear him to the group.

So Scott began to wander afield, breaking an arm on a motorbike in Bermuda, becoming an aquanaut and manning a submerged laboratory for three weeks, one thing after another. One ironic fact that bound us all together, I first observed in the case of Scott Carpenter: no matter how well or badly the astro years turn out, no matter how easy or painful the going, no astro wants to say good-bye to the job. Perhaps unconsciously, Scott was expressing an attitude that persists today: many cling to the title of *Astronaut*.

I suppose Gordon Cooper was the next to fall from grace. He gained the reputation as another guy following his own muse. He, Gus Grissom and Jim Rathman, the former Indy winner, formed the GRC Racing Team and entered a car for several years in the Indianapolis 500. They didn't have a winner, but they had the usual sponsors to cover part of the cost and they always had a good time, a month-long party, each May. The first time I went to the famous old Brickyard was to visit with them and help work on their car. Al Worden, only recently arrived in the program, took a few weeks' leave and spent them in Gasoline Alley with the GRC Special. It was a lark, although I do think we could have become pretty fair mechanics.

Gordo had already taken a turn at speedboat racing and none of this racing nonsense endeared him to the establishment. Nor did a later remark, when the NASA brass ordered him out on the eve of a race he was scheduled to drive at Daytona Beach. Gordo had a mild case of apoplexy and his withdrawal wasn't exactly graceful. "What do they expect us to be," he fumed, "tiddly-winks players?"

Cooper's rebellion was sincere, but he shouldn't have been surprised at the repercussions.

While various internal factors were affecting the career of each astronaut, the general public discriminated on a more obvious characteristic:

the distinction between those who had been "up" and those who had not. It was most apparent when filling requests for speeches or some of the frequent social invitations in the Houston area.

That was understandable. When an organization invited a dinner speaker they wanted someone who would attract as much attention as possible, a crowd-puller. It was a poor substitute when a pretender to Valhalla stood up to tell the audience about jungle training in Panama or flying the mission simulators.

At the risk of reducing our own odds of flying, we (the Apollo guys) looked forward to the arrival of the next group of astronauts so we could drop the "new" from our introduction. Having to exist in reflected glory for so long may explain why so many wasted little time establishing their own identities following their flights.

Of course, at first we were so gung-ho just to be there, it didn't matter what we were called. I recall making a flying visit to NASA about six weeks before I was scheduled to report. A friend from my Marine Reserve Squadron, Hugh Purser, and I hopped into a couple of A-4Ds and flew into Houston from Los Angeles. Actually, it was Los Angeles to Houston with a side trip to Beaumont, Texas, Hugh's hometown. Hugh and I had done a lot of low flying across the western deserts but this was his first chance to lay a "buzz" job on his own home town. We did it up right and "escaped" to Ellington Field, 50 miles west.

We parked on the ramp with all the NASA aircraft and made our way to the flight office where the fellow in charge assigned us a locker. We could look around and see what was in store for me. We admired the custom-made, hot-looking flying helmets—custom-fit to each astro's head. And custom-made Dehner boots. The flight suits were NASA blue, not those low-rent orange or green ones that military pilots wore. I was joining the last of the world's great flying clubs and it was clear that I was going to dress first class.

Hugh was dutifully impressed that they would roll out the red carpet for a neophyte like me. But the topper came when we walked through the reconditioned barracks that housed the astronaut offices and I casually waved and said hello to Al Shepard and John Glenn and the rest of the legitimate heroes. It was a sweet, heady kind of atmosphere. On that visit I not only couldn't tell that a pecking order existed, I wouldn't have given a toot that it did.

The illusion of quick acceptance was to be heightened by the genuine courtesy of John Glenn. Very soon after joining NASA, John dropped by my office and asked if I was having any problem maintaining my Marine Reserve affiliation. I had transferred to a Marine squadron at Dallas Naval Air Station where we were flying the FJ-4 Fury. It was still unsettled as to whether I'd have the use of a NASA airplane to fly from Houston on duty weekends and thereby keep the Marine Corps happy with my attendance.

John offered, "A good friend of mine, Jay Hubbard, is an aide to the Commandant. If you have any problem with the Marine Corps, let me know. Jay will take care of you." As a matter of fact, Jay did take care of me, and over the years became a good friend.

All any of us wanted was a space flight, and we rarely pretended otherwise, at least among ourselves. I doubt that any of us, in our hearts, were any more concerned with the good we were doing mankind than Indianapolis 500 drivers are motivated because they believe the risks they take will develop safety improvements in highway cars.

For a long time many of us persisted in believing that our performance in training would determine how we fared. We kept butting our heads against the pecking order until we eventually learned that performance wasn't the key. Our Apollo group had the distinction of being the first to whom Deke made a point of *not promising* a flight to everyone selected.

So the pressures mounted: to get on a flight crew, to climb out of the shadows and make your own dawn, and to appear in public without being reduced to showing the latest film of the flight of your "buddy," Dick Daring.

At the very bottom of the pecking order were the hyphenated astronauts, the scientist-astronauts. The old pros naturally assumed they would not be able to cut the mustard "with the aviator fellows." That rankled the scientists but when the second batch of Ph.D.s arrived we noticed a sub-class distinction was quickly established between the first group of Scientist-Astros and the second.

To understand how the pecking order prevailed, it's helpful to examine the careers of some who benefited from it. You can begin with Al Shepard, the first American in space. When Shepard's inner ear problem grounded him, there was only one logical position for him and that was in charge of *all* the other astronauts, save Deke Slayton, for whom this precedent had already been established.

Al was placed in charge of the Astronaut Office, a division of the Flight Crew Operations Directorate (formerly handled by one of Deke's assistants). He reigned there until his ear problem was corrected by surgery. Then he successfully moved himself directly onto a flight crew. He was succeeded as Chief Astronaut by the resourceful Tom Stafford, a second generation, Gemini astronaut, but no Mercury astronaut was ever put in a position of reporting to Tom.

When Shepard returned from his Apollo 14 comeback, he had made it to the apex of the pyramid: the only Mercury astronaut to walk on the moon. He was the king of the pecking order and would soon be promoted to the rank of Admiral. We all knew he would never wind up working under Tom Stafford. Al took back his old desk, leaving the question, what to do with Stafford, without making it appear he had been demoted? Easy. He was moved upstairs as a staff assistant to Deke.

Even the bittersweet case of Gordon Cooper was consistent with the rules of the pecking order. Gordo flew the longest (thirty-four hours) and the best of the Mercury missions. He later commanded the third Gemini flight with Pete Conrad as his crewmate, setting a new space endurance record of 190 hours, 55 minutes and making him, temporarily, the marathon champ of all the world's spacemen.

As the youngest of the magnificent seven, Cooper seemed to have the best chance of making the first lunar landing. Public sentiment certainly favored one of the original Mercury heroes taking that historic first step. But along the way it went wrong for Gordo.

He was outspoken. He complained—in print—about some of the NASA pressures. His reputation as a daredevil haunted him. He made waves. He didn't work too hard.

Cooper never flew in space again. His career was one long series of being leaned on for his transgressions, real or imagined. He paid the price for not toeing the mark.

Here was the irony of it all. Even as Cooper resisted, and the brass above turned the screws, the pecking order was religiously maintained. Gordo backed up the last Gemini flight and then, with Donn Eisele and Ed Mitchell on his crew, backed up Apollo 10.

That should have put him in line to fly Apollo 13. But when it came time to announce the crew, Al Shepard stepped forward with a clean bill of health from the medics. He was ungrounded and wanted the flight. Deke obliged, only to see headquarters turn it down. NASA management's feeling, shared by nearly all of the astronauts, was that Shepard needed more time in training.

Some fast shuffling was necessary and Jim Lovell, who had been scheduled to fly on 14, was given command of Apollo 13.

Shepard went to work with a passion. With the public rooting for him, he won his case and convinced the powers at NASA to give him Apollo 14. He picked up Ed Mitchell from Cooper's backup crew and Stu Roosa, both fifth-generation astronauts.

That cooked it for Gordo. He had done some fairly colorful, behind-the-scenes bitching to his old pal Deke when he was asked for the second time running to take a backup crew on Apollo 10. There had always been that magic lantern shining in the distance, the chance to make a lunar landing. Now there was nothing. Cooper had been passed over again, and he got the message. Everyone did.

But even then, they had to find him a place appropriate to his position in the pecking order. And they did. Gordo was moved upstairs to work with Deke, whose office was a sort of halfway house for those who couldn't, or wouldn't, work for someone beneath them in the pecking order. He marked time there until July 1970, when he left the program. Although he has never said so in public, it was no secret among the rest of us that Gordo felt his moon flight had been preempted by Shepard.

Timing is always critical to those who want to get ahead—which included all of us. The only way to beat the pecking order was with the right-place-at-the-right-time stroke of luck, such as being on a backup crew when one of the prime members bought the farm, or maybe broke a leg. It was all fate. Take for example Jim Lovell.

When Lovell successfully completed his Gemini 7 flight, he was given what could only be described as a dead-end assignment, the back up crew for Gemini 10 along with Buzz Aldrin. There was not going to be a Gemini 13 mission into which they could rotate and all the early Apollo crews would be in training by the time the two of them became available for reassignment. The only duty worse than backing up 10 or 11 was to back up Gemini 12 – and Gordon Cooper got that one.

Enter the fickle finger of fate. Elliot See, the prime crew commander for Gemini 9, stalls his T-38 on a routine landing and crashes into the roof of the McDonnell plant in St. Louis, Missouri, killing himself and Charlie Bassett in the rear seat. Their backups, Tom Stafford and Gene Cernan, inherit the Gemini 9 mission and start a chain reaction. Lovell and Aldrin are moved to back up Gemini 9 (instead of 10), which puts them in line to fly Gemini 12 in November 1966. Without this Gemini flight under his belt, Aldrin would *not* have been a candidate for an early lunar landing mission.

Normally, that date would still have left Jim out of the early stages of the Apollo program because of the overlap between programs. But fate steps in again. Two months later, the Apollo 1 crew dies in the fire on pad 34, triggering a two-year hiatus in manned space flights.

Lovell is tragically available again. After the dust settles on the post-fire reshuffling, he winds up on the backup crew for Apollo 8 with a prime crew of Frank Borman, Mike Collins, and Bill Anders. What more can happen? Lots! Collins develops a numbness in his arm from a pinched nerve and decides on surgery. His back up, Jim Lovell, is moved up, flies around the moon with his old partner, Frank Borman, and subsequently commands Apollo 13, to become the first man to fly four space missions.

As for Mike Collins, by the time he could get back on flight status, the next mission available was the first one bound for the surface of the moon: Apollo 11. Mike replaces Fred Haise on Armstrong's crew, and pilots the Command Module while Armstrong and Aldrin take their historic "giant leap for mankind."

Then there was Donn Eisele, who was originally ticketed for a spot on Gus Grissom's Apollo 1 crew. A few days before the news was to be announced, Donn throws his shoulder out playing handball and, following surgery, is required to keep his arm in a sling for several months. When the crew is introduced, Donn has been replaced by Roger Chaffee.

Few ever knew that Eisele had been slated for that doomed crew. I didn't know myself until months after the fire. We had worked together for a year and a half when, quite out of the blue, Donn turned to me one day and said, absently, "You know, Walt, I was supposed to be on that crew." That was all he said. But I knew what he meant.

Timing and catastrophes were elements beyond our mortal control. But we were all aviators and surely, we thought, how we flew, how we performed, ranked way up there among the things that counted. But just as it was unpredictable what benefited a career, what penalized us was equally mysterious.

As aviators, astronauts had the usual number of accidents for the hours we flew. A good majority of those could be attributed to pilot error: either outright poor judgment, or a poor response to a developing situation. Yet it never seemed to handicap anyone's career. Only once – in the case of Scott Carpenter—did it even appear to matter when a guy blew a space mission.

At such times the value of personal relationships was difficult to assess. Joe Engle was an air force test pilot who had flown the X-15, an early rocket plane. Joe was a great guy with impeccable credentials and, only coincidentally, one of Deke's hunting buddies. (Deke could respect you and enjoy your company if you didn't hunt, but it helped if you did. He was an outdoorsman and I suspect my stock went up a bit when Deke learned I had a brother who was an air guide in Alaska—a bush pilot who made a living hunting and fishing.)

After Engle returned from helicopter training he gained a new mobility for some of his hunting forays. Coming back alone one weekend from a hunt outside of San Antonio, Joe was running late. It was after dark when he made it back to the field—almost. A half-mile short of the runway his chopper ran out of gas. He effected a successful night auto rotation—a dead-stick helicopter landing at night—which is a good trick that no one even practices at night.

The chopper went through a rail fence at the edge of the field and all it was good for afterward was spare parts. Because Joe was a fine pilot, he walked away without a scratch. If there was ever a word of reprimand, no one heard about it. Not long after, he was assigned to the backup crew for Apollo 14.

Another X-15 veteran, Neil Armstrong, parlayed a busted Gemini 8 flight into the Buck Rogers grand prize mission, the first lunar landing. It was Neil's first flight and with Dave Scott they performed the first docking in space.

It was March 16, 1966, my thirty-fourth birthday. Two days before, Bill Anders and I, along with our wives, had flown a rented Cessna 172 the thousand miles from Houston to the Cape. The 172 was the cheapest and, unfortunately, the slowest four place airplane we could find. It was the only way we could afford to include our families in the excitement of a launch.

I was assigned to be the blockhouse communicator for the flight crew—a position we called "Stoney," the origin of which no one knows. Stoney's primary function was to handle all communications with the crew and call "lift-off," a small but active assignment that let one feel he was making progress. It was hard not to be amused by Stoney's main responsibility: counting from ten backwards and hollering, "Lift-off." It was almost that simple. Stoney did provide visual confirmation of lift-off to the crew, the key piece of information in Gemini abort decisions during those hectic seconds immediately before and after lift-off.

Immediately after lift-off, as soon as I could get released from the blockhouse, Bill and I and our wives hopped into the 172 and started our nine-hour trip back to Houston. Along the way we listened to news broadcasts to follow the progress of Gemini 8. The first space rendezvous and docking in history was taking place at 130 miles high and 17,500 miles per hour while we puttered along at one mile high and 120 miles per hour.

By the time we landed back in Houston the mission was already over. Neil Armstrong and Dave Scott had been picked up by a destroyer in the Pacific and Gemini 8 became the second-shortest Gemini mission on record. The flight was described as the first "emergency" in space. After docking with the Agena, a runaway thruster began rotating the joined vehicles. Malfunction procedures had been developed for just such an eventuality but at the onset of the problem, improvisation by Neil and Dave seemed to be the rule of the day. First, it was incorrectly concluded that the Agena rocket was at fault and its attitude control system was shut down. When the spin rate increased, it was decided to undock the two vehicles. The Gemini spacecraft rotated even faster. To get the spacecraft under control, the crew activated the re-entry control system.

The mission rules for the situation were plain: re-entry at the next available recovery area. So, less than eight hours after lift-off, they sat floating in a raft in the Pacific waiting for a destroyer to pick them up.

Of course, Neil and Dave received the usual medals. Neil went on to become the first man on the moon. And Dave Scott's career as the fair-haired boy of the third group of astronauts was unaffected. Both performed well over the remainder of their careers, but at the same time their very progress ignored the fact that their peers—and many others at the space center felt they had botched their first mission.

In such situations, we generally felt a curious mixture of relief, pride, and envy. We would regret not having enjoyed the opportunity to demonstrate how flawlessly we would have performed under the same circumstances.

As a final example of accidents that apparently had no adverse effect on a fellow's career, there was Gene Cernan's "mishap," which occurred at a time of great speculation on who was going to fly the last Apollo mission: Apollo 17.

Gene was the backup commander on Apollo 14, with Ron Evans and Joe Engle on his crew. Backing up Apollo 15 were Dick Gordon and his crew. We all knew that Apollo 17 would be the last of the moon missions and, in the normal scheme of things, Gene Cernan would rotate into the prime crew spot. But for a variety of reasons—including having the only honest-to-God space geologist, Jack Schmitt, on his crew—some were guessing that Dick would actually get it. By this time, Apollo missions were flying at such long intervals that it was no longer necessary to skip two missions in rotating crews.

Dave Scott, who commanded Apollo 15, even made a personal pitch to Deke to help Dick get the mission.

In the midst of this uncertain situation and one week before the Apollo 14 launch, Gene Cernan decided to take a helicopter training flight down the Indian River running behind Cocoa Beach. NASA had moved a helicopter to the Cape so that Gene and Al Shepard (the Apollo 14 commander) could keep their hands in at flying lunar landing approach profiles. For whatever reason, Gene wound up flying the helicopter into the drink.

While the Accident Board never said so, among the guys the verdict was that Gene had been flat-hatting—buzzing along the river—obviously too low. He may have spotted a nude sunbather, or whatever. In any case, Gene ran a skid into the river, crashed and the chopper sank. Only good fortune and quick thinking saved Gene from being killed. As it was, the shock knocked him unconscious. He came to under the water, found the bubble canopy of his chopper broken, struggled to the surface, and swam desperately through water now wild with burning gasoline. His charred helmet was found later.

Gene followed the training manual: he took a deep breath, dived, and swam under the fire, still in his boots and heavy flight suit. An old woman, fishing in a rowboat, finally pulled him out of the water.

The betting in the office on the Apollo 17 crew quickly switched—aviators characteristically do not wait for the accident report—"That sure cinches it for Dick," the refrain went. "Ol' Gene just screwed the pooch." Deke gave Gene every opportunity—hell, he practically begged him—to claim engine failure but Gene wouldn't take it. The accident board took weeks to gather its findings, took months to file a report, and finally confirmed what everyone had assumed and Gene had never denied: pilot error rather than equipment failure.

But it had absolutely no effect on the assignments for Apollo 17. Consistent with the past handling of such incidents, Gene Cernan was still designated the spacecraft commander for the last lunar landing. Chris Kraft said much later that he had accepted Deke's assurances about engine failure on the accident. He added, "If I'd known then what I know now, it might have turned out differently."

Some might have wondered what kind of guardian angel was looking over Cernan's shoulders to guide him to what can only be described as a very successful career—clearly the grandest of any in the third group of astronauts. The answer is Tom Stafford.

Gene was a lot of the things that Tom wasn't. Even before his first mission he was one of the few astronauts who could outshine Wally Schirra on the social circuit. He had all the essential graces. He quickly and easily cultivated the rich and the famous and, in turn, was cultivated by them. His beautiful wife Barbara was equally comfortable in the same surroundings.

Tom and Gene came together on the backup crew of Gemini 9 and, after Elliot See's accident, the flight itself. It established a relationship that paid off handsomely for both of them for the next seven years.

Theirs became a friendship that can best be described as symbiotic, with Gene providing the public relations, the social entree, and a Jet Set lifestyle while Tom provided the technical know-how, the hard work, the mission-oriented aspects of the partnership, as well as career control. It was a classic relationship.

Tom Stafford had arrived with the second generation of astros. From the beginning he was one of the more respected men in the program, He developed the right kind of earthy camaraderie with Shepard, Slayton, and Grissom, and rose to a position of authority over his contemporaries. This was due not only to his relationship with the Mercury guys, but also to the fact that he migrated toward centers of power. Tom wouldn't be content going from prime to backup to prime crew, ad nauseam. He had his sights aimed beyond that.

When Al Shepard finally made a successful grab for a flight, it was Tom Stafford, just back from the Apollo 10 mission, that Shepard (with Deke's concurrence) placed in charge of the Astronaut Office. The only man still in the program higher in the pecking order (but not in responsibility or authority) than Tom was Gordon Cooper. To avoid an ego crunch and maintain the pecking order, Gordo moved up to become Deke's assistant.

And Stafford became a caretaker chief, the last in a sequence of events that created at least three problems among the troops:

1. Al and Tom's good fortune was clearly Gordo's loss and even those not close to Cooper were sympathetic on that point.

2. Most of the astros resented not only Shepard's willingness but also his ability to place himself directly on a flight crew without even the pretense of embarrassment at skipping a backup assignment or showing regard for those whom he cut out of the pattern in the process.

3. Some of the second group of astros, Tom's contemporaries, were less than thrilled at his rise to a clear cut position of authority over them.

While Chief Astronaut was a paper-pushing job with little glamour, Stafford was nicely located within the "corporate" structure, and in a unique position to dispense the space center version of patronage. He could influence which public appearances were approved around the country, who was assigned world-tour boondoggles, and he could strongly influence flight crew assignments, including his own.

Stafford kept Shepard's chair warm for nearly two years while Al made the third lunar landing. Following Apollo 14, Tom turned the job back to Al, joined Deke's staff and began laying the groundwork for his own power play, à la Shepard.

The only mission for the next decade without a flight crew assigned was the Apollo-Soyuz Test Project scheduled for 1975, and Deke had his cap set on both flying again and commanding that particular mission.

Well, so did Tom Stafford, and he had learned the rules and how to play the game like an expert. After the infighting was over, the public announcement listed Tom Stafford as the spacecraft commander with Deke Slayton, Tom's boss of ten years, working for him.

Stafford, the acknowledged master at astropolitics, is a tall, balding, slightly awkward-looking fellow with a Lyndon Johnson earthiness and a taste for the technical aspects of a mission. He was ambitious and smart—except when it came to investments. He probably took more chances on dry holes and poor insurance companies than the rest of us combined.

Tom was deceptive in the impression he made on people. He looked like a Presbyterian minister and he played the "good ol' boy" role to the hilt, notably when he was testing the political waters around the state of Oklahoma. But it was a mistake ever to underrate him. He was perhaps a better Chief Astronaut than Shepard, devoting more time to the job and generally representing our interests well.

With all his other attributes, a social whiz he was not. He knew how to have a good time but wasn't much for the social charade. Thus Stafford and Cernan blended their talents perfectly.

Although Cernan prevailed over Dick Gordon on the Apollo 17 mission, one member of Dick's backup crew did make it: Jack Schmitt. That was one situation *not* resolved according to the pecking order.

In his own way, Schmitt was an interesting case. Jack was movie-handsome, dark, and short (two out of three isn't bad). He had spent a lifetime outdoors, had a good reputation as a geologist, and was considered by some to be brilliant. The two of us first met when Jack was working for the U.S. Geological Survey in Flagstaff, Arizona, at a time when one of my duties was working with the USGS to plan lunar surface activities.

From Jack's perspective, I don't suppose we hit it off particularly well in that first encounter. I recall he quizzed me about becoming a scientist in the space program and was less than encouraging. Jack didn't particularly appreciate my opinion that the timing was premature for scientists in the manned space program—an opinion borne out by subsequent events. On the other hand, I sensed that Jack felt the special skills of an aviator were overrated which I, naturally, resented.

When NASA selected the first five scientist-astros, Jack was right there among them. He had an uphill fight all the way and no one ever worked harder for his seat in a spacecraft. He finished pilot training behind the other scientists and he certainly did not graduate with honors. When Jack returned home it was two months before NASA would certify him safe for solo in our T-38s. The joke around the office at the time was "If God had meant man to fly, it wouldn't have been Jack Schmitt."

Jack was determined to keep at flying until he became an able, if conservative, aviator. Nothing ever stopped him, which was fortunate, because scientist-astronauts were firmly anchored at the bottom of the pecking order.

Jack was the only scientist in the program with a legitimate case for flying to the moon but fighting the pecking order wouldn't get him there. He became the unsung hero of one lunar landing mission after another, working tirelessly in Houston or at the Cape to prepare every crew from Apollo 11 on for their geological tasks.

As the Apollo program was drawing to a close, Jack finally got a break. He was placed on Gordon's backup crew for Apollo 15 even though it appeared to be too little and too late. Still, many of us felt the program would never end without Geologist Jack getting to the moon. He deserved it, and some of us considered Jack the strongest thing Dick Gordon had going for him in the politics to fly the last Apollo mission.

Gordon lost, but Jack did indeed get his flight. The real loser was Joe Engle, who had worked with Gene Cernan for a solid year as his Lunar Module pilot. Engle was replaced by Schmitt on the Apollo 17 crew in the only instance of violating the pecking order that comes to mind. It was surely in response to the pressure the National Academy of Sciences put on NASA—higher politics overcoming the lesser. Engle took it without a whimper. I'm not sure I would have been as gracious.

Jack Schmitt represented a victory for all of the scientists who stayed with the astronaut program through the years, many with no visible rewards. They usually got the worst details, but they stuck it out.

Of course, underlying all of our actions and efforts and ambitions was gamesmanship. If the astronauts didn't invent it, some of them sure perfected it as an art form. It wasn't simply a case of knock-your-buddy, it was also a matter of knowing when and how to "boost" him, a form of damnation by faint praise: "Sam is smart. Sam knows his limitations and weaknesses." Some played the sycophant while others were expert at the pointed barb.

Of course, in the Astronaut Office, no one was ever really secure. A space flight was such an overpowering goal that when one was at stake most of the astros became almost paranoid about their opportunities. The prevalent attitude was never to volunteer a favorable word about the way someone else was doing his job if he was even remotely considered competition. Of course, he had to be knocked *only* in front of the people who counted: Deke or Al Shepard or Chris Kraft, or any of the heavyweights up to and including Dr. Gilruth. Most important was any prospective crew commander, just in case they had any say about whom they would take with them.

Everybody was fair game in this shoot-down-the-other-guy routine, but as a practical matter it was applied most effectively with respect to our peers, those at roughly the same place in the pecking order. Recalling my own last years with NASA, those level with or above me in the pecking order received my praise only on rare occasions, but I was never reluctant to praise a job well done by those who worked for me. In terms of the system, the latter was a harmless and acceptable practice.

I never was able to spell out the process by which one made it to a prime crew assignment, but I did conclude that there was little science to it. Why Deke assigned Gene Cernan to the Gemini 9 backup crew with Tom Stafford remains a mystery, although the success of his subsequent career is not. Every rookie who flew with a veteran and performed adequately could be expected to be looked after by his spacecraft commander. The only limitations to that rule were how well the commander's own career flourished and the failure of the former rookie to perform in the future.

This process was enhanced by the fact that crew selections were dependent in many ways on availability. And after flying with one person, or serving with him on a backup crew, the two were both available in the same time frame for later assignments.

Tom Stafford's career was launched by an early and impressive performance on Gemini 6 with Schirra. Gene worked with Tom on several backup crews, rode into space with him on Gemini 9 and Apollo 10, and finally commanded his own mission on Apollo 17. When Tom was asked once why he had stuck with and, in effect, sponsored Cernan for so many years, he replied, "Gene knows how to follow orders. He'll do exactly what I tell him to do."

Alan Bean, like many of us, started off believing that competence, dedication, hard work, and attention to the job would lead to its own reward: a space flight. It amounted to being conscientious, but too much of it could be your downfall. You would expect someone who really believed in what he was doing to not hesitate to express his opinion in reviews and meetings, even if it differed from those held by the higher-ups who might not be as knowledgeable on the subject. The topic might be a change in the flight rules for the T-38, or whether the Astronaut Office should take a position different from the Program Office on a proposed spacecraft change.

All that the early, idealistic Al Bean got for his efforts was a backup position on Gemini 10 when Elliot See and Charlie Bassett were killed, and heading the Skylab effort when it was still seven or eight years away from flight. But Al was better at watching and learning than some of us and, apparently, more flexible to boot. When he decided to become pragmatic, his career began to steadily improve.

It didn't happen overnight. One didn't just knock on Deke's door, and say, "I surrender, mold me," and bingo, turn into a company man. But Al began to swallow his own opinion, to go along with the majority; he no longer volunteered compliments about his colleagues and learned to play "the game." It wasn't an accident, but a conscious effort on Al's part—if you couldn't lick 'em, join 'em—and he recommended that I do the same.

With his new approach he became an accepted member of the establishment, was assigned to back up Apollo 9, landed on the moon on Apollo 12, and commanded the second Skylab mission for fifty-nine days in space.

In my case, following Apollo 7, I was made Chief of the Skylab Branch of the Astronaut Office, replacing Owen Garriott, the senior scientist-astronaut. Alan Bean and Gordon Cooper had filled the role before Owen. I anticipated flying the first Skylab mission, having at one time been promised the assignment.

Two years later I was bumped by Pete Conrad, coming off Apollo 12. Pete was a second-generation astro with good pecking-order position as well as good qualifications for just about anything. The knowledge that Pete had the tools and experience only softened the blow for me. When

Pete took over, he wanted the flight and began looking forward to it with me as his backup. Then came the day Stafford said that if he decided against running for the Senate from Oklahoma, he (Stafford) would displace Pete as the first Skylab commander. It was musical chairs all right, but some of the players were also starting and stopping the music.

Some of us in those early years resented the "pecking order"—those who it plainly worked against. But it was in existence when we arrived and we were just so darn glad to be there, we accepted it with little complaint. Besides, in time, the politics of getting a flight would become much more Machiavellian and morale busting. In thinking back, I doubt if any of us thought of the system as corrupt but, in a sense, it was. The first astros at the trough established the ground rules and it served them well as generally better qualified astronauts followed them into the program. What was missing was outside, independent oversight to ensure that merit played a significant role in the equation. What higher authority was exercised usually carried with it some of its own brand of politics.

Within the system we lived with, a few obvious commandments come to mind, a sort of buyer's guide to how astropolitics was played:

1. If you were "one of the boys" you didn't necessarily have to be terribly competent.
2. You never worked for an astronaut selected after you, regardless of other qualifications—his or yours.
3. Physical fitness (other than injuries or death) had no bearing on your status, opportunities, or accomplishments.

4. First impressions, even those formed before you joined the program, could affect your career almost forever.
5. In bestowing rewards in the program, the rich got richer and the poor got poorer.
6. Scientist-astronauts stayed at the bottom of the pecking order.
7. Classical political influence—meaning out-of-town political influence—was counterproductive.
8. A power play was good only if you were certain you had the horses to finish it. That's why so few tried.
9. If you can't say anything good about someone, don't hesitate.
10. Do unto others as they would do unto you, but do it first.

7

Countdown to Apollo 7

OUR STINT as the Apollo 1 backup crew lasted barely two months—from the Apollo 2 cancellation in late November 1966 to the night of the Apollo 1 fire on January 27, 1967. It was a short but uniquely different experience from being in the prime spot. In theory, the backup crew is subject at any time to being placed in the shoes of the prime crew, individually or collectively, and to fly the mission. As a practical matter, this is seldom the case. In fact, it occurred only two or three times in the first fifteen years of the space program. When we were thrown into the breach to back up Grissom's crew, we had no illusions about being called upon to replace them. We had serious doubts as to whether even the prime crew would be trained well enough to fly the mission at the scheduled launch date. To be frank, we were all counting on some hardware or testing delay to cause a schedule slip, which would give Gus, Ed and Roger additional time to complete their training.

It all became academic that night in January when the fire on Pad 34 triggered a reappraisal of the entire Apollo Program. The fire investigation was hardly begun when Deke notified Wally, Donn and me that we would now be flying the first manned mission. Over the next several months unmanned testing continued and the Apollo mission sequence was renumbered to account for these unmanned tests. Our flight would turn out to be Apollo 7. Too bad we did not believe in luck.

By the summer of 1967 we still believed the Russians were ahead in the U.S.-proclaimed race to the moon. But they were having problems of their own and we were trying like hell to close the gap. In April 1967, cosmonaut Vladimir Komarov was killed returning to earth from the first manned test of the Soyuz spacecraft. The flight came amidst intense pressure from the Kremlin to reclaim the Soviet lead in the "space race." It was soon announced that the parachute of his Soyuz 1 spacecraft had failed during re-entry but we were only able to piece together the real story years later.

The four unmanned Soyuz launches had all been unsuccessful for a variety of problems in the thermal control, heat shield and parachute systems. Soviet designers knew that the Soyuz re-entry module had not been completely debugged and considered it unready for manned flight. However, the Communist Party ordered the launch anyway. May Day was just around the corner.

Komarov's death attracted its share of rumors, the most gruesome being that his death screams were recorded by American monitoring stations. Since his descent occurred in the far northwestern regions of Soviet territory not normally covered by American space-tracking facilities, it is unlikely we overheard him. The full story behind the Soyuz 1 disaster has never been reported.

The entire country seemed to be in the clutch of an emotional losing streak, of which the Apollo 1 pad fire had been a low point. The year 1967 had seen the war in Vietnam intensify. That summer the worst race riot in the nation's history ended in Detroit, Michigan, with 43 dead and 5,000 homeless. College campuses were seething. And in New York the schoolteachers went on strike for eighteen days.

The space program was getting a fresh look, from within as well as without. NASA was leaning hard on the contractors, demanding stepped-up levels of quality control and new safety practices. We decided to bite the bullet; to take the inadequate junk, represented by the blackened pyre on Pad 34, and transform it into the brilliant machine that carried us to the moon in five giant steps.

North American Rockwell transferred Harrison Storms and brought in a new team to run its Space Division, while NASA replaced Apollo Program Manager Joe Shea with a new man of their own—George Low. The program was desperately in need of new faces and a new approach. Low was an old-timer with NASA and had held many top management jobs. Both men were young and bright but there the similarity ended. While Joe Shea was colorful and somewhat flamboyant, George was serious and businesslike at all times. Joe was aggressive and doggedly pursued the solution to problems as *he* saw them, including lobbying support for those solutions. George would thoughtfully consider the views brought to him by his deputies before selecting the most appropriate course of action.

Partly because he was a contemporary, Joe was always willing to take on an astro at his own game, whether it was squash, handball, or turning a terrible pun. (His punning duels with Wally Schirra were legendary. Wally would try to overwhelm Joe with sheer numbers, while Joe would rely on quality to carry the day.)

George preferred to remain aloof and above the fray, operating in the arena of mutual respect rather than friendly camaraderie. In George's decision-making processes, logic was seldom deterred by emotional appeal. He consistently placed good men in the top jobs and knew when to go along with them.

In that year and in that climate Wally, Donn, and I found ourselves at center stage. It was no longer a backup role, not a drill, not a redundant mission. As the public saw it, the prior crew had been killed, Apollo was still trying to get off the pad, and we—the crew of Apollo 7—were the men entrusted with *doing* it, with getting the U.S. back into the game.

My whole mood changed—the confidence in my approach to problems, my daily rhythm. I slept better. Food tasted better. My wife looked better. For the first time around the office our crew was being envied instead of being envious.

The three of us were drawn closer by the irresistible challenge of a shared adventure. Wally became, in every, sense, the charismatic, complicated guy the press had been creating for most of a decade. It was *his* flight now; he wasn't standing in for Deke Slayton or backing up Gus Grissom. Until we were announced as the Apollo VII crew, and the virus really got to him, I honestly didn't feel that Wally had any real urge to make another space voyage. His mind, if not his heart, was on getting out and exploring the commercial opportunities that would be waiting for him. As Wally himself put it, "The space program devours people. I have been completely devoured by this business."

But there was one crucial circumstance that overlay his attitude—and ours. Wally Schirra was being pictured as the man chosen to rescue the manned space program. And that was a task worthy of Wally's interest.

Instead of just going through the motions, he became the wagon-master. He was going to steer us and he left no doubt about it, even in those odd times when no one else really cared who was steering.

Wally could afford to be a prima donna on occasion, because he had one precious asset going for him: people adored him. He was simply a great, convivial, sunshiny guy. When Wally walked through a plant and shook hands with people, they had the dazed glow of people touched by royalty. Donn and I walked through and they were warm, friendly, and respectful, but they were just filing our names for future reference.

Schirra was a right-now hero. He could be ambitious, serious, and contentious. He could be anything he wanted to be, including hungry or sleepy. If testing became a little hectic and Wally was not quite satisfied with a particular system, he would simply stop in the middle of a sentence and tell the engineers and the technicians to check it out one more time. "I'll be in the ready room, taking a nap," he would say. "Call me when it's ready."

Our attitude had changed and so had management's—and we weren't the only ones. Contractors became more receptive; to the point where I worried they might be too responsive to our sometimes-arbitrary demands.

Between the night of the fire and the date of our launch twenty months and two weeks would pass. During that time the attitudes of the people at North American Rockwell and in the news media, as well as strangers in the all-night diner, conveyed to us the feeling that we were something special, like a Roman gladiator or the heavyweight boxing champion getting ready to step into the ring. Except that instead of measuring the time in minutes, we had to measure it in months. It caused us to go about our work without bustle, but with a sense of purpose.

Twenty-one months is a lot of time to be soaking up applause or calculating risks. We drove ourselves, at work and at play. An airplane was always available to slip us away for a weekend of hunting on Catalina Island, or get us to Indianapolis on May 30 for a ride in the pace car at the Indy 500.

We could not afford to be invisible. The public had received a jolting reminder that there was a down side to space exploration, and it was our way—the program's way—of letting the country know we weren't running scared.

Between the weeks we lived at North American Rockwell to get the vehicle ready and the long days we spent in the simulators, we probably qualified as the best-prepared crew ever sent on the first flight of a new vehicle.

With all that time, we still used it up and needed it all. As it was with every flight, but especially a first flight, work was piled on us. Of course, no matter how many months we trained, there would still have been points not fully covered and details left undone. It was like getting married. If one waited until conditions were ideal, no one ever would get married.

The very best of times were those spent in residence at the Cape. It was a casual atmosphere, slacks-and-a-Ban-Lon-shirt, in the midst of hard work. But there was something about being on the scene that lifted our spirits. To keep it loose we worked as often as possible at a private beach house NASA provided, taking in the sun and developing the flight plan. (Actually, it was one of the private residences condemned years earlier when the Kennedy Space Center was established. Tony Broadway, our jack-of-all-trades facilities manager had rehabilitated it.) In that summer of 1967, life was a soft summer breeze.

We probably had more offices than the President. We kept one in Houston, one at Downey, California, and two at the Cape (at the training building and in the crew quarters). We spent serious time in all of them, but we also made it a point to break the desk cycle and get away to smell the flowers and hear the music. This was part of the Wally Schirra philosophy: "Take an even strain." He didn't believe in burning himself out. He thought it was important to cleanse the brain now and then and have fun.

The Cape was party-oriented, anyway. We lived it up and had our good times, usually with friends-of-the-space-family types. However much we partied, people defended our right to raise hell. They assumed it was an escape from the dangers soon to be faced. That aspect of the mission, the potential for death, was wildly over-dramatized. Naturally, we enjoyed every minute of it.

We were all playing Mr. Cool. It would be poor form not to and, besides, we really felt that way.

In the interest of maintaining our mental health (and social flexibility), we lived in town, at the Hilton or the Holiday Inn, coming and going as we pleased, but taking many of our meals in the crew quarters at the Cape.

Part of our continuing effort to keep ourselves amused focused on the infamous "gotcha," simple shorthand for a form of practical joking, a game of personal tag. Wally would walk a long way and stay awfully late to pull a gotcha. Sooner or later we all got into the act, and I was involved in what was surely one of the best.

First, you should know that the crew quarters at the Cape was the one place where astros were authorized to call home at government expense. The telephone was a way of life to us. Even if we planned to go out and party on a given night—in fact, *especially* if we planned to go out and party—we felt better for having talked with our wives and kids first.

We'd place those calls through the NASA operators and over a period of time came to know each other's voices. The most famous voice of all was that of Operator 33. She not only had a sexy, throaty voice, but a sexy line as well. Well aware that she was talking to men who had been away from home a while, she laid it on thick.

Over the years, a remarkable number of us were suckered into impulsively asking, "Hey, how about having a drink or cup of coffee after work?" The bears coming to the honey.

It would be a while before those who had actually met Operator 33 confided in anybody else what their experience had been, but the word got around. She was not bad-looking, but for all her sensual talk, she was about as sexy as Martha Raye in army fatigues. In the flesh she was large, cold and painfully shy. It was all very depressing.

There was always somebody slow to get the word who would fall for Operator 33's "professional" voice. The sucker would end up at her place having a cup of coffee and sneaking glances at his watch, listening to her say something like, "Well, you probably want to leave now." And he would feel obligated to reply, "Oh, no, I'll have another cup of coffee."

It would be days before the embarrassment and guilt would wear off enough for him to laugh about it.

One of the men who hadn't been clued in was a young astronaut on our support crew named Ed Givens, who happened to reach Operator 33 several times in a row during his calls home. We could read the signs, and at night around the dinner table the rest of us laid it on pretty heavy about what a hot number Operator 33 was.

Ed sidled over one night and asked, "Say, Walt, do you know Operator Thirty-three?"

I said, "Boy, she's a doll, isn't she? Don't miss out on that, Ed."

A couple of nights later all of us but Ed were having dinner together. Everyone had helped set the trap, and we all figured, "Tonight's the night."

Someone said, "Ed's in cleaning up and changing clothes." A few moments later, Ed came breezing down the hall and past the dining room.

"Where you going, Ed?"

He stuck his head in the doorway and said, "Well, I have an appointment in town."

Someone said, "Oh, you got a date, huh?"

He really didn't want to admit a thing, but he looked right at me and said, "You better not be lying to me, Walt."

He walked out and we sat there, nearly choking with laughter.

The next morning we were at breakfast when Ed walked in, his eyes blazing. He ate breakfast in silence. Then, looking right at me, he had one comment: "You cheap sack of shit!"

We all broke up again. I lived in dread of what he would pull to get even, right till the day Ed died in a car accident a year later.

As the months sped by, our investment in the mission grew. Each day we gave another small piece of ourselves, making the prospect of a slip-up, of losing the flight, unthinkable. We would not *allow* some vagary, of fate to knock us out of it now.

In the spring of 1968 we took my son Brian to see an orthopedic specialist about a foot problem, and I seized the opportunity to consult the doctor quietly about a worry of my own. I had developed a soreness in my left shoulder, presumably from a recent handball misadventure. The pain had persisted but I dared not visit the NASA physicians and run the risk of being removed from the flight crew six months before launch. After four-and-a-half years, I wasn't going to blow it because of an aching shoulder.

Withholding medical information from our doctors may not have been strictly kosher, but it was far from uncommon. The determination to get into space carried us beyond the point of the usual anxieties about physical discomforts. They weren't so much health worries as they were career survival issues. Every time a NASA doctor poked around he had the power to prevent you from making your flight.

My conscience didn't even wince when I sought out civilian advice on what I hoped would be a minor condition. I regarded the NASA doctors with suspicion in spite of their record of finding some way to certify just about everyone for flight. But I felt it essential to protect myself from them and any risk of a shoot-from-the-hip decision.

NASA medics had also acquired a poor reputation among the flight crews in their respect for the confidentiality of the doctor-patient relationship. Too often they had blabbed to the news media about this or that crewman's problem. We felt it was done for the notoriety, for a moment in the limelight at the expense of what should have been a private and confidential matter.

The doctor took an X-ray of my sore shoulder and after studying the picture insisted on taking several more. Then it was my turn to insist on a look at them. From the time we examined the complete set of X-rays, we began to play a little game with each other. He was concerned, I assumed, about the profusion of small blemishes, or specks, on the bone itself that the pictures showed. Well, I was no doctor, but I had been exposed to a lot of medicine, and it took me only a few seconds to realize that he was concerned about bone cancer. During the next ninety days, while he checked it out, he never once indicated more than the possibility of an osteomyelitic condition.

He was my friend as well as my doctor, and he was willing to keep our secret. He kept insisting that he didn't believe it was anything to be unduly disturbed about but, in the way of doctors, thought it only prudent to get the most competent opinion. He proceeded to ship the X-rays to three different experts in three different corners of the country. I went home thinking that I was possibly living with bone cancer and might not be around too much longer.

Two thoughts were uppermost in my mind, at least one of which, I'm sure, is common to anyone who suspects he has a fatal disease. I resolved to get my family affairs in better shape. And I hoped with all my heart that the NASA doctors would not discover the condition until after the flight of Apollo 7. Unless it somehow manifested itself externally, I felt the chances of concealing my problem were excellent. The flight, after all, was only six months away.

Three of those months passed in a kind of controlled suspense while we waited for the opinions of the three specialists. I gave little thought to dying. It wasn't the first time in my thirty-six years that the prospect was near at hand, but it had always been in the abstract or passing me by in a fleeting instant.

Living can be difficult, and three out of three people die, but there is no use railing against either. No matter how we juggle our standards of time, there are only so many hours in a day and so many days in a year. I have always believed the key is to live each of those days one by one; in doing not only those things we enjoy, but also enjoying those things that are done because we must. Mastering the things that must be done, as well as those you choose, will in time insure they become nearly one and the same.

While training continued and the doctor had no news about the X-rays, I had neither the time nor disposition to pity myself. Mine had been a full life spent in learning and doing. I had no problem accepting death, but it was going to make me mad as hell if I missed that flight. It's not how long you live, but how you live your life that counts.

Eventually, the doctor called me to his office. The findings were in and the diagnosis favorable. The condition turned out to be one peculiar to my own system. There were no other indications and I knew the bone cancer scare was behind me. I breathed easy again and, in time, even the soreness in my shoulder worked itself out.

I suppose your average fighter pilot sounds almost paranoid when it comes to his health. A fighter lives in terror of being grounded. A quirk, or a physician's pet peeve, can sometimes do you in.

I once took my flight physicals from a navy flight surgeon at Los Alamitos Naval Air Station, California. His hang-up was flat feet, and mine are so flat they can pass for rocking chair rungs. I had been tipped off about this particular doctor, and for the three years he was there I walked around his office with my toes digging into the floor to keep my arches elevated. All the while, I was aware the doctor was watching me out of the corners of his eyes. He suspected my feet were flat, which could disqualify a man for flight orders—because the regulations said so, that's why. And all this after I had been flying for twelve years. Once or twice he started to say something, but always held back. It chills me to think how easily my flying days could have ended right there. And space would have been something I'd look for in a parking lot.

As 1968 turned into autumn, the thoughts uppermost in our minds were: don't screw up and don't get hurt and dropped off the flight.

The atmosphere grew more hectic as launch day approached. It was the natural consequence of the schedules drawing to a close, with all the last-minute details and round-the-clock checkouts of the spacecraft. It was, after all, the first model of a new generation of space vehicles, and it was being checked out by a new contractor whose only previous experience resulted in a spacecraft being incinerated on the pad thirty days before launch. Finally, there was our crew that had been on the line for nearly three years, a crew that could have easily rebelled at the increasing flood of data being fed into the round computer we wore on top of our shoulders.

Particularly irksome were the last-minute additions to our flight plan and the flood of input from members of the hand-wringing society. Everyone wanted to make the mission safe, but they also wanted it loaded to make up for the long delay. Hand wringers are those folks who seem to come out of the woodwork in the last few weeks before launch with their own private concerns and reservations.

From the mission engineer: "On second thought, maybe you'd better not try that test with the computer—it might dump the REFSMAT."

A test engineer at the Rockwell plant: "We can't find in the records any mention of the overpressure on the water system last spring. What do you think about doing the following test?"

A suit technician: "That suit will be OK, but if the zipper gives you any trouble .... "

The closer to launch, the more trivial and (it seemed) the more frequently we faced what Wally called FLT's: Funny Little Things. The expression dates back to an early geology field trip with C. C. Williams. During the exercise C. C. would occasionally bend over, pick up a rock for his pack, and say, "Hey, there's another FLR."

Like any well-trained astronaut, Wally was not prepared to show his ignorance easily. But as the day wore on, and the collection grew larger, he could no longer contain his curiosity, "What the hell is an FLR?"

"Funny Looking Rock," came the reply.

We began to lose patience with the FLT's, but we knew it wouldn't end till lift-off. Everyone wanted his conscience clean when the bolts blew. The showdown on flight plan changes wouldn't come till we were actually in orbit, and it would lead to some tense moments between Schirra and the control center.

Training became more realistic. All up mission simulations included

Mission Control and the worldwide tracking network. We worked in our pressure suits several days a week. The main objective of so many suited training exercises was to become familiar and comfortable in the spacesuit. It wasn't simply a suit in the usual sense. The physical problems of living in it, especially pressurized, were like a frog learning to live in a turtle shell. Airplanes, boats, and other complex equipment can be purchased for a whole lot less than the $140,000 we paid for each suit and each crewman had two flight suits and one for training. To call them custom fit is an understatement. They were such mechanical marvels that the simple function of taking a leak was an imposing challenge.

Under some circumstances, we could be required to live in the suit for as long as four or five days, so we routinely trained in it for many hours at a time. Provisions were incorporated to handle "calls of nature" during the twelve-to-fourteen-hour days we spent lying on our backs for spacecraft tests or mission simulations. In shirtsleeves it was no trouble to make a head call every couple of hours, but for suited exercises it was virtually impossible. At those times we were damn glad they had developed a urine collection bag and a means of using it in the suit.

We attached ourselves to the collection bag through a piece of surgical tubing resembling a condom, a hose, and a one-way check valve. The first obstacle to overcome was the psychological block of "doing it" lying flat on your back. The second was overcoming the resistance of the check valve while urinating. The physical problem was sometimes easier to deal with than the psychological one. Both could be overcome with practice, but even that didn't always guarantee success. More than one astronaut was christened a "wetback" due to putting off going because of the physical or mental block, eventually going out of necessity, and finally getting the waterworks turned on only to discover too late that the essential connection had come loose. Result: No pressure to overcome, no collector, and a warm, wet feeling around your middle. But it was far better to lose your cherry and become a wetback during simulations than it was in zero gravity.

For relaxation we had our gym: handball, tennis, and any other way we could find to unwind. Wally was determined to see that we stayed loose, and despite everything, we were probably the most relaxed crew ever to come down the pike.

Astronauts were notorious for using the Cape as their own private drag strip. Dating back to the early Mercury days, the fellows had "enjoyed" many an interesting side-of-the-road conversation with highway patrolmen. Usually, these encounters ended with the cop asking for an autograph and letting the offender go, promising fervently, as we always did, "to keep an eye on it next time."

In the event they were unrecognized, some of the astros felt no compunction about identifying themselves, and leaving the impression that they were in a hurry to catch the next rocket, or had an urgent appointment with the president.

I don't mean to excuse this blatant indifference to the traffic laws. But it was an attitude that spilled over from our hours in the cockpit, where one simply felt this sense of freedom, of privilege, of answering to nobody (almost).

About a month before the launch of Seven, Wally and I spent an afternoon on the public tennis courts at Cocoa Beach. Expressing his concern that I might injure myself at handball, Wally had leaned on me to take up tennis, his game.

We were returning to the crew quarters in two cars—Wally in his Corvette, me in a rented Oldsmobile—when the inevitable happened: a spontaneous drag race. Wally floored it, gunning away almost before I realized what he was doing. I'd be damned if I was going to let his Corvette walk off and leave me (the code again). I tore after him and drifted around a curve in time to see smoke streaming from all four of Wally's tires.

He was screeching to a halt, for a reason that soon became painfully clear. Across the street, heading in the opposite direction, a police car was pulled over, and by the door a local gendarme was waving frantically for Wally, and now me, to stop.

Coming to a stop behind Schirra I adopted my best meet-the-cop pose. We were both in tennis togs. The officer was finishing a ticket for some other luckless citizen, and I could see Wally fidgeting in his car ahead of me. His brain at that moment was working feverishly, trying to dream up a story that would melt that officer's heart. We're late for launch. There's a call on the Moscow hot line. The public commissioner is expecting us for tennis.

Impatiently, Wally started out of his car, confident that two reasonable men could dispose of the matter quickly. The cop spotted Wally making his move and angrily motioned him back to the car. Finally, he walked over, circled the Corvette, and began writing a ticket. Wally realized in about ten seconds that the cop either didn't know we were astronauts or didn't give a damn.

Slyly, Wally started working a little space patter into the conversation. The officer kept on writing. Wally bore in a little harder and dropped the fact that we were flying the next mission. "Yes," he said, smiling at the cop as if he was sharing a secret, "we're flying in another month. It's a great feeling."

It wasn't selling. I was growing more embarrassed and trying hard to remain quiet, tugging discreetly on Wally's shirtsleeve. At last the cop had all he could take. "OK, both of you," he said, with a wave of the hand throwing me into the same pile of trouble. "Get into your cars and follow me down to the station."

Now, Wally decided discretion was the better part of valor. Now he clammed up, even though he felt we had been arrested unfairly. Oh, we were speeding all right, but there was no way for the officer, facing the other direction, to know by how much. All he had to go on was the dust we kicked up on the side of the road and the vapor trails we were leaving behind us.

We were ticketed and released, with a court appearance scheduled for one week before the flight. For just an instant I had a mental flash of the launch being canceled and headlines all over the country, screaming the news: "Apollo 7 Scrubbed; Astronauts In Can."

But Wally knew what to do. He called Charlie Buckley, the head of security at NASA, and asked him to "take care of it," Charlie, an understanding fellow and a racing buff himself, arranged for the court appearance to be delayed a week, which meant that it would have coincided with our second or third day in orbit. Not so good.

After a series of back-and-forth calls between Wally and Buckley—since he got us into it, I was happy to let Wally try to get us out of it—our day in court was put off until after the flight. To my knowledge, that was the last thought Wally ever gave to the matter.

But the ticket, just the idea of it; preyed on my conscience. I asked Charlie what was going to be done about it. He shrugged. "They're not going to drop it," he assured me. "You guys really ticked off that officer."

After the flight I called the judge who had been assigned the case and asked what was required of me (no mention of Wally——it was now every man for himself). The judge said, "Walt, why don't you stop in and see me and we'll talk about it."

That seemed like a good thing to do, so I hopped into a T-38 and flew from Houston to Cocoa Beach, where my first stop was the courthouse. The judge turned out to be a genuinely gracious man. He gave me a tour of the jail, which I went to some lengths to praise profusely. When we finished he said, "Well, do you think you learned a lesson from this?"

"Yes, sir," I said. "I sure have. I'll never get caught speeding in Cocoa Beach again."

"OK, then, I'll just tear it up." He pulled out my ticket and Wally's. "Tell your buddy," he said, "that I took care of his, too. Ask him to stop in and say hello when he's in town."

I promised him I would, but decided to wait and see how long it took Wally to bring it up. That was in 1968 and I'm still waiting.

It was almost time now. All the waiting, the frustrations, the misadventures, the oddball things, the pointless worries—none of it mattered now. I could even see the humor in a mild confrontation Wally and I had over my penchant for pushing myself. Two weeks before, the wire services had sent the following news story across the country:

> Cape Kennedy—Navy Captain Wally M. Schirra, Jr., who almost lost his seat on a Mercury flight in 1962 because of a water skiing accident, has cautioned one of his fellow Apollo 7 crewmembers against daredevil ski antics.
>
> Civilian astronaut Walter Cunningham has taken a couple of nasty falls in recent weeks while skiing near this spaceport. Schirra, commander of the three-man Apollo 7 ship, made it plain he wasn't happy about it.
>
> "I've chewed him out a couple times," Schirra said in an interview. "He tried to ski as well as I do and I've skied for years. But Walt, as he always does everything, was trying to catch up in a matter of months. I said, 'Walt, you can be replaced. We spent three years getting ready for this. If you want to fool around water skiing these last three weeks, go ahead. But just realize what you're blowing if you do it.' So he's got the story."
>
> Cunningham, who describes himself as a "go-go-go type," said

in a separate interview that he "has to go full throttle all the time
on everything, on or off the job." He said he took up water skiing
for exercise because Schirra had complained about his charge-
ahead tactics on the handball court.

There was one more brush with the law and one more medical crisis
to go before launch.

Lift-off was set for Friday, 11 October 1968. On the Saturday before,
at Wally's urging, we took advantage of the local dove season to do a bit
of bird shooting. With a hunting fanatic like Tony Broadway on the staff,
arrangements were no problem.

The gang of us took off for the property of a Melbourne, Florida, dairy
farmer. The party included Deke and Stu Roosa, the astro serving as
blockhouse communicator—"Stoney." It was a good hunt. Actually, we
could hardly miss. Our friends had taken the precaution of setting up
feeders in the area we were to hunt. The birds came in droves, and Tony
kept busy just driving around the field, picking up the dead birds and
dropping off another can of cold beer.

Late in the afternoon we had visitors, confirming the uneasy feeling
about all good things coming to an end. The game wardens arrived. They
didn't find all the extra birds we had shot, but they did find the feeders
and proceeded to round us up in the field. It appeared we were headed
for the hoosegow again until it was pointed out to the wardens that their
raid had netted the entire crew of Apollo 7: Wally, Donn, and me.

As usual, the astronaut mystique saved the day. We were released in
time to join the rest of the astronaut staff, our medical personnel, *and the
game wardens* at the dairy in Melbourne, where a barbecue was laid out.
The afternoon's adventure provided food for conversation to go with the
beef, booze, and watermelon.

It was one of those evenings when time doesn't seem to exist. And
then, suddenly, around 6:30 P.M. I began having a sharp, searing pain that
traveled across my chest every few minutes. By 7:00 P.M. I was convinced
I was having, or had already suffered, a heart attack.

No one has ever accused me of being a hypochondriac. On the contrary, it is all but impossible to get me to admit I am sick. Pills, including
aspirin, are something I rarely take. But now, for the second time in six
months, it seemed I was in the grip of physical disaster. From what I

could tell of my symptoms, at thirty-six I was having a coronary. Two of our doctors were at the party, but I gave only fleeting consideration to calling on them for help. Hell, in two days they would be giving me my F-minus-four-day flight physical, the big one, and I'd be damned if I'd give them any extra information they could use against me.

My immediate dilemma was solved when Dee O'Hara, our flight nurse, called out for an early ride back to Cocoa Beach. I quickly volunteered, figuring if the very worst happened on the way in, at least I'd have some medical assistance.

It was a forty-five-minute ride back to the crew quarters with sharp pains hammering at my chest every three or four minutes. After dropping Dee off at the Holiday Inn, I called a friend, Al Bishop, and asked him to arrange a discreet visit to a doctor. Bishop was close to many of the astronauts and their families and could be trusted. A contractor representative and wise PR man, Al knew his way around the Cape, understood the NASA operation, and didn't need to be told why I was resorting to such private channels.

We met at the doctor's office. After listening to my symptoms, he gave me a thorough examination. The pains had subsided somewhat and were less frequent, but they were still there. He could find no sign of a heart problem and ran through the usual possibilities: gas pains, muscle spasm, and stomach upset. If he couldn't find anything maybe NASA wouldn't either.

The doctor made his final diagnosis as we were walking out of his office. Without knowing any of the astronauts or being familiar with their prevailing psychology, he made what was for him a logical assumption: "You know, with that launch just five days away, and you going into space for the first time, all that tension you're under could be causing this reaction."

He couldn't have been further from the mark, but it was useless to argue with him, I have never spoken to an outsider who didn't assume we were all under terrific tension due to the "harrowing experience" facing us on launch day. Such is simply not the case. In eight years of watching flight crews prepare for a mission, I have observed only one or two men with even the slightest indication of being uptight.

I thanked the doctor and turned to thank Al Bishop. "Forget it," he said. "You're not the first guy in the program to ask me for help with a medical problem."

In the room that night I dropped off to sleep in spite of the periodic stabs of pain. The next day the pain had subsided and the sun was shining outside. Cocoa Beach glistened with a fresh, lemony look. "To hell with it," I said, and by noon I had joined Bishop and his family at water skiing. The pain went away and never returned. But I didn't feel comfortable and didn't relax until completing my F-minus-four-day physical Monday morning with nothing detectable on the electrocardiogram.

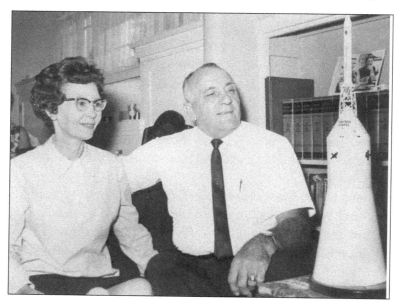

Mom and Dad watching the countdown of Apollo 7
on their black and white television.

The phone calls, the letters, the press coverage—everything was building to a climax. In Dover, England, the Flat Earth Society warned us that the round ball we would see below us would just be an optical illusion. For months, mail had been arriving in bundles from everywhere, from kids and parents and soldiers and scientists.

A lady in Charleston, Massachusetts, for reasons unknown, singled me out to send along this cheery prophecy: "When you three go up in space, the rocket is going to get on fire and you three will be scattered in dust. Dust thou art, and to dust thou shalt return."

All that last week, Apollo 7 was the major story in the nation's newspapers. A headline in the *Miami Herald* announced, "Three Astronauts Ready to Face Challenge Three Others Died For."

Then it was October 11, 1968. I opened my eyes at 5:50 A.M., ten minutes before the alarm, as I customarily do in anticipation of an early call. I had enjoyed a sound sleep since 10:15 the night before.

My first thought was, "This is it . . . today's the day." The brass ring was finally swinging my way and I was exhilarated. Not with the breathless feeling of facing your first dive from the ten-meter platform, of forcing yourself to leap because you've come that far, but with a feeling of soaring achievement that you are there because you've earned it, that you are prepared for it. It was like a first flight in the newest supersonic jet, only a thousand times better. No man had ever flown an Apollo spacecraft, and none had ever ridden as powerful a rocket.

With Apollo VII, we weren't stepping into the pages of history books. I knew that. But we would be a footnote somewhere: "First manned Apollo mission in the program to land a man on the moon." Among our peers, we were stepping to the top of the pyramid and you could feel their envy. They looked at us—and saw themselves. I felt a little self-conscious to be looking forward to the morning so anxiously.

The few minutes I had to spare were spent-talking to Lo at her motel. The family had been up since 5:00 A.M. in preparation for going out on the Banana River to watch the launch from a boat chartered by *Life* magazine. This was to insure that the magazine got the "exclusive" photos for which they had been paying since 1963.

I had remembered to send Lo a dozen roses. There really wasn't much that needed to be said, she knew what they meant. We talked about the winds and the weather. I was a little concerned about Brian and Kimberly's reaction to the flaming lift-off, but Lo assured me they were doing just fine. She wanted to hear about our little dinner party at the crew quarters the night before. The gathering had included some of our old personal friends from entertainers to business executives.

I told Lo I would call her in eleven days, keeping it casual, and rang off. By then Deke Slayton was there to wake us, and we began the unhurried ritual that would lead to the three of us standing on that swingarm outside the spacecraft at 8:35 A.M.

Our first stop after showering—our last for eleven days—was the doctor's office. Wally and I walked together while he reminisced about the same walk prior to his Gemini flight. Part of the preflight physical is the Babinsky test, a check for lesions in the upper motor nervous system—nerve damage. The bottom of the foot is scraped with a dull instrument, while the toes are observed. If the toes turn up it is an indication of nerve damage.

Wally had practiced the proper response to gain one of his famous gotchas on the doctors. When Wally's toes turned up on launch day the doctors figured he was ready for a hospital bed—not a launch pad. Wally waited until they were huddling in whispers before he broke out laughing. There was no business so serious or so important that Wally could resist the temptation of a gotcha.

We had undergone our major physical four days earlier (the F-minus-4 day). On launch day we breezed through what we called a "cold mirror" test (that's where they hold a mirror under your nose and if you fog it they know you're alive). The doctors needed only twenty minutes to draw blood, take a urine specimen, and check our hearts, throats, ears, and noses.

As Wally and I returned to the crew quarters for breakfast we passed Donn Eisele. He was late, as he had been for most of the week. Donn was never known as a hard charger, but in this last week he had even slowed down a notch; it was hard to even get his attention.

We shared some concern about his current physical condition as well as his sharpness. His performance on the bicycle ergometer (a device to measure the effect of exercise on the cardiovascular system) four days earlier had been poor enough to cause the doctors some hesitation. Wally had made a personal plea to keep him on our crew for launch. Surprisingly, his marginal physical condition had little effect on his adaptability to zero-g or the launch and re-entry loads.

We had the usual launch-day breakfast of steak and eggs prepared by Lew Hartzel, the "astronaut cook." Lew had been with us for years while his helpers came and went. Outsiders naturally assumed that he was some kind of gourmet chef. After all, hadn't he been selected to cook for the space heros? The truth was, Lew was hired between charter boats and had found a home with the astronauts. While his cooking was overrated, he was easy to get along with and catered to our idiosyncrasies. There were homemade cookies several times a week after he learned they were my favorite food.

A half-dozen guests shared our breakfast, including James Webb, who had retired the week before as the Administrator of NASA (and was actually viewing his <u>first</u> manned space launch). John Healey of North American Rockwell and Fred Peters and Ken Kleinknecht of NASA, also joined us, along with Deke and two members of our support crew, Ron Evans and Bill Pogue. Wally and Donn socialized while I (as usual) read the morning paper, with its glorious headline (in the-sky-is-falling type), "Go 7!"

The camaraderie and underplayed excitement of an adventure soon to begin made the mood warm and pleasant. I recall no uncertainty or concern.

After breakfast we made our way to the third floor of the checkout building to begin the suiting ritual. It has been compared to the ceremony at the altar under the bullring where the matador dons his *traje de luces* or "suit of lights." No suit of armor was ever more elegant than ours, or more splendid, or complex, or essential, or expensive.

Waiting for us were the suit technicians, complete professionals who had certainly gotten less sleep than we had. They were up late performing that last bit of lubrication on moving parts and checking the suits. We were each assigned a technician—Clyde Teague, Jim Lewis, or Keith Walton—and an assistant to help, if necessary. There was one final visit to the john before being wedded to the launch day urine bag. The bags would be strapped to our waists until we could get out of the suit in orbit hours later. A *solid* waste problem wouldn't dare intrude on our sensibilities during the next twelve hours.

The count was moving well. It would take a major problem between 7:30 and 11:00 A.M. for the mission to be scrubbed.

The technicians attached and checked out the biomedical harness. This "rig" consisted of five EKG sensors and the associated signal conditioners and electronics. Wally had engaged in a months-long campaign to simplify the harness. Now, on launch day, he took his last shot. "Too many sensors," he complained. "The leads are too short."

He was betting on his launch day leverage, but Deke took charge in his firm, quiet way, and everyone went with the equipment on hand. Deke and Wally agreed to iron it out after the flight. It was an issue destined to be lost in the noise of subsequent events.

Our communications were checked out and our helmets locked in place. We began breathing 100 percent oxygen to wash the nitrogen from our blood and (especially) our joints to lessen the likelihood of bends in the event the cabin didn't hold pressure during boost. At this point our interest was focused on each suit checking out every step of the way. Any big problems would mean switching to our backup suit (another $140,000) lying ready on the bench. I had logged forty hours in the suit I was wearing and had confidence in it. The pressure points were familiar. An undiscovered pressure point, in a suit rarely used, could become maddening after four or five hours in the couch.

Every flight crew has an air of pre-occupation at this time. Their minds are focused on the critical events in the ongoing count. Clyde Teague could cite examples of crewmen needing to be reminded to step into the suit, of stumbling through suiting procedures they had smoothly run through a dozen times.

One of the papers carried a launch day picture of me reclining in a lounge chair with my eyes closed. It was to stay relaxed and loose, save energy, and not get sweated up in the suit. But seeing the picture, I realized, relaxed or not, I would still have looked it. Of course, we consciously tried to project that cool image. We could, with a quick sideways glance, catch the technicians watching us, checking to see if we were measuring up.

I recall wondering if the program managers ever worried about some crewmember saying on launch day, "I've changed my mind. I'm not going!"

When we stepped into the hall to begin our walk to the crew transfer van, our co-workers in the building were lined up to shout their good wishes. They broke into applause as we moved toward the elevator. Sound was muffled inside the fifty-six-pound suits, but we waved to acknowledge their support. Many of them were apprehensive, recalling the fire twenty-one months before.

The elevator stopped at the first floor where, instead of continuing on by foot, Wally had arranged for us to climb aboard a small freight dolly to be hauled down the long hallway to the transfer van. All the way down that hall I felt foolish; we looked like three huge white sacks of potatoes. There we were, America's space gladiators, being pulled to our destiny in a freight wagon.

We stepped out into a nice day (there was a stiff breeze blowing that would come back to haunt us in a few hours). The applause from the hundreds of spectators waiting outside the crew training quarters, waving, clapping, and holding up signs, was a great feeling. But I knew that in two months there would be a new play and cheers for new heroes.

They were there to send us off and also to wonder what made us tick. If they only knew that most of them could have been locked in a capsule at lift-off and flown through launch, orbit, and re-entry, with little or no ill effect—*if everything went according to the script.*

We looked at the pretty secretaries, smiling and waving, and even spotted some new faces and shapely legs we hadn't noticed before. It was good for a few smiles on the way to the pad and it was reassuring to realize, in that moment of fine tension, our vital signs were normal.

With a good imagination, you could think of us as businessmen in an alien world, on our way to a different office, carrying a strange briefcase (the portable ventilator, with its supply of pure oxygen for the suit).

A police escort led us from Merritt Island onto the Air Force Eastern Test Range—the Cape—and past more cheering, waving crowds. How can so many people resign themselves to vicarious experiences? Perhaps Thoreau answered it best: "The mass of men lead lives of quiet desperation."

In this parade there is time to reminisce. I thought of how Wally got more livable, if not lovable, the closer we got to launch. He really wanted to go. It meant something now to make that one more space flight, to become the only man to fly each of America's three generations of spacecraft: Mercury, Gemini, and now Apollo.

We could all feel the country pulling for us. The publicity and excitement was at a much higher pitch than it would be for many subsequent Apollo missions—more than the later lunar landings would receive. The Cape hadn't experienced a manned launch in two years, and we were putting them back into the flying business.

We didn't dwell on this. We were too busy living it. We took it for granted that the VIP bleachers would be bulging with prime ministers, governors, and the big names of government, industry and show business. It was *the* place to be.

The van moved quickly over the eight miles of flat terrain to Pad 34.

Merritt Island, where the Kennedy Space Center is located, is just that—an island, with the Indian River on the west and the Banana River on the east. We crossed the Banana River to get to Cape Kennedy, which was controlled by the Air Force. The undeveloped areas on the combined 84,000 acres are covered with tropical vegetation. Much of the concern about a launch abort is related to the fact that the Cape vegetation is not uniform. A pad abort, or an abort just after launch, with onshore winds, can blow the spacecraft back to crash on sand, water, or hard palmetto stumps.

The van made one stop at the blockhouse to let out Deke Slayton and Charlie Buckley; it was their station for launch.

The blockhouse is a two-story structure of twelve-foot-thick reinforced concrete. Only a small dome protrudes above the ground. It's a sobering thought, sitting in the spacecraft with a million pounds of fuel under your butt, to know that all that steel and concrete is there for the protection of VIP's and the launch crew just in case we blow up. Little things like that explain why everyone in the world didn't really want our job, even though they might claim they did at a cocktail party.

In the blockhouse everyone is quite safe. There are two periscopes and many closed-circuit television cameras for close-up viewing of all critical areas. Stoney (Stu Roosa, that day) has a console there, as do all the Kennedy Space Center officials essential to making "go" or "no-go" decisions about launch.

Less than an hour before lift-off the five-foot-thick, solid-steel double doors of the blockhouse will be closed. Once closed, no one comes out until after our monster has cleared the umbilical tower or the launch is safely scrubbed.

The gantry at Pad 34 looms majestically above the blockhouse, even though it is a quarter of a mile away. The van complement is now reduced to the driver and those persons necessary to place our 700 pounds of human payload into the spacecraft. There is a stark beauty to the now empty area in the half-mile ride around the perimeter, to the bottom of the launch umbilical tower. I savored the thought that, at that moment, there were so many envying me the way I had envied Alan Shepard seven years before. Al Shepard was certainly among them.

The van pulls up to the base of the $147 million complex, spectacular in its bright orange corrosion-resistant trappings, and backs up to the elevator. Clyde Teague, Wally and I, still carrying our portable ventilators, unload for the ride to the 220-foot level. Donn will follow in ten minutes. We press the elevator button, and—nothing happens! My heart leaps and the old pulse rate does a somersault. We punch the button several times before the elevator starts its creaky ascent. The problem leaves Wally and me wondering about our abort posture and the launch mission rules—the elevator *must be* standing by at the White Room level for use in an emergency escape during certain parts of the countdown. It could mean a launch delay.

The White Room is a tiny, enclosed cubicle at the end of the swing-arm providing protected entry to the spacecraft. The preferred crew-escape route for critical emergencies, after strapping in, is across the swing-arm, into the elevator, and down to the ground rescue vehicle—an armored-personnel carrier, staffed by a four-man crew, which would meet us at the base of the tower to whisk us to safety. The rescue crew has just one responsibility in a crisis: to charge in, toss the three of us inside the vehicle, hang breathing systems around our necks, and take off through the boondocks. They were never needed, but they sure enjoyed those rehearsals, while scaring us half out of our wits.

There is a back-up, riskier but faster—the emergency slide wire. To take it, you slip into a harness, hook on to the wire and step off at the 220-foot level. A few thrilling seconds later you are on the ground an eighth of a mile away.

In thirty seconds the elevator rose 23 stories and delivered us to the spacecraft level; Wally was the first to step out and cross the swing-arm to the White Room. We were about to realize a dream that, for me, had been seven years in the making, including fourteen months training for the cancelled Apollo 2 and twenty-two months getting ready for Apollo 7. I would soon find out how Captain Ahab must have felt when he finally harpooned his white whale.

Wally, Donn, and I had been together three years as a crew. Nearly a billion dollars was being bet that we would succeed in taking the first of the five Apollo steps to the moon. I felt supremely confident in my knowledge of the spacecraft and my ability to perform. In the White Room we were greeted by the man we affectionately called the "pad fuhrer." Gunter Wendt, a German immigrant, had served as the major domo of the White Room for manned launches dating back to the Mercury days. His authority was near absolute at the spacecraft level where he tolerated no non-sense, from the flight crew on down. This attitude endeared him to us.

He had handled ten Gemini launches for the McDonnell Company, before North American Rockwell brought in its own people to organize the Apollo program. All of the astronauts, but especially Wally, had pulled strings to persuade North American Rockwell to hire Gunter. Some of us believed that Gus Grissom's crew might still be alive if Gunter Wendt had been on the scene that day.

We considered him a key man. North American Rockwell was new in the manned spacecraft business. They had some good men, like Skip Chauvin, the test conductor at the Cape, and John Healey, the spacecraft manager. But they had yet to launch their first manned vehicle, so it gave us an added touch of confidence to have Gunter there.

While Wally was being strapped in, my portable ventilator suddenly began to lose oxygen pressure. With efficient NASA planning, there was a spare available in the White Room at the end of the swing-arm. It was soon apparent that I must switch over or suffocate. But the technician and I both hesitated. On our minds was the elaborate procedure to avoid the risk of invalidating the earlier lengthy checkout procedure. I had been lit-erally certified, signed, sealed, and delivered. With a knowing glance between us, we switched directly over and I reported it *after the flight*.

It was quite windy now at the 236-foot level. Beneath us we could feel the vehicle and swing-arm sway. I thought how often over the last seven years I had envied other men this moment, as they climbed to the top of other rockets and rode their way into the history books. Now, as I stood on the swing-arm 230 feet above Pad 34, waiting for Wally to be strapped into his couch, the emotion just wouldn't come. The memory of Al Shep-ard's launch in May 1961 seemed more real to me than the launch day events for Apollo 7.

Looking down at that beautiful booster floating in the clouds of liq-uid oxygen from venting off excess pressure, bathing the American flag on its side in a fine mist, I kept waiting for the moment to seem real. I had the eerie feeling that it was just another drill. When would it become a reality? Standing on that swing-arm for seven or eight minutes, in a wind that felt like a gale, it never came. Was it a characteristic of the business that I wasn't to experience the pleasure of fulfillment as we stepped through the well-rehearsed script?

While I stood there in the blowing wind, only a few short miles away on the Banana River, Lo, Brian, and Kimberly were watching that same oxygen venting in the morning sun. They were following launch activities on commercial television and keeping their fingers crossed. NASA had been less than enthusiastic about their being at the Cape in the first place and we were on our own to make travel and accommodation arrangements. Ironically, they were prepared to help on the return trip— if circumstances warranted. Prior to boarding the boat that morning, Lo was notified that NASA would have a car standing by at the dock to whisk the family to Patrick Air Force Base for a government flight back to Houston in the event of a launch catastrophe. It was phrased a little more delicately but that's what it amounted to. While I appreciated the offer on learning of it later, on that morning Lo certainly did not want to think about it.

Liftoff of Apollo 7 from pad 34,
11 October 1968, at 11:02:56.

To an astronaut, the launch is getting off the ground. For which we enjoyed the fruits of everyone's labor plus the glory, the glamour and the rewards. But to the suit technician, the launch is strapping us into the spacecraft. It was their big scene in the months-long drama, as important to them as liftoff was to us.

Wally was strapped in and then it was my turn. While trying to fasten a stubborn shoulder harness, Clyde Teague cut his knuckles and worried about bleeding all over our white suits. At that stage we would not have held the count for even a cut throat, believe me.

Wally and I were able to talk with each other without the blockhouse hearing by way of a communication mode we had ferreted out in the circuitry of our radio panel. Donn, who was by now strapped in, could not reach his switches and had to content himself with facial expressions or transmit to the world.

T minus two hours and counting: John Young, our backup Command Module Pilot, had been in the cabin all morning, making final switch settings. Now he left to descend to the blockhouse. All around us people were climbing into bombproof shelters while we lay, just a little impatiently, on top of a million pounds of high-energy fuel.

Wind conditions remained the only questionable factor in our countdown. According to the Launch Mission Rules, we could tolerate winds up to 18 knots measured at the sixty-foot level. The launch director didn't want to scrub or delay the launch for high winds, and neither did we. On top of all the other unknowns this mission faced, we knew that the abort criteria had been compromised to the limit. For example, during the boost phase of our Saturn 1-B, there was a period of approximately ten seconds during which an abort would impose a load greater than 18 g's on our bodies. It was the first time such an exposure had been accepted, and then only after much soul-searching.

T minus 1 hour, 9 minutes and counting: Wally, the only one in a position to see the sky, peers out of the only uncovered window and says, "It's as blue as a bluebird out there."

T minus 50 minutes and counting: Everything is "go" for Apollo 7. The terminal count is picked up with the communication checks from Stoney (Stu Roosa). If we get into a prolonged hold, Stu can give us a direct telephone connection to our families.

It was time for the last of the pad crew to clear out. As Gunter leaves the White Room, Wally cannot resist a parting pun. "Gunter went," he announces to the blockhouse.

After the White Room is cleared out, the access arm is swung back three feet from the spacecraft. For the first time, we are able to arm the pad abort system and, if necessary, use the launch escape tower to lift our Command Module away from the booster. We are alone at last, and it is great!

It is turning out to be the smoothest final count ever for a first flight. The latest wind report is 15 to 18 knots, with gusts to 22, from the east—an onshore breeze—not good. Inside the spacecraft we are resigned to having an out-of-limit launch condition with the winds, but we aren't happy about it.

T minus 33 minutes, 30 seconds, and counting: We have our first glitch. The high-speed elevator, which is scheduled to be stationed at the 220-foot level for a quick evacuation, is stuck at the ground level after taking down the close-out crew. If anything goes wrong today, we will have to ride the wire.

We're still keeping an eye on the winds. To abort, we need only to fire the 155,000-pound-thrust launch escape rocket, but that wouldn't get us above the fifty miles needed to qualify for astronaut wings. I wondered idly what Al Shepard thought about a launch escape rocket with more thrust than his Redstone booster?

T minus 25 minutes: Wally can't resist getting his doubts about the launch winds on record and putting the boys in the blockhouse on the spot. We were convinced the winds exceeded the launch mission rules, but everybody, including us, had go fever.

T minus 6 minutes, 15 seconds: There is a hold, a minor problem costs us two minutes while the inner chamber of the second stage engine is being cooled to prescribed limits. The delay disturbs us out of all proportion to the time lost.

The count continues.

T minus 4 minutes, 7 seconds: From Skip Chauvin, our launch conductor, "Go for launch." The destruct system for the second stage of the Saturn I-B is activated. From this point forward, the ground can destroy the rocket (and anything around it) by blowing up the second stage. We all give a final "go" inside the spacecraft and stand by to go on the automatic sequencer.

T minus 2 minutes, 43 seconds, and counting: The countdown is now on automatic, with all spacecraft launch functions initiated by the computer in the blockhouse. We know we are going—finally! Each of us is fully occupied now; even five or ten seconds of idleness seems like an hour. The first two stages of the Saturn 1-B begin to pressurize with helium. The pressure is building up.

Two minutes and counting: There is little chatter on the comm channel. Donn is completing the key check in the guidance and navigation system. The abort advisory system in the spacecraft is activated. Inside our gloves, fingers are crossed against any late problems.

Sixty seconds and counting: "We're go for Apollo Seven."

Fifty seconds: The vehicle is pressurized. "The spacecraft is go!"

Forty seconds and counting: All aspects of the mission are GO. In forty seconds we will have the first fire at Pad Thirty-four since the last Apollo One test.

Thirty seconds: The booster is switched to full internal power.

Twenty-one seconds: The power transfer is complete. In eighteen seconds that monstrous Saturn 1B will roar into life and there will be 1.6 million pounds of thrust pushing up our tail.

Roosa makes the traditional count backwards from ten, until he reaches the call that would send shivers up the spine of a Greek statue:

"One—we have ignition—we have lift-off."

8

The Flight of the Phoenix

THE ROCKET RISES from the pad so slowly, so ponderously at first, that you could be imagining it even moved at all. It is an agonizingly slow ten seconds before Apollo 7 clears the tower. One million three hundred thousand pounds is balancing on an arrow of flame. Painstakingly, it climbs, trailing a fireball as vivid as the colors of hell. At the spectator bleachers, two-and-one-half miles away, the earth actually trembles. The vibrations, the noise, the shock; they roll over you in waves. And, from out of the *second* fire on Pad 34 rises our modern-day Phoenix.

I'd seen many lift-offs, but this one was different: It was the largest rocket ever launched carrying the largest payload ever placed in orbit. And, oh yeah, this time I was riding inside, not watching.

Half a million Americans lined the roads and beaches of Florida that day to watch the United States re-enter the world of manned space flight. It isn't stretching the truth or over-dramatizing to say we carried the nation's hopes with us. Twenty-one months before, a fire on the very pad from which we launched had killed three good friends. Another setback now, and our prospects of landing a man on the moon before 1970 will be lost forever.

In the cabin we have no way of sensing the actual moment of lift-off. We know our Phoenix has begun its climb from out of the fireball only because the spacecraft clock begins ticking off the elapsed time and Wally can see the altimeter climbing. Inert metal and fuel has turned into a live monster. Once quiet dials begin to move and jump. Donn has the G & N computer flashing our trajectory parameters. I am monitoring the environmental and electrical systems to insure that the cabin pressure is bleeding down according to schedule to prevent a blowup in the vacuum of space. It is the most complex machine ever built by man to be operated by man. And our job is to see that the monster does not eat us alive.

A few seconds after lift-off, we roll a few degrees to enable a pure pitch maneuver to eventually place us in the correct orbit. We continue to pitch over backwards (much like going over the top when doing a loop), which will take us into orbit upside down and heading East.

For the first two minutes and forty-four seconds, our only visual contact with the outside world is through a small forward viewing window on Wally's side and a small round porthole over Donn's head. At that point, when we jettison the launch escape tower, it carries the boost protective cover with it and all five windows are exposed for the first time. However, there is nothing to see but sky until the last few minutes before reaching orbit. Donn started rubbernecking right after the cover cleared, and we both snapped at him to keep his eyes inside and his mind on the job.

Apollo 7 was fifty miles high and sixty miles down-range when the word came from Houston, "Seven, you're looking good."

At four minutes after lift-off, Wally radios back, "Apollo Seven is go." The country's first manned flight in nearly two years is off and running, and it was riding like a dream. A few moments later our CapCom in Houston, Jack Swigert, gives us a call: "You're right on the old button."

For the first ten minutes and thirty seconds of a nominal launch, except for performing a few essential functions, we are mostly along for the ride. We're space pilots, but we aren't flying the spacecraft. And Mission Control doesn't control it. It is an on-board computer operation all the way into orbit. We're on automatic pilot. The flight path has been programmed. We monitor the instruments—as does Houston—to see how good a job Seven is doing flying itself. If it doesn't perform, we can take over, fix it or get off.

We might not have been piloting the craft, but we weren't exactly idle as we entered an eleven-day coast around the world at 17,500 mph. In those first hazy minutes in orbit, we run through the long insertion checklist, get our helmets off, retrieve some of our stowage (in particular, cameras), and—during the second pass—separate from the Saturn 4-B, the second stage of our booster.

The second time we passed over Africa there was a quick chance to look out and enjoy a little of the wonder. I look down and find myself staring at the Sinai Peninsula, just as it had appeared in drawings from the recent Arab-Israeli war, with the Suez Canal and the Red Sea on one side and the Gulf of Aqaba on the other. It was fantastic. Here I was, looking at the globe as it *really* was, and thinking, "Those early geographers, and those who made those first globes, were right all along." I took some pictures and recorded the frame data.

Once the initial activity subsided, my first sensation of space was simply one of belonging. I had lived with the thought for five years, had watched the parade of new actors step onto the stage, dominate the scene, make incremental progress, take their curtain calls, and then scurry away with new notoriety, increased self-confidence and fame. A few months later another cast, the same sudden notoriety, the press conferences, and the questions. And now, it was our turn on stage!

A fellow would have to be less than human not to have his consciousness raised during those first hours. We had embarked on the very first of what would be literally hundreds of firsts for the Apollo program. But the three most significant milestones, as we rated them, were:

1. The *first* landing on the moon.
2. The *first* circumlunar flight.
3. The *first* manned flight of the Apollo spacecraft.

We passed significant milestones with every turn of the clock: the first

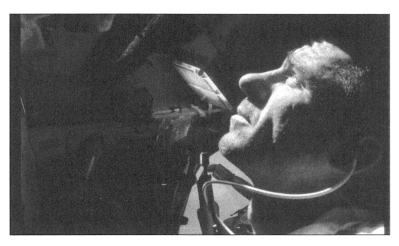

Me, observing something after a week in orbit.

American three-man flight; the first Apollo rendezvous; the first celestial navigation fix; the first manned firing of the 20,000-pound-thrust service propulsion engine.

And it all went so smoothly, so uneventfully, that any preflight doubts seemed almost foolish. At lift-off we weren't worrying about dying or having that 280-foot rocket blow up. The only worry I recall was the fear of failure. It showed itself in a little pep talk to myself, delivered aloud just before launch: "OK, Cunningham, whatever you do, *don't screw up.*"

I had always envied engineering test pilots working for the aircraft companies, the men with an opportunity to take the first hand-built model of a brand-new airplane into the air for its first flight. Now here I was in a piece of machinery, many times more complex than any airplane ever built, carrying men for the first time into a sterile, strange, and un-

Marine Corps Commandant, General Leonard Chapman,
presenting me with Navy Astronaut Wings.

charted sea. It was the first manned test of the most powerful booster in the world and its last use till the Skylab program five years later.

Since the last American space flight, the United States had lost a crew of three and the Russians had lost a cosmonaut returning from space. Confidence needed to be restored that outer space and man belonged together. The public needed convincing that our missions were not circus stunts performed by soldiers of fortune with a collective death wish.

And, of course, we were keeping an eye on the Soviets. In our efforts to keep the space effort funded, the race to land the first men on the moon was hyped for all it was worth. The world came to regard it as a great Olympiad in the sky. When Russia launched Zond 5 in September 1968, we worried that it was a prelude to an imminent Russian manned flight around the moon and, eventually, a lunar landing. By the time Apollo 7 lifted off, we knew that Zond 5 had re-entered the atmosphere in a trajectory—steep enough to heat the craft to levels that only instruments, not humans, could safely withstand. Our spirits soared. It was clear that Apollo 7 would put America back in the lead.

At home, North American Rockwell had been the prime Apollo contractor for nearly ten years without launching a manned spacecraft. They were looking to our crew to get them on the scoreboard. Beyond question, Apollo 7 was the most ambitious first flight ever undertaken. By contrast, John Glenn's first Mercury mission had lasted less than five hours and the first Gemini flight, with Gus Grissom and John Young, did no better. Apollo 7 was to be our second-longest space mission ever, right out of the starting blocks. Its planned duration of eleven days would demonstrate the ability of the spacecraft's systems to sustain a crew of three for the time required to complete a lunar landing mission. Apollo 7 was our first step to the moon.

You don't really know what togetherness is until you have spent eleven days with two other people in a volume about the size of the back seat in a large American sedan. If your buddy belched, you said, "Excuse me." We worked, ate, slept, caught colds, and performed all bodily functions in that same space. We had spent as much as twenty hours a day in the spacecraft during testing and simulations, so we were prepared for possible psychological strains. Surprisingly, other than rare outbreaks of temper, it was less of a problem than I expected.

The one factor making it more tolerable was the absence of gravity: living in a continual state of free fall. On earth we move essentially in a two-dimensional world. In a house, for example, we always compete for space with furniture, lamps, dogs, and other people. Area is constraining. Think how much roomier it would be if you could avoid all those obstacles by walking on the ceiling or the walls, or doing as we did in the spacecraft—flying across the middle of the room.

("Flying" is somewhat of a misnomer for the Apollo spacecraft, because we could always extend an arm or a leg and touch the walls on one side or the other. In Skylab, however, it became a very apt description.)

In the world of zero gravity, *volume* is the measure that restricts movement and becomes confining, not the floor area. It was ironic that as man moved into the vastness of space his own movement became more restricted—to 225 cubic feet, the interior volume of the Apollo spacecraft.

Zero gravity is a wonderful feeling but very difficult to describe. Those who haven't experienced it can't even begin to imagine it. While zero-g cannot be created artificially, it can be experienced imperfectly for 20-25 seconds during parabolic flight in an airplane. But experiencing true zero-g, or free fall, is a little like being pregnant—there is no such thing as "almost."

A feeling remarkably close is that sensation we experience during a dream of falling out of bed, or falling interminably through space, with nothing to break the fall. That "free falling" feeling just prior to awakening, with the terror stripped away, is the nearest thing to floating in zero gravity I have experienced.

Sight and feel, both conscious zero-gravity senses, adjust almost immediately. The subconscious is not nearly as flexible. It requires two to three days on first exposure to overcome that falling sensation immediately prior to falling asleep in the spacecraft.

Into that small but compelling world came the three of us. Twenty-four hours later, Wally was sick with a miserable head cold, followed the next day by Donn, only a little less severe. I never came down with a cold, although I did feel a little blah the third day. (A week before the flight I had shown symptoms of a cold, and a couple of days later Donn and I took shots for it. Wally had rejected the shot since he felt fine; he couldn't imagine himself catching a cold at such a historic moment and wasn't about to get a shot just for the exercise.)

By the third day Wally was miserable. In our on-board storage we had included a large supply of vacuum-packed tissues. They were useful for wiping off the grime, catching urine drops, or any other of the many required body ablutions. Fortunately, we had overstocked on this item. However, the used ones were not vacuum-packed and, consequently, took up twice as much space.

As soon as we were squared away in orbit, Wally began blowing his nose, and within a short time we were stuffing used tissues in every empty spot we could find. Wally showed no interest in conserving them, and Donn and I began to worry whether a tissue crisis could end the mission. When we suggested to Wally that he might try to get more than one blow out of each tissue, our pleas fell on deaf ears. We were literally up to our asses in used tissues.

For a couple of days, Wally engaged in the space equivalent of staying home sick in bed. He felt too wretched some mornings to get out of his sleep restraint beneath the left-hand couch.

After Donn developed his runny nose an impression was left with Mission Control that the entire spacecraft was rife with colds, but actually only Wally had a real problem. It was a good example of what Bill Anders referred to as "The Bull Moose Complex," from Al Capp's character, General Bull Moose: "What's good for Bull Moose is good for the world." Or, paraphrased: what was good for Wally was good for our world—the spacecraft.

There was no doubt that Wally felt he had caught the cold they were saving for Judas. He was sleeping poorly and becoming as jumpy as a frog in a biology lab. He continued to perform, issuing orders from his "sickbed," but the heavy workload at the outset of the mission, combined with his discomfort, made Wally more irascible by the day. He didn't miss an opportunity to nail Mission Control to the wall. Donn and I were amazed at the patience of those in the control center with some of the outbursts that came their way. On the ground they were well aware that every word of the air-to-ground communications was being fed directly to the press center, a fact of which we had not been informed. So Wally's bad temper was making big news back home.

The first flare-up came on the second day in orbit with the first scheduled television broadcast from space. Due largely to Wally's cold and some minor problems, we were struggling to keep up with the flight plan. "I tell you," he snapped, "this in-flight TV will be delayed without further discussion." That ended the debate and ground control agreed to let that broadcast go till the following day.

That was all the encouragement Wally needed in the rigid stand he took throughout the mission. It was also the only time his obstinacy was justified. We just plain weren't ready for a TV broadcast.

Wally's reason for canceling the early TV transmission was to concentrate on our rendezvous with the Saturn 4-B. He had reason to be a little uptight about it. We were attempting the rendezvous without radar and the things that could go wrong were too numerous to count. We fired the main engine twice: once to put the capsule in a position below and slightly behind the Saturn 4-B and a second time to bring us close enough so that we could accomplish the final match-up. It came off without a wrinkle. Donn took sightings with the guidance computer, while I made visual sightings to fill out the backup charts. Wally maneuvered to within 70 feet of the rocket and flew alongside, in perfect formation, until it was time to break away.

Eventually those daily television shows would become the entertainment highlight of the journey—for us as well as for the public. Lasting seven to eleven minutes, they came to be called "The Wally, Walt, and Donn Show." They were scheduled once each morning during a roughly 2,000-mile pass between Texas and Cape Kennedy, the only two ground stations equipped to receive the transmissions. The ham in us didn't just surface; we damn near brought back vaudeville. We began the broadcasts with a sign that read, "Hello from the lovely Apollo Room, high atop everything." And once we displayed one that asked, "Deke Slayton, are you a turtle?"

According to barroom tradition, Deke was required to answer, "You bet your sweet ass I am," or pay the penalty of buying a drink for everyone within earshot. Deke copped out by cutting off his microphone and recording the answer.

The telecasts gave us a chance not only to check out the system that would capture the first footsteps on the moon, but also to demonstrate to the people at home a few facts of space life. We performed acrobatics at one point to provide a glimpse of weightlessness in action. We showed scenes out the spacecraft windows, catching glimpses of clouds and coastlines racing by. But our best show was done completely upside down on the home screens. It was an opportunity to have fun and strip away some of the mystery. The shows also led to a special Emmy Award from the Academy of Television Arts and Sciences the following year.

Wally grew more and more impatient with maneuvers and tests he felt were not part of the original plan. At one point he said, "I wish you would find out the idiot's name who thought up *this* test. I want to talk to him personally when I get back down." Then Donn got caught up in the swing of things and began to throw a little weight around, also. Donn's complaint had to do with a test to get a navigation fix on the horizon. "I think it's rather ill prepared and hastily conceived," he said. Echoing Wally, he added: "I want to talk to the man who thought up that little gem. That one really got to us."

Finally, Wally laid down "Schirra's Law": "I have had it up here today, and from now on I'm going to be an on-board flight director for flight plan updates. We are not going to accept any new games or do some crazy test we never heard of before."

I think that would have been a little tough for Wally. Fifteen to twenty mission controllers work for the Flight Director. The Flight Director is authorized to "take any action necessary for crew safety and mission success." According to one of the most capable, Gene Kranz, "The name of the game in mission control was teamwork—both the 'I' and the 'we' of teamwork. It means stepping forward when called upon and then stepping back as part of the team. Members checked their egos at the door."

Wally never checked his ego—for anyone!

We learned later that at the next press briefing, a newsman stood up and said to Glynn Lunney, the prime flight director for Apollo 7: "I've covered sixteen flights, man and boy, and I don't recall ever finding a bunch of people up there growling the way these guys are. Now you're either doing a bad job down here, or they're a bunch of malcontents. Which is it?"

"I would be a little hard pressed to answer that one," said Lunney, and dropped it.

The flight controllers in the trenches—the rows of consoles where the various spacecraft systems were monitored—tended not to pay a whole lot of attention to Wally's testy exchanges, or chose to look the other way and ignore the embarrassing situation they created. Lunney, like the other flight directors, was faced with that press conference every time the shift changed. He was on the hot seat with the media at least once a day. He later confided that he didn't feel it affected his judgment or performance, but during every slow period he caught himself dwelling on the effect Wally's indulgence was having on the professional procedures and rapport between astronauts and flight controllers so carefully built over the years. He felt it was so obvious to both astronauts and controllers that he speculated on whether Wally's buddies would take him out behind the woodshed and shape him up when he got back.

When Lunney felt things were really bad he began tapping his pencil; George Low, the Apollo program manager, would try to calm him down by talking about other things. Deke, who was also highly incensed, contributed by telling jokes.

Our backup and support crews working in Mission Control also suffered during the mission from defending Wally's actions in some pretty indefensible situations. For guys like Jack Swigert, Bill Pogue, and Ron Evans it may have had a carryover effect on their future crew assignments.

There's no question that it had a significant impact on the mission. The flight directors were very reluctant to send up anything additional, new, or different in the way of tests or checkouts even though there was plenty of time toward the end of the mission for such additional tests. They felt that such additions would only present further opportunities for embarrassing exchanges on the air-to-ground loop or that some worthwhile test would not be understood by Wally, which would then trigger an outburst.

In retrospect, the exchanges weren't all that significant, but in a mission as routine and boring as Apollo 7 turned out to be, the media was desperate for any angle.

Wally saw each encounter as a challenge to his authority and judgment as captain of the ship. He never felt he was behaving like an ass, but rather that he was defending a principle. My own attitude was cautious, if not downright cowardly. I did not participate in, nor did I believe the poor behavior and air-to-ground abuse was justified. I also realized that all three of us would be tarred by the same brush. So when the exchanges became heated, or threatened to, I would disengage myself, stay out, and later play the apologist for mission control's position. I was not known for my diplomacy, making the situation awkward and difficult for me. The new tests *were* sometimes poorly thought out and *did* add to our workload (which was not excessive), but they also produced valuable data.

In the end, the mission left a bitter residue with the support people and controllers who had worked with so many crews before. In Glynn Lunney we had perhaps the best flight director the Johnson Space Center ever produced, and his patience was tried to the limits. The technical success we achieved on the mission was blemished to a great degree by the reputation we earned for being difficult. Then, too, our mission objectives were accomplished so routinely that the news media had very little to report except those "human interest" items.

In retrospect, at least four factors combined to make the flight a pressure cooker for Wally Schirra: his age (he was forty-five at the time); his preflight lack of interest in the details of many of the test objectives; the nuisance of his head cold, the effects of which were heightened by zero gravity; and the long duration of the mission. His longest previous stay in space had been twenty-five hours, and Wally was noted more for his quick style and grace than for his endurance.

When one considers the strange sleeping and eating cycles we endured, and the closeness of our quarters, it's remarkable that more tensions didn't result. On our first day in space we were up for twenty-three hours straight before getting to sleep. NASA liked to get its money's worth from every crew—and did, especially at the beginning of missions.

During training, I had fairly well sorted out what it was going to be like in a spacecraft for eleven days, including how I would behave and respond. Working with Wally and Donn for nearly three years—prime, backup, and prime crew again—I knew their strengths and weaknesses. If they were paying attention, they knew mine. I had anticipated certain problems and knew what I intended to do in such cases.

"I'm the navigator," Donn, our navigation expert, liked to joke, "and I've got a right to know where we are." But he knew the guidance and control system and had a good grasp of the mission and its objectives. Together, the two of us had developed the procedures to accomplish our mission objectives. We had cross-trained enough, including flying many re-entries, that we were confident there was no aspect of the mission the two of us couldn't handle. If anything happened to Wally, we felt we could cover for him in every area. It wouldn't surprise me to find out each of us had privately reached that same conclusion about each other's jobs.

As a practical matter, Donn's and my jobs did not revolve around life-or-death situations. The time-critical decisions that dealt with our very necks were Wally's. He was in command of the vehicle. It was his hand on the abort handle during boost; he flew the spacecraft and handled the attitude control system 90 percent of the time. A dumb mistake by any of us could blow the mission or, worse, the spacecraft. But if everything went according to Hoyle, as we expected it to, neither Donn nor I was in a position to cause or react to time-critical problems. Wally was in control at those crucial times when our necks were on the line and that is where he placed his training emphasis.

The catch was that Wally hadn't exactly immersed himself in the other objectives of the mission prior to the flight. Donn and I fully expected that some of those objectives would only sink in during the flight, causing him to raise questions, reservations, and complaints that should have come up months before. Development of all in-flight procedures had fallen to Donn and me by default.

Wally was never a detail man, and at least part of his testiness during the flight was caused by his discovery, for the first time, of some of the details of the tests we were to perform. Then there was the added stress of a bad head cold and the realization that if the mission had to be aborted, there was a risk that his eardrums would be damaged in the subsequent re-entry. It all added up to Wally being an irascible fellow most of the trip.

I had decided to do something very untypical of me; to roll with the punches and catch as little flak as possible. That left me in several instances acting as a mediator between Wally and Donn. Now, I'm not noted for my diplomacy, but the only real on-board confrontation of the mission taxed what little I had.

Every mission has literally hundreds of test objectives to be accomplished and, invariably, one task runs right up against the next. On our ninth day, Donn was required to verify the midcourse navigation program in the Apollo guidance computer. This involved maneuvering the spacecraft to a prescribed attitude (requiring a budgeted expenditure of fuel). Then Donn, using the sextant and computer, was to track a star on the lunar horizon.

During the following night-pass, Wally was scheduled to check out a backup alignment system by maneuvering to several stars using a sight placed in his window. His task would be expensive in terms of fuel expended and, therefore, was scheduled to be performed only *once* during the mission.

Donn's task was going slowly—it had never been attempted even in the simulator—and Wally kept chipping at him to hurry. I tried to point out that we still had twenty minutes of darkness left, but Wally barked, "Wrap it up. I've got this backup alignment coming up."

Donn had been working hard on his test and had just one more sighting to make. He finally got fed up and snapped back, which for him was uncharacteristic: "Okay, if you insist, I'll wrap it up. But we've already spent the fuel to get here and I could be finished in another five minutes. I just want to put it on the tape that we're knocking off this test because you ordered it."

Wally didn't even blink. "OK," he said. "You just do that and when you get through I'm going to put on that same tape that you threatened mutiny." The ground wasn't the only target for Wally's ill-temper.

I was over on my couch trying to make light of it and get a word in edgewise, as a peacemaker: "Well, Wally, why don't we just wait a couple more minutes." And, "Donn, we can come back to it."

It all blew over rather quickly, with Donn making one more sighting. They spent a frosty day pouting and saying as little as possible to each other, and then the air just cleared. Donn knew there was no room for bad blood in the six-foot cockpit, and Wally, I suspected, felt a bit foolish about the whole affair. At any rate, not another word was ever mentioned again, during or after the flight. None of it ever appeared on tape, either.

Donn and I were curious about Wally's impatience with the navigation test. We assumed he had wanted to start a slow, fuel-conserving maneuver to line up his stars—a bad guess. Apparently, Wally felt uneasy about performing his alignment-one try only—under the watchful monitoring of Mission Control on the next night-pass. He had decided to rehearse the entire procedure, ignoring the fact that there was no fuel in the budget for it. With darkness running out, he had to really burn up the fuel to get his practice alignment completed. An hour later the real event went off flawlessly, and to this day, ground control hasn't figured out what happened to the forty pounds of fuel that came up missing during the ninth day of operations.

What surprised me most about the episode was that for the first time in three years, Donn had stood up on his hind legs and said, "Just a damned minute, Mr. Schirra." It was something Donn should have done a hundred times in the past rather than laugh along with Wally and compromise a point during training. If he had, the two of us would probably have been able to force a better balance inside the spacecraft when we finally flew the mission.

By the fourth day the romance was really over. We had grown accustomed to some of the most spectacular sights in the universe. In the beginning, if we weren't tied up on a task, each of us tried to view any unique or spectacular sight that passed by one of the five windows—typical tourists. With attitude control fuel in short supply, we spent most of our time drifting and taking potluck as to when and what would be in view.

On day four, as we slowly tumbled around our orbit, the window on my side of the spacecraft was pointing toward the earth. Wally, trying to decide whether to push his nose against the window, asked, "What can you see?" Without thinking, I responded casually, "It's just those damned Himalayas." Wally went about his business, but a few seconds later we both burst out laughing when we realized how jaded we had become. Many years later, I wish I had that view just one more time instead of the few pictures we took to remember that grand sight.

It is not as easy as one might think to get good pictures from an orbiting spacecraft. That is why, after forty years, we have so few good ones. Flight crews return and immediately begin to share their photos even though, in most cases, they are the least important and lowest priority of our activities onboard. Most mission activities are so complex that it is difficult to share them with laymen. Since anyone can appreciate a good picture, it is easy for the public to inflate the importance of their role on a mission. I do know as the years pass and the memories fade, I am glad to have the photos to keep the experience alive and real.

It was difficult to find good subjects and get good photos. The Himalayas were in view because one of our five windows was pointing toward the earth under good viewing conditions. The five small spacecraft windows were spaced around a sector of about 150 degrees. The largest was about nine inches across. Since we were randomly drifting most of the time there was 210 degrees of the spacecraft circumference that could be pointing toward the earth with *no* viewing ports.

What other factors restricted our picture taking?

The most important one, and one that impacted many other objectives, was the orbit in which we were flying. Our orbital inclination—the angle between our orbital plane and the plane of the equator—was about 31 degrees. That meant we traveled back and forth between 31 degrees North latitude and 31 degrees South latitude, restricting us to the equatorial zone around the earth. Every 90 minutes we flew over the same path in space but, due to the earth's rotation, our ground track had moved 15 degrees farther East.

Each 90-minute revolution was split between 45 minutes of daylight and 45 minutes of darkness. The nighttime earth can be very beautiful but it is hard to get a meaningful picture of Hong Kong in the dark.

If you are oriented with a window pointed down and *if* it is daylight, there is still the problem of the heavy cloud cover in the equatorial belt.

When you are both inclined and able take a picture, it still must be taken through two panes of 3/4" thick quartz glass separated by a small, evacuated space. It was the best glass money could buy but it was, nevertheless, an obstacle.

The pros on the ground preferred we not take pictures immediately after sunrise and just before sunset due to the bad color balance. That meant a three or four minute reduction at each end of a 45-minute day.

Lastly, it was strongly recommended that we take pictures not more than 20-25 degrees off of the vertical. Otherwise, we would be looking through too much atmosphere to get good detail.

With all these limitations, I am sometimes amazed we got any good pictures at all.

By day four we had also become accustomed, as well as we were going to, to our irregular sleep cycle. This was the first spacecraft in which the crew was free-floating while asleep—free falling is more apt. During all previous flights crew members had gone to sleep strapped in their seats with their fingers clasped across their chest to keep from inadvertently flipping switches—a technique I dutifully practiced in the month before launch. We had sleep stations beneath the left-and right-hand couches. The sleeping restraint functioned as a cocoon, which merely prevented the sleeper from floating around the spacecraft while asleep.

The first couple of nights were less than ideal, but I adjusted by simply deciding to quit worrying about being strapped down in order to feel something against my back. The third night was the first one that I really slept soundly, for six or seven hours. The sensation of falling asleep without having a bed—or anything else—under you is one I can best compare to the nightmare of falling through space and never hitting. Just prior to dozing off our subconscious would signal the falling sensation and we would be instantly awake with arms flailing. But after we finally adjusted to zero-g, it was better than any Posturepedic or feather bed I ever slept on.

We never slept three at a time, in order to keep one man on watch. Wally and I did sleep simultaneously—he always made a joke of insisting that we didn't sleep "together"—following Donn's sleep period. The three of us would share a watch for eight to twelve hours; then Donn would begin his sleep period. When he woke up, Wally and I would sack out. When our sleep period was up, Donn would wake us and we'd start the cycle again.

Normally, no one slept his entire period; I was invariably up before it was time. After a couple of problems developed while Donn was on watch, Wally and I began to sleep with one eye open.

Sixty-one hours into the mission, while Donn was on watch, we had a malfunction in the electric power system that threatened a complete electrical shutdown. Wally and I were supposed to be sleeping, but I was so near to consciousness beneath my couch that I was able to rouse myself and correct the situation before Donn could get involved. The electric power system was my specialty. A day or two later, Wally and I each awoke at different times to find Donn asleep during his watch. We found him floating asleep up in the docking tunnel, in the zero-g fetal position: legs, back, and arms all slightly bent. It was not the best way to watch over the spacecraft. On later missions it became standard practice for all three crewmen to sleep simultaneously, so in retrospect it wasn't critical. But on this first mission it didn't make Wally and me feel very secure, knowing the spacecraft was brand-new and unforeseen problems could arise at any moment.

In defense of Donn, he had a more difficult time than Wally and I in at least two respects. The only time the spacecraft was completely quiet was during long portions of his watch. Inside a vehicle that small, every little noise is heard throughout. Equally important, the cessation of any "normal" sound can create an instant alertness. With very little activity— little conversation with the ground, few pictures to be taken, and little movement in the cabin—it wasn't too difficult for Wally and me to get a good night's rest. But for Donn, the long quiet periods made it difficult to stay alert and awake. When Donn was supposed to be asleep there were two of us at work and moving about in the spacecraft. The level of activity was reduced, but Wally wasn't the kind to accept gracefully too many restraints on what he could do. There were whispered conversations between Wally and me, as well as periodic communications with ground control, all of which made sleep difficult for Donn and caused him to be up three or four times during every sleep period. Naturally, that left him still tired during our sleep period which followed.

Halfway through the flight we had already accomplished more than 75 percent of our objectives—missions were always front-end loaded—and, rather than exult in the days, we began to just check them off. The flight plan dictated when the day ended. When it said, "sleep," the day was over. But the start of our sleep periods were moved around the clock, from 5:00 A.M. on the first day (really, the morning of the second day), to 5:00 P.M. on the tenth day. (We continued to reference our on board time to the Cape, where we had spent our last several weeks and would return after splashdown.) At the end of each day we would scratch a mark through the date on the calendar. But by October 17, the seventh day, Wally was counting the days so anxiously that he began crossing them off soon after we finished breakfast. There is no question; we were beginning to anticipate that eleventh—and final—-day.

Mealtime was not one of our highlights, just another item on the flight plan. Often we ate on the run, with one guy eating while another did the work of the moment, then trading off. We were on a four-day menu, which then repeated itself. By the time we hit the first reruns it was trading time, knocking the hell out of a planned menu that probably cost millions of dollars to develop. But we ignored the diets and kept trading—I swapped my banana pudding for Donn's chocolate—trying to create a little variety and to keep our interest in eating alive. This certainly didn't thrill the doctors, but our crew—and most others—looked at eating pragmatically. We treated it primarily as body fuel and only secondarily as a medical experiment.

We had one piece of luck. In the suit room before launch we had each placed several small packets of food in a pocket of our pressure suits, including some freeze-dried, bite-sized bacon squares. This was in case the mission had to be terminated early and we were unable to unstow the food. On the ninth day we discovered that the mission planners had actually slighted us one complete meal apiece, in effect leaving us without breakfast on the eleventh day. We re-allocated our remaining food, in order to have the right number of meals, even if they were smaller. The last few meals were looking a bit lean when, on our last full day in orbit, we remembered the packages stashed away in our flight suits. We dug them out and our morale leaped when we saw the bacon. Happiness was finding dried bacon squares for breakfast on the eleventh day.

The same mix up that left us one meal short also resulted in the spacecraft being shy one of the canisters for removing carbon dioxide from the atmosphere.

For the most part we existed on freeze-dried, reconstituted, and bite-sized foods, plus liquid drinks. We didn't have the instant foods that were available on later flights, the kind that were spooned out of an open container. The only hot food we had was what we could mix with the hot water on board, but by the time it was thoroughly dissolved it was no longer hot. It was interesting that after the first couple of days in orbit we began to handle water and bite-size morsels exactly the same. No matter which way we faced, we could just as easily put the water in our mouths before or after the bite-sized dried food. After eating, of course, we brushed our teeth—which felt great in spite of having to swallow all of the toothpaste afterwards.

Another big surprise was finding that the flight plan we had lived with for so long had Wally and me waking up, from the fourth day on, and eating, not breakfast, but dinner.

Our work-rest cycles made for one giant case of jet lag. The real workday on Apollo 7, that is, where the lion's share of activities was concentrated, began after Wally and I completed our sleep period. This was at 9:00 A.M. on the second day and moved all the way back to 1:00 A.M. on the morning of splashdown. Donn's problem was compounded. In order for all of us to get adequate sleep, Donn had to be hitting his sleep restraint as much as sixteen hours *before* Wally and I were scheduled to wake up. That wasn't so bad the first night; Donn went to sleep, or I should say, to bed, around 9:00 P.M. Within a week, when Wally and I were waking up at midnight, Donn was scheduled to hit the sack at 10:00 A.M.—a virtually impossible adjustment, even for Donn, who could usually sleep any place at any time.

By the ninth day, Donn was so punchy, and all of our days so screwed up, that Wally and I were able to convince him that it was 10:00 P.M., and that he was overdue to hit the sack. He was headed under the couch before we called the gag and admitted it was really 10:00 A.M.

More than once during my own sleep period I recall looking up with one eye to peek at the instruments for the critical electric power system and finding Donn floating above the couch, sound asleep with a pencil in his hand, looking for all the world as if he was working.

After the sixth day it became obvious that we would run short of film before the flight was over and we began restricting our picture taking to sights that were, well, meaningful. So what happened? Wally or I would wake up in the middle of our sleep period and there would be Donn, clicking off pictures of the islands out in the middle of the Pacific. One time the movie camera was cranking away as though there was no tomorrow, filming a path across the Pacific, and all we could see down below were clouds.

Our first order of business on waking up (naturally) was to play Pass the Urine Bag (technically, the UCD, or Urine Collection Device). After it was filled, a series of valves permitted us to dump the contents of the bag overboard.

Now, *that* was something worth taking a picture of. If one dumped just at sunset, the flecks of ice coming off the urine dump nozzle would look like a million stars and it would be impossible to take star sightings for about five minutes.

Of course, it's a real experience to see your own urine take on a cosmic quality in space. But it is eye-catching and every crew has taken pictures of it. The ice particles are quite beautiful, the very phenomenon that caused John Glenn to rave about the "fireflies" at sunset. It was considered a mystery at the time of the first reports, and I don't think space officials ever released a clear explanation.

Believe me, just *doing* it was no simple process. A modified condom was attached to one's penis and a storage bag was filled through a valving system. After the bag was dumped overboard, we allowed it to drain for a while to insure all the moisture was out of the system. We were forever forgetting to close the overboard dump valve, and it would eventually bleed down the pressure in the spacecraft enough to trigger an alarm, indicating an air leak. After several days' use, this alarm came to mean simply that the last one at the john had left the urine dump valve open. When time was short, it was possible to urinate straight through the system, but with a perfect vacuum at one end of the hose and an essential part of one's anatomy on the other, we tended to be a mite careful in manipulating the valves.

Here is probably as good a place as any to answer the other half of the second or third most popular space question. It was the *solid* waste management problem that we all dreaded. Before Apollo most missions were less than four days in duration and it was possible to go on a low residue diet and avoid the problem entirely. On Apollo 7 we made it to the third day before anyone had to answer the call of nature. Following my first experience, I wrote the following memo in my logbook to help follow-on crews preparing for their maiden voyage.

Use of Waste Management Bags

Clear out as much room as possible in the lower equipment bay and reserve at least forty-five minutes. The key to this exercise is setting everything up prior to commencing the main event.

The rear door in your long johns is too small to allow a good placement of the bag. I suggest dropping your drawers and getting comfortable. This means disconnecting the biomed harness. I have done it both ways and the latter is best. Separate the outer bag and stick it to the wall. It will be used to hold all the little pieces of paper that collect. Lay out at least 4 folded paper towels and the wet wipe that comes with the bag. These paper towels will be used, folded, and used again. Wet one of the towels *and* the wet wipe, which always seems to be dry. These should be placed within easy reach.

Remove the chemical biocide packet and place in the bottom of the bag. Stick the bag to the appropriate spot on your rear as accurately as possible. Try to keep the one finger glove out of the way. Now attach the urine collection device to the other end and you're ready to go (pardon the pun).

Use the finger of the bag to push and hold everything to the bottom of the bag. Leave the bag stuck where it is while you clean up the urine portion of the job.

Unless you have been singularly unfortunate you should be able to safely remove the bag from your posterior and attach it by one corner to the couch. Use a couple of the dry towels judiciously and shove them carefully into the bag. Next apply the wet paper towels and more dry ones as necessary. Finish with the small wet wipe and close the top of the bag *except* for a small hole. Break the chemical container at the bottom and mix well, trying not to let too much of the chemical get soaked up by the paper.

Knead the bag until well mixed (or as long as you can stand it) and roll it up tightly, forcing the air out the hole you have left at the top. Place this in the outer bag with all the little pieces that have accumulated.

Remove the inner seal cover, seal it, and roll up the outer bag. Remove the protector on the outer sealer, roll the outer bag and store it in the fecal storage compartment.

Good luck.

There was more than one thing a fecal bag could be used for. Along about our fourth day in orbit, I encountered a bag of chocolate pudding that had failed at the seams. In attempting to eat the pudding it was getting squeezed out at several places along the edge. That was an impossible problem in zero gravity and Wally suggested a fecal bag as the perfect solution where it wouldn't smell or possibly explode as it decomposed.

All used fecal bags were sealed, rolled tightly and stored in a special compartment that could be vented to the outside to remove disagreeable odors. By the end of the mission we had thirteen little nuggets stored in the compartment and we didn't give them another thought until the day after splashdown. On that morning, the three of us climbed aboard an airplane for a two-hour flight from the carrier to Cape Kennedy. The only cargo besides the flight crew on this special mission was a large plastic bag containing those thirteen "nuggets" for early delivery to the doctors back on the beach. Depending on the individual scientist, it was debatable which part of the cargo the doctors were more interested in. That plastic bag would capture our own attention three days later.

With no shaving for eleven days, our ablutions were pretty simple. They were followed by dressing for the daily "Wally, Walt, and Donn Show." With only one change of clothes for eleven days, we got dressed and undressed a surprising number of times. For sleeping we always got out of our inflight coveralls but stayed in our Constant Wear Garments (long johns). If possible, we peeled down each morning to enjoy the luxury of a sponge bath. To answer the call of nature three or four times during the mission there was only one way to go and that was strip all the way down.

We were not exactly in a state of euphoria, but with the exception of those rare moments of tension and concern, our spirits remained high. Every innocent thought or act seemed to inspire some kind of reaction. When Wally held up another of our printed signs to the on-board TV camera "Keep those cards and letters coming, folks"—it was no time at all before the CapCom radioed a frantic SOS from Wally's secretary. She was being swamped with mail.

Early in the flight, Eisele reported an intriguing experience with a "mysterious" radio signal he was picking up. The transcript of his conversation with ground control went like this:

EISELE: We have some music in the background. Is that you?

GROUND: You must be picking up the twilight zone there.

EISELE: Is someone trying to plug in a radio program to us, or are we just picking that up spiritually?

GROUND: That must be a spurious signal. No, we don't have anything like that.

EISELE: OK, I'm getting a hot tip on some hospital insurance plan from some guy.

GROUND: Maybe they are trying to tell you something.

EISELE: Yeah. Maybe they know something I don't.

And so it went: peaks and valleys, a little mischief and, occasionally, a sense of the universe we were now exploring. Our universe had contracted to the spacecraft and the mission in which we were immersed. Oh, the world went on around us, but it seemed to exist outside the crystal ball in which we were living. The war in Vietnam was a hot election issue ("Don't take any pictures over Hanoi") and Jacqueline Kennedy announced her engagement to Aristotle Onassis.

Seven's response to that news was classic Schirra, "Beware of Greeks bearing gifts."

Throughout the mission we compared notes on what we were experiencing. We never got any clear agreement on whether it seemed like we were flying inverted over the earth or flying upright and diving down under the planet. In fact, at different times, we each experienced a variety of impressions. I came to see the spacecraft and the earth as two unique bodies moving through space on more or less equal terms.

Other subjective effects which we discussed and investigated as time permitted were the "break-off phenomena" and space sickness syndrome. In the early sixties psychologists hypothesized that man was psychologically dependent on an earth-centered frame of reference. Detaching one's self from this reference, as in space, would supposedly create a lost feeling—a melancholic effect. Supposedly it would be even more pronounced in circumlunar space. That one was so far out we had trouble even identifying with it. During our mission, I concluded that man existed in a *self-centered* frame of reference. Through his visual sense (primarily) and his brain, he can relate himself to any convenient external reference system.

Nausea, or space sickness, is a very subjective experience. Half the Apollo crew members had some manifestation of nausea early in their missions. Yet, Donn and I attempted to induce nausea with no success.

Finally, Wally marked off the last day on his wrist calendar. And after wondering in the early stages how the time would pass, it *had*.

As we approached our retro-fire burn, deorbit, and re-entry, Wally braced himself for one of his big moments of the mission, second only to the abort responsibility during boost.

An aviator earns his pay by landing the airplane. The degree of success with which he can perform this function, under *any* conditions, is a fair measure of his worth. In flying the Apollo spacecraft the opposite was true. Landing the spacecraft—flying the re-entry—is a more-or-less routine, manual-control task, although a certain mystique has developed around it. Furthermore, re-entry can be flown just as well, if not better, by the on-board computer.

On the other hand, many problems could trigger an abort during boost, with endless factors affecting the decision. Only two of these problems could initiate an *automatic* abort, when an emergency could occur so rapidly that there would be no time for men—either in the air or on the ground—to analyze the situation and react. Those were vehicle rotation rates exceeding limits, or two of the eight engines shutting down. In either case an escape rocket would blast the spacecraft free and return it to earth. This automatic system was disabled 61 seconds into the launch.

When to abort and when not to are judgment calls that most times are at the total discretion of the spacecraft commander. In this role, Wally was

virtually flawless. On Gemini 6, he was awarded a medal for not aborting during an unsuccessful launch attempt. When the Titan booster
belched smoke and flames without lifting off, Wally correctly decided
that there was no danger of an explosion. He made a split-second decision not to pull the seat ejection handle when few would have faulted him
for doing so. A few days later, Gemini 6, still intact, blasted off, carrying
Wally and Tom Stafford to America's first space rendezvous.

Our retro burn was computer controlled, and if it came off properly
we would be down in twenty-nine minutes, come what may. The most
critical requirement was to be in the proper attitude at the time of the
burn. The only activity on board which even resembles flying an airplane
is maneuvering the spacecraft. Consequently, we showed a distinct bias
for performing maneuvers manually whenever possible. Maneuvers were
planned well ahead and performed slowly to conserve fuel. It wasn't
unusual to acquire the proper retro attitude well in advance. With that
detail taken care of, the crew's mind was freed for other critical procedures. Besides, it gave one a warm feeling of reassurance just to be there.

When it came time for Wally to maneuver into retro attitude, which
would trigger all the events for re-entry, he did just as everyone else had
before him. He started early—and it was a good thing, too. Before we
made our retro burn, Apollo 7 had been in three different retro attitudes.
Twice Wally was pointed 180° from where we belonged. And twice Donn
and I, by nudging and eye contact and hemming and hawing and mum-
bling a lot, managed to disconcert Wally until he discovered the problem
and finally went to the proper retro attitude.

For Donn and me, those were the most awkward moments of the
flight and potentially quite fatal. We were spared great embarrassment by
the fact that we started early and were out of ground contact for the entire
time we were stumbling around. It also gave us a new appreciation of
why one goes to the retro-fire attitude early.

The retro burn itself came off almost as an anticlimax. A few minutes
before 6:00 A.M. on October 22, 1968, Apollo 7 made its last pass over
Houston, at a height of 76 miles, a small, swift dot of light in the morning darkness. Schirra, staring out a window, reported, "We're flying a
pink cloud." And then, his final quip of the flight: "Our landing gear is
down and locked."

From the time Apollo 7 started her long slide down the pike, I was already feeling melancholic and cheated. Something I had gloried in and had truly loved was being taken away. It would be a long time, I thought, before I would experience that feeling again. I didn't know, at the time, that I would never return to that unique world. Before the experience was even over, nostalgia was sinking in.

Twenty-four minutes after we started re-entry, the chutes opened in a solid overcast at 10,500 feet over the Atlantic. Then we were in the water, and eleven days in space suddenly seemed like eleven minutes.

The voyage was already assuming that dreamlike quality of a moment long ago in another place, as though I was remembering scenes from an old movie. In the post flight debriefings it would be easy to describe events or tests or incidents that had filled our time, but impossible to describe the experience itself. It had happened to another Walter Cunningham. Trying to recapture just the wonder-world sensation of zero gravity seemed hopeless.

Eleven days of living together, three men in a super powered thimble; zero gravity; being for one chunk of time THE news the world over, and a focal point in the lives of people throughout the world—it was already history and beginning to recede fast from my consciousness. The letdown from Olympus had begun.

Splashdown came at 6:24 A.M. We slipped into the water as cleanly as a newly launched ship. We had pulled it off and were pleased. Probably 90 percent of the most critical events of a space flight, from the standpoint of crew safety, occur in those last thirty minutes. A safe landing requires retro-fire going off smoothly; satisfactory separation between the Command and Service modules; a properly executed re-entry; ejection of the cone covering the parachutes; deployment of the drogue chutes at 45,000 feet, the pilot chutes at 25,000, and main chutes at 10,000 feet; and finally a good splashdown.

In normal circumstances there was little the crew could do to improve performance but a lot we could do to screw it up. Our re-entry was nominal, and we were down. I piped up with the fighter pilot's wry comment; "Well, we cheated death again."

We might have laughed, except that immediately after hitting the water, the Command Module began a steady and rapid rotation, flipping us upside down—-or at least three-quarters. It left us hanging from the couch straps and looking out the side windows at a very choppy sea. But we had procedures for this. After letting the spacecraft cool for seven minutes, it took an equal amount of time to inflate the uprighting bags that would return us to an even keel. This was more than enough time for us to get sicker than dogs in spite of the motion sickness pills we had taken just prior to de-orbit.

There was a post landing checklist we still had to perform, but for now we were just hanging on, waiting for the spacecraft to upright. We also had planned on removing our pressure suits and slipping into our cleanest set of coveralls. After hanging inverted for three or four minutes, with each man keeping his own counsel with his stomach, one is not only hesitant to move but even to speak. Then Donn asked, "How do you feel? You going to get sick?" Without waiting for an answer, he added, "I think I'm going to throw up." From that moment on I really had squirrels dancing inside my stomach. Even Wally was a bit concerned, and he had cast-iron guts.

Donn, bless his soul, had the most difficult assignment of all. As soon as possible after landing it was his job to get out of the couch, go down to the lower equipment bay, and connect a VHF radio antenna. It was close quarters, head down in the bottom of the craft, with no air circulation. During training, Donn would invariably get sick before the job was finished and it would fall to me to complete it; and within a few minutes the chances were good that I'd be as sick as Donn. But it was all academic this time. Donn got sick just hanging in the straps, while Wally and I fought off nausea until we finally got the hatch open.

We had a brief spell of apprehension after noticing water pooling in the lower end of the spacecraft, and seeping between the inner panes and the exterior windows around the shell. We couldn't tell if the water had leaked in through a ruptured pressure vessel or through a ventilation fan, or if it was simply condensed moisture. We kept an eye on it, until each of us stepped happily over the side into the frogmen's raft. The Command Module was a great spacecraft, but on the water it reacted more like a cork than a boat.

In the chopper we began to realize how fortunate we were that re-entry had been accurate and divers were standing by at our splash-down. The weather was reported 600 feet overcast, with two miles of visibility, in rain showers. It was no problem, but it had cheated us out of looking up and seeing the gorgeous sight of our three main orange-and-white parachutes drifting down against a background of blue sky.

Once we stepped onto the deck of the carrier *Essex,* I began to shake off the postorbital remorse (which must be akin to postnatal depression). After eleven days in space, seeing the U.S. Navy turned out on a carrier deck brings it home that millions of souls have been sweating out your success and your safety. My feeling at that moment was, "Thank heaven we came down in our prime recovery, area." It would have been unthinkable to disappoint all those people by landing in the Pacific Ocean.

Then there were the cards, letters, and telegrams waiting for us on board. They dramatized how many people had shared our flight as a personal ordeal—and triumph. It made me wonder what I could possibly have done to warrant such support and how to justify all the faith invested in me.

Physically, the one overpowering sensation we experienced was one of heaviness. When the postflight medical checkup got under way and I lay down on the examining table, it felt as if I were going to sink right through it. I felt as if my body were made out of lead. This feeling persisted until the following day.

As I lay there, looking up at the overhead, which was several feet above, it seemed strange that I couldn't do what I had done for eleven days: push off from the table with one finger or by flexing my shoulder muscles and simply float to the ceiling. I imagined myself sitting up there, upside down, and holding to the pipes to keep from floating away. No more, not anytime, no how!

Exiting the helicopter on the USS Essex
following splashdown of Apollo 7.

Even our clothes seemed heavy. When we stepped out of the heli-copter onto the carrier, we all had the uneasy feeling that our pants were going to fall off. I hitched mine up and the three of us grinned crazily as we realized why.

I began to feel weary: not that spaghetti kind of weary, where you just want to melt to the ground, but the kind where all your bones send you a message of a physical job well done. The scuttlebutt around the office had been that an early prime crew might be recycled for the first lunar landing. But I had no illusions at that moment and I knew it wouldn't be us. It was virtually impossible for any crew to fly two of the big missions. I made it a point never to kid myself. Unfortunately, it is possible to spend a decade in manned space flight, as happened to some of my friends, without leaving a mark on it. The first manned test of the Apollo space-craft offered an opportunity to be counted and who has a right to ask for anything more? I'd rather die than not be counted.

A near-perfect mission was behind us. Suddenly the goal of landing men on the surface of the moon was very close. After a two-year hiatus marked by tragedy and then triumph, Donn and I were Astronauts. For the next sixty days, until Apollo 8 lifted off, ours would be the voice of authority. We had been there! We had joined the "Brotherhood of the Right Stuff." No longer would we go out to show training movies and talk about our buddies' space flights. From now on our reports would be first hand.

9

Riding the Hero Trail

THE WRITER Tom Wolfe once referred to it as postorbital remorse. The astronaut most often cited as the classic example is Buzz Aldrin, who, in the opinion of his admirers, including himself, was unable to cope with the hero's role and the adulation that followed the moon landing of Apollo 11.

To all of which I say, *"Hogwash!"* Buzz signed into a hospital when he found himself heading for what he labeled "a good, old-fashioned, American nervous breakdown." It took nerve to do, and even more to make it public. But I don't believe the "incessant round of appearances," the glory, or the applause were Aldrin's problem any more than they were for the rest of us. The problem came when he began to hear his own kind of music, liked it, and then, perhaps, realized it wouldn't last forever.

It is easy to get the impression from the story of Buzz Aldrin that all astronauts were vulnerable to some kind of postflight depression. Let me set the record straight.

If there was a letdown it was professional, not personal. We had completed the mission, a goal for which we had trained and dedicated and sacrificed most of our lives, but there was no way to know if we'd have another. And besides, part of our training, by design or not, included traveling and making public appearances. If the public obligations and social fanfare were the sources of the problems some experienced, we would have seen examples before flying and possibly some would not have lasted through the program.

Early in the Apollo program, it became standard practice after each mission for the flight crew to take off on a grand tour covering key cities in the U.S. and abroad. The obvious aim of these dog-and-pony shows was to spread good will for the space effort and for the United States. In

The glamorous astronaut after 11 days in space
without a shave.

NASA's efforts to squeeze the maximum value from these excursions, their imagination was limited only by the degree of cooperation they could expect from each flight crew. To a degree, the flight crew could influence the scope of these postflight activities and they were in a fine position to bargain. They might show a little more enthusiasm for NASA's desires in return for the approval of an appearance or a speech that could help a friend, or a business contact.

The real prize in the postflight reward league was the grand tour. These were not just sun-and-fun-filled vacations out of some travel folder; most of the days were long and tedious and filled with official functions. But I never heard of a crewman, or a crewman's family, who wasn't anxious to make one.

How elaborate a tour was laid on depended on NASA policy at the time, the national and international interest generated by the flight, and just plain timing. Certainly the Apollo 11 crew, the first lunar expedition, was in more demand than any group or individual since Charles Lindbergh. Their tour represented a masterful job of planning by NASA and the State Department. Phileas T. Fogg would have wept with envy. And I suspect Buzz Aldrin wasn't as reluctant a passenger as he made out. The tour is described ad nauseum in Buzz's book, but it can be summarized as twenty-three countries in forty-five days—with a footnote for what Joan Aldrin characterized as "three kings in two days."

That was heavy company and the schedule *was* hectic. But other crews—notably Apollo 13, whose narrow escape from misadventure captivated the public—endured schedules equally as daunting. The Apollo 11 crew did carry the brunt in 1969, but in the years immediately following, the number of flights was cut in half while astronaut appearances nearly doubled.

It was briefly a mystery to Donn and me why the flight of Apollo 7 inspired so little post flight activity after such tremendous preflight interest. The exchanges between Wally and Mission Control had turned off more than a few people but I also knew that NASA had to keep the bandwagon rolling. Requests for the crew were being fielded, as usual, by the public affairs office at NASA headquarters. As rookies, Donn Eisele and I were not too proud to venture out among the natives to receive a little homage. Maybe a little parade, or something. Wally, on the other hand, after three missions, had ridden in enough parades to last him a lifetime. Anything short of a New York tickertape parade, with the Radio City Rockettes in his lap, would probably not have been acceptable. The one parade being pushed by NASA was in San Francisco, California, which happened to be my home state.

Without our knowing it, Wally had left orders at NASA headquarters that all postflight activities were to be channeled through him. When the pitch was made for the San Francisco parade, Wally quickly vetoed it. Poor cooperation wasn't going to improve a reputation earned in flight as NASA's tarnished heroes and we eventually coasted through one of the least demanding postflight calendars of any Apollo crew.

The closest Lo and I came to a "grand tour" was a ten-day swing through Australia and New Zealand in May of 1969. As a kind of mini-junket, it was representative of the treatment astronauts received abroad, and the itinerary was a challenge. It was among the more memorable experiences of our eight years in the space business. The occasion was the annual celebration of the Victory of the Battle of Coral Sea, in which American and Australian forces fought side by side in a naval engagement that became a turning point in the Pacific war. The battle began May 4, 1942, ended four days later, and saved Australia from invasion by a Japanese armada.

We were there in a unique diplomatic-social role. It had been traditional for high-ranking military officers to represent the United States at the anniversary celebrations that took place throughout the Australian continent. The year 1969 found tensions rising over certain political issues, including the war in Vietnam, and in an effort to play down the anti-Japanese implications of previous ceremonies, the Australian government had indicated that a civilian representative would be preferred. An astronaut was a likely candidate, which is where I came in.

Other departures from the past promised to make the trip a trying one. In prior years, the dignitary of the moment—an admiral or four-star general—would tour the seven largest Australian cities over a period of three weeks, reinforced by vessels of the Pacific fleet or the air force band, with appropriate regalia. In 1969 it was compressed to five cities in seven days; there would be no Pacific fleet or air force band, but only what we could muster in the way of support from the U.S. Embassy. In effect, it would be *a cappella*. Then, too, there would be a number of school appearances, added in deference to the intense interest of youngsters in space exploration. And, finally, we would be traveling without the usual entourage of protocol people.

Throughout our visit Down Under, we traveled in style in the personal jet of exploration. And, finally, we would be traveling without the usual entourage of protocol people.

Throughout our visit Down Under, we traveled in style in the personal jet of Prime Minister John Gorton. His BAC-111 became the flying command post for our entourage, which varied between six and a dozen people. The significance of my role was brought home when the captain of the aircraft requested my permission in Melbourne to carry the Minister of Supply—the equivalent of a cabinet post—with us to Canberra, our next stop.

Wherever we went, the schedule was laid out with stopwatch precision. The first stop, Brisbane, offered a typical agenda: tea and biscuits with city officials and officials of the Australian-American Association; a press conference; a parade; the laying of a wreath to honor the dead of World War II; a luncheon with speech and receiving line; a visit to the local racetrack for two races and an introduction; an appearance at a rugby match with a parade around the field at half-time; a presentation to a combined assembly of local high school students and talk show audience; back to the hotel to tidy up and dress for a black-tie dinner-dance and speech; then to bed around midnight to be up the next morning to start all over again in another city.

In Sidney, I was able to sneak away (with two detectives in tow) for twenty minutes to buy a sweater. It was cold down there in May. That day was topped off with *two* formal dinners. I mean real formal—cutaways and tails! The second followed on the heels of the first and neither sponsor was supposed to know about the other.

The Australian people are open and friendly, very much like those in the American Southwest. Most of them felt a strong identification with the American people and the space program. The first person to greet us on arrival in Brisbane was the Right Honorable Lord Mayor, Alderman Clem Jones. His first words to me were, "So you went to UCLA. Well, I graduated from there myself."

That proved to be typical of the Aussies in their attitudes toward Americans. I encountered nothing but friendliness, even though the Australian government at the time was embroiled in problems concerning the use of U.S. Air Force tracking sites in the interior and a controversy over the purchase of American fighter planes.

I did finally get my very own "hero's" parade through downtown Adelaide, and it isn't one I'll quickly forget. To begin with, Australians are a rather blasé folk not given much to pomp or finery or frills. Their idea of a good time is to drink their share of beer and watch a little "footy" (Australian rules football). We were driven into town in an open Rolls Royce, which had been brought "down under" expressly for the transportation of Queen Elizabeth on one of her visits. As we approached the town center at mid-day, our instructions were to stand up and wave at the spectators. It was immediately obvious that the spectators could care less whether we were there or not. It was a Saturday, and they were clearly intent on their shopping chores. We drove through town trying to attract attention by waving and smiling and otherwise looking silly while the good folks of Adelaide went blissfully about their business. Our Australian hosts must have felt that a touring astronaut was entitled to a parade. It was nice to be thought of as parade material but the awakening was in finding out that we weren't.

Parades, of course, are for the little kid in all of us. But at times they can get hilarious. The Apollo 12 crew came back from their world tour telling about a parade they had in Iran where the local Communist party managed to put out some false information on the parade route. Pete Conrad, Al Bean, and Dick Gordon found themselves headed down the parade route while the crowds were lined up one block away wondering where the astronauts were. In some of the countries they visited many of the people don't read. They may know nothing of world events and haven't the foggiest idea why those idiots are riding along in those great huge cars.

From Australia we flew to New Zealand for three more days of celebrations and a civics lesson. New Zealand is probably the most socialistic country in the world, and plagued by the frequent strikes that are characteristic of that form of government. There were several such "industrial actions" going on during our brief visit. The one that attracted my attention involved the pilots of Air New Zealand. The salaries of the captains on Qantas, the Australian airline, had recently been increased to $28,000 per year, while the Air New Zealand captains were making $12,000 a year to fly the same equipment over the same routes. They felt justified in striking for equal pay.

At a luncheon our first day in New Zealand I sat next to Prime Minister Keith Holyoake, to whom I had presented a New Zealand flag that had traveled with me on the five-million-mile trip of Apollo 7. While making lunch talk, I happened to mention—tactlessly, I suppose—how surprised I was to learn that captains on Air New Zealand earned only $12,000 a year. He replied, "That places them among the highest-paid people in 'New Zealand." Then he went on to ask me, "How much do you get paid in a year, Mr. Cunningham?"

That caught me off guard, but I answered, "Oh, eighteen to nineteen thousand dollars." The Prime Minister then informed me that was about $6,000 more per year than he was paid. He received the equivalent of

$12,500 a year in salary with an additional household and entertainment allowance of about $6,000. The "first family" lived in their own home, run by his wife, with no outside help. He made his point. From his perspective, the airline pilots were asking for $5,000 more a year than the combined salary and allowances for the chief executive of the country.

From New Zealand, we were headed to the Far East for a tour of military hospitals in the Philippines, Okinawa and Japan. The Vietnam War was heating up and our hospitals were just beginning to fill up with casualties. But, first, we passed back through Sidney for our one day off in the month of May. It was here where I gained a little insight into the entire celebrity syndrome.

There seems to be a kind of orbit in which celebrities move. When one has reached a certain level of notoriety, for whatever reason, he somehow becomes "worth knowing." Total strangers know who you are, or think they do, and assume that a sort of fellowship exists among so-called public figures—that they all know each other, or would like to if they don't.

We checked in at the Chevron Hotel in Sydney on Sunday night to find the lobby swarming with people. The manager explained, "Tom Jones is opening tonight in the lounge."

I brightly asked, "Who's Tom Jones?" The name meant nothing to me.

The first show was due to start in thirty minutes and when someone asked if we'd like to see it, we jumped at the chance. They were filling that room, six hundred seats, three times a night, standing room only. Now someone had half an hour in which to find a table for six, front row center.

In the meantime, the manager insisted we meet Tom Jones, assuming, of course, that it was a courtesy to us both. While we were unpacking, Jones was brought from his room, past the throng of teenybopper groupies camping in the hall of the penthouse floor, and to our door. I knew nothing about Tom Jones, and he had obviously never heard of Walter Cunningham. We shook hands and tried to make chitchat. We really had nothing to say to each other; the one thing that passed between us having any sincerity and meaning was our mutual appreciation of the awkwardness of the ritual. We both knew that each had been dragged through that same routine many times before, and no doubt would be again.

My sympathetic neutrality did turn quickly to admiration when he proved to be a superb showman.

The eagerness of the hotel manager was a common affliction. The public is familiar with the attraction and popularity of an entertainer and they tend to identify with that part of an astronaut's life as well or think they can. With an entertainer, the public sees not only the personal acclaim but its reason for being—the public performance. It's the same with an athlete: a Michael Jordan, or an A. J. Foyt, or a Pete Sampras.

With an astronaut it's not so simple. The acclaim may be the same, but the only direct exposure the public gets is the few hours in an astro's life when he is "on stage" during his mission. And, even then, what he is doing isn't clear to most, let alone what he does with the other 99 percent of his time. The astronaut mystique more closely resembles that of a nationally known politician than that of an entertainment or sports figure.

The ego trip provided by the worldwide attention lavished on astronauts returning from space can be intoxicating stuff. It's easy to get high on the flattery and flourishes and the self-satisfaction of a job that is unique. No one is totally immune. The trouble comes when one forgets that the acclaim is not so much for the individual as it is for the event—for the accomplishment. When the applause dies down, as it always does, the withdrawal symptoms begin.

That is what happened to Buzz. At least that is the consensus of those of us who lived with him through the Apollo program. More than that, Buzz has spent his life since Apollo 11 keeping the memory of the landing alive—as if it needed it. He was actually making sure that the public did not forget Buzz' role in that singular event. He went so far as to legally change his name from Edwin E. Aldrin to Buzz Aldrin.

There is no question that Neil and Buzz, with their greater notoriety, were under a lot more pressure than the rest of us and everyone handles pressure and fame in their own way. Neil tried to stay out of the limelight and to live, as much as possible, a normal life. We have all been proud of the manner in which Neil handled being the first man in history to walk on the moon. I have never heard one story critical of Neil's behavior except to wish he would not be such a recluse. Probably everyone who flew in Apollo has wondered if he would have handled the celebrity half as well.

In Buzz' case, the unflattering stories are legion. His celebrity as second man on the moon was a double-edged sword; he complained mightily about the pressure of being in the public eye yet continued to do everything possible to stay in the limelight. In 1991, he was one of the principals in a project to build a monument in which he and Michael Jackson would be honored and from which he would also benefit financially. Buzz was probably the only astronaut who did not find the concept tasteless and inappropriate. It was never built.

We have all heard stories from some new acquaintance that begins with, "Do you know Buzz Aldrin?" We answer with a cautious "Yes," knowing we are in store for yet another bizarre or embarrassing tale of an encounter with Buzz. Our next reaction is the hope that this new acquaintance doesn't think we are all like that.

Buzz is a very bright guy with the most imaginative ideas for future space exploration of any of the astronauts. When it comes to non-technical matters and his personal relations, he just doesn't know the impression he makes. For some astros, just like some athletes or fading Hollywood stars, they don't know when to quit blowing their own horn or when get off the stage. Buzz finally endeared himself to the rest of us when he slugged some conspiracy theorist who was trying to get Buzz to swear on a bible that he really had landed on the moon. That was in 2002, 33 years after the first landing.

The military hospitals were a grim awakening to reality for me. What little we saw of the local scenery was overwhelmed by the sight of brave, young men, some blind, some missing limbs and all trying to make me feel comfortable in the wards as I talked about spaceflight and home. I thought of Bob Shumaker, my roommate during astronaut selections, and wondered if he was still alive in some Vietnamese prison camp. Here I was, riding the hero trail but I knew who were the real heroes. I could have—should have—been there. There but for the grace of God.

It was on the Australian trip where I began to take stock of the isolation booth the space program had become for me. That month that Lo and I were together represented the longest continuous period of time we had spent in each other's company in six years. I had felt that our marriage was healthier than most and well able to withstand the various pressures of the program. Now I became conscious of how wide the gulf between us had grown because of my job and what had been happening to me, and how much Lo had been shut out of it. We had damn near gotten out of the habit of communicating. I made a note to myself to back off and get a better perspective on the things that counted, starting with my family.

There were times during our Australian swing that I thought of how Lo had made things easier for me in so many ways. The weeks immediately before a flight are loaded with stress factors for an astronaut's family. A wife's reaction can either ease that pressure or compound it. Lo came through beautifully. She was lighthearted as the days passed and on the morning of splashdown her first comment to reporters was, "Walt's just been away for a couple of weeks and now he's back."

During a mission, the crew wives are the focus of continuous media interest. Often a dozen or more reporters and other media representatives would be camped on the front doorstep. They were interested in getting pictures of the family, anything: the wife, kids, goldfish, parakeet. A brief chat with the lady of the house made their day. This sometimes led to embarrassing moments for some of the families. Foot-in-mouth disease was not unusual among a group of women who had never been given any briefing on the handling of a press conference. During the mission, however, NASA did provide a protocol officer to coordinate their contacts with (and protect them from) the media.

Sometimes a wife's behavior during a mission would catch some criticism, if not from her loving husband, then from the other astronauts. It was with some trepidation that a returning crewman caught up on the newspapers that had collected in his absence. He might find himself thinking, "My God, did she really say that?"

I was relieved to read the papers and discover how skillfully Lo had handled herself. She had acted with composure and dignity, had kept the kids under control, and in all the photographs came across as the beautiful woman she is. I marveled at her poise and was proud of her. The flight consumed us all, of course, but Lo avoided the impression some wives gave that the fate of civilization was at stake. She treated it all with just the right touch. It occurred to me just how great an adjustment she had made over the years. We both came from poor backgrounds, with no exposure to fame and high society. Today Lo can hold her own anywhere.

The only surprise I received in scanning those back newspapers was the account of a press conference conducted by General Sam Phillips, the headquarters chief of the Apollo program, immediately after we had splashed down. The general was the first to hail the mission of Apollo 7 as "a 101 percent success." The media picked up the phrase, and the headlines and stories over the next several days spread the word.

My first reaction was that the remark had been taken out of context during the press conference. If not, it indicated that the mission was being appraised, for public consumption at least, on the basis of our technical accomplishments and not the angry exchanges between Wally and Mission Control. Yet I could not honestly reconcile that judgment with my own. After spending the last three of the eleven days doing practically nothing except existing, I could hardly conjure up a picture of a performance above and beyond our objectives.

This probably requires some explanation. After all, you can't understand the score if you don't know how the game is played.

The success of a mission is measured against a comprehensive list of mission objectives. Flight crews are aware of this and are particularly sensitive if they have flown earlier missions that didn't yield the magic number of 100 percent success.

In the early days when nothing was known of man's capabilities in zero gravity, and NASA was not yet numb to the cost of doing business in space, every effort was made to have an action-packed mission. The voice of moderation in workload planning has always been the astronauts'. It didn't take us long to realize the surest way to guarantee success was to insure before launch that the objectives were neither too many nor too difficult.

Our competitive motivation to always look good was consistent with NASA's image-building efforts, and a trend was established that would sometimes produce mediocre workloads and high scores for success. There were both good and bad reasons for keeping certain experiments and objectives off the flight. Without extremely close scrutiny by the flight crew, many half-baked and useless ideas would have been added to many missions. There were always proponents of collecting information—-any information—simply because space is a unique environment. Some information was sought long before anyone had conceived of a way to make use of it.

Such tests, as well as those with a useful but perhaps subtle application, were frequently dismissed by flight crews as gee-whiz experiments. Looking ahead to a triumphant return from the "perfect mission," it was

easy to become overzealous in eliminating useless, unclear, difficult, medical, or scientific objectives. The best way to avoid failure on a complicated test was to eliminate it from the mission.

Astronauts are generally thought of as adventurers, gamblers, and
risk-takers; quite the opposite is true. Our philosophy was to reduce the
risk in all aspects of any operation. Not taking on questionable tasks was
consistent with that philosophy. Never mind that that attitude worked
directly against some worthwhile experiments and engineering tests such
as those with complex protocols and above-average chances of being
screwed up; experiments whose past efforts may have contributed to
embarrassing the flight crew; experiments in which the crew served as
guinea pigs; medical experiments; and scientific experiments, depending
on the prejudices of the particular crewmen involved.

The most diligent efforts of some crews came in the sensitive area of
preflight planning. It kept out the more wild-eyed ideas and insured
flights where mission success was guaranteed before lift-off. The price for
such success was that many valid experiments were dumped and many
days during the latter part of a mission were spent with little to do except
count the hours to splashdown. But the system produced an unparalleled
string of successes.

This attitude gained strong momentum during the early days of Apollo. The crew of Gus Grissom, Ed White, and Roger Chaffee had their own
order of priorities for what was to have been the first Apollo mission.
They went at it as an engineering test flight and, applying that definition,
eliminated anything that even hinted at being scientific. Since they hoped
up to the very last to undertake a mission that would break the fourteen-
day space endurance record, they looked with disfavor on anything that
might compromise that personal objective.

When our crew was scheduled for Apollo 2, we fell heir to everything
they had dumped. With Wally even less enthusiastic about science and
scientists than Gus, his interest sank with each new blivet we inherited.
After the fire investigation and the Apollo program restart, we had
enough leverage for Wally to pull a re-run of the Grissom "engineering
test flight" bit all over again. Minimizing the chance of failure was the criteria applied to eliminate those objectives most demanding of time or talent.

The major effort in flight planning is blocking out the scheduled times
for different activities. Failing to complete an experiment in flight is a

major embarrassment, especially when everyone and his brother can perform it in the 1-g environment on the ground in much less time. Things do take longer in zero gravity, but the contingency times we built in could sure add up when the experiments ran smoothly.

Ground planners get their licks in another way as well. The actual duration of any mission is really an unknown and many things can cause it to be terminated early. To cope with this possibility, not only are more important tests scheduled early, but the entire workload is shifted toward the early part of the mission. That is particularly true (and justified) for the initial flight of any new spacecraft.

So while General Phillips and others described Apollo 7 as a 101 percent success, I always felt we lifted off with a workload planned to about 60 percent of our real capability. We would have accomplished a great deal more had we scheduled twice as much activity and completed only 80 percent of it. Some equipment acceptable to us on the canceled Apollo 2 mission (such as the scientific airlock) were rejected for Apollo 7 and didn't fly until the Skylab missions five years later.

Not all crews approached flight planning and activity scheduling in the same way. They ranged from a very hard-nosed attitude by the Mercury astronauts ("how to go into space without risking public criticism") to the second group of scientist-astronauts ("lay it on me"). Those late arrivals were unaware of their strength vis-à-vis management, were not prima donnas, were responsive to a broader spectrum of requirements, less aware of in-flight problems, and more willing to be judged on how much, rather than what percentage, they accomplished.

The debriefing period encompasses a minimum of ten days of hectic activity. It begins immediately after the shipboard reception, a phone call from the president, a physical examination, and a shower that can only be appreciated by those who have had to bath for two weeks in less than one glass of water. We started our first debriefing tapes before dinner, aboard the recovery ship. These tapes were completed and transcribed and became part of the postflight report.

Verbal debriefings, in some ways, are comparable to a suspect's position in a sordid criminal investigation. They come at us in relays. It began with an all-day show-and-tell with the top brass: program managers, center directors, headquarters people, and the prime contractors. That was followed by special debriefings with the systems engineers and those involved with specific mission experiments, then another daylong session with the other astronauts. In that one we let our hair down, talking and laughing about everything from individual idiosyncrasies on the urine collection device to the things that went wrong which we don't want anyone else to hear about. By the time the media gets hold of a crew, its act has been pretty well polished and the world gets very few surprises.

The serious work of debriefing was interrupted by one humorous incident. While engineers were analyzing systems, Rita Rapp, the nutritionist, was analyzing each of the empty food bags to determine exactly how many calories each man had consumed on the flight. That was going to be a little tough since a fair amount of horse-trading went on after the fourth day in order to maintain our interest in eating and to minimize our weight loss.

Rita was a shy little woman in her forties, very prim and proper. After three days of weighing and measuring, she finally gave up and called us pleading, "Okay, I give up, where is that last food bag I'm missing?" None of us knew what she was talking about until it was identified as chocolate pudding. The one leaking package, wrapped in a fecal storage bag, could be pictured now lost among the thirteen others that had been used for their originally intended purpose. When we told Rita the bad news that it could be found with the boys analyzing the other end of the food chain, she gave a small groan.

We didn't hear for several days. Finally Rita called to say she had located the lost pudding in the *last* of the thirteen bags, which she had carefully unwrapped in pursuit of her data. If that isn't dedication I don't know what is.

As the debriefings continued, we worked on our postflight pilot's report, one of two dozen sections in the official NASA Mission Report. This document receives a wide distribution, which probably accounts for the fact that NASA likes to keep it pretty well laundered and the content consistent with the space agency's desired image.

Consequently, NASA edited out of our crew comments anything that might reflect negatively on planning, hardware design, or poor performance by any individual. Not even self-criticism was acceptable. My primary responsibility was for all of the subsystems except the guidance and navigation system, and I addressed myself to those areas in the pilot's report. Writing that "accurate, on board gauging of the maneuvering thruster propellant system should be a *requirement* for future space vehicles," *requirement* was changed to "great asset" in the final report. When I wrote that part of the cooling system (the evaporator) was over-serviced with water—my goof—and thus not available for use during re-entry, the self-criticism was deleted in the published version.

When reference was made to a mission rule that had been knowingly violated during the flight (the recharging of re-entry batteries which resulted in a potentially dangerous condition when we separated for re-entry), the final report deleted the entire paragraph. The omnipotence of the astronaut and the infallibility of NASA had to be maintained.

Another part of the postflight ritual was less sensitive. After the flight it was routine for each crewmember to be decorated for contributions to manned space flight with either the Distinguished Service Medal (the highest) or the Exceptional Service Medal (second highest). A particularly noteworthy or unique contribution would qualify for the DSM. When the Gemini 6 crew experienced a power kill on the pad, Wally Schirra's decision not to abort—thus making it possible to re-schedule the mis-

The White House Signing of the International Space Treaty in November 1968 with Apollo 7 and Apollo 8 crews, also included Charles Lindbergh, President and Mrs. Johnson, NASA Administrator James Webb and Vice President Humphrey.

sion—earned him the Distinguished Service Medal. The time, place, and person making the medal presentation were determined by NASA's attitude of the moment, the media coverage available, and the political situation. When it was all sorted out, the Apollo 7 crew was to receive its medals from President Johnson at the LBJ Ranch during the first week of November 1968.

I was pleased at the prospect not only for the honor but also for a basic, old-fashioned reason. I was excited that Lo, Brian, and Kimberly — as well as my parents, who were flying in from Los Angeles for the event—were going to meet the President of the United States. On the appointed day the crew and families of Apollo 7 climbed into a NASA Gulfstream and headed for the Texas hill country. President and Lady Bird Johnson greeted us at the jet strip, which had been built on their ranch. Our crew piled into a Lincoln Continental, with LBJ himself as chauffeur, for a quick tour of the ranch. The wives went ahead in another Lincoln with Lady Bird, who chatted with the President by radio.

Later we toured the small ranch house where the Johnsons lived. The place was immaculate and filled with a quiet Texas charm. It was the first opportunity we would have to enjoy the warmth and hospitality of Lady Bird Johnson. We would repeat that pleasure on a number of occasions over the next several years, and each time we were impressed with the ability of this very busy woman to make her guests relax and give the impression that she had nothing else to do except make them feel comfortable and at ease.

The ceremony went off smoothly, with awards going to the Apollo 7 crew and to others, including Tom Morrow, president of the Chrysler division responsible for producing the booster we used. Wally made a brief speech and presented the president with a picture of central Texas, where the LBJ Ranch is located. I had taken the photograph on our second revolution, but unfortunately the ranch itself was hidden behind the Saturn booster in the foreground. After the ceremony, Wally, Donn, and I went with the president to leave our handprints in some concrete stepping stones freshly poured for that purpose. Many such squares, inlaid with visitors' handprints, were used as walkways around the ranch house.

When it was time to leave we had to round up Brian and Kimberly, who had been exploring the ranch with the Eisele kids. As we all walked back to the airstrip, Lo and I knew it had been fun for Brian and Kimberly, but we wondered if they had any understanding of meeting the president and visiting his home. It was important to us that the significance of the visit not escape them.

We need not have worried. At the plane, the president was saying good-bye and shaking everyone's hand. When Brian's turn came, he reached up, took the president's big hand in his, and said, spontaneously, "Thank you for inviting us, Mr. President."

Oh, yes, the medals. We were each presented the Exceptional Service Medal—-NASA hero, second class. We were proud to accept them and they are cherished to this day. At the time, Donn and I discussed what effect Wally's bad temper in orbit might have had on the choice. There was no way of being sure, but later events left little doubt that it was indeed a factor. Every other Apollo crew, ten in all, as well as the nine people who flew in Skylab, received the Distinguished Service Medal.

I knew I had not participated in any of the temperamental exchanges between Apollo 7 and the ground. It was simply not my style but, more importantly, I had too much respect for the flight controllers with whom I had worked so closely for three years. The transcript of all air-to-ground communications bears me out. No doubt, the emotion of the moment and the situation, in general, overrode any desire to draw a distinction between crewmembers. Then, too, there were bigger fish to fry—following the success of Apollo 7; we were going to the moon.

Because I had been so thoroughly embarrassed by Wally's behavior several times during the mission, one of the first things I did on return was to call those people I had worked with and respected at Mission Control. Personally, and for the entire crew, I apologized to John Aaron, the systems engineer who had worked with us in developing the malfunction procedures; Glynn Lunney, the best flight director in the business; and others. Without exception, they assured me that they knew where the problem had been and seemed genuinely glad I shared their sensitivities to the situation. If the working troops who had taken the brunt of Wally's tirades knew and understood the situation, I assumed that those on up the line must understand also. I began to doubt that assumption, however, when I realized some of the guys in our own office weren't too sure whether it was all Wally's show or Wally, Walt, and Donn.

It was months after the flight when I first learned of a rumor that

Chris Kraft (at the time head of flight operations) had been overheard to say—during one of the mission's acrimonious exchanges—that he would see to it that none of our crew ever flew again. It was a difficult story to track down, and not one that Chris would have been happy to know was being passed around. At the time, as Chief Skylab Astronaut, I was working on a program not scheduled to fly until the lunar landings were over. In that respect, it was definitely not a plum assignment. On the plus side, my boss, Tom Stafford, had assured me that my efforts would result in command of the first Skylab mission. With that in the offing, Kraft's animosity could be a fatal obstacle. Very few doubted he carried that kind of influence. After all, who could forget Scott Carpenter's short career?

In the spring of 1969 I decided to confront the rumor head-on and met with Kraft. I laid my cards on the table, told him of my concern, and asked if there was any truth in what I had heard. His reaction wasn't exactly outraged innocence, but he did deny making the remark.

Valid rumor or not, I thought about it when Wally resigned (shortly after the mission), when Donn Eisele was eased out after backing up Apollo 10, and again when I resigned in 1971—all of us without flying again. I still believe the entire Apollo 7 crew was tarred and feathered due to the actions of Wally Schirra during those eleven days in October. We were never collectively hauled on the carpet, and, according to Lunney, no one ever really took Wally individually to task either. The feeling was, well, it's over and it probably will never happen again. The only ass-chewing I'm personally aware of is the one Deke delivered to Wally five minutes after we had returned to the crew quarters at the Cape from the recovery carrier. Donn and I weren't invited but we had the impression Wally did a whole lot of listening.

The motivation, attitudes, and behavior of two-thirds of that Apollo 7 crew were different from Wally's. If two of us felt so differently why couldn't we have changed the atmosphere in the spacecraft during the mission? It is necessary to understand the command structure essential to such complex and demanding operations, the military upbringing of the participants, and Wally's personality to appreciate the difficulty in effecting such a change. The roots of the problem and NASA's willingness to accept the situation can be attributed to the prima donna attitude that was allowed to develop around the Mercury astronauts. Wally was legitimately in command of the spacecraft but he attempted to expand that authority over the entire mission.

I might have done more to effect a change in Wally's attitude during those eleven days. On the other hand, Donn didn't seem particularly sensitive to the reputation we were generating and I could very well have ended up alone in the effort. A full-fledged campaign to change Wally's attitude, if unsuccessful, could have created an untenable atmosphere on board that would have been very detrimental to the mission. It could even have led to early termination. When three people are confined in a 225-cubic-foot cabin for eleven days, nothing seems quite so essential as cooperation and getting along. As the situation actually developed it was extremely embarrassing to me, but my persistent, low-key efforts to keep a lid on it did not disrupt the harmony onboard. Apollo 7 was able to accomplish more than originally planned, although at a cost I did not like. Where professionalism is the name of the game, our crew was labeled as crybabies. To this day, Wally does not feel he has anything to apologize for.

It may sound trite but, for me, the mission came first.

The fame the early astronauts earned really belonged to the job, rather than to individuals. And the ways in which the public confuses individual astronauts helps to keep us humble. The public frequently has no idea which one you are, and they may not even know if you ever flew in space. If you flew a mission, they won't know which mission it was; if they do know, they won't know or care what your assignment was; they won't know if the mission was in earth orbit, or went to the moon, or landed on it. Yet each of us from Apollo is generally referred to as "a man who walked on the moon." They usually feel awkward at not recalling the mission, but even I sometimes have trouble remembering who flew what, where and when.

I have been introduced hundreds of times as a man who walked on the moon, although I have been only 300 miles closer than the reader. After a while it is simpler to not correct this misconception and simply say, "Thank you." Once in a while we give in to our feelings. In 1976 I was in Los Angeles giving a reading of "Madrigals for Space" in a concert performance of the Roger Wagner Chorale. On the sidewalk outside the theater, as I hurried to the performance, one of the musicians in the orchestra caught up to me and asked, "Are you the astronaut?" To which I answered, "Yes." His immediate response was, "Which one?"

I couldn't resist replying: "This one."

It is part of a familiar phenomenon. We are recognized, but not identified. I am most frequently mistaken for Gene Cernan or Scott Carpenter, both of whom I resemble faintly, and sometimes for Alan Shepard, which puzzles me. I don't have Al's steely-eyed stare, so maybe it's the reputation we share for being blunt and often brusque.

Sitting one morning with Louie Welch, then the mayor of Houston, in the coffee shop of the Houston airport, I was asked twice within five minutes for my autograph—once as Scott Carpenter and once as Alan Shepard.

It would be easy to get caught up in the American way of fame. But the postflight glamour is temporary; it's only the fallout, not the main event. We were standard bearers during the lull between flights. It was a little like being the annual winner of a perpetual trophy. The winner's name goes on the silver punch bowl and possession is retained for a short while, but when next year's winner emerges, former accomplishments are returned to perspective as a line of type alongside last year's date.

If these things are forgotten while the spotlight is swinging to the next crew, especially if one begins to believe that he is the anointed one, the letdown can be traumatic. For some it isn't too much too soon, but rather a case of too little for too short a time.

That's why I can say NASA's postflight schedule wasn't to blame for Buzz Aldrin's breakdown. In the opinion of his peers, Buzz was more concerned about having to get off stage than he was at being on. In that hectic Apollo 11 postflight period, there was some exploitation going on, but there was also a lot of capitalizing. When an option was presented, Buzz volunteered for more appearances than most. One of the girls working in the office described it as a "my public deserves to see me" attitude. When it began to wind down, he may have felt someone was stealing his thunder.

I believe the biggest single cause of Buzz's problem was even more fundamental. He was the only member of the Apollo 11 crew who did not feel extremely fortunate and appreciative at their unique role in history. From the time they finished post flight quarantine, Buzz always seemed to be doing a slow burn. He wasn't pleased to be the second man on the moon; he was annoyed as hell that he wasn't the first.

Looking back, I suppose the mental health of all of us would have been better if we had opened an occasional window and let in more of the outside world. Once the echoes of Apollo 7 had faded, I realized I had missed the entire 1968 Olympic Games, held that year in Mexico City. They never even existed for me, and yet as a sports fan I had always followed the day-to-day results hungrily. But with the hectic days before launch, and our days in space coinciding with the games, they just disappeared into the woodwork. My only recollection of the entire spectacle was one message from ground control, reporting that there had been a twenty-nine-foot broad jump by Bob Beamon and an eighteen-foot pole vault by Bob Seagren. Come to think of it, Apollo 7 probably stole a few headlines from the Olympics that year.

10

There's One Born Every Minute

WE WERE ON a magic sleigh ride, soaring above the rooftops and across the heavens, but, unlike Santa, we were taking on baggage, not delivering it.

In the glory years of manned spaceflight, what the country kept forgetting was that we were people. Each of us was, in fact, four people: adventurer, social lion, would-be business tycoon, and political object.

The one thing we did not see ourselves as was heroes. We didn't look in our mirrors each morning and see the Little Shepherd of Kingdom Come. That was something the public craved and the media had created—not that we didn't enjoy the myth, we just never fully understood it.

In whatever we did there existed one universal thread: competition. If we took up handball to stay in condition, friendly matches became bloody tournaments. We hustled to see who could plunge faster and deeper into the more complicated business deals. If we had to take a urine test, we tried to see who could fill the biggest bottle. (Once, when a nurse asked Schirra to leave a urine sample, he obtained a five-gallon jug, filled it with water, poured in a bottle of iodine, and left it on her desk.)

If any of us felt some higher emotion about our work, we did not freely express it. We still don't. I've tried to unravel that in my own mind because any idiot knows we had a special place, at a special time in the history of this country. Could it reflect a subconscious fear that if we admitted this, even to ourselves, NASA might somehow discover they had the wrong guys?

In late July 1973, Al Shepard appeared as a guest on William F. Buckley's television show, "Firing Line." Naturally, they looked back over the years of space exploration and measured the worth of that effort. At the end, questions were invited from an audience that was mildly hostile—well-behaved but anti-space. One young woman asked Al if the astronauts had made a spiritual commitment to this "adventure" in which they were taking part. I believe Al understood the question as having to do with religion—did the astros experience some kind of revelation? And he dismissed it rather quickly. The question was valid and, watching on television, I reacted to it, almost eagerly. It went to the guts of what I consider another astronaut myth—the bland, plastic, programmed human machine myth.

We did, in fact, have a spiritual commitment to adventure. To some of us it damn near was a religion. We were well aware that in the final third of the twentieth century, there were few frontiers left to raise the vision of man. From our unique vantage, space represented the last frontier, the last chance "to strive, to seek, to find and not to yield" until we had found another world. There will be other last frontiers, but this one was ours.

Spiritual? Hell yes! I can't imagine anything more spiritual than the desire and drive and dedication to identify with the heavens, to achieve a oneness with the universe. All the emotion-charged phrases that people usually reserve for religion apply here. The job required that kind of commitment. You had to believe in it. It made you willing to risk your health, your family, your life, and even to lie about things that might kill you, just to experience the exhilaration of exploring whatever was out there. I think Al missed the point there, because if any of us reached it, Al did. But while we were in the program we didn't let such thoughts surface.

We weren't nearly as discreet about the kind of things that tended to chip away the hero's armor. We certainly didn't pay much attention to the words of Satchel Paige: "Go easy on the vices, such as carrying on in society. The social ramble ain't restful."

I had never owned and had rarely had occasion to rent a tuxedo prior to arriving in Houston, but the old hands told us it was a high-priority item. That was an understatement. We were invited to so many social engagements, to so many charity affairs, to so many official (meaning, "by direction") functions, and into so many wealthy Houston oil-gothic homes that we would joke about it, insisting that the program needed a special category of astronaut to handle the night life. We would call them "partynauts."

The social life contributed to the impression that we were living the fat life, that the government was pampering us. But the extent of the government's largess for the "high-living" astro execs while on the road was a magnificent per diem allowance of $16 a day. If it was worked carefully that could support an astro for a whole day in New York—if he slept in Central Park. The point is that astronauts did not get rich in the program, but we did enjoy a standard of living and social life that greatly exceeded our income.

There were constant invitations to spend summer vacations at private guest ranches, holidays at Acapulco resort hotels, and one private game hunt after another. One aspect of this tempting schedule never stopped bothering me: as astronauts, we were usually the focal point in the crowd—and frequently the only ones who couldn't really pay their own way. We were mixing with a crowd that was socially and financially way above us. We enjoyed their standard of living through some kind of artificial insemination.

The new astronaut, of course, was like the little kid pressing his nose against the candy store window. He got an occasional lick of the peppermint stick but when it came to the bonbons, he usually went away hungry, and envious. He might wonder, "Why don't I get invited to the posh affairs? Why can't I get some of the goodies?"

We received so much adulation, for the mere fact of being selected, that it was sometimes difficult to remember what we came to call John Young's Law: "One wasn't really an astronaut until he had been in space." Among those in the know, we were regarded merely as candidates. The guy they wanted for their parties, their balls, and their homes, was the astronaut who had been in space. Then they could ask, "Howazit? What did the earth look like from *up there?*"—all the things that made for good cocktail party, talk. In Houston in the 1960's, nothing dressed up the decor quite like an honest-to-God astronaut. Potted palms had nothing on us.

But the law of supply and demand also applied here. When there weren't enough real live heroes to go around, the new guys would get their chance to fill the cocktail party conversation breach.

As astro pledges we would get such questions as: Is it hard to get in the program? Is the training difficult? Do you think you'll get a flight? What's Al Shepard like? To this day, thirty years after joining the club, I encounter strangers and even old friends I haven't seen in years, who will ask with honest curiosity, "Do you *know* Neil Armstrong?"

It would have been much the same anywhere else, of course, but the fact is that most of it happened in Houston. What happened to us was flavored by the unique texture of that city, its oil riches, its friendliness, its love affair with the big deal and its admiration for those who make them.

And don't forget the Astrodome, Texas' answer to Xanadu. We had damn near carte blanche to whatever might be going on at the "eighth wonder of the world": "Have your secretary call, we'll leave your tickets at the box office." It was partly altruistic, an eagerness to do something nice for the local heroes, and partly just a public relations reflex. The pound of flesh would come when a message would flash on the Astrodome's two million dollar scoreboard, "Welcome Astronaut So-and-so." Then there was the time we and the Schirras were attending a concert at the Houston Music Theater—on passes. We were introduced just before the show started and as we sat down Wally smiled and whispered, "We just paid for our tickets."

In a convoluted sort of way, NASA encouraged our socializing. We were mixing with the community and selling the program. Only rarely did anyone question whether the carefully contrived astronaut image was being well served as we made the rounds from Houston to Washington to Hollywood. Once someone approached Schirra at a party and asked if the drink he held in his hand might not be a bad example for the youth of America. "My son is over twelve," replied Schirra, tartly, "and he's the Boy Scout now."

We were always being shown to the best tables and the best seats. Our first year in town Lo and I were invited to a charity performance by Marlene Dietrich. When we noticed the $100 price on the stub of our complimentary tickets we were stunned. In our travels we were frequently someone's guest at dinner—a politician, a government contractor, or a friend of the space program. That type of entertainment was accepted by us all and we certainly didn't considered it influence peddling. One fallout was that some enjoyed it so much that they expected to be entertained and ceased being appreciative. That attitude helped turn off the faucet for those who came after.

Despite our modest $16 per diem, we were able to really stretch our money. We frequently stayed at the better places, where we enjoyed not a commercial rate, not a military rate, but an "astronaut rate." We couldn't accept free accommodations. Besides, we felt that we should pay *some-*

thing. Our hosts were willing to oblige our pride, and a dollar or two a night struck us as a nice democratic figure — until NASA put a halt to it.

The more experience one gained and the wider his exposure, the more contacts he made. Favors and gifts, ranging from the casual to the substantial, became a habit. It began almost from the day we arrived. The big daddies of Houston opened their hearts, their homes, their offices, and their promotional schemes to us. When the Mercury astronauts landed, they were each offered a *free* home by a millionaire land developer destined later to become the center of the hottest bank and insurance scandal in Texas history. NASA, deciding that such an offer went beyond the bounds of friendliness, said No.

Soon the space agency was in the position of a blocking back, trying to fend the deals off. They kept coming, and though NASA mowed down quite a few, some got through.

Many offers, of course, were honestly made and seemed reasonably unselfish, and we accepted them. The insurance company that provided 4 percent mortgages on our homes never publicized it. It was one more way for me to live beyond my means.

Even before I left California to report to Houston, Al Shepard told me about the "brass hat" cars available from the local Chevrolet organization. These were management-driven cars sold to favored friends at approximately dealer cost, a price so sweet we could drive them for a year and sell them for nearly as much as we paid. We, the third group of astros, were cut in because when it became time to place orders for the new models, the total number was still small, and the deal was big enough to share the goodies. Besides, the parking lot would have looked funny with sixteen haves and fourteen have-nots. As it was, the parking lot looked like Chevy Town. A few years later when our ranks doubled, we went bipartisan—Ford and Chevrolet.

Those were the first brand-new cars most of us had ever owned, and they had an immediate effect on our lifestyles. Corvettes blossomed like crabgrass, setting a pattern for years to come. I ordered a sedan even before I arrived, passing on the Corvette only because I already owned a Porsche. The new Chevy was waiting for us the day we touched down in Houston and I decided, "We're in Fat City. This I could get used to." We weren't cut in on everything, but enough to let us think we were insiders.

When I had learned we would share in the Time-Life and Field Enterprises publishing contract, to the tune of an extra $16,250 for the next several years, Lo and I began to reshape our plans for a modest home in a community adjacent to the space center. Within weeks we went through the exercise of moving from a home in California that had cost $14,500, to talk of buying a new one for $25,000, to consideration of building one for $50,000. Admittedly, that was a wild dream for a rookie astronaut making $13,000 a year, but I went for the better home, gambling on an ever-improving future. It wasn't a sure thing, but it was a helluva good bet.

If we rationalized the favors we accepted, it was on the basis of the most fundamental of all reasons: money. In the cage formed by our media image and NASA obligations, we felt a desperate need to participate and still break even. We were expected to travel all over the map, look great, talk great, act great, and all on $13,000 (or less) a year! To varying degrees it was a conflict that unsettled every man who came into the program. Gordon Cooper once explained it to a writer from *Esquire:* "Being a celebrity is something new to all of us, at least on this scale . . . it isn't always pleasant. We were being used as a kind of shot in the arm to the nation." And Gordo added, "The *Life Magazine* money is all that has kept our heads above water."

Poor *Life.* I doubt that anything they ever printed about us got more publicity, than the contract itself. And poor Field Enterprises. By the time my group got in on the action, Field was shelling out nearly twice as much money as *Life,* but everyone still referred to it as the Time-Life contract. By whatever name, it was, as Cooper said, a godsend to the astronauts. Without it the temptation to moonlight would have been much greater. Rather than contributing to the grubby scrambling that came later, I think it actually held it off till the contracts had expired.

From our point of view, of course, it was a near perfect deal: no reporters hounding us, $100,000 in life insurance provided by the two publishers, and a cash bonanza that, for a couple of years, exceeded our government salaries. And, best of all, there was little we had to do for it.

The initial four-year term of the 1962 contract included an option for four additional years. At first each astro was assured $10,000 a year from Field Enterprises plus $6,250 from Time-Life. However, since the contract called for a maximum total annual payment, equally distributed among all active astronauts, the last year anyone received the full amount was 1965. It looked as though each of us was worth an extra $100,000 over the next eight years—*if* the option was picked up *and* the group didn't grow. Unfortunately, the option was not exercised by Field Enterprises and we grew to seventy-three active astronauts.

But a significant part of all this, one that was consistently overlooked in the debate over the ethics of our accepting money for stories some felt already belonged to the public, was the insurance coverage. The cash was fine, and most of us liked it only a little bit better than our right eye, but at that stage in space travel it was impossible to find an insurance company that would write a policy on an astronaut's life. We weren't covered under the government employees' life insurance policy and when NASA had the opportunity to include us several years later, they elected not to because of the added cost to the thousands of other NASA employees. Fortunately, any of our existing policies that included an "aviation rider" were apparently still in force.

Ironically, it wasn't long after we joined the program—that is, the third group, the Apollo astronauts—that the publishers paid $100,000 death benefits on the lives of Ted Freeman, Charlie Bassett, and Elliot See.

Field Enterprises was particularly generous in their administration of the contract. Even after they had elected not to pick up the four-year option, they continued to pay the widows the full contract benefits as though it were still in effect. It was a no-strings gratuity on the part of Bailey Howard, the Chairman of Field, and reflected the generosity of the entire Field organization toward the astronauts.

In some ways, the contract haunted everyone who touched it. I don't think any of us ever felt that the stories—those by *Life* or Field Enterprises World Book Science Service—did justice to the situations they were intended to describe. We always came out bland, plain vanilla and pretty much alike. Of course, every story, had to be approved by NASA, and that arrangement discouraged anything that looked interesting or spicy.

The writers, all of them, made it as convenient as possible. In a sense they worked for the house. They were friendly and openly rooting for us. Yet time and again they were writing the same stories, under the same conditions, and it was inevitable that we would turn out to be almost indistinguishable from one another. As Robert Sherrod, one of the *Life* writers, was to put it later, "The astronauts came out, as usual, deodorized, plasticized, and homogenized without anybody quite intending it that way."

We weren't too pleased with the results but we salved our critical perspective and our consciences with the money. The publishers were less than thrilled with the results, also and pleaded constantly for more access to the astros, better insights, more honesty, more exclusivity. Various books have been published from the material, including *We Seven,* about the original seven astronauts, and *First on the Moon,* the story of Armstrong, Aldrin, and Collins. Both bombed.

The seven Mercury astronauts each received approximately $25,000 a year for the duration of the Mercury program from *Life,* which turned out to be the only serious bidder for their personal stories. By 1962, when the second, or Gemini, group of astros had been selected, President Kennedy had decided that that contract would not be renewed. The ethics of the whole deal bothered a lot of people but most notably the press, whose sense of moral outrage is always heightened in situations involving its own interests.

The authority for the astronauts to sell their personal stories dated back to the Eisenhower administration. Before the controversy ran its course, just about everyone had taken sides; the press, the public, right on up to the President of the United States.

John Glenn, who had become a particular favorite of the Kennedy family, probably saved the contract. One of the arguments advanced against the sale of our private stories was the obvious one: soldiers in combat also take grave risks, but don't, as a rule, get paid for talking about it. When the president asked John about his feeling on the decision to shut off the *Life* contract, he cut quickly to the point. "I did not deny the old argument that a soldier going into combat might share an equal danger with astronauts," John later explained, "but I felt that if there was enough interest in that soldier's home life, background, or childhood, then he, too, should have the right to receive compensation for opening his home, his family, and his innermost thoughts to public scrutiny that would not otherwise be available."

Although by 1970 the payments had dwindled to less than $3,000 a man, and in 1972 it was $64, the contract was one of the few things in which all astronauts shared equally. Other windfalls were a different story. Some astros had what the marines facetiously call the Semper Fi attitude: "Pull up the ladder, I've got mine."

No one was handing out uncut diamonds or GM stock but Gordon Cooper, for one, was always willing to share, whether it was free Firestone tires or arranging for everyone to own a diving watch. Tires, watches, cameras, and other assorted items came our way occasionally. Some passed them up but a few freeloaded on everything that came their way.

Wally appropriately labeled the activity *"scamming"* and those astros who were really good at it came to be known as "scam artists." Wally, for a long time, had the dubious distinction of being one of the best.

I doubt that any of us ever agonized over any deeper implication of the favors, gifts, and services that were lavished on us over the years. It simply meant that America loved us, and our wives. It would be ridiculous to presume it could influence anyone's judgment; besides, we were never involved in contract awards.

For the lift-off of Apollo 7, I wanted my family to see and understand what it was for which I was willing to invest five years of my life. And I wanted them to feel it emotionally, not just read about it. Since I hadn't broken myself completely of the old-fashioned habit of paying my own way, when NASA wouldn't provide my family government transportation—they couldn't (or wouldn't) draw a line between an astronaut's wife and those of other NASA officials—I automatically booked them on a commercial flight out of Houston.

When I asked a friend to meet them on arrival, he was appalled—I mean, shocked—that the flight crew's family had to fly to the Cape like everyone else. Over my protest, mild though it was, he picked up a phone and arranged for them to be picked up by one of the many corporate planes headed for Florida. Every Apollo flight drew a veritable air force of private jets owned by corporations and business honchos and Texas oilmen. Many of these aircraft were only partially filled and the owners were glad to be personally involved with the mission and its participants. Following my mission, Lo (and sometimes the kids) traveled to or from the Cape on airplanes belonging to Rockwell, Ryan Teledyne, Howard Hughes (courtesy of Bob Maheu), and others.

Although the wives had a lot of legitimate complaints about the neglect and loneliness resulting from their husbands' being totally wrapped up in their jobs, they shared in many of the perks as well. They grew accustomed to the privileges and fringe benefits of the program. They got to fly around the country in plush, private jets. They were the center of attention at club meetings and social functions they attended. In general, they were treated like queens. Some wives found that life harder to give up than the astronauts themselves.

The endless Las Vegas jackpot spitting out all of these good things only created more problems at home. It was a monster that had to be fed. As our standard of living rose, the pressure for a greater cash flow grew. It generally fell to our wives to cope with the monthly budget. The independence they had to develop sometimes further agitated the troubled home life of a family separated half the time.

As each astronaut became more embroiled in the supermarket of life—it was like one of those shoppers' sweepstakes on TV where the wife races up and down the aisles pushing a grocery cart and grabbing meat and canned goods against the clock—the more tempting seemed the business offers that others kept dangling in front of us.

No, not every business acquaintance was out to exploit us, but it paid to suspect that he was. And there was more than one way to exploit an astronaut.

On the one hand, he could know that he was being used and not mind it, because the situation provided what he wanted in return: income or contacts or the promise of a future connection in the business world.

The easiest way to fall into a cesspool of trouble was to be naive enough to always think that they—the big operators—really needed us. That they admired our brains, not just our bodies. That astronaut hero image was directly convertible into dollars if handled right, but no one wanted to be obviously exploited. We saw ourselves as astute and preferred to believe we were being solicited for that reason. Actually, it was nearly always because of our commercial value. The deals usually came to us sugar-coated in order to sell us on *their* program.

In the early seventies, Alan Bean became a director of an insurance company in what appeared to be a really fine deal. Bean is extremely cautious and he negotiated for a nice piece of stock at a very friendly price, on borrowed money, at a brother-in-law interest rate. A few months later he improved on the original deal and it looked like he was on his way to making a killing. The next thing I heard the stock was down, he still owned a lot of it, and he was hoping to get out whole on the deal. In the meantime, the company not only had the services of Alan Bean as a direc-

tor but a whole lot more. He had given the grand tour to company principals at JSC and Cape Kennedy, and entertained them in his home with
the astronauts. The company, in turn, had been able to parade the "company astronaut" when necessary or useful. Just one more astro business
deal that didn't strike gold.

The older hands were always cautioning the young astros against
being too gullible, with a dash of one-upsmanship or gamesmanship lib-
erally applied here and there. Guys like Schirra or Stafford might bad-
mouth a deal simply to give the impression that what you had working
wasn't nearly as good as theirs. And generally it wasn't.

None of this, I hasten to add, was illegal or even shady. We weren't
running guns to the Middle East or filling orders for the fleshpots of
Cocoa Beach. But unless one thought the whole world was a cream pie,
he had to know that when a company tacked your name onto their board
of directors, they intended to use you. Few of our guys had any real business training, and almost no one had experience in the commercial world.
But we knew our reputation had value and figured we should be getting
a quid pro quo.

Looking back, it is remarkable how many of those early associations
ended in disaster. Almost all of us, at one time or another, wound up getting burned. And I can't say we weren't warned. There were Federal Civil
Service rules limiting the business activities in which we could engage.
But, in addition, the NASA administrator distributed a three-page letter
early in the game listing further restrictions that applied to astronauts.

We received a fairly steady stream of the-sky-is-falling memos intended to alert us to the dangers. In essence, we were not to accept part-time
jobs, consulting or lecture fees, or gifts, and we were not to involve ourselves in any way with companies competing for government contracts.
NASA was concerned not only about what we were doing but what we
might *appear* to be doing. Human nature being what it is, the warnings
and restrictions did not eliminate all such activity. That's one of the reasons adultery is so popular, because it's forbidden.

Some of the boys were amused by the fact that the virtue-and-purity
lecture became the duty of Al Shepard, then Chief Astronaut and in the
mid-sixties on his way to becoming a millionaire in banking and real
estate. Actually, there was nothing in the NASA rulebook that said an
astronaut couldn't invest in business, and even participate, so long as it

didn't involve huckstering. When his ear problem grounded him, Al quietly used the contacts he had developed in Houston to build a handsome investment portfolio. Through friends in auto dealerships, banking, and the construction business, Al became a partner in a couple of banks and an investor in shopping centers and discount houses.

Al is a little sensitive to the suggestion that he got rich on NASA's time. But he was able to handle his office responsibilities with about half his energies. He never stopped fighting to get back in line for a flight, and when it came—Apollo 14—he shed most of his holdings and all of his directorships. Of all the Mercury Seven, Shepard's career was the only one aimed well enough to get to the moon. He stuck it out. He survived. I don't doubt that Al would have made a pile of money in or out of the program.

At any rate, neither the memos nor Al's lectures really discouraged us. We felt that NASA was intruding too much into our private lives, including our precious American right to be screwed by some hard-nosed business promoter. It was the old story of Big Brother trying to protect Junior, only once the kid has been to town and seen the bright lights he's not interested in being protected.

Part of the romance of the big deal is being involved with the high rollers. We found ourselves moving with the likes of John King and Clement Stone, Robert Maheu and other men who controlled sprawling business empires in the sixties. But the high rollers weren't immune from catastrophe either. King lost control of his own King Resources and Maheu was fired by his invisible boss, Howard Hughes, in a weird sequence of events that created slightly more publicity than the first moon landing.

In the early days it hardly occurred to us that millionaires were also subject to bad moves and wrong guesses. We learned quickly that if we gave it the personal touch, turned on the astronaut charm, and touched their lives, it was easy, for such men to become enamored of the space program. They became fans and space buffs. Casual contacts with influential people could deepen into friendship but it generally started with that first impression, that big flash, of getting high on the astronauts.

I submit with some regret my first extracurricular business involvement as a classic example of the whole process, better than some in our office and worse than others. It began with the purchase of stock in an electronics company on the recommendation of a lady broker who, it later developed, was dating the president of the company. One of their products was a briefcase telephone, an item that never quite caught on with the masses. The stock was rising, and at the urging of the broker I met with the president of the company, one of the original founders of Litton Industries. He was impressed, he said, by my background; my technical knowledge, my charisma, and, of course, my good judgment in having bought his stock. He invited me to become a director and a consultant, at a retainer of $1,000 a month. That was roughly the going rate for astronauts in the corporate marketplace and not an unusual consulting fee.

This was my first brush with the commercial corporate world, and as near as I could see (not far past the $1,000 per month) the deal looked good. I began unraveling the NASA red tape required to affiliate myself with the company, making the usual declarations that they wanted me because I was such a smart apple and not because I was an astronaut. I also warranted that there would be no exploitation of my position in the company's advertising. The application had to be approved at three levels, up to and including the NASA Administrator, James Webb. (Such approval was required even if no compensation was involved. To become an unpaid director and organizer of the nonprofit Earth Awareness Foundation, I had to go through the same process.)

Though it wasn't made easy for us, NASA tried to not shut the door completely and, except in those cases where a conflict of interest clearly existed, the applications usually went through. The agency could have said a flat "no" to any outside activity. And, given the big club it carried—control of the flight assignments—most of us would have gone along with a minimum of kicking and screaming.

I got my approval, happily pledged my allegiance to my new business "friends," and plunged right in. The company was based in California, and since I was flying back and forth regularly to North American Rockwell, it was convenient for me to stop in occasionally to shake hands or catch a directors' meeting or offer a little advice.

The relationship proceeded so smoothly that I actually did receive a check for the first month's consulting services. For subsequent months, to help the company out, I agreed to accept stock in lieu of salary.

I had originally purchased several hundred shares of stock on the open market. As luck and destiny and my own sense of timing would have it, my one good shot at getting out with a fat profit came during the flight of Apollo 7. The stock doubled in price, reaching its all-time high during our eleven days in space. Several other astros had bought the stock, including my crewmate, Donn Eisele, so we worked out a code through Jack Swigert, one of our CapComs, to pass on the latest quotations. As the price kept rising, Donn and I squirmed, trying to think of some creative way to pass the word to our broker to sell—we never did.

It took six months to realize most of the directors were no better equipped to oversee the business than I, and less prepared to learn. The company began to flounder. The stock fell, and I watched in vain for signs of improvement. As financial problems mounted, the company decided to do a private placement, with the stock offered at "bargain prices." A number of the fellows jumped in with me on the offering—Armstrong, Collins, Bean, Kerwin, Weitz, Anders, Schweickart—-even though I pointedly made no effort to tout them on the stock. But with fine logic, they figured ol' Walt was a director of the company and assumed I wouldn't be there if it wasn't a good deal, so they bought in. It left me feeling like I had sold a used car to a friend, and I kept my fingers crossed that it would all work out.

Next the company became the target of a take-over attempt. An elderly woman, who held a major block of shares, was being romanced by an equally elderly flim-flam man, then under indictment in Los Angeles in connection with another company he owned.

To attack the present management he tried to get at me, planting tips with the television networks and several newsmen that I was a "front man for a bunch of crooks." It was an uncomfortable time. Even though none of the stories was ever aired or printed, I felt trapped.

It took eighteen months for me to wend my way through the following scenario. Phase 1: "I'm just a neophyte at this, so I'll sit here in the board room and see how the big boys do it."

Phase 2: "My God, these guys don't know any more about what needs to be done than I do."

And Phase 3: "Are they honest? I really shouldn't be involved with these guys, but since my friends and relatives have invested I'd better hang around a while to see what I can do."

I finally did resign, and a few months later the company filed for bankruptcy.

I wound up with ten thousand dollars invested in worthless stock, plus a bucketful accepted in lieu of salary, plus the pinched conscience of knowing that friends and relatives had blown some dough as well.

I was not the only astronaut to take such a bath. For men so astute at their jobs, with reasonably good heads, to be taken for such rides in business, can only be attributed to the most naïve assumption of all: we trusted people not to screw an astronaut. In the late sixties this was the cornerstone of many of our business deals.

There was Shepard, operating out there with the captains and kings of industry, and here were the rest of us, losing our lunch money. Tom Stafford was teased about his bad oil deals although he actually only invested in one dry hole. Jim Lovell had his name dragged into Texas' largest bank stock fraud. Frank Sharp, the principal in that one, even promised to make Jim the President of Braniff Air Lines, except for one small detail—he forgot to buy the airline.

Shepard, Slayton, and on up to the line, they must have shuddered each time one of those special requests hit their desk. The topper came when Buzz Aldrin, catching up on things after Apollo 11, sauntered in one day and plopped down on Al Shepard's desk a whole handful of requests to become involved in outside business deals. After that, the agency began to take a harder line on the nature and number of such activities.

Another favorite sport was the stock market.

Occasionally some insider would attempt to ingratiate himself by giving one of us a hot tip on the market. Incredibly, the first five years I invested in the market I never lost a cent. Either I was always listening at the right time or the market was fixed. Whatever, the next four years I never picked a winner and I learned about market cycles.

None of us were what you might call big plungers. If I heard about a stock selling at 5, and I bought a hundred shares and sold at 8, I had made a score, $300, and I was damn glad to get it.

Typical of the way we operated was the tip that Roger Chaffee passed to several of us in 1965 on a company called Liquidonics. Couldn't miss. Roger already had his little edge. He bought it at 4, tipped us at 5, and sold out at 7 1/2. I dumped mine at 7 3/4, on the assumption that Roger had to know what he was doing. And besides, I had made my $200 or so. Liquidonics continued all the way up to 70 and, though none of us exactly ate our hearts out, we did chew a little on the left ventricle.

You could walk down the hall of the astronaut offices and find behind each door a desk piled high with work and an astro—if he was in town. We all seemed to have a phone growing out of our ear and if it wasn't space business, there was a good likelihood we were talking to a broker or lawyer or to some home-state politico about a personal appearance or opportunities on the home-grown political scene.

As an example of this hectic activity, in early January 1969, immediately following his flight around the moon, Bill Anders and I were walking toward his office. As we passed his secretary's desk he called out without even thinking, "Jamie, get Dirksen on the phone." It seems that Everett Dirksen, the Senate Minority Leader, had been trying to reach Bill for several days.

Bill's casual remark, as he stood there in pinstriped suit with vest, struck me as totally incongruous with the "cruddy shoes" Anders selected as an astronaut with me five years before.

Looking back on the heyday of Apollo, I marvel at our collective innocence. An astro would return from a space flight. He would be invited to his home state to speak at several banquets. He would take the standing ovations, hear the cheers, and gaze out upon those adoring faces. Local politicians would see the tremendous crowd appeal and suggest that he run for office. In his head he would suddenly be hearing "Hail to the Chief" or something. It was the siren call of "public service," and the victim would think, "Why not?"

The irony of it was that most astronauts were military men and had lived for years under the Hatch Act restrictions, which prohibited political activity. They avoided national politics, considered themselves transients, rarely took part even in local issues, and were usually absentee voters from their own home districts. Most of them were politically unaware and could be described as *apolitical.* But they had been exposed to the great white light in Washington; visiting in the White House; testifying before Congress to defend the budget and sell the space program. The smell of the power and the glory was a strong attraction.

This astronaut-as-political-prospect began with John Glenn.

By the time I reported to NASA, it was already rumored that Glenn would return to Ohio to run for the Senate seat held by Stephen Young, a seventy-four-year-old Democrat. John was perceived as a hand-picked Kennedy candidate. He was the talk of the office, and the bitterness I sensed among his old Mercury teammates was disturbing to me. I learned later that it stemmed from two causes. John had been the program's straight arrow, pure of heart, the fellow who kept insisting that astronauts had an obligation to the American public not to misuse the fame and power that would surely come their way. We had to set examples. Well, some of the boys wondered if the Senate was where you went to set an example.

I'm sure they felt that John had let them down, that he had capitalized on his stature as an astronaut to launch his political career. John was the first but not the last.

There was another aspect of John's ambitions which bothered them. After that first orbital flight, the country—and the White House—simply adopted John Glenn. Of all the astronauts, he was the one with the most magic goofus dust on his shoulders. While the others were off training for the next Mercury missions, and probably bitching a little about the work load, they could pick up the paper and see photos of John and Annie Glenn skiing with the Kennedys, weekending at Hyannisport, or riding the rapids somewhere with Bobby Kennedy. Scott Carpenter and Wally Schirra felt he should have been at the Cape helping. How much of their feeling was fraternal and how much was simply envy, I couldn't tell. Before it became obvious that the political bug had smitten John, they honestly worried about "the team" breaking up. Wally Schirra was the one who brought it into the open, declaring in a television interview that John's public relations activities had just about washed him out of the space program. He was hopelessly behind.

At the beginning John was about as political as a Saint Bernard. Though he had been given the Kennedy liberal stamp, he was like most military guys, at heart, conservative. I even caught him once with a copy of *Human Events,* a conservative organ, in his mailbox. John simply believed in the old-fashioned virtues: flag, honor, a strong military establishment, and short hair. You can know a career officer all his life without ever being aware of how he votes or if he does. It's like when Eisenhower came home from Europe to run for president. His platform was his grin. No one knew for sure what he was; and he could just as easily have run as a Democrat than as a Republican.

With most military men there is room for growth, and this was true of John Glenn. By the time he made his second race for the Senate in 1968, he actually believed in and supported the liberal issues that his mentors had assumed he favored all along. He had developed his own political consciousness, and it had been shaped by those around him: Bobby and Ethel Kennedy, and McBundy and Sorensen and the rest of the Kennedy crowd.

None of his Mercury fellows could get involved in the campaign and they were probably relieved by the restriction. Rene Carpenter did go to Ohio to campaign for him. I suspect the others were gun-shy and nervous about what such political exposure would mean to them in terms of the program; they were inhibited by all those years of military political isolation. They also must have resented John for making them feel politically uncomfortable.

It really wasn't so surprising that he made the decision to enter politics. When he flew the first U.S. orbital flight he was pushing forty, and he knew the odds were against his making another. As for landing on the Moon, that was way out of range. Given his clear status as the crowd pleaser, the program's Number One hero, there was a feeling in the establishment that John should not take any more risks. As he himself finally put it, "The idea of becoming the world's oldest, used, permanent-training astronaut does not strike me as very good career planning."

John was the tip of the iceberg; then the floodgates opened. Both parties became aware of us as a virgin talent pool, would-be candidates for national office who came with something almost as valuable as a name or money or a famous face. We had charisma.

You could sense it as a guy finished postflight activities or moved into his late thirties. All over the place astros were preening themselves, posing on imaginary runways like beauty contestants, waiting for the phone to ring.

To take the fruitcake, it seemed those who saw themselves as attractive (irresistible?) candidates, all wanted to run for the Senate! They weren't our future sheriffs and city councilmen and justices of the peace. No, sir. These were unselfish men, and if the country needed them to serve in the United States Senate they would not disappoint the public.

There was always scuttlebutt around the office or in the gossip columns about this one or that one considering a plunge into politics or being courted to run. Al Shepard, who may honestly be the only one of us with no such ambition, was sought after in both Texas and Virginia.

At one time Tom Stafford was all but barnstorming across Oklahoma, trying to make up his mind about a race for the Senate. Jim Lovell was the subject of a constant stream of rumors out of Wisconsin. Jack Swigert "confided" that he had been approached to run in Colorado (for the Senate, of course) as was Charlie Duke in North Carolina. Don Lind, a Mormon with no space flight and no charisma, was touted as a prospect in Utah.

Who was Don Lind? A good question that illustrates the depth of the astronaut charisma. Lind was a civilian scientist-astronaut, with ten years of experience and scant prospects of ever lifting off the pad any time soon. He came into the program in 1966 as part of the group which dubbed itself, tongue-in-cheek, "The Original 19." He was pleasant, bright, a naval reserve aviator with better scientific credentials than operational flying experience. He was a classic example of how promotable the image was. If the public were to rank astronauts on accomplishment and recognition—like football's top twenty-five—Don Lind would be listed among "the others." Not a glamour boy, he would toil more than twenty years before making a flight. And yet, in 1971, key people in Utah were encouraging him to run for Congress. As far as his co-workers could see, he had only two things going for him: he was an astronaut and he was a devout Mormon.

In a very real sense, Lind was "Utah's astronaut." That was one of the quirks of the program. NASA had a penchant for sending a guy back to his own state for speeches and diplomatic errands, and naturally we did nothing to discourage it. In some places it magnified territorial pride into something really fierce. (For an occasion I've long since forgotten, I once made a banquet speech in Milwaukee, Wisconsin, Jim Lovell's home state. When I was introduced, I simply said, "I bet you didn't know NASA had more than *one* astronaut," and the place collapsed.)

All of which led to a little disappointment around the office. Some bright opportunist would listen to all the political gossip, assess his own qualifications and conclude he was both electable and draftable. Then he would wonder why a group in Wisconsin was trying to run Jim Lovell for office when his own state had yet to realize they had this hot property waiting by the phone down at Clear Lake, Texas.

For all the maneuvering, real and imagined, that was going on, we engaged ourselves in precious little political dialogue. This was due to military conditioning as well as discretion in getting involved in matters

NASA might regard as too controversial. No prohibition of it, just the ever present sword of crew assignment hanging over our heads.

In 1964 I was one of two astronauts openly supporting Barry Goldwater in the presidential race. The other was Elliot See, who caught some hell about the "Pilots for Goldwater" pin he wore on his lapel. Goldwater had not been a supporter of the space program and that worried most of the people at NASA, even those who identified with his other positions. Favoring Goldwater wasn't a popular thing to do just then, but between being a civilian, a reservist, a near-scientist, and a fresh rookie, popularity wasn't going to be my strong point.

The partisan conversation was sterile and the political activity almost nil with a few exceptions. On the morning after Martin Luther King was assassinated, Buzz Aldrin was leading a memorial parade in downtown Houston. Under the circumstances it was a nervy thing to do, and Buzz caught a lot of flak for it and no end of criticism from the rest of us— behind his back, of course. It was mistakenly assumed by the public that he represented the astronauts when he only represented Buzz Aldrin.

By and large no one knew what the astronauts stood for (other than God and country and the space program), sometimes an asset in itself in politics. There was also the clean image and the fame and romance that went with being space heroes. It's ironic that so few effectively harnessed all that. Only three have managed to get elected: John Glenn on his third campaign for the Senate, Senator Harrison Schmitt on his first try and, many years later, Jack Swigert to congress. My own flirtations, I must admit with a slight blush, were set just as high. My political ambitions grew out of my career as an astronaut, and I wouldn't think of setting my goal any lower than Congress. I was conservative, politically informed, and willing to take a stand and argue a position.

The kind of show business glamour that attached itself to the astronauts had never been a handicap in my home state of California.

Right after joining NASA, I had planned my life around a loose timetable: devote my twenties to education and my thirties to space flight; in my forties, I would work to provide financial security for my family, and in my fifties, assuming I could afford the luxury, I would consider going back into public service. Politics almost rearranged that schedule in late 1970.

When word began to circulate that I was thinking about leaving

NASA, I was approached by several influential groups about running for Congress from California. The attention was flattering, and the notion of running for the House of Representatives seemed more appropriate for a beginning politician than a bid for the Senate. I was immediately faced with the same questions as a Hollywood actor who is criticized for taking a shot at politics; there's glamour and a name but what about the know-how and everything else it takes?

It's a legitimate question, and the only answer I ever heard that made sense came from John Glenn: "Why not, I'm honest, I'm intelligent, I'm capable."

I had the same attitude. The country needs honest men, who can resist pressure and who are reluctant to compromise what they believe in.

An astronaut establishes some valuable contacts. From mine the encouragement was widespread, firm, and consistent. Redistricting had created five new seats in California and I had inside information that the incumbent republican (and a fellow Marine) for the Silicon Valley area was not going to stand for reelection. Considering what Silicon Valley became, passing that one up may have been the biggest mistake of my life.

I was also intrigued with the prospects in my old home district around Santa Monica, where the incumbent seemed to be in trouble. I had delivered newspapers on those very sidewalks, worked at the local RAND Corporation, was considered something of a hometown hero, and would have the backing of the local newspaper.

After a lunch and several other meetings with then Governor Reagan's "kitchen cabinet," I backed off simply because I did not want to run as an astronaut. I knew I would be forced to exploit the space hero image to a far greater degree than I was prepared to. Public service seemed much more attractive when being an astronaut was, perhaps, the brightest of my accomplishments, but not the only one. Politics also takes money. Raising money requires compromising and money has never been a good enough reason for me to modify my beliefs.

When I failed to become independently wealthy in my forties, I came to my senses and eliminated politics from my life's plan.

The fact that there has been so much sound and motion about astro political careers, and so little substance, suggests several things. It might have been our own good judgment winning out. By training, astronauts weigh their chances and don't take unnecessary risks; they calculate the odds against their own capabilities and train it down to a tolerable risk.

Again, those who approached us may have been more astute—or more cautious—than we gave them credit for being. It takes a lot of right answers before those with the connections and the money throw in their support. Perhaps they discovered that "their" astronaut didn't have really strong convictions. Or maybe they were looking for a man who could be steered, molded, and controlled, and that isn't an astronaut's strong suit, either.

Don't be surprised if several more astronauts end up in Congress, and maybe a few statehouses as well. The astronaut charisma won't disappear altogether. There isn't a one of us who hasn't learned to stand up in front of strangers and make an effective speech, the kind that brings them to their feet or brings a little puddle to one eye.

Who knows whether the hero worship, the romancing, the gifts, and free plane rides led to later embarrassments. I can't be sure. Maybe collectively we crawled along, taking what came our way, until a really motivated guy like Dave Scott reached a point where selling envelopes he had carried to the moon didn't seem wrong.

It is easier to get a perspective on the public's reaction. NASA went so far out of its way to paint an image of us as clean and pure, with hearts made of precious metal, that however we slipped it would seem like a fall from grace. As the saying goes, watch that first step. It's a lulu.

11

Don Juan the Astronaut

IT WAS APPARENT that the astronauts had truly arrived as national figures when, in the spring of 1974, a letter about our sex lives appeared in one of America's most widely read columns:

> *Dear Ann Landers:*
>
> *I am curious about a certain aspect of our space program that has never been discussed publicly. Will you try to lift the veil?*
>
> *Since our society has become so sex conscious, and any married man who abstains for an extended period of time is considered an oddity, what measures are taken, if any, to minimize or curb the astronauts' desires?*
>
> *Their "sexual sabbatical" should serve as an incentive to wayward husbands who find it necessary to be away from their wives for extended periods of time. It might help them reassess their motives before they decide to stray.*
>
> Not in Orbit

Ann Landers replied, almost indignantly, that not all men who travel are faithless, and she went on to develop this interesting theory for two paragraphs. But the question went begging. "As for the astronauts," Ann concluded, "only THEY can answer your question. Anyone in Houston want to respond to the lady's question?"

As far as anyone knows, Not in Orbit is still waiting. For what it's worth, the answer is a simple one: Nothing was done to curb our desires. However, we probably thought less about sex during our missions than at any other time. There was little opportunity and, as the scientists might put it, no stimuli.

But that letter wasn't to be laughed off. The question about celibacy in space turned the public's attention to the conflict between our public, Boy Scout image and the party-time gossip. The first clue we received that our extra curricular activities would be grist for the rumor mill was when Deke Slayton delivered his lecture on, "Be a straight arrow or be damned careful." He completely overlooked the "law of unintended consequences." The unintended result was to make us even more aware that the job offered fringe benefits yet unrealized.

In January 1964, as the fourteen of us prepared for our first visit to the Cape, Deke called us together and cautioned us to go easy on the social vices. His immediate concern was the recent arrival in Cocoa Beach of a correspondent for a keyhole rag called *Confidential*.

"You're all big boys now," Deke began, as I recall, "and I'm not going to tell you how to behave, but I will point out a few special pitfalls. Most of you, I hope, won't need this lecture. Most of you are bright enough to know that if you are out screwing around you'd better be damn discreet about it. But all of you are going to get a lot more play from the girls now, and you're going to find that some of the precautions that kept you out of trouble before won't save you here.

"Apparently, the people from *Confidential* have heard that we swing pretty loose and easy around Cocoa Beach. We hear they've now got a man watching the lobby of the Holiday Inn, seeing what they can dig up for a juicy story. They're also watching the rooms in the back at night to see who is coming and going. If you think they'll ignore you because you're new, forget it. So if any of you have hanky-panky in mind, you'd better also think about this: we didn't bring you into this program to be smeared all over some scandal sheet. Any time your outside activities are more important to you than this job, just let me know and we'll arrange for a change."

No one spoke. Deke was to make it clear, time and again, and not just on the subject of chasing girls, that we were expendable. It wasn't so much a threat as a fact of life. We were all selling our services and NASA was the only buyer. They didn't just own us from nine to five, either. They bought us hat, ass, and overcoat, and it was a buyer's market. The fear that they could and would cut us loose before we had flown a mission was what kept us in line. The ever-present threat didn't prevent us from engaging in certain irregular activities, but it did take a little of the fun out of it, and it sure kept us on our toes.

What we didn't realize at the time was the particular pedestal on which the media had placed us. In the years ahead they would contribute to protecting our reputations in a manner usually reserved only for national political figures. Over the years astronauts acquired a kind of underground reputation for bedroom athletics. It never really broke into the open; couldn't damage the White Knight legend, you know. Stories circulated about wild parties (orgies), and the names of some were linked with well-known actresses and entertainers. A brief epidemic of divorces about the time the moon landings were ending raised more than a few eyebrows.

There were some who led the kind of life Hugh Hefner might envy. And there were others who stuck by their marital vows and subsisted on milk and apple pie. But let's face it, we had a lot more opportunity to go astray than the average Rotarian.

What those around us should have understood from the beginning was that, first and foremost, we were fighter pilots. The observation of one friendly psychologist, early in the space program, was quite valid: "They really burned the candle at both ends. They had a tremendous vitality. They would work hard, train all day, and party all night. They did a lot of partying. They drank. I'd try to follow along on some of their activities. I couldn't keep up. I'd just pass out." Aviators have a saying: You can always spot a fighter pilot. He's the guy with a huge watch on his wrist, trying to cash a check at the bar in the officers' club, and ready to swing with the nearest good-looking doll. It's an image which fighter jocks have worked hard to earn.

One of the qualities for which the astronauts were selected, supposedly, was self-discipline. Not everyone was seduced by the lifestyle, but you can believe that all were tempted. I'm only surprised more didn't succumb to the easy times and promising nights.

As a group, I suppose our moral code was about what the national average would indicate—if there is a national average. It is even possible, under the circumstances, that our behavior was better than the gossip and suspicion implied.

Sure, there were astronaut groupies who were not much different from those who tracked rock groups and baseball players. They called and wrote notes and stood ready on a moment's notice to whisk us off to paradise. Some even specialized in only the well-known, a most devastating kind of discrimination to the unflown rabble. The "specialists" might not recognize us if we fell in their laps, until the instant we returned from a flight and qualified for their target list. There was one young astro who hungered after a certain long-legged beauty at the Cape, a good "friend" of the big boys. She wouldn't give him the time of day. However, the very night of his return from his first space mission she jumped at his invitation to a quiet little party for six. When the couple returned to his room at the Holiday Inn her clothes were off before he could turn the covers back. She literally jumped into his bed. She was one of several who managed to collect at least six or eight of our gang. With some women it was clearly a sport, and they were proud of their scorecards.

One woman supposedly presented herself at the offices of *Life* magazine, in New York, offering to sell a story that she obviously thought was a blockbuster. It was her proud boast—which she planned to document in vivid detail—that she had taken to bed every one of the nation's astronauts. She claimed to have batted a thousand. *Life* doubted the authenticity of her claim and, besides, she hardly squared with the image the magazine had promoted of the astronauts as America's Galahads.

Later, when an unofficial survey was taken around the office, there wasn't a single astronaut who even recognized the lady's name. It's possible some could have forgotten.

Miss Tell-It-All wasn't the first to seek publicity for notoriety that may not have been deserved. Every so often we'd pick up a gossip column and read that one of us had a little action going with this or that celebrity. For the next few weeks the wives would be on the hot line comparing notes. After a while they learned that one of the best measures of a story's lack of substance was the very fact that it had appeared in print. No astronaut needed that kind of exposure, but the woman involved always did.

One item in the "you'd-never-guess-who-has-been-seen-together-lately" category involved astronaut Charles (Pete) Conrad and singer Keely Smith, Louis Prima's ex. I first heard about it the way I usually got such information—through my wife. Naturally, she wanted to know if there was any truth to it. It wasn't like I knew for sure but I dutifully took the party line. It sounded absurd and I told her so, but I did take the time to ask Pete how such a story could get started. "It's easier than you think," he said, with a pained grin.

The whole thing began a week or two before. Pete and some friends were having dinner in a Los Angeles restaurant. During the evening a friend at another table had brought Keely Smith over for an introduction. They chatted for about five minutes and, as she was leaving invited Pete to stop by at a birthday party she was giving for one of her children the following Sunday: "The kids would love to meet you." Pete made a polite but non-binding response—"Well, I'll try"—and finished his dinner. Their paths never crossed again. End of story.

Two days after that story circulated I was speaking with Lo from St. Louis, and she eagerly gave me the latest bulletin. "Betty called," she said, giggling uncomfortably. "She heard we were splitting up because you've been dating Keely Smith!"

That's where I came in. To some of the public, all astronauts looked alike!

A more persistent story was one that linked Neil Armstrong and Connie Stevens, a former wife of Eddie Fisher. The story popped up several times over a period of months and always in the region where her act was booked. It was a little out of character for Neil, both in terms of his own behavior and his sensitivity to public opinion. This isn't to portray us as some kind of underdog, but in these circumstances the astronaut had little to gain and virtually everything to lose. For the entertainer, the major consideration was to get her name spelled right.

The bachelor astro was only slightly better off than his married compatriots. His personal life might be able to stand the heat, but he still had the space agency looking over his shoulder. Gossip of any kind made NASA very nervous.

When it became public knowledge that one of the first scientist-astronauts, Dr. Duane Graveline, was having domestic troubles, NASA didn't hesitate to get into the act. Not long after his wife filed for divorce claiming uncontrollable temper, the agency quickly asked for and received his resignation. That was as dramatic an example to the rest of us as a neck attached to a swinging rope was to horse thieves in the Old West.

There were other examples of how NASA took a personal interest in the private affairs of the astronauts. When John Young became involved in a long romance, he was summoned, or so we heard, for a fatherly chat with Dr. Gilruth, the Director of the Johnson Space Center. No one knows what was said behind Dr. Gilruth's door, but the rest of us watched closely to see if he would remain in the flight rotation. He did. (And he married the woman.)

At times we welcomed the help and influence of Big Brother. On one occasion Wally Schirra suddenly found himself with a second wife he knew nothing about. The lady had signed herself in at a Cocoa Beach motel—partly owned by the seven original astronauts—as Mrs. Wally Schirra. She began spending money, cashing checks, and advising everyone within earshot that she was the second and genuine Mrs. Schirra. People were beginning to wonder, and Wally finally turned the matter over to NASA security. They exposed the woman and sent her packing. No one knew where she had come from or where she went.

Over the years, the astronauts also acquired a semi-straight following that mostly parked in the motel lobby and looked at the scenery. We referred to them as "the little old ladies," although in truth they ranged from teenagers to the Grandma Moses type. Most of them were tourists, and they were content just to be where the astros hung out. To avoid a big autograph scene, we developed a technique of hurrying into the lobby, registering on the run and heading for the room without looking left or right. Looking back, I'm sorry now we didn't take a little more time to oblige them. What those ladies had in mind was motherly love, and you didn't have to play games to earn it.

Part of the way we lived was a response to the pressure, the hours, and the womanless world in which we worked; part of it was biological. But much of it was purely fun and games and did not always lead to the boudoir. In fact, we often fumbled away opportunities—opportunities we had angled to get.

Once, I was to speak at a UCLA alumni dinner in Los Angeles, at a swank department store where NASA had placed on display some of the Apollo 11 moon rocks. (Coincidentally, some of them were stolen that night, the first such theft of samples brought back from another heavenly body.) A striking blonde, whom I judged to be about twenty-five, caught my eye during a fashion show that featured some of the local socialites. I was at the head table, sitting between the wife of the UCLA chancellor and the very proper lady who was the evening's program chairman. When the fashion show ended I was surprised and flattered to see the blonde I had singled out walk straight toward me. She held out a program, smiled, and said, "Could I have your autograph for my children?"

This was one of those times when it was anything but annoying to sign an autograph. Returning the smile I said, "My pleasure. What are their names?"

She began rattling them off so fast I did a double take. "Just a second. How many kids do you have?" "Five."

I was stunned. '"Well, how old are they?" I wasn't just being curious. Before writing down, "Eat your spinach" or "Study hard," it helped to know if the kids were five or fifteen.

"The oldest is seventeen," she answered.

"I don't believe it," I said. "How could you have five kids under seventeen?"

"Oh, it was easy," she responded. "I just screwed a lot."

I ducked my head and started writing as fast as I could, not daring to glance at the chancellor's wife. I muttered something inane like, "That's nice," and handed back her program. She smiled and walked off. It wasn't easy that night to pay attention to the program.

The story that probably best illustrates our collective attitude produced an enduring line that could almost have been our motto. Conrad, Gordon, and Bean (the Apollo 12 crew) were friends long before they were teamed up as astronauts, and they were a pretty unflappable combination. They seemed to enjoy themselves regardless of the occasion. After making the second lunar landing, they were guests at a press luncheon in Oklahoma City. Through some private signal, they had called each other's attention to an attractive female reporter in the audience. There was a lot of smiling back and forth, and when Al finally caught her eye he threw her a wink. She caught a lot more than Al was pitching, because when the conference was over and he walked through the lobby, there she sat, waiting for him.

Al paused only briefly. "Sorry honey," he said. "Just testing."

Testing or not, an astronaut generally expects a woman to accept if he asks her out. And she generally does.

We never lacked for vicarious thrills, and some that were not so vicarious, but we tried not to confuse romance with matters of life and death. Jobs that involve some degree of risk seem particularly appealing to men who believe in their own machismo. Most of us like to think that we have a little Don Juan in our blood, if only we had the time. The other wives teased Dick Gordon about his sex appeal, his animal magnetism. But I'm not sure Dick appreciated it when someone dubbed him "the animal."

At the other end of the spectrum were guys so straight that you didn't know whether to admire them or have them stuffed and shipped to the Smithsonian Institution as the last of a vanishing species. The likes of Frank Borman, Stu Roosa, Bill Anders, and the late Ed White represented both a challenge and a threat to the lovers in the group. They were a continuing reminder that no law of nature said you had to be a swinger. Some of the wilder ones would have felt more secure had they been able to bend the straight arrows by offering them favored phone numbers. Then there was the time a particularly tempting dish was delivered up to the door of Ed White's room while we were working in Miami. It could have been thoughtful consideration but was, more likely, an attempt to insure that Ed was "one of us." I really don't know if they ever succeeded. And that was all right, too. Regardless of our preferences, we didn't preach or make moral judgments.

Any group of seventy-three reasonably normal males placed under a microscope could produce results not unlike ours: some fell in love; some broke up their homes; some ran up the score; some kept the faith. Few could resist the battle of wits.

One well-known astronaut was warned by a high NASA official that his reputation was getting out of hand. He was told to be more discreet. A few nights later, to be safe, he drove fifty miles south of the Cape to take a lady friend to dinner. When they sat down and looked around the room, the first face he recognized was that same headquarters big shot, quietly dining with his own beautiful companion.

Another time, several of us had the somber job of cleaning up the personal effects of an astronaut buddy who had died. As we went through his desk and files and closet, his closest friend let out a wounded yell and held up a small address book. "That son-of-a-gun was screwing my girl."—a relationship for which we coined the term "Peters-in-law."

With all the competition that went on and all the potential that existed for mischief, the astronaut record of seven divorces in sixteen years wasn't very remarkable. The seams of several other marriages did undergo great strain. The wonder is that more didn't tear apart.

Of the first forty married astronauts to fly in space, seven were divorced by the mid-seventies —roughly 18 percent. Six of those divorces occurred within a two-year period, leading some critics to suspect we were coming back from space with some kind of social disease or a post-orbital melancholy.

Time, and the fickle interest of the public, have made it possible for an astronaut to get a divorce today and not make news. But it wasn't always so. In fact, the first astro divorce—which took place in 1969, after ten years of manned space flight—was a landmark case for us.

Although he wasn't the first to consider such a move, Donn Eisele was the first to divorce his wife. Harriett had joined the program with him, had enjoyed the good and put up with the bad, and she had been a part of *Life Magazine's* happy-home-life image. Donn's friends didn't judge the merits of his action or try to decide who was at fault. We saw it as a test case to determine whether an astronaut was free to get a divorce without endangering his career.

At the heart of this cause célèbre was a lovely young woman whom Donn had met early in 1968 at a Cocoa Beach party. This was the year we practically lived at the Cape and were regularly involved in the social scene. Susie, who was single, was friendly with the local married set that so often played host to the astronauts. She had been to several of the parties before Donn met her, and some of us knew her as a pretty and intelligent young woman. At the time Donn and Susie met, he was experiencing deep personal problems at home. Harriet Eisele wasn't known for her understanding about the travel and other demands of Donn's job and she carried the added burden of loving and caring for a Down's syndrome child with leukemia.

One night the Eiseles entertained the Apollo 7 crew, and most of our wives attended. Jack Swigert, a bachelor, was there with a new girlfriend (we seldom saw Jack with the same woman twice). As the evening wore on and the drinks flowed, our wives began commiserating about their sorry lot and how particularly tough it had been with their husbands traveling so much. Jack and I were standing to one side listening. Finally, Jack had heard all he could take. He got on his own soapbox and took a position for which most of us privately applauded him. Most of his remarks were directed right at Harriet Eisele.

"You wives are foolish as hell," he said, "if you take this attitude every time your husband comes home. Yeah, we've been off all week in the land of milk and honey and beautiful secretaries. But we're also working our tails off. Your husbands look forward to coming home for a little loving relaxation, not a lot of nagging. You should make them feel great when they get back to town, not like they're taking a dose of medicine. If you don't, some weekend when he's faced with a choice of staying where he is or flying home, he isn't going to make the right decision."

I looked at Harriet Eisele. She seemed amused, certain that Jack had over-dramatized the situation. The other wives weren't so sure.

I thought of Jack's brief lecture in the days when Donn began to lose his enthusiasm for rushing out of the simulator at the Cape on Friday afternoons and making an early takeoff for Houston. He began to volunteer for more than his share of late Friday and weekend duty. We knew what was happening: he was getting serious about a relationship we had all assumed was a casual fling. From time to time Wally or Tom Stafford or I—in fact, all of us—offered him some unsolicited advice. We suggested he go slow.

I don't believe Donn resented our interest. He knew we thought we were looking out for him. At that point, no one suspected that he was headed for a divorce and a new marriage. His extra curricular activities at the Cape did not interfere with his job until the last two weeks before the flight, so we really couldn't butt in too much. He had been around long enough to know that his behavior was more typical than not.

As launch day approaches, the flight crew tries to block out the outside world. That effort reaches a peak the final week. As October 11 and the lift-off for Apollo 7 approached, we weren't getting home at all. Wally and I became concerned that Donn was feeling too much pre-launch pressure or Susie or both. That last week he zipped into Cocoa Beach at every opportunity; the last two days he wasn't even available for several scheduled activities. We were worried, not because he was wrapped up in a girlfriend, but because at that point his mind should have been on a mission that was only hours away. We had obviously underestimated just how serious his affair was.

Following the flight of Apollo 7, Donn was assigned to the backup crew for Apollo 10, then training at the Cape. The romance continued to flourish. When word got out that the Eiseles were getting a divorce, the first reaction around the office was that Donn had fallen overboard. He had violated the first rule of philandering: "It's okay to fool around but don't fall in love."

If the story was only of passing interest to the public, it really got our attention in the office. An astronaut divorce, especially the first one, was bound to attract the notice of the national media. I suspect that Donn already had a timetable in mind for his departure from the space program when he filed for his divorce. Susie wouldn't be just a new wife, moving into the tight little space colony. She was a woman who had traveled in the same social circles as the guys when they were at the Cape. Susie knew us living the bachelor life of men away from home, and it just plain scared the hell out of some, the idea of her getting chummy with our wives.

Not that they really needed to worry. Under the circumstances, when their paths crossed, most of the wives treated Susie as though she were Typhoid Mary. In their view the new woman on the block was married to the "bum" who walked away from his responsibilities—including a retarded child. They could identify all too easily with Harriet.

The Astronaut Wives Club held regular monthly coffees and Susie Eisele's move to Houston had to be the most exciting topic of conversation to reach their tables in years. A few, like JoAnn Carr, and Beth Williams, C. C.'s widow, were in Susie's corner and felt she deserved to be received with courtesy in spite of any negative feelings toward Donn. But there was no way the majority of them were ever going to accept Donn's second wife.

Susie Eisele turned out to be a fighter. After she recognized the frosty, reception in store for her, she quietly passed the word to cool it—the old "people in glass houses" gambit. Many of us, whose Cocoa Beach behavior was not exactly spotless, implored our wives to thaw things out a little. But a few of the diehard wives went so far as to schedule parties when Donn was out of town, so they could avoid inviting Susie and having to speak with "That Woman."

We were all interested in the fallout of Donn's divorce. There were several astronauts, including Scott Carpenter and Gordon Cooper, who had been holding failing marriages together, hoping for another flight. Even those of us with solid marriages waited for the aftershock. Would it bring on a surge of divorce filings? Would life go on? Would NASA try to put as much distance as possible between itself and any culprit who besmirched the Boy Scout, white hat, All-American boy image which they had so carefully nurtured and protected?

Donn was an unlikely candidate to challenge the system. He was not one of the "in group," and most of us in the office could identify with his position in the pecking order. We watched fascinated, not by the personal drama, not with deep concern over the breakup of a family, but with morbid curiosity about the effect on Donn's career and, ultimately, the implications for the rest of us.

It was Donn's casual performance as Apollo 10 backup more than the divorce that alienated the powers that be in the office. His career was definitely not upwardly-mobile. Deke called Donn in and told him he had a couple of months to find another job.

Fair or not, when Donn married Susie it was inevitable that he would resign. He was encouraged to do so by some of the fellows, who were uneasy about how much Susie knew and whether she would respect their confidences once introduced socially to their wives. Tom Stafford was Chief Astronaut at the time and, until then, Donn's good friend and neighbor. The fraternal efforts to keep our family skeletons in the closet at the Cape fell on Tom's shoulders, and he did his best to influence Donn's thinking. When Tom began to hasten the process, Susie paid him a visit. Susie was a bright and tough lady. She reminded him that she knew where a lot of the bodies were buried at the Cape and if he didn't back off she would make sure a lot of others would know too.

Donn knew the score and, I suspect, felt he was keeping faith with his friends when he decided to move on. That decision was hastened by the systematic exclusion and a growing disenchantment with his job. It was greeted with relief from most quarters. He accepted a position with NASA at Langley, Virginia, and a short time later left to join the Peace Corps.

Donn Eisele didn't exactly become a martyr to his fellow astronauts, but at least he had broken the ice for those who felt trapped in dead-end marriages. The prevailing opinion in the office had been that our position as public figures and NASA's obsession with the astronaut image demanded a willingness to tolerate domestic pressures. Now it was different. No one envied Donn his fate, but at least the earth hadn't just swallowed him up. The agency hadn't gotten directly involved in any obvious way. He hadn't been forced out directly over the divorce. He might even have gotten away with it if he had not immediately married an old girlfriend and settled her in Houston and then laid down on the job. It was a scenario that looked rather attractive to those who wanted out of a collapsed marriage.

Think what this meant. Holding things together was part of the price each of us was willing to pay for that ticket into orbit. All of us had been willing to suppress personal feelings, desires, even a home life, good or bad, to keep the gods of space happy. Now someone had crossed the line. It was emancipation day.

By the mid seventies, forty-one married astronauts had gone into space at least once, and it was from this experienced group that the divorces came. Among the thirty who had not flown, only one, Don Holmquest, had cut the cord from his original wife. It could not have had an effect on his career. That was already on the skids.

For a time the favorite question of the news media was: Did space flights somehow change us, make us restless, looking for new directions, new hopes, new wives. The answer is really quite simple. It was a case of men who were used to taking charge, finally returning to the helm of their own lives, and making decisions they had postponed in order to protect their careers. Each astronaut took the step at the end of his flying career.

Scott Carpenter, Gordon Cooper, John Young, Donn Eisele, Ed Mitchell, Al Worden, and Buzz Aldrin were the astronauts whose marriages broke up within 24 months. All seven had made at least one flight, and only John Young would make another. Curiously, after Eisele made the big move none of the later divorces caused much of a ripple around the office or the home front. Donn and Susie had a solid relationship until he died in 1989. It isn't the kind of thing they give medals for, but Donn did make it easier for the others to pursue normal alternatives to their married lives.

Most of the marriages were strong enough to withstand more than the usual load of bumps and shakes. Those who strayed were prudent enough not to let it affect their families—with the exception of Donn and John Young, who divorced his first wife to marry a woman he had loved for years. Those who did obtain divorces followed the usual pattern of eventually remarrying. Does anyone really find anything sensational in these figures? Or is it a fair cross-section of human behavior, given the odyssey we all shared?

The most publicized astronaut infidelity was a crisis in Buzz Aldrin's marriage. He told his wife about the other woman, and in his book, *Return to Earth,* he told the world. My reaction was that Buzz had shown some guts, but little headwork. Buzz thought he was in love. His wife demonstrated patience, and they worked it out—*on that occasion* (Buzz later divorced and remarried—several times). What else is there to judge?

Society, has come a long way since the days when Elizabeth Barrett Browning wrote, "How do I love thee? Let me count the ways," to a time when Masters and Johnson did the counting. My only other reaction to Aldrin's published confession was surprise that so many people seemed unprepared to learn that astronauts had human appetites. Somehow, I don't believe it weakens the great technological achievements won in space to know they were accomplished by living, breathing, emotional, human beings, and not by cold, programmed automatons.

Whether it was the Pressure cooker of the early space program or just the kind of individuals brought together to accomplish its goals, their marital record continued to deteriorate. Of the 23 survivors in the first three groups of astronauts (seven died in the program.), fifteen were divorced before reaching their golden years. I don't know what the current statistics are for the Astronaut Office but, hopefully, they reflect a higher state of marital bliss.

Soon after my own selection I came to realize that being an astronaut would elevate, in some vague and unbiological way, my own sex appeal and social status. The first indication came the day after I was selected. The headline in the next edition of the Santa Monica paper read, "RAND SCIENTIST SEIECTED AS ASTRONAUT." The next morning I had a phone call from a woman I hadn't seen since high school, fourteen years before. In the intervening years we had each married and settled in the same city, yet had never bothered to contact each other. Now, it was as if the ninety-seven-pound weakling had turned into Charles Atlas overnight. Carol came by the office; we had lunch and then strolled along the beach reminiscing about our high school days, when we had dated. I could almost feel the sparks flying, even though I was the same craggy-faced, studious fellow who one day earlier would not have received a second glance. Nothing had changed, except for one story in the evening newspaper. I went back to my office that afternoon feeling slightly heroic.

What makes this subject so delicate is the fact that nearly all of the astronauts were married, although some were married in a very limited geographical sense. During this period, to be an astronaut and a bachelor, well, that was as good as life could get. Just imagine, to have the test pilot swagger, an ample salary (with little overhead), a jet airplane to hop around in, and the highest professional respect. Prize bait in the social fish bowl.

Among the legitimate astro bachelors—C. C. Williams, Jack Schmitt, Ken Mattingly, and Jack Swigert—only C. C. and Swigert took advantage of the great potential of the situation. When C. C. got married toward the end of his first year at NASA, it was up to Swigert to carry the flag.

Jack's coast-to-coast girl chasing was in legendary bachelor style. For short periods Jack would have someone special in his life, someone he thought a little more of than the others, someone to act as hostess at his annual wine-tasting party, someone our wives might recognize from one social function to the next. Jack was part swinging bachelor and part confirmed bachelor. He was a fastidious housekeeper, who complained little about living alone and always seemed informed as to the best buys on meat and canned goods.

Lo and Jack had always gotten along famously, and on occasion she would fix him up with someone we knew. Once Lo arranged for Jack and my younger sister Charlotte and the two of us to go out for dinner. My only concern was whether Charlotte could take care of herself. After all, Jack went through women like Sherman went through Georgia. But no cause to worry. On the appointed evening Jack resembled the Tony Randall character in "The Odd Couple" more than the *Playboy* image of a bachelor. Rather than exchanging teasing banter with his date, Jack and Lo spent the half-hour drive to the restaurant discussing the comparative costs at local supermarket chains.

It is no betrayal of fraternal trust to say that Jack carried on a relentless investigation of the he-she relationship. He covered the full spectrum of female companionship, from White House file clerks to Hollywood starlets. Jack was the kind of fellow who could work all day in Houston or at the Cape and casually make a date for the same night in Los Angeles—and keep it. In his job he was dedicated; in his private hours he was indestructible. It wasn't that Jack scored every time—if he had, his body would now be in a jar at the Harvard Medical Laboratory—but no one ever devoted more time or energy to the chase.

In some respects, Jack's MO—as they say in police work—was the envy of his peers. He had probably collected the fattest telephone book of anyone I have ever known. Whereas many of the guys simply indexed their black books by state, Jack's was truly a living file. One imagined a steady stream of names moving from the category of hot prospects to active players to recently retired. And sometimes he would recycle them as oldies but goodies.

Anyone who traveled with Jack was witness to part of his technique at refueling stops around the country. Typically, we would have just enough time to take a pee, grab a cup of coffee or a candy bar, and file a flight plan while the ground crew refueled our T-38. Whenever Jack pulled into the line, he was in just as big a hurry as the rest of us, but his rush was to the nearest telephone. It didn't seem to matter whether we stopped in Atlanta or Point Desolate, Maine. There was no place beyond the reach of Jack's little black book. If he had the time, he would check in with every girl in the near vicinity, those he had dated and those he was still *"auditioning."* It was a quick, friendly "just-passing-through-and-thought-I'd-say-Hi," but it went over big with the lady of the moment. We rode Jack unmercifully about it, but he seldom missed an opportunity to make a call.

To his credit, Jack never neglected his job, even though he was constantly trolling for a new catch. The impressive thing about Jack was his ability to operate coast-to-coast, thanks to the instant mobility provided by the T-38. I'll never forget one of Jack's four-day grand tours in the summer of 1968. He was working at the Cape, helping us prepare for the Apollo 7 mission. We had a long holiday coming up—the Fourth of July weekend—and as we talked one day Jack proudly related the man-killing schedule he had laid out for himself. Of course, it was planned as a triumphant march across the continent, from the mountains to the prairies to the ocean white with foam. On Wednesday night he would fly to Miami to audition a new prospect he had met down in stewardess heaven. On Thursday it was back to Cocoa Beach for a date, to Atlanta for a hot one Friday night; into Denver, the old home town, for a Saturday night special; and then the big windup Sunday in Sacramento, California.

When Wally Schirra wondered when he had found the opportunity to line up a girl in Sacramento, Jack's answer was right in character. "Remember the press conference we held at the Aerojet General plant last year?" he asked. We all nodded yes. "Well," he said, grinning, "you remember the nice-looking female reporter who followed us around on the tour?"

We all nodded and understood. Jack had kept her on the back burner for ten months, and Sunday night was *the* night. We could hardly wait till Monday to see if he was still alive.

Jack lived through many such trips with no ill effects. He was single-minded and methodical in affairs of the heart, but his success was in no way comparable to his efforts.

Still, among the bachelor astros, he was clearly the team leader. C. C. Williams was active, without being obvious. Ken Mattingly gave the impression that being an astronaut was part of a larger pattern. He was self-disciplined and led an almost ascetic personal life. Then there was Jack Schmitt, who seemed almost wary of the astronaut reputation and the women it attracted. Schmitt was short, dark, handsome, and sometimes alarmed by the more aggressive, liberated females. Office gossip had it that more than one good-looker had been told by Schmitt, "Look, I'm not that kind of a guy. I don't just tumble on the first date. It means more to me than that." To my knowledge, Jack maintained that simon-pure attitude until he married at the ripe old age of fifty.

Swigert was the predatory male in the classic sense. And though we had few bachelors, he wasn't without competition. It came from the few really swinging married guys who, on occasion, worked the same territory as Jack. This was a source of continuing irritation to Jack, who felt his flanks constantly threatened. Whenever he learned that a married buddy was dating one of his girls, Jack would lecture her solemnly on the moral implications of her conduct. "Look," he'd say, "you shouldn't be dating him. He's married. He has kids. You should be dating someone single. Someone without obligations. Someone like me." How much of an impression this appeal made often depended on whether she was herself married.

I don't recall the competition ever turning surly. No punches were ever thrown in defense of any lady's honor, real or imagined, and in a way that's odd when you consider how much sharing was going on. The married guys were amused by the earnestness of Jack Swigert. They were in it for the thrill of the sport, as one of them made clear one day when he made a pass at a secretary in our office.

In the friendliest of gestures, he patted her on the fanny and said, "Say, when are you and I going out to dinner?"

She looked at him innocently. "I couldn't do that," she said. "You're married."

"That's okay," he assured her. "I'm not looking for a wife."

If we begin to sound like so many traveling salesmen, that may not be a bad analogy. We were selling ideas, to engineers or managers or to the public. We were on the road half the time. Our territory was all fifty states and points beyond. We had a shine on our shoes and a smile on our faces. We had one advantage no traveling salesman ever enjoyed: the T-38, our favorite fringe benefit. The "beautiful people," and their private jets had nothing on us.

Pilots would describe the T-38 as a very sexy aircraft. It was hard to look ordinary climbing out of the cockpit of that airborne white stallion, decked in full flight regalia. The T-38 was to many of us the symbol of the astronaut scene, embodying everything essential to the definition of glamour. And rare was the lady who was immune to a personal guided tour through the cockpit of this sweet airplane—in the middle of the night, if necessary. Such was its impact that it eventually gained the unofficial nickname "the golden leg spreader."

I can see where we developed a kind of split personality. There was the astronaut image; the pursuit of a life-style that in other places or other times would never have been accessible to us. Then there was the side that shrank from the image and the fanfare, when we reminded ourselves that at the bottom we could be dull men, sent to do a technician's job.

If we revved our engines at times it was partly to change the pace, partly out of restlessness—our way of burning off excess fuel. More often than not we sought the company of trusted friends, who sensed our moods, knew our rhythms, could keep a confidence, and didn't go bananas if they discovered us in a pub having a drink with one of the local beauties.

That's what we liked best about Cocoa Beach. It encouraged a casualness, an almost barefooted earthiness, that is common to small Florida towns. But there was action if you wanted it. An astronaut could run wild within the limits of his own endurance and the concern he had for his reputation. (Some had very little.) I was standing at the check-in desk of the Holiday Inn one day, when the rather plain clerk behind the counter nodded across the room and said, "Isn't that so-and-so?" referring to one of the more popular astronauts. "Yes, I think it is," I said. She shrugged. "I bet I'm the only woman in Cocoa Beach that hasn't been to bed with him." I went away wondering if she was bragging or just feeling neglected.

It wasn't all Ban-Lon shirts, happy hours, and souped-up sports cars.

Most of us developed friendships with local couples who made us feel comfortable and provided a kind of sanctuary when we needed it. We could let our hair down with the Bishops or the Johnsons (if our hair had been long enough to let down). In their company we could get snockered if we had a notion to and not read about how we disgraced ourselves in the local gossip columns.

They were friends who made no demands and asked few questions. They were always ready to throw a party or babysit with our kids or roast wieners over a beach fire while someone strummed a guitar. One woman, we shall call Gayle, always had a reserve of attractive friends, some married and some single, who were part of the scene. The price of this friendship was to be gossiped about in the parlors of what passed for Cocoa Beach society. There were enough stories floating around about the astronauts to indict any woman seen in the same room with them. Generally, these activities were about as sensual as the Andrew Sisters and the Stage Door Canteen.

We dubbed Gayle and her court "The Vestial Virgins." They would flirt and dance and have a good time, but they'd depart early for the home fires while we dragged ourselves back to an empty room at the Holiday Inn or tore up the highway back to the crew quarters at the Cape.

We also had great times at the home of Al Bishop, a space contractor field representative during the heyday of the space effort. I'll never forget one blast of a party, the night before a launch, that lasted almost to liftoff the next morning. The highlight of the evening was when Donn Eisele decided to swim his way back to the Holiday Inn, a distance of three or four miles. Donn dove into the canal behind Al's house while the guests looked on, their moods ranging from disbelief to hilarity. He splashed out of sight before it occurred to anyone that in his inebriated condition he could drown himself. A search party spent the next hour and a half patrolling the water's edge. We finally discovered Donn fast asleep in a neighbor's backyard.

The crew quarters NASA supplied at the Cape served as a combination dormitory and locker room. Until the preflight quarantine became mandatory after the measles scare of Apollo 13, we lived there more or less at our own convenience. It was handy during late night testing or long schedules, or just to take a breather from the social vices. The crew quarters had just two knocks against it: if we stayed there we lost our per diem, which had been increased to $25 a day, and it was 25 miles away from the action on the beach.

NASA management, of course, looked upon the crew quarters not only as an amenity, but as a means of exercising control and cooling down preflight shenanigans. Even the location and design contributed to that end. They were located on the third floor of a building devoted to engineering, testing, and office space, with people coming and going at all hours of the day and night. But through skill, cunning, and a high degree of motivation, we still managed to bring off an occasional party. There was always a hard core who felt that a failure to do so would constitute a waste of available resources. The traffic in the building and the launch period presence of as many as fifteen astronauts did little to discourage such efforts. For months afterward, the boys were still talking about a social gathering that must have taken place shortly before the last Gemini launch. Late into the night, or early into the morning, they must have gone into the sauna en masse to bake out.

No one might ever have found out except for two clues discovered by the housekeeper the next morning: an empty wine bottle and a bra. Of course, it was possible that someone planted the evidence for a good laugh or to cast suspicion on the crew of Lovell and Aldrin. Incidents like that didn't endear us to management, needless to say, but they made life a lot more enjoyable.

Let's face it, when a person decided to exploit it, the sexual fallout could be a significant fringe benefit of being an astronaut. While the temptations were great to measure up to the picture of the glamorous fighter pilot, man on the move, we did not all succumb. Some stayed clean because of their moral character and others for practical reasons. Traveling so much at night and working during the day could put a big dent in the number of opportunities to make whoopee. It was tough enough trying to keep up with your homework. There were times when one's resolve would be sorely tested by the situations in which he found himself. We didn't have to have a roving eye to find the action. A man not usually inclined to play the game could still be a pushover for a woman who fell into his arms. It still takes two to tango, and a lot of women wanted to dance with an astronaut. They acted like sleeping with him was something special indeed.

Keep in mind it was a small club; most of us knew what the other guy had going. Some of the guys developed their own unique reputation. One of the older heads was known for the great quantities of tail he collected, while another focused on quality with only a small sacrifice in numbers. A third gained a reputation as a man who would screw a one-eyed snake.

Against that background of overachievers there's no doubt about one thing; after some astros left the program their wives' sex life picked up while their own took one hell of a beating.

It should be noted that I have not attempted to justify the way we lived and how we behaved. Whatever the space program achieved in the 1960s, whatever it meant to the American spirit, was made possible by men who responded superbly under extraordinary conditions. The American public wanted heroes, and heroes they got. I just don't believe it dulls their achievements to know that the men who became living symbols of the program were otherwise quite normal.

12

Footprints on the Moon

FROM THE MOMENT their boots made contact with the lunar dust, on July 20, 1969, Neil Armstrong and Buzz Aldrin stood on a new plateau for all mankind. Though each subsequent landing would be increasingly more difficult technically, all would come to be regarded as a kind of encore—a reworking of the path Apollo 11 had blazed before them.

Yet somewhere between Neil Armstrong's small step and mankind's giant leap, came the strides taken by Apollos 7, 8, 9, and 10, enabling America to go that last historic mile. Of the twelve crewmen involved in those first four Apollo missions, only three (Scott, Young, and Cernan) would return to walk on the lunar surface. But all of them—all the men of Apollo—would leave their footprints on the moon.

The lunar landing was one of those stellar events in history, whose success was attributable more to the system than to the individual players themselves. Perhaps it was because of the magnitude of the challenge, or the complexity of the system put in place to accomplish it, or the large number of participants—400,000 workers at the peak. It's hard to imagine anyone doing a better job than Neil Armstrong in man's first landing on the moon. He was near perfect. But so were John Young and Jim McDivitt and Bill Anders and all the others who didn't fly but put Apollo 11 in position to plant the American flag on another body in the universe.

At the height of our national rapture over the landing, Olin (Tiger) Teague, the portly congressman from Bryan, Texas, had an idea. Teague called Deke Slayton and suggested that he, Teague, should get the ball rolling to recommend the Apollo 11 crew for the Congressional Medal of Honor.

Deke gulped. The crew of Apollo 11 had already received the Medal of Freedom, our highest civilian award, personally from President Nixon. Honors were being showered on them at a rate which may have surpassed any other single achievement of man. The general sentiment was that all were deserved.

Slayton listened quietly as Congressman Teague pointed out that the precedent had been established forty years before when Charles Lindbergh became the first man to fly the Atlantic.

It must have been a delicate moment for Deke, whose pride in the success of Apollo 11 was equal to anyone's. But he would oppose any move to single out one astronaut or one crew for the nation's highest honor, and he said so to Olin Teague as firmly and gracefully as possible. He maintained that such an act would be a slight to the rest of the team who had, in effect, run interference for Neil and Buzz and Mike Collins.

There was another consideration, Deke's own awareness, shared by a few others, that the roles of Armstrong, Aldrin, and Collins in this historic event had been determined largely by chance—by the luck of the draw. Years later, as the Apollo program was ending, Deke confided to me that he believed he had prevented the Apollo 11 crew from receiving the Congressional Medal of Honor. It wasn't hard to read him. Deke had wrestled with his conscience at the time, and he was still a little troubled by it.

In no way do I intend to minimize the achievements of Apollo 11, a flight that was a premier event in the long saga of man. But unlike Lindbergh and Columbus, who struck out on their own, without promise of success, Apollo 11 would be selected in an impersonal way to do something immortal.

Sir Edmund Hillary, with Norgay Tenzing, made the first successful assault on Mount Everest by walking in the footsteps of their predecessors. Many with Hillary worked their way to the upper camps where it was decided who would make the final successful push the last short distance to the summit. Armstrong and Aldrin were the Hillary and Tenzing of the Apollo program. The landings which followed Eleven all traveled the same path in space. They used the same building blocks, though each made a slightly different excursion at the end. The first to put together all the building blocks of the four preceding missions was Apollo 11.

I would characterize those five giant steps in the following way:

Apollo 7.   Successful engineering test flight but left a bad taste; con-
            firmed the Command Service module was safe to fly.
Apollo 8.   Public relations success and confidence builder. There was
            even time to say a prayer at Christmas.
Apollo 9.   Unsung test of the Lunar Module. This time the prayers
            were for Rusty Schweickart to get well enough, soon
            enough, so the mission would not have to be repeated.

Apollo 10. A full dress rehearsal around the moon. We spat in the eye of
            the man in the moon.
Apollo 11. Success! The only part of the mission that was performed for
            the first time was the last 50,000 feet to the moon's surface.
            Now, that was a very important 50,000 feet.

In the mid-sixties, who would have thought that the fifth giant step
would put a man on the moon? Certainly not the astronauts. We were too
smart. Oh, yes, we were aware of the plans which, if successful (and it was
a mighty big "if" in 1967 when the mission sequence was formulated),
would place Apollo 11 in a position to attempt the first landing. We just
never expected success to come that smoothly.

From October 1968 to July 1969 we were caught up in an inexorable
string of successes, almost as if it were beyond our control. There was no
time to figure out what we were doing right, only time to keep on doing
it. With each lift-off we were only two months away from the next mission.

When Apollo 7 lifted off on October 11, 1968, on the most ambitious
first flight ever attempted, it all boiled down to one objective: demonstrate
that the Command and Service Modules comprised a safe vehicle for
man's longest voyage beyond the earth's atmosphere. The task was not
only the technical one of testing each and every one of the spacecraft systems. We also had to address any psychological barriers that still
remained. It was essential that confidence be restored in a vehicle born to
problems and disaster. We had remade the Apollo spacecraft, incor-
porating every operational and safety modification for which a case could
be made. The Seven crew believed in it. All that remained was to take her
out of the barn and fly.

Our success, of course, was crucial to the established mission sequence. The space agency had quietly decided a month before our own lift-off that Apollo 8 would travel to the moon—*unless* we turned up something unexpected. At the time, this seemed like our only chance to reach the moon before 1969 and take a clear lead over the Russians in the space race.

From that point on, the Apollo 8 crew would be hanging from the light fixtures until they heard us say, "No sweat. It's a great bird and you can count on it." And that's precisely what we reported.

The Apollo 8 decision was a sound one. The CSMs looked like they were in great shape, while the lunar modules were all slipping behind due to a broad range of problems. We wouldn't have a Saturn V with CSM and lunar module before the spring of 1969.

Coming as it did, before we had even flown a manned Apollo spacecraft, Gene Kranz describes the Apollo 8 decision as "another example of the high-risk, high-gain leadership present at NASA in the 1960s."

Recall that Seven was only the second *manned* Apollo spacecraft and the first one had burned on the pad. Seven accomplished its job by eliminating any lingering apprehensions, which permitted Borman, Lovell, and Anders to set sail for the moon with confidence.

For the first time, on Apollo 8, men in space would be not just thirty minutes away from terra firma, but as long as four days away from their home planet. To achieve that milestone they were prepared to accept even higher risks than the NASA managers who had to give the final go-ahead.

Apollo 8 provided a tremendous emotional boost to the space program for insiders as well as spectators. It proved we could go the lunar distance and, for the first time, the country *knew* we were going to beat the Russians.

In 1968 the Soviet Union was still battling us neck and neck to put the first man on the moon. They had launched the Zond 5 space probe around the moon and back in September. Two months later, they would repeat with Zond 6. The Russians had upstaged us so often that the agency was scared silly they would attempt their own manned circumlunar mission prior to our first lunar landing. We had a way to head that off and give the Russians a show for a change. The Lunar Module might not be ready to fly for several months, but we could send men *around* the moon with what we had.

There was little more that could be accomplished on a circumlunar flight than had been planned for the original high apogee earth orbital mission. The only things new on board were some of the programs in the Apollo computer. The one factor added to the Apollo 8 mission was the distance from the earth—and the potential for a long, slow return in the event of an aborted mission. Everyone was hell-bent for going to the moon, including the Apollo 8 crew. The go-ahead was given.

In its journey, Apollo 8 would experience two sights never before seen by man: the dark side of the moon and the planet earth in its full global splendor. How I envied the crew! In those moments when I had allowed myself to dream of a private experience to carry with me from my years at NASA, it was always of the first view of our planet suspended in its pristine beauty against the black velvet fabric of space.

The first landing on the moon was simply beyond my imagination. The flight sequence was against me, and I dared not covet an honor that seemed beyond ambition. Besides, I asked myself, why should fate place its fickle finger on me? I would assume that most of us went through a similar monologue. It was a way of preparing oneself for the disappointment if the plum fell to someone else—as it did. *Sic transit gloria mundi.*

The big guessing game had been accelerating ever since the office summit meeting of April 1967, when Deke called in the prime and back-up crews for the first three Apollo missions. In his customarily direct way he announced, "The eighteen of you are going to fly the missions that get us to the moon, including the first lunar landing."

We proceeded to lay out two plans; one optimistic and the other *very* optimistic. The first plan called for a landing on the fifth manned mission *without* a prior close approach to the moon's surface. The very optimistic sequence showed a landing on the fourth mission, likewise without benefit of a close approach, (See chart) but no one ever really took it seriously.

At the time, none of us knew on which mission a lunar landing could be safely attempted or how many unsuccessful attempts might be required. Deke wanted an experienced nucleus from which to make crew assignments. Those crews would then rotate their way toward the top of the pyramid. We had the feeling we were reaching the climax of a grand competition. Actually, we had as much control over our futures as lab mice.

Mission

Command Module only in earth orbit.	Apollo 7	Apollo 7
Command Module and Lunar Module in earth orbit.	Apollo 8	Apollo 8
Command Module and Lunar Module in earth orbit. Lunar mission simulation with a 4,000-mile apogee.	Apollo 9	Apollo 9
Command Module and Lunar Module in earth orbit. Lunar mission simulation.	Apollo 10	
First Lunar landing attempt.	Apollo 11	Apollo 10

The way it figured to work was this: if you flew 7, you could back up 10. If you backed up 8, you could fly 11, and so on down the line. The system was subject to change and would, in fact, be modified on several occasions. Coming out of the meeting we knew, when it came time to announce a lunar landing crew, it would be desirable—if not essential—to have all three pilots flight-experienced and through the Apollo training cycle at least once before.

So there it was, down to the eighteen finalists, although several of us—Schweickart, Anders, Eisele, and myself—would be making that qualifying flight a little late in the game. Two of the crews—the Apollo 7 backup of Stafford, Young, and Cernan; and the Apollo 8 backup of Armstrong, Lovell, and Aldrin—met all the qualifications. Only one crew, Seven, had two rookies, Don Eisele and me. (What had Wally Schirra done to deserve that?) But the Apollo 7 mission was the only one cast in concrete and it would be the first out of the chute. Conspicuous by its absence in either plan was a Command Module only mission in lunar orbit—what came to later be called the Apollo 8 mission.

Looking over our group of eighteen, I didn't need a computer to realize I was one of the longest shots in the room. Low in experience, popularity, and political instincts, it had been a long shot just for me to be there. I simply shut off that vision of myself making the first lunar landing. The first view of the planet earth from an altitude above 10,000 miles definitely seemed a more attainable goal.

That one of course fell to the Apollo 8 crew.

Frank Borman is a man capable of success in whatever he attempts. He is a doer and a born leader, but he can be an imperious martinet to those who work for him. He seemed to glow. He wore the smug look of one who knows he will be the anointed one to do *"it,"* whatever *"it"* may be. In many ways he was like Wally Schirra, but smarter and more effective in pursuing his objectives. He made decisions quickly and rationally.

Jim Lovell is an easygoing fellow who delivered uninspired but competent performances. I was first introduced to him as "Shakey," a nickname bestowed on him early in his flying career by his friend, Pete Conrad. Jim's career at NASA was marked by his singular ability to be in the right place at the right time. It carried him to several space endurance records and, in the process, the distinction of being the first man to fly on four different space missions.

But Jim didn't win every hand. The break that made his flight on Apollo 8 possible (Mike Collins' back problem) broke the rotation and cost him a seat on the big one. He would have flown to the moon on Apollo 11 with Neil Armstrong's crew. Instead, the Apollo 13, spacecraft which he commanded, miscarried and his planned lunar landing had to be aborted.

The third member of the Eight crew, Bill Anders, was bright, dedicated, and one of the few people I ever met as stubborn and as serious as myself. A good Catholic with six children, he liked to tell his friends, "In my family there is a king, queen, and serfs." The two of us shared another distinction: we were the only two astronauts to carry the title Lunar Module Pilot with no Lunar Module to fly.

Apollo 8 was another precise, nearly perfect, giant step to the moon. Its unique accomplishment was in removing any psychological barriers associated with escaping the earth's gravitational field—if, in fact, they ever existed. Everyone who could squeeze into Mission Control and in the viewing room behind—some two hundred of us—watched tensely as Apollo 8 disappeared behind the moon for the rocket burn that would commit three lonely human beings to lunar orbit. For nearly an hour, while they passed behind the moon and out of radio contact, back on earth we could only sweat it out. No human power could reach them; no ear could hear their call. And then, at the precise moment they were to appear on the eastern rim—if they had successfully entered lunar orbit—the CapCorn tried to reach them. "Apollo Eight Houston... Apollo Eight Houston, over."

For seconds that seemed like minutes there was silence. Then Jim Lovell's voice confirmed they were in lunar orbit. "Go ahead Houston, Apollo Eight."

He then provided us with man's first impression of the lunar surface: "The moon is essentially gray—no color looks like plaster of paris—sort of gray sand .... "

Anders added, "Looks like a sand pile my kids have been playing in for a long time—it's all beat up—no definition—just a lot of bumps and holes."

It was Christmas week 1968, the second greatest Christmas story ever told. Borman's crew pulled off the public relations coup of the century when they gave a shared reading of the first chapter of the Book Of Genesis on Christmas Eve. Who could help but be moved when Frank began the first of ten verses from the Bible: *"In the beginning God created the heaven and the earth..."*

That moment established Apollo 8 indelibly in the minds of millions of TV viewers around the world as the Christmas mission. Today much of the public thinks of it as the first flight in the Apollo series, an impression that—I am frank to admit—-causes me an occasional twinge. It was a beautiful touch but took a little selling by Borman to get Anders to read from the King James Version of the Bible. Lovell's participation seemed a little incongruous, but he came through loud and clear.

Gossip at the time had it that Borman got the idea from a friend of his with the CIA. That seemed little more than an amusing footnote. Had it been a few years later, of course, the religious reading would have instigated an investigation. The suggestion for the reading actually came from Si Bourgin, of the U.S. Information Agency, who correctly predicted the worldwide reception would be overwhelming.

The Scripture reading was universally well received, with the exception of Madalyn Murray O'Hair, the militant atheist from Austin, Texas. She filed a lawsuit against NASA and the government demanding equal time, or something.

On the tenth and final trip across the back of the moon came the most suspenseful moment of the space program to that time. Shortly before reestablishing contact it was necessary to burn the service module engine for two and a half minutes if they were ever to return home. Talk about a pregnant pause—that was it. Waiting for radio contact at the proper acquisition time, we all held our breath, and when they appeared on time with the spacecraft tracking for home, a loud and spontaneous cheer went up that would be repeated each time this scene was re-enacted in the years following. It seemed only minutes later that Borman reported "Lovell is already snoring."

In the control room we were all laughing then in that nervous way caused by excitement. Borman, Lovell, and Anders had hung their fannies over the cliff and had been able to bring them in on cue. It was not the cheap thrill of a circus stunt or of forcing oneself to dive off a thirty-foot tower or submitting to an impulse to walk the edge of a tall building, but rather the satisfaction of accomplishing an objective, which entailed a lot of risk, professionally, and under control all the way.

Apollo 8 also chalked up another first. After years of dedicated pessimism by the NASA doctors concerning the ability, of man's body to withstand the physiological shock of zero g, they almost had their heyday at the beginning of the mission. For the first time a flight was close to termination because of on-board sickness. The problem had plagued the Russian cosmonauts, but we had never experienced any hint of zero-gravity motion sickness through the six Mercury and ten Gemini flights. Yet, shortly after leaving earth orbit on their way to the moon, Frank Borman became ill with nausea, vomiting, and diarrhea. The symptoms could have spelled real trouble.

Frank later attributed it to a reaction to a sleeping pill he had taken—or maybe a twenty-four-hour virus. Mainly it was a mess. He wasn't throwing up on the floor because there is no floor in zero gravity. When you get sick in space, it's three-dimensional. Lovell and Anders were worried about Frank, but they were also worried about living in a pretty funky spacecraft for seven days as well. Ground control didn't learn about Borman's problem until some ten hours after it struck, when the contents of the on-board tape recorder were played back on the ground. By that time, Frank was coming out of it and no one wanted to terminate. They toughed it out.

NASA doctors had a running frustration trying to impress on us the potential for nausea in a spacecraft in which it was large enough to move around. We considered them prophets of doom and ignored them. (During the first day of our Seven mission, I had personally gone to some lengths to perform my own little experiment, going through all manner of head gyrations in an effort to approach the point of malaise.) None of us felt any motion sickness, even with Wally's cold, and we filed it away as one more bogeyman raised by Chuck Berry's medical troops. It was to become a much more significant problem on Apollo 9.

Borman's crew was the first to receive the full-blown hero treatment since John Glenn, a world tour with international acclaim and honors. I was able to share the public's reaction two months later when Bill Anders and I were inducted into the Explorers Club in New York City. The Eight crew had carried an Explorers Club flag on their epic journey and Anders was to return it at this annual dinner.

We found ourselves on the program with an assortment of explorers: Sir Edmund Hillary, the first man to climb Mount Everest, Jim Fowler, who brought his own giant condor from South America, and another gentleman who traveled by snowmobile to the North Pole. Bill and I felt like kids in the company of such seasoned campaigners, in the kind of room where you'd expect to find Vincent Price playing the organ while the draperies burned. It was Old World.

But I doubt that any of the members had ever been more deserving of honors than Bill Anders was that night. Bill presented the flag and then I listened with envy as he gave a travelogue of his journey to the doorstep of the moon. The slide projector, clicking off photographs taken on the outward-bound journey, created the illusion of an adventure shared. The slides were actually monotonous, all showing the same picture of the earth occupying an ever-smaller portion of the frame. (Enroute to the moon, the spacecraft is oriented such that only the heavens and the earth are visible out the windows. The moon is not seen until passing behind it.) Then he flashed one picture of the earth on the screen and said with studied casualness, "Here we are, one hundred sixty-five thousand miles out."

The room was so quiet you could hear the proverbial pin drop. I realized at that moment, among all those illustrious explorers, that Bill Anders was perceived as the greatest of them all.

I envied Bill as I had envied no man. It gave me pause, knowing that my friend would never seem exactly the same to me again. I'd have given anything to have been able to deliver the lecture Bill was making, but my assignment to Skylab had eliminated my chance of flying anything but an orbital mission in the future.

I felt then, and still do, that Apollo 8's role in the moon landing sequence was more form than substance—a work of art rather than a pushing back of boundaries. But it caused an emotional binge, a soaring of the spirit in a very real sense. In the context of man in space it was unique and wonderful, but if it had never occurred, I feel sure Apollo 11 would still have attempted the first landing. It may have eased any psychological barriers associated with Apollo 10's dress rehearsal around the moon. Of course, that opinion is open to debate.

Chris Kraft, the head of flight operations at the time, has stated that Eight was the keystone of the Apollo program. And countless Americans, to this day, think of it as the first manned Apollo mission.

After Eight, there remained but one important piece of hardware to be tested, the most important piece: the Lunar Module (LM, pronounced "lem"). The first one off the line was christened Spider, an apt description, and took to the air with the Command Module (Gum Drop) on an unheralded mission early in 1969. It was to be flown by one of the better-trained crews ever launched. Jim McDivitt, Dave Scott, and Rusty Schweickart had been in training as a crew since January 1966 when they were assigned as the original backup to Gus Grissom's ill-fated Apollo 1. Jim and Rusty, were the first two assigned to follow the production LM's out of the factory, and a great chunk of their careers hinged on that early decision.

This crew would give the Lunar Module a thorough shakedown. To accomplish this, they would be in the unenviable position of the first to fly a spacecraft in earth orbit *without a heat shield*. The LM was designed for landing on the moon where there is no atmosphere and, consequently, no need for a heat shield. After separating the LM from the Command Module, the only possible way back to earth was to rendezvous with their Command Module, which had the heat shield protection to withstand reentry.

The members of the Apollo 9 crew were looked upon around the office as fair-haired boys, and sometimes referred to with some cynicism as "the rah-rah boys." Through all the ups and downs and changing of gears early in the Apollo program, somebody up there always seemed to look out for McDivitt's crew. With personnel transfusions into Apollo from late Gemini flights, the pad fire, and mission changes due to hardware problems, some astro fortunes rose and others fell but one thing remained constant. From the time we started training for Apollo in early 1966, Mac's crew was assigned the first Lunar Module and, by damn, they would fly the first Lunar Module.

No one was more deliberate or meticulous than Jim McDivitt; no detail was too small if it affected his mission. He eliminated problems by working them to death. When he presented his case he had the facts—the antithesis of Schirra's patented emotional appeal. Most of Jim's contemporaries considered him the "anointed one" among the nine Gemini astros. Looking back it does appear he was given every chance, break, prerogative, and option, beginning with command of the second manned Gemini mission.

Rusty Schweickart would be the LM pilot and perform the first EVA of the Apollo program. He was bright, an idealist, at the intellectual end of our spectrum. As the only civilians in our group of fourteen, he and I spent a brief period after our arrival at NASA as pseudo scientists, sops to the National Science Foundation, which was then lobbying to get one of its own into space.

The third member of this trio, with nearly as much going for him as McDivitt, was Dave Scott. He was the fair-haired boy of our group; well-educated, athletic, with boyish good looks (and frequently an attitude to match). Above all, he was a fine aviator, and his career, too, seemed to have been made in heaven.

There was more reason to be apprehensive about the safety of the first Lunar Module crew than for the passengers on Apollo 8. If things went awry, Jim and Rusty, could find themselves adrift in space in a machine with no capability of returning to earth safely. In that unlikely event, Dave, flying the Command Module, would be called upon to make the first rescue and single-handed space rendezvous. You can believe Dave spent one hell of a lot of time practicing in the simulator for such a contingency.

The Nine mission filled several squares, although Rusty's EVA turned out to be only a shadow of the original plan. This was due to the one major problem experienced during the flight. What had been debatable with Frank Borman on Eight was an indisputable fact with Rusty on Nine: he was sick as a dog for four days. Only determination and drive enabled him to stick it out through some of the most miserable hours known to man. It was the granddaddy of space sickness cases, at least until the Skylab launches in 1973.

Only those who have experienced it can fully appreciate what Rusty suffered, 200 miles out in space, weightless—or what it took to finish the mission as planned. They didn't have weeks or months to adjust, as Skylab would have. To the contrary, their first five or six days were typical of all the Gemini and Apollo missions; overloaded on the front end in case of an early termination. Not yet fully recovered, and still wary of further sickness, Rusty piled himself into his pressure suit, climbed out of the Lunar Module, and performed what little he could of his scheduled space walk.

Nine was a crucial step to the moon, a well-executed engineering test flight. But rare is the layman who recalls there were two missions in the Apollo program that *did not* go to the moon.

Nine left its imprint on Rusty Schweickart. The motion-sickness experts at the School of Aviation Medicine in Pensacola, Florida, found him a cooperative guinea pig in their search for a cure. He threw himself earnestly into helping them develop a conditioning program for those with similar tendencies (although there is still no way to predict who might have them). But when doctors eventually prescribed a head-motion exercise to be followed during the first hours in zero-g, some blamed it for subsequent stomach "awareness."

Rusty's efforts earned him countless rides on a rotating chair at high rates of speed while making a terrific number of head motions. But I don't believe he was ever again seriously considered a candidate for future space flights. His role as a backup commander in Skylab held out the prospect, but it never came to the test. Later events—meaning a wave of zero-g sickness among the Skylab crews—indicated it would not have been a smart gamble. After his return from Apollo 9, Rusty never appeared all that enthusiastic to revisit the scene of his misery. The code required an effort and he made one. If it took a bit of his spark out, no one held it against him.

It was becoming apparent by now that the zero gravity brand of motion sickness was very subjective. It remains a major physiological problem that must be solved if the dream of universal space travel is ever to be realized. Traveling to other planets without a solution will surely make the barf-bag manufacturers rich.

Even before Nine lifted off, the flight crew assignments through Apollo 12 were obvious. It hadn't been determined yet which mission would attempt the first lunar landing, but most of us were guessing that Twelve would catch the brass ring. It still seemed improbable that we could put together the success record necessary to let Apollo 11 go for it.

An Apollo family portrait would picture Nine as an engineering student standing between Eight and Ten, two strapping glamour-boys who traveled to the moon. Politicians advise in any group picture to avoid standing on the end because it is easy to be cut off and forgotten when the results are printed. That is where Seven stood. Apollo 10, next up, was a full-dress rehearsal of the lunar landing.

Just seven months after the flight of the Phoenix, our backup crew of Stafford, Young, and Cernan was ready to fly their own Apollo spacecraft. Apollo 10 carried a veteran crew. Stafford and Young had each made two Gemini flights and Cernan one.

Being a backup crewmember is not the easiest assignment. The responsibility is a great deal more than just training man-for-man and as a unit to fly the mission. It is a support role to the prime crew, handling tasks that the prime crew cannot (or chooses not to). Human nature being what it is, there is a tendency to follow their own downstream mission plans and hardware as closely as possible. They must also train for their role in mission control during the flight. On the one hand, getting the prime crew launched demands everyone's concentrated effort. On the other hand, the key to a backup crewmembers future is more dependent on how well his own anticipated mission goes. It was small consolation to get one's prime crew launched only to find your own mission had gotten completely screwed up before you arrived on the scene. Conscientious efforts at backup training were more than justified if one had to step in and fly the mission, but for this to happen one must wait for his buddy to break a leg, catch the measles, or worse. You couldn't help but feel like a vulture occasionally.

Protocol and historical precedence tend to restrict a backup crewman from knocking heads with the prime crew over an issue, in spite of the fact that the backup crew may be at a higher level of training or experience. When these three backed us up on Seven, their thoughts were frequently on flying Ten to the moon and back. Tom Stafford had lived through two tours of Wally's "even strain" approach to training on Gemini and served as Wally's backup for two years on Seven. He knew Wally well and was better versed on our mission. There were many times when I wished he had pursued his views more energetically when they differed from Wally's. In his capacity as backup commander, he seldom chose to ruffle Wally's feathers, even when he agreed with Donn and me and knew we could use all the help we could get. But Stafford is a politician and his counsel did ease Donn and my pent-up frustrations during the months of working with Wally.

John Young, who backed up Donn, was old reliable. There was nothing spectacular about his work, but John would do anything for which he was called upon, anywhere in the country, on whatever schedule was necessary. He was one of the most uncomplaining, hard workers I have ever known; thorough in his analysis and no-nonsense in his conclusions.

When asked in mid-1967 to evaluate a beefing up of the spacecraft couches to survive a land "landing" (the couches not the crew), he concluded, "Make no mistake, we will be lucky to survive a land landing in this beast. A NORMAL LAND 'LANDING' CAPABILITY DOES NOT EXIST IN THIS VEHICLE. To provide it will cost us two years and many megabucks. It is recommended that we admit this fact and that crews push others to quit adding weight internal to the vehicle that cannot begin to improve crew survivability, in a land 'landing.' And let's go FLY."

Gene Cernan was the other end of the spectrum from John. He met the schedule and filled the squares, but we never got the impression he stayed up late worrying, or working on the problems of Apollo 7. The job was so stimulating and satisfying that most of us were rarely able to put it completely out of mind. Gene never seemed to have this problem. Gene and John kept their counsel with Stafford more than with Wally, and operated more in the role of the Apollo 10 prime crew than the Apollo 7 backup.

With one wild exception, Ten was a perfect test flight. For the first time in three trips no one got sick. Every phase of the LM mission went without fault, except for the final ten minutes of powered descent phase.

Their Lunar Module trajectory took Tom and Gene to 47,000 feet above the surface of the moon where they were setting up for an ascent on the backup guidance system rather than the more sophisticated primary guidance system. They had probably performed this procedure dozens of times in the simulators but when it counted they just got sloppy.

According to Gene, in his book, *Last Man On The Moon:* "I reached over with my left hand and switched navigational control from Pings (primary) to Ags (backup). . . . A moment later, Tom reached out with his right hand and instinctively touched the same switch, knowing that it needed to be changed from one setting to another, and moved it back to where it had been a second before (primary)."

On separating from the descent stage, all hell broke loose. The ascent stage went ass over teakettle. In an operation where everything has been planned to a gnat's eyelash, the unexpected can really scare the pee out of a fellow. With all the conversation going live to the ground, Cernan let out an expletive that was not deleted. In fact, it was heard around the world. "Sonofabitch," Gene blurted, "What the hell happened?"

Tom, mistakenly thinking they were in Ags, threw the switch once more. This actually put them back into Ags and totally confused the computers. After 15 seconds of pure pandemonium and spinning madly, Tom took over manually and stopped the world going around. They made the ascent burn on Ags and flew the rest of the way home uneventfully.

After learning the reason for the outcry, Gene's language seemed quite reserved. Unfortunately they could have been killed by their self-inflicted emergency. It never should have happened.

Once more the unexpected and less important became the trademark of the mission. Apollo 10 was to be remembered as the flight where an astronaut swore while the whole world listened.

Back on the ground, Apollo 10 was serving as the swan song for the youngest of the original seven astronauts, Gordon Cooper. Frustrated, fed up with getting what he took to be the short end of the stick, and weary with NASA's continued intrusion on his private life, Gordo too often seemed to be just going through the motions. Many of us had viewed his case with sympathy, but at this point he lost the support even of those in whom the loyalty instinct died hard. He was getting a raw deal, but that does not excuse giving less than your best.

With Cooper on the Ten backup crew were Donn Eisele, who was always quick to adopt the behavior pattern of his leader. Therefore, he was also operating at less than full speed. Ed Mitchell, the rookie of the crew, was the newest, the youngest, the brightest, and the hungriest, and he went at the training grind as though it were a contest. His performance did not go unnoticed and secured him a seat on Al Shepard's Apollo 14 crew.

With the launch of Ten it became official that Apollo 11 would attempt the first manned landing on the moon. The entire country was examining the crew of Armstrong, Aldrin, and Collins as the products of an exhausting search among the astronauts to find the crème de la crème—to settle on those individuals among all the rest who would be most apt to perform the best job on the most demanding mission in history. They had good credentials and it would be nice to reassure everyone that there was a science to selecting the crew for such a momentous event. But it just wasn't so! In the end, it was more the rotation than the competition that decided which mortals would be the first to land on the moon.

They were not picked by computers, nor by accident, but by a human process that fell somewhere in between. Deke Slayton liked to insist that any of his boys could do the job; that the crucial selection had not been for crew assignments, but to qualify for the job in the first place. We would learn much later that Deke had, from the beginning, reserved the center seats on Apollo for graduates of test pilot schools. The rest of us were headed for the right seats. The only exceptions to Deke's "rule" were by Gene Cernan and Ron Evans on Apollo 17 and only after a gutsy gamble by Gene.

In theory, everyone started even. Fate, politics, and performance, more or less in that order, took over from there. It's politics when the three active Mercury astronauts could take their pick of the Gemini missions, leaving the generally better-qualified Gemini astros to work in behind them. Grissom the first one, Wally the glamorous first rendezvous mission, and Cooper gets the best of the rest of the early missions. In the jockeying for position at the start up of the Apollo program politics took a back seat to fate.

When the original Apollo flight schedule (in 1966, before the fire) got underway, half of those who would eventually fly on the first six missions were still tied up on tail end Gemini crews. Training for the two programs overlapped by more than a year. But when the Apollo 1 fire caused a twenty-one-month delay, all of the Gemini crewmen, including Armstrong and Aldrin, became available for the restart of Apollo.

Even the fire had less effect on the order of things than an earlier shake-up at the end of the Gemini program. When Elliot See and Charlie Bassett, the prime crew for Gemini 9, were killed in St. Louis, the impact on flight crew assignments was the most significant ever experienced. With the first two crew assignments in Apollo already made, astros who had been counted upon to follow in line suddenly became unavailable because of Gemini crew shake-ups, while others who had been expected to be tied up on Gemini for another six months came on the market. Stafford and Cernan, who were scheduled to fly Gemini 12, the last Gemini mission, moved up to Gemini 9, giving them an early bailout to join Apollo. Jim Lovell and Buzz Aldrin, stuck in dead-end spots backing up Gemini 10 (with no Gemini flight to go to from there), moved to Gemini 9 backup and then inherited the last Gemini mission. This twist of fortune gave Buzz the necessary flight qualifications to be considered for the first lunar landing. The subsequent availability or non-availability of many early Apollo crewmen could be traced to this accident.

Ours wasn't the first business where members of a small group found their careers enhanced by the misfortune of a respected peer. Though we never got used to it, we never looked back, either. If we had, we would have noted that while Armstrong was assigned a dead-ended position on Gemini 11 backup, his Gemini 8 crewmate, Dave Scott, had been moved directly into Apollo on Grissom's backup crew. If Armstrong already had a ticket to the moon, it would have made better sense to give him the Apollo experience. So which of the two was the fair-haired boy?

Hardware problems caused still other changes and delays. From the beginning, the first Lunar Module had been the responsibility of McDivitt's crew and they were the most experienced on the LM. Borman's crew had the second LM on the third Apollo mission, which would have taken them to the highest altitude above the earth ever attained: 4,000 miles.

No one was very surprised before Apollo 7 when it became clear that the launch dates for both the McDivitt and the Borman crews were threatening to slip due to delays in manufacture of the first Lunar Modules. One solution to maintain the regular launch schedule was to fly a second Command-Module-only mission, and slip each of the Lunar Modules back one mission. When management committed to that decision, Deke knew it would necessitate switching some crews around. The realignment was obvious. Deke claims he did the courtesy of asking for McDivitt's agreement to drop back to the third mission, and that the single-minded McDivitt's characteristic response was to stick with the LM his crew had lived with for two years. *Afterwards,* he notified Dave and Rusty of his decision. (McDivitt later said Deke had never offered the circumlunar mission to him.)

Borman, always an opportunist, went enthusiastically for the prospect of a circumlunar flight. So, months before a commitment was made to attempt a landing with Apollo 11, we had a crew line-up that looked like this:

Apollo 8.	Prime: Borman, Collins, and Anders
	Backup: Armstrong, Lovell, and Aldrin
Apollo 9:	Prime: McDivitt, Scott, and Schweickart
	Backup: Conrad, Gordon, and Bean

Now we can play the what-if game. If the LM hardware hadn't slipped, or if Jim McDivitt had insisted on flying the second mission, then the following events would have taken place: Borman's crew, with Mike Collins recovered from a back operation, would have flown an earth-orbital mission with Apollo 9; their backup crew of Armstrong, Lovell, and Aldrin would have rotated to Apollo 12, the second lunar landing; McDivitt's crew would have gone around the moon on Apollo 8; and Pete Conrad and Alan Bean, from their backup crew, would have been the first two men to set foot on the moon. The what-ifs for the See-Bassett and Apollo 1 accidents are too much to attempt.

Overriding all of this speculation was a factor that most of us would only learn of years later. Deke Slayton, Bob Gilruth and NASA headquarters had made an agreement, prior to the Apollo 1 fire, that one of the Mercury astronauts would have the first chance at being the first on the moon, if possible. That meant, the first man to walk on the moon would have been the only Mercury astronaut still flying—Gus Grissom.

In early 1968, when all this was taking place, it would have been interesting to know the odds on Apollo 11 winding up as the first moon ship.

That would have been easy compared to parlaying the See-Bassett accident, the Apollo 1 fire, hardware schedule slips, and several individual physical problems to predict which astros would come up with the Apollo 11 brass ring: Jimmy the Greek, where were you when we needed you?

By the time the mission got off the ground, Neil Armstrong, Buzz Aldrin, and Mike Collins had lived for six months with the historical significance of what they were about to attempt. They were an interesting study. Mike had undoubtedly adjusted smoothly to his role and contribution to the mission. Neil could paste an Alfred E. Neuman smile on his face, content in his assignment, and worry, about what he should say on that first small step, while Buzz must have been seething and bubbling inside like a caldron.

Professionally, they made a good team. Mike was pragmatic, Buzz was the theoretician, and Neil was the one with a feel for the hardware and the cool judgment. Everything Neil did was low-key. He flew the X-15 rocket plane early in its development, yet I never heard him mention it. He never seemed to get involved emotionally in an issue and, when he spoke, his tone and delivery gave the impression that his words had been rehearsed. His face has a softness, a pinkness, that will keep him looking younger than he is. He was one of the least athletic of the astronauts; if he felt the urge to exercise he'd lie down until it went away. To those who knew him, Neil wasn't the type to become involved in the super spectacular. Whatever he did, he seldom made mistakes. He was the right man for mission commander.

Like Neil, Mike Collins rarely got involved in office politics or in the issues the rest of us campaigned for. He had a casualness that struck some as laziness, but he was a better technician than he claimed in his book. His EVA on Gemini 10 was the most effective of the program. Mike's one emotional involvement came as a leader of the thriving anti-doctor clique among the astronauts, resisting any attempt to use us as guinea pigs. He was also the best handball player in the office, a ranking I frequently challenged... unsuccessfully.

Buzz Aldrin, the LM pilot, was a puzzle to most of us from the time our group first came together. His dedication to the science of space rendezvous was almost legendary. He was personally responsible for many of the initial steps and later innovations that brought rendezvous to the level of success it enjoyed prior to Apollo 11. Many of the essential aspects of the mission were dependent upon computer software, another of Buzz's fortes.

It was obvious that Buzz was doing a slow burn when the rumors began that Neil would take the first step on the moon. He seemed to have presumed that he would be the first man out, possibly because a very early version of the checklist called it that way. There was never any mystery to the process by which Neil was accorded that honor. The sinister-influence theory—the idea that forces in Washington wanted a civilian to do it—struck me as ludicrous. Neil was the command pilot, a member of the second generation of astronauts. Seniority, the pecking order, and all the sacred cows required that he go first—if going first was the desirable thing to do.

Aldrin's efforts to checkmate Armstrong, which took the form of behind-the-scenes lobbying, much of it aimed at Tom Stafford, irritated many of us. Stafford was deeply involved in the mission planning and Aldrin, as the Lunar Module pilot, was pushing for the final mission plan to show the LM pilot stepping out of the hatch first.

Meanwhile, Aldrin's dad was trying to shake a few trees in Washington to correct the "injustice" of Buzz not stepping out first, perhaps to the embarrassment of Buzz. It wasn't the first time that the elder Aldrin's good intentions had muddied the waters of his son's career. Before Gemini 12, the old colonel had injected himself into the question of the spot promotion, which then *Major* Aldrin would receive after his first space mission. It had become a tradition after a first flight for the parent service to advance their military astronauts to the next higher rank. His Dad's efforts won no friends for Buzz, nor did Buzz's own campaign to beat Armstrong to the moon dust. The whole issue resulted in at least one confrontation between them, but it did not visibly affect their ability to carry out a beautiful mission. His father was still writing letters to the editor months after the flight while Buzz developed a stock response, reminding people, "We both landed at the same time."

The fact is, Neil's footprints are many years older now. That may be a speck of sand in the hourglass of time, as the saying goes, but it is fortunate for the country. The reason is basic. No one knows how Buzz would have handled that pressure, including Buzz himself. But Neil did so with dignity and grace and then retreated to the quiet, scholarly life he had always wanted, as a faculty member at the University of Cincinnati.

The scene at the Cape on the morning of July 16, 1969, resembled a carnival more than the beginning of man's greatest adventure. What a vast difference it must have been from the sailings of the fifteenth- and sixteenth-century explorers, or the dignified departure of Lindbergh's *Spirit of St. Louis* from fog-shrouded Roosevelt Field, Long Island, forty years before. For this trip most of the world was watching. In fact, most of the world seemed to have descended upon Cape Kennedy, squeezing into the firing room and overflowing the VIP bleachers. In living rooms all over America, parents were telling their kids, "Shut up now and watch. The men in that rocket ship are going to the moon," the words sounding not quite believable even to their own ears.

But we believed. Regardless of what else they had going at the moment, most of the astronauts found some excuse to be at the Cape with a million others to watch the United States send its missionaries to another world. At lift-off we pushed with our hearts and our heads, as we had for all the other missions, but we knew that nothing new and earthshaking would take place for three and a half days. Until the final descent and landing, every event, every maneuver, had been performed previously from one to four times.

We reserved our apprehension for the landing, the one thing that had yet to be demonstrated. That's what created our suspense. For the first time, Apollo would go the last 50,000 feet. At Mission Control, shortly after 4:00 P.M. on Sunday, July 20, 1969, we waited as that final 12 minute descent began. We watched displays that even the crew could not see and listened silently for sounds that had yet to be uttered. If a man so much as cleared his throat a hundred other voices shushed him.

I thought, "They are actually going to pull it off." Followed quickly by, "Men that I know are actually landing on the moon." I looked around the room and realized that each of us was separately absorbed in private thoughts of the moment. It was what we had each been working for all those years.

Sitting there in our Walter Mitty world of Mission Control, the private thoughts of each man were penetrated by two events in the final descent. About four mnutes after initiating final descent, Eagle, plunged rapidly toward the surface of the moon, Neil and Buzz began getting a persistent alarm from one of the computers. They were being read on the ground also, and each time Aldrin sang out, "Another twelve-oh-one alarm,"

Cap-Com would come back with, "Roger, alarm." It was the signal for a computer overload, which could play hell with its job of calculating the LM's altitude and rate of descent and it was conflicting with radar data. Simply put, to land safely they had to know how fast they were descending.

The alarms were creating doubt, one of a pilot's deadliest enemies. Confidence had to be restored that the problem would correct itself or that the landing could be accomplished in spite of it. There was no time for discussion. A young engineer named Steve Bales concluded that the computer would clear itself in a few moments. If he felt any hesitation, his manner didn't betray it. In the stillness of the room he nodded and said, "Go, flight," and 6,000 feet from the surface the Eagle was cleared to continue. It is no exaggeration to say that, at that moment, the landing could have been aborted, unnecessarily. The quiet "Go" of young Bales was undoubtedly one of the most crucial decisions ever made in Mission Control.

It is relatively simple to make a life-and-death decision when it is your own life in the balance; making that decision when someone else's life is at stake is a different thing entirely. Bales would confess later, "I was scared to death." He had the knowledge and the guts to make his decision, and for that judgment and decisiveness he would be awarded a Medal of Freedom at a White House ceremony standing alongside the crew of Apollo 11.

At 3,000 feet, Eagle is hit with a couple more 1201 and 1202 alarms but this time it was easier for Bales to give a "Go!"

In spite of the tension and the packed viewing room of VIP's looking over their shoulders, the flight controllers were their usual picture of calm, efficiency and decorum. The viewing room is not unlike the observation level in a hospital when a famous surgeon is operating. People walk softly in and out but the room is always overflowing with professional experience and pride.

Even during the deadest midwatch there is rarely any trivia heard over the two communication loops monitored in the viewing room. Yet within two minutes of landing there was brief consternation and then laughter at a wisecrack heard over the internal loop (within the control center only). Unable to resist the purely American instinct for a gag at the most solemn and critical moments, a young engineer had injected a comment that was cynically in context, yet, in the pressure of the undertaking at hand, outrageously funny, "The president is go for landing," came loud and clear over the speaker. It was triggered either by Mr. Nixon's eagerness to get into the act (he was standing by, via telephone, to talk to them on the moon) or the fact that everyone (including the president) was but a spectator to what was transpiring in our world at that moment. While the world watched, Neil and Buzz made their historic landing. Neil's transmission sent goose bumps around the globe: "Houston, Tranquility Base here. The Eagle has landed."

Charlie Duke, the CapCom, replied, "Roger, Tranquility, we copy you on the ground. You got a bunch of guys about to turn blue. We're breathing again. Thanks a lot."

Make no mistake; the significant event was the landing, not man's footprint in the lunar dust which came several hours later. That was show biz. The first footprints were symbolic, but when that ugly, spidery contraption—"like a praying mantis," as Mike Collins described it—touched its claws to the moon, man had succeeded in one of his most difficult undertakings. It came at the end of a long and tenuous chain of man-made circumstances and occurred nearly two years late by the original timetable. Special credit is due the amazing pieces of machinery that got us there and the thousands of brilliant minds that conceived them. Many call it luck. I have said we were "lucky" to do it in only five flights, but there was no luck involved in getting there. It was the best-documented example in history of science and skill overcoming superstition and ignorance.

As Neil and Buzz were shaping that chain of circumstances to a touchdown with barely seventeen seconds of fuel remaining, they were experiencing the very essence of what living is all about. While science and skill gave them the tools to control their own fate, they, nevertheless, were walking the tightrope that separates life and death. Many men walk that tightrope during their lives, but this time they were coming down the chute to an adventure so fine, it was out where the meter doesn't even register. With the slightest misstep they could find themselves in oblivion as martyred heroes.

All of us who watched and waited thrilled at the vicarious experience of those first two humans walking on the moon. The USSR was the only country that did not air the live broadcast of the first ever moonwalk. Neil was his usual laconic self but Buzz described the scene as "magnificent desolation." The two of them planted an American flag after great difficulty getting the staff far enough into the surface to support itself.

When it came time for lift-off, Mission Control was packed once more, but the atmosphere was not the keen, almost metallic sense of anticipation that grew as the landing neared. Now came the collective urgency of getting them back. It was as though "we" had put them into their hole and now, by God, "we" had to get them out by our concern and prayers. We strained as the Eagle ascended from the moon. Buzz said he looked up long enough at liftoff to see the flag fall over. The LM was climbing away from the surface because everything worked as advertised, including the crew. While Neil and Buzz were still in the boost phase of their departure we were faced with the fact, incredible as it seemed, that the United States had actually pulled it off. We had put a man on the moon within the time promised and nearly within the cost advertised. When it came right down to it, that fifth giant step was easier than we had expected. Maybe, more correctly, the crew and the hardware made the impossible look easy.

In eight short minutes the LM was in lunar orbit and Mission Control began clearing out rapidly. What the hell, the rest had all been done before. We could watch it all on television and have a drink while doing it. Frankly, we assumed the remainder of the mission would be a piece of cake for the guys—relatively speaking, of course. How quickly we take for granted what so recently seemed impossible.

13

A Beaten Path

THE NATION suffered a letdown after the first moon landing, not unlike what a baseball team and its fans must feel when the pennant has been clinched but there are still games to be played. The old team spirit may get bruised but it's a good time for personal goals and controversy and touches of temper.

That was the sense of what happened to us after Apollo 11. That first landing, the beginning, had become an end in itself. What were we to do as an encore? Space agency planning had produced nothing more than a series of ten, basically me-too missions to the lunar surface over a period of approximately thirty months. Each would go to a different site, always a compromise between scientific curiosity and mission risk. Mobility on the moon's surface would be increased and some variation in the science package would be introduced with each landing. To the American people the moon was likened to the old story of the elephant investigated by blind men: whatever they grabbed, wherever they touched, they got an entirely new impression. The moon was being sold as our great gray elephant.

Once Armstrong's crew brought home their color photos and rocks and moon dust, we really didn't expect to get all that many surprises, and Congress, it turned out, wasn't all that interested in unlocking the secrets of the solar system. The space program wasn't selling, which was why the public relations boys began to place more emphasis on the benefits to everyday living that would result from our space discoveries. It was like trying to convince racing fans that the purpose of the Indianapolis 500 was to develop safer passenger cars.

Congress, too, must have concluded that the missions were repetitious, and pressure from that quarter forced NASA, in late 1969, to cancel Apollo missions 18, 19, and 20. There were a lot of wounded squawks when the cuts came and two of the loudest came from the astronauts and the geologists. Up to then the geologists had pretty much treated the moon as their own private sandbox. We, of course, saw nine seats to the moon flying out the window when our life's work was to fly in space.

In my opinion, the cuts were a sensible, prudent move. This country's first space station suffered for five years, while the lunar landings were draining off the lion's share of the space dollars. Had the lunar missions been reduced to, say, five, Skylab would have been in the air two years earlier.

Against this backdrop the ever more challenging missions did seem boring—until Apollo 13. That is why the mission story frequently took a backseat to circumstances surrounding it, before or after.

There was never any question about flying Apollo 12 and it was born in a thunderstorm in November 1969. While Seven had splashed down in the worst weather ceiling ever (200 feet), the record for bad weather at lift-off belongs to Twelve. Visibility was barely two miles, in a hard rain, and by the time the rocket had reached 500 feet only the fire from the engines was visible, burning its way through the clouds. At 1,000 feet the rocket was struck by lightning and the spacecraft was automatically switched to backup battery power. Thirty seconds later it was struck again, and the on-board computer began displaying garbage from the navigation platform. It was not exactly a happy-go-lucky lift-off for Pete Conrad, Dick Gordon, and Al Bean. One more strike and our guys might have been singing "Nearer My God to Thee."

Pete Conrad is a compact five-foot-six, but he had that special presence that stood out in a crowd. Early in the program we thought he was a half-million-dollar-better bet to be the first man on the moon than anyone else in the office. That was when we were working with the Grumman engineers on a "super weight improvement program" for the Lunar Module. NASA was willing to spend $30,000 a pound on any change that would lighten the Lunar Module, and Pete weighed at least fifteen pounds less than any of the rest of us.

He was a Princeton graduate and a career naval officer. As an instructor at the Naval Test Pilot School, he had counted among his students his two crewmates, Bean and Gordon. Pete was bright without being an intellectual, in good physical condition without being a jock, and an independent and outspoken thinker without ruffling too many feathers (a trait I envied). He even got involved in car racing, without catching the flak that Gordon Cooper did for the same hobby.

Pete had the confidence and judgment to be an ideal spacecraft commander. The closest thing around to Pete was Air Force Captain Charles C. Charles, a character, dreamed up by Milton Caniff for his "Terry and the Pirates" comic strip. If you were going to make a movie about an astronaut, Pete is the one you would pick to play the lead.

At least one observer was willing to bet that Conrad would be the first man on the moon. Gerry Morton, of TRW, after wagering $100 on it with a friend, told Chris Kraft about it. Months later, after the first two Apollo flights, Chris was at Gerry's house for dinner. Casually, he said, "Looks like you won your bet, Gerry. Pete will probably be on the first lunar landing."

Buzz Aldrin must have thought so. Years after the fact, Pete told some of us that Buzz had tried to "bribe" him to "dump" Al Bean and put himself on his crew. I am sure it was based on Buzz's perception of his greater capability—especially with rendezvous. When Bean heard it from Pete years later, he, characteristically, just laughed it off.

The timetable then pointed to Apollo 12 as the earliest possible attempt. But as the early missions continued to perform without a serious hitch, Kraft, George Low, and Wernher Von Braun became convinced that the landing would be possible with Apollo 11 and it should be attempted. They believed it enough to carry the plan to the administrator of NASA — Dr. Tom Paine. Paine bought it and, as developments were to prove, their judgment was correct. Of course, in the process, Pete lost out as the first man on the moon.

Dick Gordon is short, dark, good looking, with a raw sex appeal that many of us envied. He is gregarious and cocky, in sharp contrast to his crewmate Bean.

Alan Bean was a thoughtful, cautious type, with the gaunt, balding looks to match. He had a body hardened by college gymnastics and was still in good shape. He was famous around the office for stubbornness in pursuing his own ideas, generally in the area of crew comfort and procedures. He was a native Texan, from Fort Worth and the University of Texas. His instincts frequently clashed with the military system, and while he could always be expected to drop the public pursuit of an idea at a senior's suggestion, he would usually continue to push for it in private.

Pete once said, "When you think you have the door closed on one of Bean's ideas, you had better keep running around to all the side doors to see that he's not slipping it under one of them."

It was a good crew.

While Pete's boys struggled to recover from the lightning strikes and save their mission, Sue Bean and some of the rest of us went to a birthday party for Vice President Spiro Agnew. The party had been organized by Al Bishop, the RCA representative at the Cape. Bishop was about to begin working for Robert Maheu and the Howard Hughes organization but he would remain a regular at each launch, always escorting a mob of Hughes' (or I should say Maheu's) guests attending their first space shot. He also worked with the Secret Service, as an advance man for the vice president's appearances around the country.

The party was to be one of those small, intimate affairs for Agnew's retinue and a few of the astronauts, but it grew to resemble the cast of *Ben-Hur*. To find a spot large enough to handle the crowd while maintaining privacy and security, Bob Maheu shelled out $8,000 to bring a 120-foot yacht up from Miami to Port Canaveral for the party. Once on board, Agnew talked politics and Vietnam and played the piano while the rest of us lounged about and sang. He and his wife Judy were relaxed and delightful company. Years later I thought of that party, sadly, when Ted Agnew resigned from office, a ruined public figure.

At Mission Control that night they wrestled with the question of just how badly wounded was the Apollo 12 spacecraft. For the first time in my recollection, both the flight director and mission director began to shed their ultra-conservative approach. They elected to allow Twelve to continue, while assessing the impact of the lightning strikes. Given a string of unqualified successes, they were moving closer to the crew's go-for-broke attitude. Twelve went on to one of the most impressive technical achievements of the program.

In 1968, NASA had landed an unmanned Surveyor spacecraft on the moon for the purpose of soil sampling and on-the-spot analysis for transmission back to earth. That now-dead spacecraft was resting in a small crater nearly a quarter of a million miles away. One of Twelve's objectives was to return to that site to determine the effect of time and exposure on the Surveyor and to confirm the conclusions reached by that earlier probe.

It was a real challenge to determine the precise location of the Surveyor from a distance equal to ten times the circumference of the earth and then to land within walking distance of that spot. It would be comparable to dropping a grape into a Coke bottle from the top of the Empire State Building.

The general area where the Surveyor had landed was known, but there were hundreds of small craters in the region, any one of which could be sheltering it. Before its demise, the Surveyor had transmitted panoramic, 360° pictures of its surroundings. What followed was the kind of celestial detective work that made the Apollo Program the success it was.

A geologist at the U.S. Geological Survey in Flagstaff, Arizona, studied these and other orbital photographs of the area and identified those craters, which could conceivably have been the nesting place of Surveyor. He then, painstakingly, reconstructed what might be seen, for 360° around, from each of these sites. It was then a matter of matching the photographs from Surveyor with the artist's conception of the view from the crater. The landing site was a bull's-eye, with Pete bringing the Lunar Module down within sight of the Surveyor.

Conrad's words were less than historic but in character when he became the third human being to set foot on the moon. Only Neil Armstrong knows how much thought and rehearsal went into his memorable quote, but we were all impressed with Pete's spontaneity as he paraphrased it. Having safely dropped from the last rung of the ladder, which was still several feet short of the surface, he gulped and said, "That may have been a small step for Neil, but it was a giant leap for Pete."

Years later, Pete told me that he made his non-historic statement to win a $500 bet—a bet still uncollected when he died.

That was Pete—down to earth and practical. What Aldrin saw as "Magnificent desolation," Pete described as, "This is what is known as dirt dirt." Back in space, this "dirt dirt" floated everywhere and left the odor of gunpowder in the cabin.

The Russian space, military, and political establishments probably viewed our accomplishment on Twelve—pinpointing an object and then flying to it from a quarter of a million miles away—as second only to a successful lunar landing itself. The military implications of such a guidance capability were obvious.

A new wrinkle had been introduced for the Apollo 11 post flight routineæquarantine. The crew of Apollo 12 was the second to undergo this experience in the Lunar Receiving Lab, an exercise that was a waste of time and tax money. Most of us believed it was a medical boondoggle by the U.S. Public Health Service, an attempt to get a piece of the lunar action. To justify it, the medics had to first raise the fear that some germ, or some alien particle, would attach itself to the moon walkers and, after hitchhiking to earth, contaminate our planet. It was the stuff of science fiction.

The twenty-one-day quarantine of the Apollo 11 crew had been noteworthy in that by the time they checked into the Lunar Lab, the story of their adventure had already preceded them. When Mike Collins settled into his bunk, sitting at bedside was a paperback copy of *We Reach the Moon: The Story of Apollo 11,* by John Noble Wilford. The book had been written in the weeks preceding the flight and waited only for the successful (or unsuccessful) return to be printed.

Of course, it was easier to get things into quarantine than to smuggle them out. There were several "accidents" during the first use of the lab's biological barrier, and a parade of people were exposed to the quarantine area. Each "victim" was dutifully confined on the other side of the barrier to become a part of the growing in-group. The list included one young lady technician whose motives we jokingly questioned. By the time the three-week sentence was served, the place was just about filled to capacity.

The crews took the quarantine with relatively good humor. "There wasn't a whole lot to complain about," summed up Alan Bean, "and if there was we couldn't do anything about it, so you might as well relax and enjoy it. Besides, it wasn't a bad way to get post flight paper work out of the way. Our debriefings and pilot's reports got finished much more efficiently without the home and office routine."

Eventually even the diehards admitted that exposure to the moon posed no threat to humanity. No germs. No plagues. No blobs percolating in some scientist's back closet. Following Apollo 14 the crew quarantine section of the Lunar Receiving Lab was quietly converted to more useful purposes.

Meanwhile, back at the office, speculation continued about the crews of Apollo 13 and Apollo 14. Some serious political maneuvering was in progress, resulting in Gordon Cooper bowing out to a desk job and Al Shepard becoming America's first and (briefly) last man in space. The same events enabled Jim Lovell to become the first to fly four missions.

In the usual scheme of things, Cooper's crew, having backed up Ten, would fly Thirteen. Lovell's team, backing up Apollo 11, would fly Fourteen. Keep in mind that, even while training for a particular mission, the prime crew feels a certain anxiety until the crew is announced publicly four to six months before the flight. When an unusual delay held up the Apollo 13 announcement, we began to suspect that something was afoot. The gamblers in the office were all betting that Shepard would be taking the ride.

No one argued with Al's right to fly again, but there was near unanimous objection to the way he went about it. The plan began to surface when it started to fall apart at the seams. Shepard's rare inner ear problem had disqualified him from space flight since 1963. He was only allowed to fly NASA aircraft with a second qualified pilot on board. For a man of Al's temperament, ambition, and ability, this kind of dependence had to be a helluva blow to his pride. Al had never let his duties as Chief Astronaut absorb all his time and energies. The excess he channeled into a few personal goals: banks, real estate, and other business activities around Houston.

Since his fifteen-minute sub-orbital flight, Shepard had carried the title of "America's first man in space." Perhaps *tolerated* is a more apt word, in the same way Deke Slayton tolerated such references as, "one of the Original Seven" and "the man who trained the men who went to the moon." As crew after crew took the big ride, Al must have felt like the boy left to guard the sheep while the hunters went after the fox.

In 1969, Al saw the opportunity to remove any question about his ability, real or imagined, in his or anyone else's mind, and he took it. In Los Angeles, he underwent a new and risky operation to correct his inner ear problem. The surgery was kept a secret, but we soon noticed that Shepard was flying the T-38 without a second pilot. He stepped up his physical fitness program and began to disengage himself from his outside businesses.

Some of us got the message that Al was back and he was going to the moon. The next opportunity was Apollo 13, and Al was obviously moving himself into the driver's seat in Cooper's place. It was a power play, pure and simple, with the horses to back it: Al Shepard and Deke Slayton. Al was pushing for what he believed to be rightfully his, while Deke was eager to establish the precedent that a man wasn't eliminated from space flight just because he was older, or just because he had been grounded, or just because he had been relegated to a desk job for ten years. It was also a popular cause with many on the NASA team. The public, predictably, was even more sympathetic to Al's side. It would do more for men in their late forties, emotionally, than all the Geritol and lunchtime jogging combined.

For those of us off working on the Skylab program, it was like listening to the noises of a distant crowd. For those in the arena, such as Gordon Cooper and Jim Lovell, their futures were at stake. Inevitably, the rest of us began to take sides as a matter of principle. If "they" could screw Gordo in this way and establish a precedent, "they" could screw any of us—which should have been news only to the most naive.

It was obvious to anyone sensitive to office politics that Gordo was fighting for his life in the astronaut business. He had not flown a mission since 1965 and had served two successive assignments on a backup crew. He was being had, and he knew it. During the period when he had expected to be in prime crew training, Cooper was flying a T-38 back and forth to Washington, trying to rally support at NASA headquarters, trying to save *his* moon flight from the sentimental wave now building for Al Shepard.

It was a fruitless effort. During the years when Deke and Al had been shaping the organization and working with all the people who counted, Gordo had generally pursued an anti-establishment course. The chickens were coming home to roost; all the trips to Washington and all the appeals to the lords of the manor were to no avail. Gordon Cooper, the youngest of the Mercury, astronauts, the one who had flown the best of the Mercury missions, and the one considered most likely to prevail in the contest to reach the moon, had closed out his space-flight career with Gemini 5—-five years earlier.

In a big mismatch, Shepard had beaten back the challenge of his old friend, Gordon Cooper, but he still wasn't home free.

Jim Lovell had Apollo 14 sewed up, and the makeup of the Thirteen crew hardly seemed to affect him. But he was indignant that anyone, even his boss, could inject himself into the middle of the flight schedule without having served the same apprenticeship as those who were taking their turns in the rotation. We heard one day that Jim had threatened to resign over it, and we waited for the next round.

At this point, all the Shepard assignment lacked was approval from headquarters: specifically, the signature of George Mueller, the associate administrator. With time growing embarrassingly short for the crew announcement, Mueller made his decision. He didn't like the procedure any more than we did. There was no way that Shepard would be on Apollo 13. Mueller did not approve of the one-giant-leap-to-the-prime-crew tactic, and felt there was too little time for Al to reach the proficiency of prior crews.

Immediately after that, Deke Slayton approached Jim Lovell at the mission debriefing for Apollo 11, and asked, "Can your crew be ready for Thirteen?" Jim, who had just finished backing up Eleven, gave him the obvious answer, "Yes!"

Shepard still had to secure Mueller's approval for the mission for which he had been quietly training for at least six months. Through the efforts of Dr. Gilruth and his buddy, Deke, Al was able to get a headquarters OK for the Apollo 14 assignment. He had lost one and then won one, a fortunate sequence, which was to insure the success of his efforts to land on the moon. Al's perseverance was exceeded only by the successful sixteen-year campaign of Deke Slayton. It was great for Al, but the waves rippling through the Astronaut Office left some long-term hard feelings.

Mine were not among them. It is to the credit of those who selected the Mercury Seven in 1959 that both these men, Deke and Al, were able to maintain that self-discipline and control which fulfills great ambitions.

Lovell was still living right. If Jim fell in a creek, he'd come up with a trout in his pocket. Those instincts would certainly come in handy before Apollo 13 was over. He was now going to become the first man to make four flights into space.

It was a fluke that Jack Swigert happened to be onboard with him. Thirteen was to have been Ken Mattingly's mission. He had lived through all the work, problems, and excitement that go with a prime crew assignment. Then, three days before lift-off, it was learned that one of astronaut Charlie Duke's kids had come down with the measles, and Mattingly had been exposed on his last visit to Houston.

Ken was one of those rare birds who had never contracted measles as a child. When Chuck Berry and his medics found out, they threw themselves into the problem with abandon. Here was a live crisis at a crucial time, practically on the eve of a flight. Well, a potential crisis. A near crisis? By the time the doctors got through, we knew there would be some kind of crisis.

The ruling was clean as a scalpel: Ken was grounded for the next ten days. The fallout was unreal. A disease little kids get had set the space program spinning. These were the options: the mission could be postponed a full month to meet the next launch "window" for the selected landing site on the moon; the backup crew could replace the prime crew and launch the mission on schedule; or Mattingly's backup, Jack Swigert, could move up in a one-for-one substitution and launch on schedule. They were fortunate to have a second talented Command Module pilot on the team.

Crewmembers had never before been replaced individually. More importantly Jack had spent most of the preceding thirty days not training, but playing social secretary for the prime crew—the tedious but accepted chore of arranging rooms, invitations, and tours for their guests at the launch. Regardless of what was at stake, not one of us ever expected to see a crew broken up two days before launch. Some mixed-crew training was always done, but essentially we existed as a unit. The last six weeks before lift-off, the backup crew concentrated more on getting the prime crew ready than on anything else. So when the decision came to move Jack up, it was a stunner. Henceforth, backup crewmembers knew that any one of them could, at the last minute, be tapped to fly the mission.

Ken Mattingly was a meticulous guy, trained to a fine edge, while some questioned Jack's ability to step in and adequately replace him. Those of us who had worked with Jack had little doubt. He had worked with our team preparing for Apollo 7, had picked up hundreds of hours of simulator time in support of Apollo 10, and, finally, had served nearly a year on the backup crew for Thirteen. For all those credentials, and in spite of the pressure he faced, the top brass ordered a demonstration of his proficiency. It was to be a full-up simulation—a sort of *mano a mano* with Mission Control. In a twelve-hour ordeal his performance was flawless.

Jack Swigert was a real pro. We first met when Jack was a Pratt & Whitney test pilot going through astronaut selections in the summer of 1963. He was a friendly, appealing guy, big for an astronaut (a former college football lineman), with an unusual walk that was considered his trademark. His feet were so flat one expected a slapping noise when he walked, as if the soles of his shoes were loose. He walked along on those paddle feet as if he were behind a mule and a plow.

Jack was passed over that summer of '63, with hints that he was deficient in both test-flying experience and academic background. He set out immediately to correct it. Jack enrolled at Rensselaer College and acquired a master's degree in aeronautical engineering. He then went on to fly the test program on the inflatable Regallo wing for Rockwell when that technique was being considered for incorporation into the Gemini program. With that to round out his credentials, Jack was selected the next time he applied. He brought to all of his activities the single mindedness of a train running down a railroad track.

No flight was to be more hounded by irony than that of Apollo 13. Swigert was to jump in without any of the usual privileges of a mission, without time to even invite his friends and family to the Cape. He would be sent off to the moon in a Command Module that would explode before it got there, while Ken Mattingly brooded at home without ever developing the measles. It was a sad and unnecessary change creating near unanimous resentment in the Astronaut Office.

The third member of the crew, Fred Haise, certainly deserved more from his career than the unfinished mission he finally flew. Like Neil Armstrong, he had been a NASA test pilot before joining the astronaut corps. The year he reported to Houston he had won an award from the Society of Experimental Test Pilots for the best technical paper. In a business where the glamorous, high-speed jets usually stole the show, Fred's paper was on a test series he had conducted in civilian light aircraft. He was with NASA for a career, not just a leap into space. (That career looked like it would take a new direction a few years later when Fred crashed and was badly burned while ferrying a replica of a World War II Japanese aircraft for the Confederate Air Force, a flying air museum based in Harlingen, Texas.) On Apollo 13, Fred was the resident LM expert, and he was scheduled to walk on the moon with Lovell.

When an oxygen tank exploded on Apollo 13, it plunged Mission Control, America, and the rest of the world into a general alarm. The planned mission was cancelled by acclamation, leaving one question: can they make it back alive? My personal confidence in the safe conclusion of the mission was based on the presence of Jack Swigert. Mission Control's performance during that period, the four days following the immediate crisis to splashdown, was probably its finest hours. But in many respects, it was a flight-crew show.

Within fifteen minutes of the first report of the explosion in the Service Module—and only minutes after ABC television's Jules Bergman had painted a vivid picture of the crew expiring before making it back to earth—Dave Scott, Rusty Schweickart, and I were seated in the Mission Control viewing room Monday-morning-quarterbacking what was taking place. Bergman, one of the better science reporters on television, was still about one-tenth as knowledgeable about space as he thought he was. His reporting on that particular evening was irresponsible.

When we arrived, the flight controllers were still huddling, going through their usual crisis drill: What happened? Where do we stand? What are we going to do about it? As we monitored the air-to-ground loop, it was obvious to me that the crew had taken all the essential actions even before those sitting safely in Mission Control had called their first meeting. While the ground was debating whether to power up the undamaged Lunar Module—and if so, what systems—the crew, recognizing there was no alternative, was standing by for the official go-ahead on the inevitable decision they had already begun to implement.

Thirteen's safe return was strictly a question of consumables—was there enough oxygen, water, and electricity remaining to sustain three men for the sixty-five hours it would take to reach splashdown in the Pacific Ocean? It was as simple as that. The flight crew was concerned with those actions necessary to stabilize and resolve the immediate problem. The *degree* of success was academic. They were like the mouse that no longer wanted the cheese; he just wanted to get his tail out of the trap.

From the moment of the explosion, the situation steadily deteriorated. Within minutes the flight crew was aware of what questions had to be answered to determine if they might die of old age or considerably sooner—possibly within hours. This was a moment for which their years of training had prepared them. They were attuned to it. Living in a spacecraft, moving through the hostile environment it was designed to tame, one develops additional sensitivities. You become as aware of your supply of electricity, water, oxygen, and (especially) cabin pressure, as a businessman is of the weather when he rises in the morning, or of not cutting himself when he shaves, or of not walking in front of freight trains.

All of which points up the difference in perspective between a crew in space and the earthlings in Mission Control. Flight controllers are rarely in a position to contribute to time-critical decisions that may confront an astronaut as he whistles through the galaxy. The most critical action Mission Control was faced with was to devise a means to align the navigational platform on the spacecraft in the 13 hours before the vehicle would swing behind the moon. Without a good platform you cannot accurately fire the engines for mid-course corrections. Their solution involved up linking the best possible state vector and then the crew checking it by a sextant sighting on the limb of the earth at precisely the time the spacecraft was expected to emerge from behind the moon.

What Mission Control can do, and do superbly, is monitor each of the instrumented points on the spacecraft (it would be impossible to display all of these to the crew). This information was fed to three of the largest IBM computers in captivity, manned by the most competent technicians with the collective memory of all preceding missions at their fingertips. This was at once the strength and the weakness of the system. While it takes time to digest all the information available, this same delay enables a precision that obviously can't be achieved with an immediate response.

Of course, an astronaut in trouble isn't looking for precision—at first. At that moment he is worrying about what road to take, not how far the road will take him. This is not a reflection on Mission Control since many mission phases, and objectives, could not be accomplished without the ground controller's precise long-term data. The information available on board is never as complete and rarely as accurate.

The Apollo 13 crew performed those steps that would guarantee the security of their spacecraft and then began powering up the Lunar Module to keep vital systems operating. It was a relatively long time, by their scale, before the ground was able to provide a confirmation of their actions, suggest some improvements, and confirm that they would, in fact, make it.

As Scott, Schweickart, and I studied the situation, it became apparent that the flight crew had done all they could. All that remained was to trim it up a bit and wait for the trend information that would let them know just how much they had to tighten their belts. Ten minutes after we arrived I returned home and went to bed.

Out of those initial strategy sessions at Mission Control minutes after the explosion, came a detailed procedure for the Apollo 13 crew to follow to the safe conclusion of their aborted mission. It was designed to conserve the remaining resources and get them home in the shortest possible time. The crew wasn't exactly in Fat City, but they were alive and they were coming home. Thanks to the expertise of the boys in Mission Control, they were able to relax a bit.

The team in Mission Control was able to get the spacecraft powered down to 100 watts (the same power consumed by the light bulb in your lamp) for the 3-day return. A single light bulb does not put out much heat and the temperature reached as low as 35-37 degrees during the trip home.

The attention of the world was captured by this accident in space. The oxygen-tank explosion was an occurrence so unlikely that NASA had not even considered it a subject for contingency planning. The contingency plan, born in real time, enabled the world to watch Apollo 13 splash down in the Pacific—closer to the aircraft carrier than any prior mission. They had six hours of life support remaining and one of their three batteries failed just as the chutes opened. Many regard the Apollo 13 recovery from disaster as a major technical miracle and NASA's finest hour.

Since the Thirteen crew had not been exposed to lunar dust, they were spared at least one burden: quarantine. The last crew scheduled for that treatment was Apollo 14 (the ground rule was a clean bill of health for three crews to get quarantine cancelled). Those of us who knew Al well waited for the explosion. Stick Al Shepard into isolation for twenty-one days? We had to see that.

We underestimated how badly Al wanted that mission. No more emotional battles for him. The czar of the office, he of the steely-eyed stare, had decided to concentrate on his training and tilt no windmills. He accepted the three weeks as part of the job. He didn't even whimper when they attached a three-week pre-launch quarantine as well. The Apollo 13 measles scare had taken its effect.

George Mueller had made the decision on whether Shepard would or would not be ready for Thirteen. But now Al was back in control of his own destiny, and he wouldn't be found lacking when the bolts blew on Apollo 14. In the years when he was flying very little, due to the second-pilot restriction, he remained a fine aviator. (A prime example of my belief that being a good aviator is not simply a learned manual skill but a state of mind.) That same ability, carried several steps further, is essential to prepare for a space flight. Al went at it with a vengeance, including his physical conditioning program. By the end of the mission he was right up there with George Blanda and Lawrence Welk as a hero of the Geritol set.

Redheaded Stu Roosa, the Command Module pilot, was an air force major when he flew to the moon with Al Shepard. I say "with," because Apollo 14 was Shepard's mission. America gave it to him like a necklace in the same way that Apollo 7 was always known as Wally Schirra's mission.

Stu was an avid hunter and a great bird shooter who had an earnest boyishness about him that would do justice to Huck Finn. He tolerated the occasional carousing of his friends, but he was a straight arrow.

Ed Mitchell was the third member of the crew, a navy officer, bright, articulate, and an independent thinker in a place and time where independent thinkers were not in demand. If it had not been "Shepard's flight," the news media would have gotten all the copy it craved from Ed Mitchell, who was into ESP and psychic phenomena.

By the time Apollo 14 was ready to roll, Ed had suffered his share of frustration and was fed up with many parts of the NASA system. He had other goals to pursue and was intent on re-ordering his life—which included the first of several divorces. Several months before the flight, he let it be known that he would be leaving the astronaut corps shortly after the mission was completed.

That posed no problem for Deke; he simply made it plain that he had planned for Ed to back up Apollo 16. If Ed couldn't wait around that long then someone else who could would be given the opportunity to fly Fourteen in his place. Ed stayed for both assignments. No one thought less of him for changing his mind. We all had a commitment to our dreams.

One of Al Shepard's dreams was to hit a golf ball on the moon. But spacesuits make golf a challenge. His first drive went about 3 feet. He took a "mulligan," dropped a second ball and hit it with his third swing. Shepard claimed it went, "miles and miles and miles," but, according to Mitchell, it landed in a nearby crater

The last four missions, beginning with Apollo 14, were technically a string of near-monotonous successes—beautiful jobs on ever more difficult missions that few would remember were it not for some relatively unimportant fringe developments. The one that attracted the most notice, unfortunately, tended to characterize this two-year period in manned space flight.

The most complete scientific explorations of the Apollo program were carried out by the crews of Apollo 15 and Apollo 16. Yet Fifteen is best remembered (when it is at all) as the crew that carried envelopes to the moon. It was the dog days for the space program and a tragedy for the Apollo 15 crew: Dave Scott and the two rookies, Al Worden and Jim Irwin.

Dave was a three-time veteran who frequently acted as a self-appointed conscience of our group in the face of commercial temptations. He often advised restraint when so-called "good deals" surfaced, though his counsel was mostly ignored. So it was with bitter irony that so much adverse publicity for NASA was generated, so many careers shaken, and so much of the carefully orchestrated astronaut image blown on the fallout of Dave's mission. Little did we know, it was a foretaste of stories that would make the news in his post-NASA career.

To most Americans, stamps and postal covers (envelopes) are a national pastime, but to serious collectors and dealers they are big money. Scott had been an amateur philatelist, like many of us, but with the Apollo 15 "great postal caper" he was turning pro in a big way.

After the post flight tributes died down, the three of them settled in for another year of serious work as the backup crew for Apollo 17, the last of the lunar landings. At the completion of the program, Worden and Irwin planned to resign at their convenience and move on to other careers. Scott could have been expected to do the same, unless he wound up running the Astronaut Office or some other division of the Johnson Space Center. Instead, at the height of their professional achievement their futures turned sour.

In the fall of 1971, NASA became aware that a brisk philatelic business was being conducted in Apollo 15 first-day covers that had been taken to the moon. By the spring of 1972, NASA had completed an internal investigation and initiated disciplinary action. By June or July of that year the news media, exercising the public's so-called "right to know," were publishing details of a full-blown scandal.

The picture that slowly emerged was of a crew that had carried at least 630 special first-day covers to the surface of the moon on board the Lunar Module *Falcon,* nearly all of them unauthorized. All of them returned with the crew and carried postmarks at critical stages of the mission, including on board the recovery carrier *Okinawa*. During the long return flight from Hawaii to Houston, Scott, Worden, and Irwin had signed each of the covers, further enhancing their value. At the first opportunity, one hundred of these covers were shipped off to a German stamp dealer where they quickly sold out at $1,500 apiece, which eventually raised the red flag.

NASA's first comment came from John Donnelly, head of Public Affairs, to the effect that there was no profit motive on the part of the crew and therefore the moon missions were unsullied.

When asked why, Donnelly replied, "Why, Dave just wouldn't do a thing like that," reflecting the high regard and simon-pure reputation Scott had carefully nurtured. There was obviously a darker side of Dave to which NASA had not been exposed.

Next came word that the three were to have split $21,000 as a sort of "transportation fee" for the 100 covers sold to the stamp dealer. The plan was to set aside the funds for their kid's education. As the scandal grew, the crew "recognized" the apparent impropriety, returned the money and apparently did not profit from this particular deal.

Of the remaining 540 envelopes, 88 were really Apollo 12 covers belonging to Barbara Gordon, Dick's wife. The balance of 450 were the personal property of Scott, Worden, and Irwin. At the (then) going rate, $1,500 apiece, they would have been worth a cool $675,000.

If any of us realized how big and lucrative the philatelic business was (or could be), it was Barbara Gordon. But her efforts also reflected the kind of harmless nuisance most of us took stamp and cover collecting to be.

During the Gemini program, Barbara set out to collect for each of her six children a complete set of first-day covers marking each of the space missions. She would become much more ambitious. When autographed by each of the crewmen, the collection would not only serve as an attractive souvenir, but should also appreciate handsomely in value over the years—a thought that no doubt occurred to Barbara.

I had to admire her tenacity in persuading her husband's friends to keep signing stacks of commemorative covers from their flights. I lived just one block from the Gordons and, periodically, our household could expect a call from Barbara asking if I would be home for a few minutes.

A short while later she'd pedal up on her bicycle with her latest Apollo 7 covers to be signed. Her biggest haul came after Dick's last flight, on Apollo 12, when she circulated more than a hundred first-day covers for signing by Dick's crewmates.

There was a growing market for Apollo first-day covers, stamps, post-cards, and other such items, and I doubt if Barbara Gordon missed a set in over six years. With what she collected, and the trading potential, it was probably the most complete and valuable collection of space items in the postal universe.

My first reaction when the scandal leaked out was shock, not so much that the incident had occurred, but who the perpetrators were. It did shed some light on a memo that Alan Shepard had sent to all astronauts only a month earlier warning us to be alert for the commercialization of vari-ous articles which we autographed almost daily for collectors around the world. Attached was a one-page newsletter from a big collector and small-time dealer listing some of his wares for sale. A few examples:

Agnew, Spiro—Vice President—signed card.....$10.00
Armstrong, Neil—Historic photo of the Wright Brothers' first flight signed by Armstrong . . . photo is a NASA print.....$50.00
Allen, Joseph—Scientist Astronaut—very scarce FLOWN COVER carried on a T-38 by Allen on a training mission, this is one of a few rare flown covers to be offered on this list....$50.00

(*Flown?* Houston to Cape Kennedy for Christ sakes—in an airplane!)

I could feel sorry for the entire crew, but with Dave it was a little iron-ic. He had always set high standards, not only for himself but for the rest of us as well. If he failed one had to wonder if it were really possible for virtue to triumph, ever. Dave is the kind of guy who would carry any shadow on his career like an open wound. Maybe we all have a little lar-ceny in our hearts. In this case, it was an indicator of future compromis-es with integrity.

Dave and I had been getting along better for several years. Almost from our first meeting I had had mixed feelings about him. He in turn seemed to resent my whole approach to the job. I admired his talents and dedication, but could live without his self-righteous, holier-than-thou attitude. We had a personality clash that reached a climax of sorts the day of the Phantom Buzz job. It was an incident that reveals a bit about both of us.

I was returning to Houston from Patrick Air Force Base one Saturday morning, near the end of the training grind for Apollo 7. It had been a hard week. The sky was clear and seductive and my adrenaline was flowing.

It is a biological fact that the more an aviator is enjoying his flying, the more susceptible he is to the temptation of flat-hatting. One hundred miles out, I dropped the nose of my T-38 and pointed it toward the community of Nassau Bay, where many of us lived. Over my house (and a block farther, Dave's) I leveled off at about 100 feet and 500 knots. When I pulled up the nose and hit both after-burners it was like a bomb going off. At 5,000 feet, I did an Immelman out and swung quickly into my approach to land at Ellington Field.

About twenty minutes later, I was walking through my own doorway and the phone was already ringing. Stu Roosa had landed a little ahead of me and was calling from the hangar to warn me that complaints were coming in and I was thought to be the culprit. On Monday morning, Deke summoned me for the traditional commanding-officer-to-young-lieu-tenant-lecture ("Knock off that childish bullshit") and sent me away to sin no more.

The topper came when Scott, obviously still burning, came storming into my office.

"Walt," he demanded, "were you flying at eight o'clock Saturday morning?"

I frowned, as if trying to remember that far back. "Yes, come to think of it. I flew in from the Cape."

"Was that you who buzzed Nassau Bay?"

Sheepish grin.

"Dammit, you scared hell out of Lurton [his wife]. If I ever catch you doing that again"—he glared at me—"I'll . . . I'll have your wings yanked."

For once in my life I was speechless. What a self-righteous hypocrite! It wasn't just that Dave was a hot-rod jet jockey himself and should have known better. It was his attempt to throw around weight that he didn't have. I mean, he wasn't a general yet. It was like threatening to make a citizen's arrest because some guy had parked in your space. (Esthetically, it was a pretty good buzz job, but it was the last one I ever made—in Houston.)

Our differences were largely the result of poor chemistry, which seemed to straighten itself out during the Apollo program. I could take no pleasure from Dave's misery in the envelope case. For one thing, quite a few of us would get our cuffs muddy before the dust settled.

Dave was younger than each of his crewmates but in a sense was the "old man" of the bunch. Besides being the commander, he had already been through the training routine several times and was expected to keep the two rookies from making mistakes, both technical and ethical. Instead, there were indications, as well as insinuations by Worden and Irwin, that they were following Scott's lead.

Deke had few alternatives and no reason to hesitate. In 1972 he had astronauts coming out of his ears and damn few missions to fly. He could afford to purge all three and did. They were relieved of their duties as the Seventeen backup crew, and reassigned or non-assigned. Jim Irwin moved his planned retirement forward six months and went out to preach the gospel with his own Operation High Flight, an organization incorporated about the time of Apollo 15. Here was a man who was truly mission-oriented. His message, "I felt God's presence with me on the moon." provided a tremendous boost to what would otherwise have been just another lay preacher's efforts. After the censure, Irwin rebounded by weaving the moral lesson of the first-day cover temptation into his sermons. He also admitted publicly that NASA had no alternative. High Flight lasted almost twenty years.

Worden was on a geology field trip in Arizona when he learned that Deke had arranged for the Air Force, his parent service, to recall him. He had been waiting for the other shoe to drop, but this move stunned him. He had little enthusiasm for leaving NASA or playing Wild Blue Yonder again, at least until he had completed his twenty years' federal service (for retirement) as an astronaut. How are you ever going to get them back on the farm, after they have seen the lights of Cape Kennedy?

Worden decided to fight. I heard he called a congressman or two and then went over the heads of Deke and Chris Kraft to argue his case with Dale Myers, the deputy administrator for manned space-flight. Myers gave him a reprieve, long enough to find a slot at NASA's Ames Research

Center to finish out his twenty years. This came at a time when Worden was getting a divorce and reorganizing his own life so it suited him just fine.

The fallout seemed to bewilder Dave for months. He nearly dropped from sight but when our group was together he was more subdued and congenial than I had ever known him. Within a year Dave found himself at the NASA Flight Research Center at Edwards Air Force Base, California, where he was eventually made Director. Strong and capable, he seemed to bounce back.

Scott's actions in the envelope case I can only attribute to a lapse, one that, no doubt, Dave doesn't understand himself. He was in for the duration and he brought pride and ambition to his work. Therefore, the consequences of his folly were far worse than for the others. Dave's fall from grace may have partly accounted for the questionable behavior that marked his career over the subsequent 30 years.

In private industry, Dave had entrepreneurial ambitions and some pretty good ideas. He always seemed to be raising money for one "can't miss" deal or another. In one of those, according to the judge in the case, Scott had raised money for one company and then used a series of deals to funnel some of it into other companies and partnerships he controlled. Nine investors had sued Scott for "fraud, intentional misrepresentation and breach of fiduciary duty" and the judge awarded the plaintiffs $400,000 in damages.

Not to fear though. Eleven years after Apollo 15's infamous personal envelopes were confiscated, Al Worden successfully sued the federal government and they were all returned. The last one I saw auctioned at Christie's cost the buyer $9,200.

Apollo 15 may have been the first crew to commercialize on first-day covers, but it was not the first to carry them. I later learned they were carried on every flight from Apollo 11 on and the practice may have started even earlier. From Twelve through Sixteen they were obtained through Al Bishop, then of the Howard Hughes organization. They were limited orders of a few hundred, featuring the crew emblems in the left corner and were the nearest thing to an "official" cover available. The crews carried only a few and usually returned a couple to Al, signed, with gratitude. To my knowledge, Bishop never sold any and never made a dime off his relationship. He was simply a fan.

To Al, Apollo 15 was no different from any other flight, except for a phone call he received from Hal Collins, the Astronaut Office manager at the Cape. Collins told Bishop that the crew would like to know whether he could obtain some very *lightweight* envelopes for them. Al said that he'd be happy to do so. He was unaware then that many of them would be smuggled on board the next lunar flight.

Al was trusted. That's why many of us imposed on him with our problems, special requests and, sometimes, matters which we would rather not share with NASA—like my doctor's appointment four days before launch. In that respect, we often took advantage of him. This time Al was badly used and he emerged as a scapegoat.

Hal said that they wanted to print twelve hundred of them, and asked whether Al could handle that.

Bishop told him that this would present no problem.

After the flight, when it became apparent that the deal had backfired, Bishop got another call from Collins. He began by warning Al that a big stink had developed over the envelopes.

When Al asked him what he was talking about, Collins told him that he would let Dave explain it to him.

Dave never called. No member of the Fifteen crew ever did. But Bishop's name got dragged through a Senate hearing as though he were the Mr. Big of an international stamp conspiracy. It made headlines in Las Vegas, where he lived, and eventually cost him a good job. His taxes were audited and most of his astronaut "pals" dropped him like a load of barnyard manure. It took Bishop several years to recover from his helpfulness.

I resented the news media's implication that the near-perfect job performed by the Apollo 15 crew was any less an accomplishment, just as I had resented the implication that we were all affected by Buzz Aldrin's public acknowledgment of a nervous breakdown.

It would be nice to say the rest of the astros were indignant, but the truth is many of us were living in glass houses. During the course of the investigation other "lapses of judgment" came to light. One that compromised most of us was a series of "business deals" with the same middleman that proposed the moon cover caper to Scott's crew.

My own involvement began with a 1969 phone call from Walter Eiermann, whom many of us had met socially in Cocoa Beach. Eiermann said he was negotiating with many of the astronauts to sign 500 plate blocks of stamps issued to commemorate the individual's flight for a payment of $2,500. My answer was probably typical: "Yes, I'd be interested if others in the group were doing the same thing." The money was enticing and it wasn't explicitly against any regulation, but I was *not* interested in becoming a trail blazer.

Three months later he called with a list of those who had already committed. His goal was to sign every man who had flown an Apollo mission, and he seemed well on his way.

I suppose we could argue that the money went for a good cause. Mostly it went for living expenses of families accustomed to the added income from the *Life* contracts, which had dwindled to nearly nothing. Some of it went to charity at the time, and I know some more did after the story broke. The investigation by NASA and the justice department may have resulted in a few amended income tax returns as well.

There were only a half dozen Apollo astros I was ever certain did not take the bait. There may have been others. Among those of us involved, the only one I know that ever received any obvious disciplinary action was Jack Swigert, and then it was not for signing (which apparently was not illegal).

Jack's problem was that when NASA investigated the whole affair, he at first denied having signed the stamps. He did so to protect his assignment on the U.S.-Soviet mission—and it ended up costing him that very prize. He had already been selected for the crew, along with Stafford and Slayton, and was happily enrolled in Russian language courses. There only remained the official public announcement.

A few weeks later Jack had a change of heart or conscience, or maybe someone advised him to clear the air. He went to George Low, the acting administrator of NASA, and admitted that he had signed but said he'd given the money to charity. Low's decision to remove Jack from the mission was based on the fact that Jack had lied—how could he be trusted? Needless to say, Jack was shattered.

Was it illegal to sign the stamps for profit? No. Was it morally wrong? Maybe. Was it a mistake? Hell, yes! At times it still has the echo of a bad joke, but it added to the growing media picture of heroes with feet of clay. Yet, with all the times we could have exploited our careers on the wild deals that held the lure of big money, the stamp signings seemed a relatively innocent and safe way to earn a modest sum.

Our image wasn't enhanced any by other things that were brought to light on the periphery of the Apollo 15 investigation. The Franklin Mint got a grubby hand involved in the Apollo 14 mission after being partially successful on Thirteen. The mint wanted to commercialize on medals that had flown to the moon. Getting them on board the spacecraft was apparently not too difficult; flight crews have always commissioned and purchased, exclusively for their own use, commemorative medals, some of which were carried on the flight.

Prior to the Apollo 13 flight, the crew was approached by a middle-man with an offer of several hundred free sterling silver medals in exchange for returning to the Franklin Mint, fifty of those which had been to the moon. The mint would melt down these fifty and coin 130,000 medals that had "been to the moon." When Thirteen aborted without landing on the moon, Lovell returned the single medal he had carried in his flight suit which caused the scheme to fall through. I later heard that Shepard and the Fourteen crew agreed to more or less the same deal. It was rumored around the office that Apollo 14 carried a personal package on board weighing forty-two pounds.

Both Lovell and Shepard attempted to hold down the exploitation, but with little leverage they were unsuccessful.

Still another flap involved a now-famous sculpture called, appropriately, "The Fallen Astronaut." Dave Scott and Jim Irwin, with the purest of intentions, placed it in a small crater on the moon on August 2, 1971, together with a plaque listing the names of the fourteen astronauts and cosmonauts who had died in the effort to explore space. The tiny aluminum statue now seems a symbol not only of those men but also of the crew that carried it there.

The sculptor flew to Florida two months before the flight to offer his sculpted figure to Scott and his crew as a memorial to those who had perished. NASA's approval was obtained with the understanding that there would be no commercial exploitation.

At the postflight conference, the crew disclosed the project and Dave made public a photograph of the plaque and statue—without identifying the sculptor. Three months later, the sculptor, who had been doing space themes for twenty years and now resented being ignored, broke his silence by offering 950 copies of the statue to the public at $750 each as "exact replicas" of the first work of art on the moon.

In no way did any astronaut profit, nor was it ever meant that they should. Of Scott, the gallery director said, "He was a shit about some things, but he was the one who got the goddamn thing on the moon. He was sincere, but nervous about the publicity. He [Scott] was the one who really wanted to be a general."

So it didn't begin with the first-day covers; they were just the key with which the dirt was dug up. Sometimes we were willing accomplices (as in the case of the two watches of a major manufacturer which were "evaluated" on Apollo 15), but more frequently we were naive or just plain outsmarted.

It was about this same time that Deke sent the names of his proposed Apollo 17 crew to headquarters. Most of us suspected the Apollo program would not end until a geologist had walked on the moon, meaning Jack Schmitt, who was backing up Apollo 15. That could mean there would be an Apollo 18 or Deke could assign Gordon's crew with Schmitt to Apollo 17. Instead, he stuck with the system that had served him so well in the past—he rotated Cernan's Apollo 14 backup crew into the spot.

When Washington and their scientists objected strongly, Deke was forced to put Jack Schmitt on the mission. If Cernan wanted to land on the moon, he would have to go with Jack Schmitt. The crew was announced—Cernan, Evans, and Schmitt—with unexpected consequences from one quarter.

When Jim McDivitt, the Apollo Spacecraft Program Manager since his Apollo 9 mission, heard the announcement he was incensed. Jim couldn't believe he hadn't been consulted on the crew assignment. According to Chris Kraft, Jim's reaction was, "Cernan's not worthy of this assignment, he doesn't deserve it, he's not a very good pilot, he's liable to screw everything up, and I don't want him to fly." He summed it up with, "If you don't get rid of him, I'll quit."

It was too late. There had been a public announcement. And a few months later McDivitt did resign.

Coincident with the flap over the astronauts' postal enterprises, Apollo 16 flew and became the most forgotten of all the missions. Probably not one in a hundred can name any of the three crewmembers, and yet in terms of execution and scientific returns—it rates along side of Apollo 15 as one of the most productive. No scandals, either. The flight was commanded by well-trained, super-trained, always-training John Young, who (glory be) hadn't even signed any stamps.

Apollo 16 was a clear demonstration of the waning interest in space (although Apollo 17, as the final act, would inspire a brief sentimental revival). The clues had been coming for some time: less congressional support, budget cuts, reduced TV coverage, smaller crowds at the Cape, and to me, at least, a change of attitude in the make-up of those crowds. The earliest launches were viewed mainly by those involved in the program or on the fringes of it or diehard space buffs. Toward the end we were drawing more tourists, more families, and there was more of a county fair feeling. Cocoa Beach was in a state of transition, with the people, the merchants, and the money moving from the Fantasia of space to the reality of Disney World, 40 miles down the road at Orlando.

So, with a minimum of pomp and fanfare, John Young, Ken Mattingly (the only man to toil through two consecutive prime crew assignments), and Charlie Duke went to the moon aboard Sixteen. Young drove the Lunar Rover about 17 miles on the Moon before the Apollo program was down to one.

Apollo 17 was described, repeatedly, as "the end of the beginning." It was a nice play on the words of Winston Churchill who used them first in November 1942, following the British victory at El Alamein in World War II: "Now this is not the end. It is not even the beginning of the end. But it is, perhaps, the end of the beginning."

Apollo 17 broke new ground in at least three respects. As the first night-time launch, visible for 500 miles in any direction from the Cape. It was the first time a scientist-astronaut, Jack Schmitt, would fly in space. And, finally, tight security was instituted around the astronaut families throughout the final training period.

That latter item reflected a frightening new development in world politics: the age of terrorism. Not long after the slaughter of the Israeli athletes by Arab terrorists at the Munich Olympics and rampant terrorist acts elsewhere, NASA wisely reappraised the security, for its last Apollo launch. It was the kind of theater that could easily have tempted such madmen.

Gene Cernan, the spacecraft commander, and Schmitt were joined by Ron Evans, the middleman in the spacecraft, who had worked on our Apollo 7 support team and four years later was finally getting his own flight.

There was a feeling about Apollo 17 of a graduation day for the class that had enrolled, fourteen of us, nine years before, and a recognition of the last hurrah for lunar flights.

Seventeen had a beautiful midnight sendoff. Mingling with the crowd, as an alumnus, I made a voice recording of the final count. You can hear it over the clamor of the crowd noise, the monotone voice, no more emotional than the public address system at an airport telling you that Flight 52 to LaGuardia is ready for boarding. But my scalp tingled. I heard my own voice whispering, "Come on Seventeen, let's go," and it didn't sound like me. At lift-off the roar of the crowd was spontaneous— pure excitement. You could feel the vibrations. And as they hit us, the sound rolled over us. Dammit, people cried! How do you tell anyone that you saw the earth tremble?

On their return from a good mission, Cernan, Evans, and their wives, along with the bachelor Schmitt, made the last astronaut "grand tour." Gene sounded a lot like a politician at a Fourth of July barbecue. He had his speech down pat, a sweeping discourse that touched all the bases: pride, humility, patriotism, the worldview, family, and a heartfelt thanks to anyone who had anything to do with the space program. It was a speech that didn't make you think very hard, but it did make you feel good. Gene was quick on his feet. He reminded people of those forget-table last words uttered on the moon just as their Lunar Module was lift-ing off, "Okay, let's get this mother out of here!"

Jack once complained, tongue-in-cheek, that when he would inject something new or clever in his own brief talk, "the next day all the good parts would wind up in Gene's speech, and I'd be left with nothing to add."

Ron Evans became the comic relief who would do an entire night club monologue, along with gestures, on the astronauts' best-kept secret: "How To Pee-Pee and Poo-Poo In Space." If it sounds coarse, it was, and in five fast minutes Ron provided the audience with an empty, if funny, view of a man in whom the government had invested $5 million. It was an embarrassing performance to many of his friends, but Ron was the hit of the show wherever they went.

Jack Schmitt was a quiet, private fellow who never appeared totally at ease with his crewmates. He didn't relish the public relations aspects of the postflight scene, and easy camaraderie wasn't his bag either. As the first scientist-astronaut to fly in space, Jack Schmitt held his own, accomplishing no more (and no less) than anyone else. If the lunar scientists expected Jack to carry the flag for them, they were wrong for at least two reasons. One is the rather narrow view held by the scientific community that most of the astronauts were nothing but "dumb fighter jocks." Secondly, they failed to recognize that the success of a mission was controlled more by operational constraints than by the particular skills and serendipity of an individual crewman. Add to this the hard facts of life of operating in a pressurized suit and the environmental constraints, and one can readily see that the real triumph is in just being there and moving around.

Schmitt's scientific training did cause him to do one thing, which no one had done before. On one of their moon walks he came upon some orange rocks and was elated. Eureka! Jack had found the moon's youngest rocks—-or so it seemed at the time. He proudly proclaimed their age as "less than twenty-five million years old." After the rocks and soil had been analyzed at home, it was determined that Jack missed in his on-the-spot observation by a mere three and a half *billion* years. I dare say, a "dumb fighter jock" would not have ventured such an ad hoc assessment.

That mistake didn't affect the fervor and eloquence with which Jack expressed his feelings about space flight, as he did when the Apollo 17 crew addressed a joint session of Congress.

"I would like first to tell you about a place I have seen in the solar system, the Valley of Taurus-Littrow," he began. "The Valley has been unchanged by being a name on a distant planet, while change has governed the men who named it. The Valley has been less altered by being explored than they who have been the explorers. The Valley has been less affected by all we have done than have been the millions who, for a moment, were aware of its towering walls, its visitors, and then its silence."

It was a magnificent way to describe the completion of the greatest technological achievement in history.

As I look back over the years of Apollo, there were a few surprises in our third group. That Dave Scott would fly three missions startled no one, but that he would share that distinction with Gene Cernan could not have been predicted. Gene ranked as one of the two miscalculations in my

1964 peer ratings. As events unfolded, the first seven of our fourteen went into space in this order: Scott, Cernan, Collins, Gordon, Aldrin, Eisele, and Anders. That line-up, of course, reflected the changes caused by the See-Bassett accident and the Apollo 1 fire. Were it not for those fateful accidents, the order of flight would have been: Scott, Bassett, Collins, Gordon, Cernan, Chaffee, and Eisele. Which is precisely the order in which they appeared, relative to each other, in my peer ratings.

The most glaring discrepancy between my ratings, and the order of baptism, came at the top. Alan Bean was ranked Number 1, but he flew tenth—and last. Possibly friendship got in the way of judgment, but I prefer to think that later events on Skylab proved my assessment to be a better appraisal of his ability than those who made the assignments.

The Apollo program was over. The midnight launch that December 7, 1972 was the last time that most of the astronauts would be together to celebrate the years in which we rode that great flame into the heavens. We had competed, we had argued, we had often let ourselves down, and we had never gotten there with that poet everyone kept wishing we could take along to help us find another word besides "fantastic." But there were moments of undiluted joy and good company, and, finally, we did give science a shot at the moon. It was, after all, only the end of the beginning.

14

The Hyphenated Astronaut Comes of Age

THE REAL CLASH in our space world, though it existed largely behind the scenes, was between the pilots and the scientists—the goals of technology against those of science.

Take Skylab. In the beginning, NASA assigned fresh astronauts to Skylab in much the same spirit the early Russians threw one another off the back of the sleigh to slow down the wolves.

To the surprise of no one, thirty-two American fighter pilots traveled into space before the first scientist. The string was broken by scientist-astronaut Jack Schmitt on the last Apollo mission. Of the next seven to fly, three were trained scientists before they became pilots. It was the beginning of a transition from career aviators—generalists, trained to do whatever was necessary on the mission—to scientists, doctors, or other specialty passenger types who could wring the most out of a given area of investigation once they were carried aloft.

Scientist-astronauts were brought into the program as far back as 1965. It was clear even then that they would outnumber the aviators some time in the future. The arrival of those first six scientist-astronauts created a stir around the office. This was a new kind of animal to be integrated into the system, and the older heads studied it warily. We quickly decided that the new breed was inferior, and worried that Congress and the public might not know the difference, or even care. Contact around the office was cordial enough, but it was clear that the scientists had bigger handicaps to overcome than just the usual new-guy-on-the-block syndrome. They contradicted the public image we enjoyed as the John Waynes of the space frontier. No milquetoast academic types would fit into that picture.

My own reaction to their arrival was relief, for virtually the same reasons most of the others were distressed. Until they arrived, the closest

thing to resident scientists in the Astronaut Office were Rusty Schweickart and myself, both having reported to NASA straight from the campus, and possibly Buzz Aldrin, with his Ph. D. in Astronautics. I can't
speak for Rusty, but I worried about being a part of the team; I mean the
varsity and not some kind of token to the scientific community. I confess,
my initial contact emphasized my scientific credentials, which seemed the
most unique card I had to play. I would have exploited anything possible
during the selection process, but once in, the thought uppermost in my
mind was to remove any question about my flying credentials and to
escape the stigma of "scientist."

By 1965 the argument between the National Academy of Sciences and
the Astronaut Office (notably Deke Slayton and Alan Shepard) had grown
quite heated on the subject of what qualifications best suited a man for a
trip into space. Deke maintained that a highly experimental flight test
program like the development of manned spacecraft required specialists
who had dedicated their lives to the operation of the closest related kind
of equipment. The program could not afford the luxury of anyone who
couldn't carry his own weight in such a flight test program. Furthermore,
Deke's boys could handle just about anything that would interest the scientific lobby, and get the spacecraft back to earth as well. To fill a technical job, one sent the best technicians available.

Deke wasn't alone in that opinion. The rest of us were cheering like
mad—this was no time to be unselfish. The National Academy of Sciences
was just as provincial as we were. Space was such an appealing and unex-
ploited area of investigation that the subject simply precluded objectivi-
ty. The Academy's position seemed to be that anyone with a yen for
adventure could be a pilot, but only God could make a scientist.

There was no way, of course, that the scientists were going to be shut
out of the space odyssey. They had a big hammer. At a time when the
NASA budget was headed toward $6 billion annually, the agency need-
ed all the friends it could find, particularly in Congress, which held a
generous respect for science along with the other things it didn't understand. When the flak began to fly about spending $20 billion on a "moon-
doggle," NASA took the prudent course and caved in. Deke had lost the
battle. Slayton wasn't acting out of prejudice. He was simply the one closest to the heat and no one knew better what the crew requirements would
be for the next ten years. NASA was projecting the first lunar landing for

late 1967 or early 1968, with repeat trips every two months thereafter, and was hoping the first Skylab would fly in 1968.

It would have been politic for Deke to man up on the basis of those projections, but as always he took the most realistic view. He also had, I think, the best appreciation of the kind of man needed to perform the job he would be expecting. It must have struck him as a waste of time, money, and talent to recruit scientists into the program so early, knowing at least five years would pass before any of them would fly. (That forecast turned out to be painfully conservative. Those who hung in there from that first group took their rides in their seventh, eighth, and ninth years of training. It was almost like being a career cadet.)

The scientist selections took place in an atmosphere that resembled a jury trial, with the defense and the prosecutors each applying their own standards to select the jurors. The National Academy insisted on screening the applicants down to the final round, at which point NASA could apply its criteria. The Academy proposed an aggressive solicitation for Scientist-Astronaut candidates, when those of us already selected had aggressively sought the job. Deke was eventually able to insist that the newest candidates begin their careers in the same way.

The Academy purists gave little attention to a nominee's prospects for passing the NASA screening, concentrating instead on the totems of scientific manhood, such as a Ph.D., numbers of papers published, and years of research. Not surprisingly, otherwise good prospects who lacked the purebred scientific pedigree were disqualified early.

When it came NASA's turn, what remained to be judged were each candidate's motivation as well as his qualifications to meet the demands of his new discipline. Additional screening assessed their ability to measure up to the years of screening and filtering that each of the pilot astronauts had endured even before applying. One experience, for example, was to expose their zest, or aversion, to the job ahead. That was the one-hour, aerobatic flight in a T-38, which consisted of spins, loops, dives, and other fun maneuvers. That alone eliminated some candidates—I mean just the idea of it, not the actual flight.

When the first selection was over, NASA found acceptable only half the number of scientists it had expected to bring into the program, which left precious little margin for further attrition. In retrospect, the internal politics and the outside pressure acted as a dose of bitter medicine that was good for what ailed us. The outcome was surprising and, in keeping with the other NASA successes of the sixties, the result of both a lot of effort and a little luck. We acquired the services of five very atypical scientists out of the six who reported that year: a medical doctor, a geologist, and three physical scientists.

There was a nucleus of aviator types. Curt Michael had been an air force pilot before earning his Ph.D. Joe Kerwin was a navy flight surgeon as well as a naval aviator. Owen Garriott, a university professor with no military experience, had still logged about 400 hours of civilian flying time. Ed Gibson was brash and bright; a hard-charging youngster who, in many ways, reminded me of a Roger Chaffee with no flight experience. Jack Schmitt was a non-flying specialist in lunar geology and the only one with a good case for inclusion in the Apollo program.

The last of the six was the unfortunate Dr. Duane Graveline, whose domestic problems forced his resignation even before flight school. His wife made it a "NASA or me" issue, and in the divorce filing that followed, she accused him of "an uncontrollable temper." That was hardly appropriate for an astronaut, and the good doctor was asked to return home.

So then there were five, who might as well have spent the next seven years in a vault for all of the space exploring they got to do. Nevertheless, the felony was compounded in 1967 when NASA was again pressured into admitting another group of scientist-astronauts (eleven this time), whose scientific specialties once more ranged from geologist to medical doctor. They were collectively almost devoid of operational experience, and some appeared to have no real interest in acquiring it.

This was the group, quick on the uptake, that identified its own future by dubbing itself with the fine, military-sounding name of XS-11 (excess eleven). Some of them would contribute in other areas, but it would be more than fifteen years before any of them would fly in space and some of them never would.

One scientist who was more than willing to play the astronaut game was Story Musgrave. His background was rather unique even in that fast company. Story was a high school dropout who enlisted in the Marine Corps and four years later returned to get serious about life. Before joining NASA, he had managed to accumulate the following academic credentials:

Bachelor of Science in statistics
Bachelor of Arts in chemistry

Master of Business Administration (Operations Analysis And Computer Programming)

Doctor of Medicine
Master of Science in biophysics

He was working on a doctorate in physiology when selected. In his spare time he had found time to accumulate 1,500 pilot hours and 200 free-fall parachute jumps. He also started a family of five children—all this before his thirty-second birthday.

For him, air force pilot training was a ball. On the side, he was giving flying lessons and commuting to Denver, Colorado, on every free weekend to complete an internship in surgery. After pilot training, Story went to work for me on Skylab and my biggest problem was not how to keep him from playing scientist, but how to keep him out of an airplane cockpit long enough to get some work accomplished. In 1997, when he retired from NASA, he had flown six Shuttle missions and added a few more degrees.

At the other end of the spectrum was another medical doctor, Don Holmquist. Making a king-sized judgmental error, he threw in with the wrong side of a power struggle that had been going on for ten years. Holmquist was bright, young, and very immature. From the beginning, I watched him curry favor with the medical directorate at NASA, assuming they would be an asset in his corner at crew assignment time. Little could he know that that was like waving a red flag in front of a bull. He never did figure out what we expected of medical astronauts, and he was eventually asked to leave.

The senior doctor in the group was Joe Kerwin, who had precisely the opposite effect on the troops as Don Holmquist. From the beginning Joe set out to be accepted as an unhyphenated astronaut. He treated his medical background as I had the study of physics: as an adjunct, a tool to be exploited within the broad guidelines of a new profession. His medical skills undoubtedly suffered while he concentrated on his new career, but many of us looked upon him as our "personal" physician more than we did any of the NASA doctors. There were damn few astronauts who didn't hide medical problems from our NASA flight surgeons, but seldom was anyone reluctant to discuss those problems with Joe. Judged by the way doctor-patient confidentiality was respected, the doctors at NASA with the highest professional ethics were those in our own office.

Dr. Kerwin was always willing to make a house call for a sick child, even if NASA doctors were available. I'll never forget calling Joe one night when Brian had a fever of $104°$ and we couldn't locate the NASA doctor on duty. Joe lived only two blocks away and he rushed right over. We both got a real laugh when the stethoscope he pulled from his bag was rusty. Joe didn't get much time for doctoring.

A few of those with their impressive scientific credentials were just as enthusiastic about learning the profession of astronaut as any of the pilots. It didn't take long after their arrival to spot those scientists having trouble making the adjustment and some just plain didn't make it. The most famous scientist-astronaut dropout was 26-year-old Brian O'Leary, who gave as his reason for quitting, "Flying isn't my cup of tea." True, he was afraid of flying, but he was also out of step even with his associates. In the six months he spent in our office he gained no understanding of what motivated us, but it was apparently long enough to convince him he did not like the whole setup, including the city of Houston. When he found out pilot training scared him to death, his mind was made up. He left the impression, "Well, I just wanted to see if I could get selected, and I did." No motivation!

O'Leary's case was an obvious failure of the selection process. The selection board, from Deke Slayton to the psychiatrists, may not have fully appreciated the difference in motivation between the John Waynes who volunteered to kick the program off and the scientists who were recruited ten years later. It was much more difficult to maintain a good batting average when dealing with the raw, unfiltered bunch that constituted the scientist applicants. Pilot-astronauts had successfully passed through many filters in a dangerous profession before their application for astronaut training.

The guy who got by the longest before the astronaut equivalent of firing was Dr. Curt Michel, who left NASA to become chairman of the Space Science Department at Rice University. He had little more desire for the job than Brian O'Leary and no more understanding of how to fit in (if he ever wanted to) than Don Holmquist. He had applied for the program partly at the urging of friends in the academic community who felt his air force flying experience, along with an excellent academic record, would insure success. With the National Academy of Sciences endorsement, he seemed like a good bet even to NASA. After reporting in 1965, he was the most conscientious in maintaining a schedule of one day a week at the scientific laboratories of Rice University. In that respect, he was dedicated to his real vocation, but it hardly improved his cynical and casual approach to the astronaut job. In 1969, after Curt took a year's leave of absence to devote full time to his scientific pursuits, it was quietly turned into a permanent arrangement.

When scientist friends asked me about the space program in those days, I tried to be honest. "It's the most exciting thing going today," I said. "If you want to be a part of it, then make application. But if what you really want is an opportunity to do 'good science,' then you'll be better off investing your time elsewhere."

That was the sadness, the failure, of the role designed for these men. The skills of most went unused while they underwent training that would be years in paying off, if ever.

The box score reads: seventeen scientist-astronauts forced on NASA by the National Academy of Sciences in a span of two years. Three quit before the end of their first year and two more were dropped as soon as it was convenient. The dozen who remained toughed it out over a course that had to be more frustrating than the path followed by the rest of us. Deke had been right when he said it was premature to recruit that many scientists into astronaut training.

Some hoped to beat the system by transforming themselves, through attitudes and actions, into *aviators.* Several graduated first in their pilot training classes, even though they were looked upon by the other cadets as old men. Those who endured did so knowing full well the low likelihood of ever being assigned a mission. As a group they compiled an excellent flying-safety record: no casualties. Did this reflect the natural caution of the scientific personality? By comparison, of the first fifty-four pilot astronauts selected, eight died in accidents (and only nine had not flown a mission by 1975).

Skylab was the vehicle that carried the last three members of the original scientist group into space. My interest, of course, went beyond that of an ex-astronaut turned civilian spectator. Skylab at one time had been my baby.

Late in 1968, Deke had summoned me to his office to inform me of my new assignment. I had been mildly curious since a month before the flight of Apollo 7, when we learned that Donn Eisele would be going to back up Apollo 10 and Wally Schirra announced his pending retirement. I was left the only crewmember of Apollo 7 with an unknown future.

At various times, Deke involved me in science related activities, and I had a suspicion what the new job might be. What I couldn't yet decide was whether it would be a good deal or a loser. It was obvious that Deke didn't look upon it as a plum or he wouldn't have hesitated so long in breaking the news. I suspect he didn't want to risk affecting my attitude before the flight with the news I would be inheriting the mess that Skylab had become.

Skylab—or Orbiting Workship as we called it in those days—was the poor relation of the manned space program. It was conceived around 1965 as a way to utilize the surplus Saturn 1-B hardware purchased for the development phase of Apollo. The Saturn 1-B was a slightly smaller and cheaper booster that we used for the earth orbital missions and tests of the hardware, launch escape systems, and heat shields. As schedules slipped and we grew bolder with each successful mission, some of the planned development flights were deleted, leaving extra hardware in storage.

The orbiting workshop was conceived to utilize an empty booster fuel tank as a rudimentary, space station, within which crewmembers would perform scientific experiments and gain experience at long duration missions. Its originally scheduled launch date was 1968.

In the beginning, all flight-experienced astronauts were working on Gemini or Apollo, and Skylab floundered from one false start to another. Alan Bean was the first to head the Skylab branch of the Astronaut Office and (in time) was promised command of the first mission. Al was rescued from this thankless pioneering when he was called on to fill the vacated seat on the Apollo 9 backup crew after C. C. Williams collided with the ground at a speed of Mach 1 plus.

In 1967, Gordon Cooper took over Skylab on his road to nowhere. Here at last was some sorely needed experience, but the program had little direction and was the first to suffer from the perennial budget cuts. Besides, Gordo's heart really wasn't in it. When he took over, it was scheduled to fly within two years. And when he left, a year later, lift-off was still "a couple of years away."

With most of the astronaut manpower thrown into Apollo, Skylab fell next on the shoulders of Owen Garriott, the senior scientist-astronaut. Owen was conscientious and hard-working. He had a personal interest in the results: it would be his only possible chance to fly. But his was an interval when whoever ran Skylab couldn't win; he could only hold down the score. Garriott had the dual handicaps of limited experience and minimal support in our office because everyone's attention was focused on the flying program—Apollo.

He received little guidance for two reasons. First, there was little interest in an earth-orbital program that would be manned by scientists. Second, there was the astronaut syndrome of having the ultimate last word. This attitude could be characterized loosely as, "Let them have their fun for now; when we assign a flight crew we'll straighten it out. Hang the cost. If they don't fix it, we won't fly it." To the old pros, the scientist-astronauts were just keeping the books, so they would know where the problems were when the heavies arrived.

When I arrived, engineers from the Program Office were having a field day in areas which were formerly our exclusive province. Earth-locked engineers, with NASA since the early days of the Mercury program, were still designing for 1-g rather than taking advantage of the zero-gravity environment. As a result, at the end of 1968, Skylab was saddled with such bizarre concepts as:

1. *Compression walking,* which presumed that man would move around the workshop by pressing his hands against a "ceiling" and his feet against a "floor" and execute a movement as close to walking as possible.

2. *A cargo transfer device* requiring that a monorail system be fabricated in orbit (Tinkertoy fashion) through each of the modules between the spacecraft cabin and the crew quarters in the workshop—a distance of 110 feet. This was to enable our puny crewmen to maneuver large packages that would be transferred back and forth in the vehicle—all of which were weightless, of course.

3. *A pelvic restraint system* in the wardroom, designed to keep us from "flying" all over the place. It consisted of a metal arm, extending from the wall on a universal joint, which clamped securely around one's pelvis.

It would hold securely, yet allow movement at the end of a boom.

4. An honest-to-God *settee* along one wall of the same wardroom (I assume for those who wished to sit out a dance).

5. *A bicycle-seated, pedal-powered carriage* mounted to a pole running the length of the cylindrical workshop. Through an arrangement of gears, pulleys, and extension rods, an astro was expected to pedal himself to any spot within the twenty-one-by-seventy-foot tank, and thus solve his problem of getting around in space.

If these descriptions make Skylab sound like a can of worms, don't let me mislead you. It was! It would have been easy to feel I had been exiled to a program staffed by has-beens, never-wases, and never-would-bes attempting to fly a bunch of leftover junk. My own appraisal was much more hopeful. If one didn't have a flight, the next best thing was to have autonomy, responsibility, and authority. That was almost impossible to come by in our office, but it was available in the Skylab assignment. The lack of interest around the office insured little interference, all the authority one was able to assume, and enough privacy to get the work done.

All that, and problems big enough to satisfy the most aggressive and ambitious manager. The challenge was to get a program flying that could never have gotten off the ground as it was conceived in 1968. What it lacked was operational input and effective management.

While I did not exactly do cartwheels off the nearest curbstone at the new assignment, I wasn't discouraged either. It was an opportunity to produce, and those two years at the helm of Skylab became my real contribution to manned space flight. Two events took place that made it possible to turn things around. Within a year, the program manager's job was turned over to Kenny Kleinknecht, a veteran of the Mercury, Gemini, and Apollo programs. At about the same time, the air force canceled their Manned Orbiting Laboratory (MOL) program and the Astronaut Office was forced to accept the seven youngest of their astronauts. The seven went to work for me and we were off and running.

As rapidly as possible, I reassigned the scientist-astros to their areas of greatest competence and credibility. For most of them, that meant working with the experiments and experimenters. They may have lacked experience, but they were among the brightest people in the office and they were working on a program whose success would be judged on scientific return. By channeling their effort into the right areas, we could guarantee that the experiments—90 percent of the mission—would be the most useful ever carried into space.

I returned decisions on operational hardware to those with a pilot background—depending heavily on the seven MOL pilots. The Rube Goldberg concepts were eliminated. We forced the science fiction view of living in space to give way to a realistic approach based on 1) coping with the slightly off-center world that existed in zero-g, and 2) achieving the possible. I prodded management to switch from the empty fuel tank workshop on a Saturn I-B to a "dry," engineered workshop launched on a Saturn V until they were convinced.

In perhaps the most important step of all, our little group brought together the five widely dispersed hardware manufacturers involved in Skylab and took a unified approach to all of the spacecraft systems and controls. We initiated cross-pollination of ideas instead of letting each company huddle in a corner with its own piece of hardware.

Overnight, I became part of that "other program" no one in the office seemed to care about—the one that was going to fly on a date uncertain but always two years away. My beaten path, my own personal orbit, now moved from such lifeless spots as Los Angeles, New York City, and Cocoa Beach to such exciting cultural centers as Huntsville, Alabama, and St. Louis, Missouri. My first trip to Huntsville was spent in a four-hour critique of the orbiting workshop mockup before the engineers could clutter my mind with all the reasons why it had to be the way it was.

At lunch that day with Wernher von Braun, I shared my conclusions, including the ridiculous concepts already mentioned, and he carried them higher. That session stirred some juices in Houston, and the program people complained to Deke that I had gone over their heads. The important thing was that Skylab had begun to move. I found myself thriving on the variety of problems that arose.

It was hard to get anyone interested in Skylab when crews were landing on the moon every couple of months. We went about our business, and the rest of the office went about theirs. The fellows I had entered the program with were now all involved in Apollo, soaking up the glamour, the lunar landings, the world tours, and the awards. And over in the corner there were fifteen to twenty of us working on Skylab in near-CIA secrecy.

One of the small benefits of Skylab was the opportunity for periodic contact with Wernher von Braun, one of the pioneers of rocketry and a man I had come to enjoy, admire, and respect. Von Braun was one of those people who fills a room, a large man, with great self-confidence. My first exposure to him had been in early 1964 when our group of fourteen toured the Marshall Space Flight Center at Huntsville, Alabama. On that occasion von Braun held court in a huge conference room, big as a ball-room, with three rear-projection screens behind him and his staff around the walls. What impressed me most during those eight hours was that no matter how technical our questions, he seldom had to refer them to his deputies for an answer. He not only ran the complex, but he knew what it was all about as well. All through those early months of Skylab we worked with von Braun and his team at the Marshall Space Flight Center.

I think of those early months of Skylab as good months, full and hectic, wound tight with the business of pushing ahead. All through this period there was great apprehension on the part of the scientist-astronauts, a feeling that at any time the project could be canceled and they would miss their moment in space. By late 1969 their worries were pointless. Skylab had reached that enviable point at which it would be more expensive to stop than to keep going.

Now it was my turn to wonder. I went to Chief Astronaut Tom Stafford looking for some assurances that I wasn't putting in two years of hard time only to get pushed aside and have someone else take over. "What does it look like?" I asked. "All bullshit aside. If I'm not going to fly Skylab I want to get back into Apollo and a flight to the moon. I don't plan to wait around developing the hardware just so someone else can cash in."

Tom knew the signs. "If you stick it out," he reassured me, "you'll be commanding the first Skylab mission."

I reminded him that the same promise had been made to Al Bean. The pressure was building within me to get that one more flight every pilot craves or to get on with the real business of life. It was getting impossible for my family. I was traveling more, bringing home a briefcase full of work every night, and I couldn't even assure them that I was doing it for a reward that was even in sight. I was gone for days at a time, and when I came home my contribution to family life was to play the disciplinarian for the first half-hour. It was the only consistent part of our routine.

Almost anything can be tolerated so long as your wife and kids love you and are willing to put up with it, too. But Lo was having trouble understanding why I stayed with Skylab when no one could even predict a flight date.

At the office, Apollo 12 was history, and we speculated about Pete Conrad's next assignment. He could either take over the Astronaut Office, if Tom Stafford resigned to enter Oklahoma politics, as some thought he would, or he could become Deke Slayton's assistant. The pecking order, you know.

My concern was a third possibility that no one mentioned: Pete could decide to take over Skylab. He not only was senior to me, he also had the horsepower and the know-how and was respected by everyone. I rooted like hell for Stafford to declare his candidacy for the Senate, creating an appropriate job for Conrad. My encouragement fell just short of making a campaign contribution. Unfortunately, Governor Dewey Bartlett decided to make the run and Stafford pulled out.

I could see the old skywriting on the wall, but it didn't happen overnight.

Late in 1970, two years after taking over Skylab, I was having frequent conversations with Pete Conrad. He was showing a growing interest in how Skylab functioned. We never really got to the short hairs. I sensed what was coming and didn't want to be an ass about it. We discussed the possibility of Pete's retiring and trying one of those big money jobs waiting for us out there like fruit hanging from a tree. But the market was down, the economy was shot, and we both knew it wasn't the right time to bail out.

I tried to convince myself that even if Pete took over Skylab, I might still get the flight, since he had already made three and this one had been *"promised."* Or, for sure, I'd get the second Skylab mission.

In August, word came down that Pete had been assigned as the new director of Skylab. There was no reason to be bitter toward Pete. He was taking it because it was the best job available, and he did it in a fashion that was characteristic of the way all of the astronauts worked. Each of us had confidence in his own judgment and ability. When Pete moved in he had no qualms about diving right in, setting up his own system, and doing it his way. All of which left me feeling like a fifth wheel.

When crew assignments started flowing out of Deke's office, my apprehensions were confirmed. Pete would fly the first one and my crew was scheduled to back him up. Al Bean, Pete's old crewmate, would fly the second. What now? Hold out hope for a rumored flight with the Russians four years hence? It was one more straw and contributed to a decision that was almost painless. I resigned from the program.

Skylab had been put on track and was now able to fly, but on bowing out I confess to pessimism on at least one objective. Knowing the engineering compromises accepted, the poor program management it had labored under at the beginning, and the impact of low budgets on key decisions, I doubted that all three missions could be flown as scheduled. There was doubt in my mind that the workshop would operate for the full ten months of the program. I expected the crews to have problems in orbit—not life-threatening but an accumulation of small, nagging ones that would add up until the spacecraft would simply not be able to function.

Skylab came to its moment of glory in May 1973, and one hour after launch it looked like a death blow had been struck at the long-struggling program. Some of the electrical system and a large portion of the thermal and meteorite protection shield had been torn away during boost. My first thought was of the agency's awful task of explaining to Congress and the nation how a $2.5 billion program failed to come off. My second was of the running battle fought (and lost) by astronaut Bob Overmyer and myself with the McDonnell-Douglas engineers on the reliability of the very hinges that failed during boost.

Those thoughts came rattling back to me when I watched the Skylab 1 crew return to earth five weeks later. Not only had they salvaged the entire program with their successful—I damn near said *heroic*—efforts at repairing the electric power and thermal protection systems, but they had performed many tasks for the first time in a space environment. When they packed up and left the workshop in orbit, we could be optimistic for a Skylab 2 mission. And Skylab 3, for the first time, looked to me like a good bet.

Joe Kerwin, our medinaut on Skylab 1, became the first doctor to make a house call in outer space, but unfortunately—or fortunately, depending on your point of view—he had nothing to treat. However, he would have come in handy on Skylab 2. That first space-station crew suffered some early discomfort but nothing that really affected their efficiency. The Skylab 2 crew—Al Bean, Owen Garriott, and Jack Lousma—were pretty sick boys for the first few days, and Garriott and Bean had to tread lightly for the first week.

They started out behind the power curve but at the end of ten days they were clicking along pretty well. As they approached the end of the mission, eight weeks later, their workload was running at 150 percent of the original flight plan, a record untouched by any other flight crew.

Everything was running so smoothly that they began a small campaign to extend the mission past the originally scheduled fifty-eight days. They would call home twice a week on a VHF radiophone connection to convey impressions and keep up with family activities. Most of the conversations were reduced to standard husband-wife dialogue.

On the crew's forty-second day in orbit Sue Bean, Al's wife, called to invite Lo and me to a going-away party, for the Dave Scotts. I asked Sue how it was going.

"Oh," she said, "I'm in the middle of cleaning the darn swimming pool, the lawn is out of control, and Amy has a cold. It's sure getting old, and today they asked for a ten-day extension. I sure hope they don't get it."

I had to laugh. Al was away on "man's greatest adventure" and Sue was complaining about cleaning the pool.

The third Skylab spacecraft carried an all-rookie crew, the first since Gemini 8. Gerry Carr, Bill Pogue, and Ed Gibson had their hands full. The discipline and logistics of the crew training routine is tremendous in scope. It takes place at sites spread all over the country, sometimes around the world, and calls for a great deal of discretionary judgment by the crew commander. Pete Conrad, as the chief of Skylab, faulted himself for not spending more time after his own mission working with the Skylab 3 crew on training priorities.

Whatever the failing, the fellows had their troubles right from the start of their three-month stay. They didn't feel well, suffering a rather well-publicized siege of first-day vomiting, and ran continually behind the flight plan *and* then behind the revised flight plan with its reduced workloads.

Ground controllers and the public became aware of the loaded barf bag in the same fashion as on Apollo 8—the on-board tape recorder. In that earlier case, it was intended; on Skylab 3 it was an unfortunate accident. In all live communications they had chosen not to mention that Bill Pogue was sick enough to throw up. Their mistake was in discussing what to do with the bag and what not to tell the ground while the on-board tape recorder was taking down every word. The tape was later routinely "dumped" to a ground site and many hours later replayed at Mission Control. Flight directors, medical doctors, and management all the way up to Chris Kraft were understandably less concerned about the vomiting incident than they were about the subterfuge. The riot act was read to the crew, but the incident compromised both their credibility and their relationship with the ground for the remainder of the eighty-four days.

It was a tough rap for the crew because it was not a self-serving decision, even though it appeared that way to observers. The period just before their flight, in late 1978, was marked by congressional budget hearings on funding for the Space Shuttle program. NASA was happily describing a twenty-year program of sixty to eighty flights a year, each lasting from seven to thirty days. Some legislative critics were just as blithely knocking the program in the head, especially the planned seven-day missions. "Hell!" they said, "it takes a week before the crews adjust enough to perform useful work. On the second Skylab mission it was nearly ten days."

All this was in the papers. NASA could not refute some of the criticism, but they were placing great emphasis on medical means of adapting to zero g as early as possible. It was a very sensitive issue. No one at NASA told them to be deceptive, but the fact remains that Carr, Pogue, and Gibson believed they were helping the agency in an hour of need. It was even discussed on the same tape that let the cat out of the bag on the vomiting incident. That part of the accidental communication was either suppressed or not considered newsworthy, and it was assumed that the crew was merely protecting a macho image.

Carr's crew eventually recovered from their stomach problems, and what had originally been planned as a fifty-six-day mission was stretched to an important eighty-four days. The endurance mark set by Pete Conrad in four missions was surpassed by Alan Bean in two, then placed out of reach for many years to come by three rookies on their first, last, and only mission.

Through knowledge gained during the earlier missions and adjustments made to the on-board regimen, the third Skylab crew was in much better physical shape on return than the second. Their accomplishments give us greater confidence that when the hardware is available for travel to the planets, man will not be found lacking.

Apollo, the moon flights, and all the steps leading up to them were for the poets, for the ages—a climax to the forty centuries in which man had dreamed about and finally reached the moon. But Skylab was for people; it was for *now*. It was what the champions of space exploration had promised would be there when the United States ended its celestial trade with the moon—our billions for its rocks.

Much of Skylab's success was the result of contributions made by the scientist-astronauts. Their disciplines were more applicable to Skylab than Apollo, but more important, Skylab was better structured operationally to accept their contributions. Their own reactions were mixed.

Don Holmquist, the M.D. who was an early dropout: "The most stimulating group of people ever, but overall, it was a stifling experience." He resented the way we responded to the space-flight carrot dangled before our noses. "Top management," he added, "was incompetent."

Phil Chapman, a member of the infamous XS-11, was a scientist in spirit as well as in fact. His career moved from MIT to NASA to a research position in industry. He was among the first to take a realistic view of the scientist's lot in the Astronaut Office, yet he stuck with it for five years. "At NASA," he said, "I was out of the mainstream of science, but I don't regret the time."

When I suggested that the National Academy of Sciences had been premature with its political pressure, Phil disagreed. "They should have proceeded with the selection on an assumption that the lunar landings would be easy, meaning scientists could fly sooner. The first group should have been solely geologists, for the lunar missions. NASA was a classic example of the system: management with total control and the astronauts with no bargaining power."

I agreed that the first scientists should have been geologists, but I'll be damned if a lunar landing was ever easy. Each landing was always the *first one* for the crew that was making it. Astronauts actually had a great deal of power; it was in program management that we had little responsibility or authority.

Owen Garriott's first mission, Skylab 2, came after an eight-year wait. "The whole thing should have taken half that long," he said. He felt, on balance, that the eight years were well spent, but he was not completely satisfied with what had occurred in that time. He thought the flight crew training had been overdone—but after eight years, who wouldn't?

Owen went on, "None of us really change after a flight—we only have the freedom to do more of what we want. Before the mission, each one has to concentrate so much on a single goal he is unable to be an individual."

In spite of the successes of Skylab, the public remained completely apathetic. Part of the problem from the outset had been the inability of the masses to understand exactly what was being done and what could be achieved. Explanation isn't easy when most people are still trying to figure out how a radio works. But even the average taxpayer can—or should—understand the need to observe our lands and oceans and to control our environment.

The casual attitude toward Skylab could be interpreted as confidence in NASA, but the course of the program was anything but routine. Salvaging the schedule after the damage on the station launch was one of NASA's finest hours, challenged only by the successful return of the Apollo 13 spacecraft. Had we been unable to send crews into Skylab, we would been designing our next generation of space stations (and selecting crews) without ever subjecting man to a really long stay in space. Man's investigation of the sun and of the earth's resources would have been delayed for another ten years. The phenomenal capability of NASA's technical experts was demonstrated during the thermal shield failure of Skylab 1 when they correctly diagnosed the problems from 270 miles below. In less than ten days, apparatus was built to solve the problems plaguing the spacecraft, making it habitable and useful for the ensuing ten months. Conrad's crew was launched in time, carrying with them one primary "fix" and two backup solutions.

As astronauts, we saw it as a revolution of sorts in the thinking of mission planners and flight directors. Historically, flight crews trained long and competitively on all phases of a mission and were not allowed to perform any task that had not been through a lengthy certification and practice cycle. We were over trained to the point where even crucial operations seemed routine. Now, overnight, it was accepted that Conrad, Kerwin, and Weitz would perform all manner of circus stunts under conditions formerly believed too risky even to consider.

The successful repair of Skylab 1 emphasized the value of real-time decision-making by broadly trained crewmembers.

Dollar for dollar and pound for pound, Skylab was one of America's most important space achievements: for what it added to present knowledge in solar astronomy and material processing, for the new ground it broke for future exploration of the earth's resources, and perhaps most important, for the study of man's long-term adjustment to the environment of space. I look back on it as a great comeback from the edge of disaster and one of the space program's brightest moments.

15

The Dispensable Astronaut

SYSTEMS ENGINEERING has been called the science of tradeoffs. In the early 1980s we began flying a few women in space, and when we did those first few "Astronettes" were the result of trade-offs.

There is just no way to get into this subject without sounding like a grand champion male chauvinist, yet I don't believe God formed women out of a pound of barleycorn. Nor do I wish they would all quit being hysterical and go back to decent jobs—like working as manicurists.

It is a demonstrated fact that women can do many of the tasks in space as well as any man. It is also a fact that it costs more, can create new risks, and further complicates the operation. Logically, the proper time for a woman (or any other category of crewmember) to take a seat in the spacecraft was when the added costs and other mission impacts were balanced by the benefits gained by their presence.

Logic, of course, had little to do with it. Since we live in a society ruled by lobbies, women flew in space long before the time was right simply because social pressures compelled it. There was, in fact, only token opposition. The public considered it fair, the politicians said it was the law, and those most intimately involved, the other astronauts, found the idea of a mixed crew . . . well . . . intriguing.

Voyages to other planets in our solar system will be measured in years, not days, and one is more likely to attract volunteers—among the astros I know—if the crew is coed. Of course, mission planners will expect all members of such long-duration flights to be qualified in special areas of science. But honesty compels me to point out that most of the eminent women scientists are not renowned for their *Playboy* centerfold bodies or their sophisticated views on sex. Thus, we have the beginnings of a conflict basic to the human experience. After, say, a year in space, your average male astronaut could fall in love with an avocado. But the idea of being used, or even thought of, in romantic ways is frequently not acceptable to the liberated woman's view of equality.

This wasn't exactly the major problem confronting the space program in the eighties and nineties, but he/she chemistry being what it is, sex can't be ignored. A spaceship is a damned small room and, even under the most detached circumstances, you get to know each other better than you want.

During my tenure at NASA, I lost count of the number of times we were cornered by flag-waving feminists: the woman physicist who had competed with men for years, the pilot who felt that her flying skill was enough of a qualification, the physical culturist who was prepared to arm wrestle, winner take all. Each had the same challenge: Why are there no women in space?

My reaction was always the same: Are they motivated by a desire to challenge the unknown . . . . or simply to challenge what they see as the male establishment? They frequently argued, "The Russians sent up a woman, why can't we?" But the question wasn't why couldn't we or why didn't we, but why *should* we? The Russians prided themselves on being able to launch and recover their spacecraft through completely automatic methods. This enabled them to fly dogs, civilians, and even the first woman, a parachutist named Valentina Tereshkova. The American space program didn't operate that way. The first astronauts successfully fought for a higher degree of human involvement and control of the spacecraft, so-called "man in the loop." The thought of an automatic deorbit and recovery was no more appealing to an astronaut in 1960 than the idea of an automatic landing was to a passenger on a commercial airliner. Any time the job at hand can be best performed by a woman and, other qualifications being equal, a man gets the assignment, I'll stand up and holler, *"Foul!"* I'll be on her side. But when a woman is launched into space merely to demonstrate that we can do it, as was Valentina Tereshkova, then I denounce it as blatant tokenism and a poor justification for spending the taxpayer's money. To those of us who bought the tickets and took the rides in the first ten years of the manned space program, it never occurred to us that we had to be *socially* relevant.

It was inevitable that the demographics of the original space pilot corps—the seventy-three crewmen selected between 1959 and 1969—would become an issue. It was hard to ignore what we had so visibly in common: except for a handful of Catholics, we were all white, Anglo-Saxon Protestants (WASPS). We were almost exclusively middle class and mostly from small towns.

I don't know why there weren't any black astronauts. For that matter, I don't know why there weren't any Jewish astronauts or Chinese or Hispanic. I only know that the absence of a black astronaut was not due to discrimination or to a lack of political pressure from, as they say, "the highest levels." In the 1960s, it was the fervent hope of those at the space agency that a well-qualified black pilot would apply. That would have solved the political problem painlessly. But to be told to "find one" and, if necessary, stretch a point here and there to enroll him, was an affront to all the extremely able men who had already been passed over. Beyond that, it would have been repugnant to the men entrusted with the selection process. I can only guess at Deke Slayton's reaction at being told to bend the requirements in order to desegregate space. "What do you mean? I *have* to take a black astronaut? We take the best we can get, and if one qualifies we'll be glad to have him—if not, and they still insist, they'll have to find someone else for my job." Deke's only prejudice was

Flying gunnery at Saufley Field, Pensacola, part of
Navy Pilot training, 1952.

against failure, but he was one of those people who resists pressure. If someone insisted on lowering the standards to meet a political objective he would have told them in a most clinical way how far to lower them and where, and then he would advise them to find another man to do the selecting.

I don't say these things casually. We went through a period in the late sixties when even the word *qualified* became a kind of code word for racial discrimination. On that score, I don't believe the space program really needs defending. As late as World War II there were only a few black military pilots, and it wasn't until the late 1950s that a major commercial U.S. airline began hiring black pilots. That was one factor working against them when the United States was ready to explore other worlds. For a long time, the men who flew, who tested new airplanes, and who were motivated to fly in space were white.

Aviation simply didn't attract minority applicants in any real numbers until the war in Vietnam. During my eighteen months in Navy flight training, in 1952 and 1953, only three of my fellow cadets were black. Out of the 300 fully qualified applicants for the fourteen astronaut openings in 1963, there were only two black military jet pilots.

In my time, the man who came closest to breaking the barrier was a young air force captain named Ed Dwight—but not without a little help from his friends. In the early 1960s, Dwight attracted attention not only in the Air Force, but also within several civilian groups actively working to break down racial barriers in the United States.

When Captain Dwight was attending the Test Pilot's School at Edwards Air Force Base, not very subtle political moves were taking place to see that he would be graduated into the Aerospace Research Pilot School, successful completion of which would qualify him to apply to become America's first black astronaut.

Fifteen years before all this, another young air force captain, Chuck Yeager, became the first man to exceed the speed of sound in what were then the farthest reaches of flight. Now a colonel and commanding the Aerospace Research Pilot School, Yeager's career had crossed paths with this appealing young captain who hoped to penetrate the boundaries of space.

Someone in President Kennedy's administration proposed to Yeager that a special effort should be made to include Dwight in the Research

Pilot class then being formed. Yeager's response—as I got the story—was in character with the man I know and his sense of fair play. "We will take Captain Dwight," he said, "but if we have to lower the standards to do so, I will also enroll all those between the usual cutoff point and Dwight's class standing." Not coincidentally, the next class at the Aerospace Research Pilot School—usually eight in number—was the largest in history, with thirteen members. Not too long after that, Dwight was way down among the also-rans in the selections for our group of fourteen, the Apollo astronauts.

From what I was told by people who knew him, he was a capable enough aviator, only one of the categories of qualification. His appointment would have pleased those who saw it as another battle to correct society's ills and it would no doubt have been splendid public relations. In spite of pressuring calls to NASA from then Attorney General Robert Kennedy, Dwight was not selected, and for honest reasons. Every improvement, every success, every new horizon in the history of flight has been governed by one rule: for a technical job, you get the best technician available. The whole idea of tokenism, or a quota system, was alien to a program that sets out to challenge the best that man can muster. Keep in mind, that of all the *qualified* applicants for the astronaut corps, over 95 percent have been rejected. To my knowledge, the selection process has always measured the applicants against each other and against the requirements of the job objectively and in complete disregard of an individual's race, color, creed, or national origin. Of course, that all changed in the late seventies when "diversity" crept into the national vocabulary and into the astronaut selections. It has been, and I hope always will be, damned difficult to be chosen whether the candidate be black or white, male or female.

Four years after Dwight, Bob Lawrence, an air force major, was selected into the Air Force Space Program—with no special concessions. The first (and only) black astronaut up to that time was killed in the crash of an F-104 only a few months after selection.

One point needs to be made here. All during my years in NASA, race was never a factor in astronaut selections. It was not an issue until the politicians made it one.

Race and gender in astronaut selections are, on the face of it, a contrived issue on the order of demanding that women and blacks be allowed to compete in the Indianapolis 500; both long since a reality. They have the same right to risk their necks as anyone else—so long as they can keep up with the field.

Of course, it isn't possible to talk about such things without sounding as though one were trying to integrate the Masonic Lodge or liberate some exclusive, all-male bar. When minority pressure groups zeroed in on the space program, they invariably made it appear that someone was being deprived of a basic human right. The public always pictures an astronaut in terms of the flight itself and the attendant glamour. Few stop to consider the four to eight years' grind necessary to get there. It takes that long because of the inherent nature of space exploration. Our decision to prepare for the flights in such a meticulous fashion has proven to be correct. There will be some changes and the time may be shortened, but it will continue to be a marathon of preparation. The selection process, as much as anything, is to determine the person with the drive and dedication to endure those training demands.

The long training ordeal was not without hazard. The first astronaut was killed in space in 1986—after we had lost eight during training for spaceflights. We were probably spared earlier fatalities in space because Grissom, White, and Chaffee paid the ultimate price in the Apollo 1 fire. The fact that they could, and did, accept the risk was essential to the job. In this respect, being an astronaut is as much a state of mind, or attitude, as an occupation. The Apollo 1 fire and its aftermath became a part of our cargo, one of those flash happenings that shape us in ways we cannot always explain. But it reinforced my feeling that there had been no place for women in the space program until room was found to take along specialists and passengers.

Grissom, White, and Chaffee were each survived by a wife and several children, and all accepted their loss according to the code—for a while. A couple of years after the fire, Betty Grissom filed a lawsuit against North American Rockwell, its subcontractors, and the space agency over the death of her husband. Betty had her reasons and we— Gus' teammates—were in a poor position to judge how imperative they must have seemed to her. But around the office the reaction was pretty unanimous: Gus Grissom had to be spinning in his grave.

Our view of the deaths was simplistic. The country had not recruited us to take the risk and accept the rewards *if* successful—and to file a lawsuit if it was not. We were professional pilots whose careers were built on assessing the risks, minimizing them, and tolerating what we couldn't control with eyes wide open. No one was more aware of the poor state of the original Apollo spacecraft than Gus Grissom. Our failure to stop the schedule and demand that the flaws be corrected was our biggest collective mistake during my eight years with NASA. But our own attitude— the fighter pilot mystique, "We can fly the crates they came in"—kept us moving toward a first launch date that could not be met except with disaster.

With all that, Gus would have been the last to ask for retribution. Betty saw it differently. She sued. And we claimed it was a breach of faith with Gus. At least that's how I felt about it. Being a realist, I held my breath for several years following the fire, expecting someone to sue somebody. We live in a litigious society and the fire was an ideal situation given the known condition of the spacecraft, the conclusions of the investigation, the political climate, and the concerns of a large aerospace contractor for its public image. North American Rockwell settled the suit out of court in 1971, for $850,000. It happened rather quietly. Only a few paragraphs appeared in the paper without the public noticeably recoiling at the idea of a cash value being placed on an astronaut's life. A short time later, at the initiative of North American Rockwell, a similar settlement was bestowed on the widows of Chaffee and White.

All things considered, Rockwell was undoubtedly relieved to close the books on a tragic episode for such a nominal amount. The company never tried to defend itself against many of the charges made against it— many totally wild and unfounded. The settlements to the surviving families came long after the Apollo spacecraft had been transformed into one of the most remarkable pieces of machinery ever built by man.

In a way, that action, that lawsuit, the idea of a hero's widow going public contributed to the transformation of the astronaut image then taking place. To be sure, other factors affected it more, including the fact that NASA itself was in a state of flux and undergoing a period of self-criticism—and, of course, the Apollo 15 envelope caper had shaken the tree. In earlier days, the astronaut image had been rather easy to control. But, by 1970, there were too many of us and too many sources for leaks and cracks.

As difficult as it was to get into space and join those exclusive ranks, getting out wasn't all that painless, either. Even so, by 1970 the exodus of older astronauts was nearly equal to the rate at which we were recruited eight years earlier.

It wasn't until months after leaving the program that I tried to define the reasons for my own resignation. It was something one had to think about: the subject came up in every interview. It boiled down to family—looking up every few months and realizing that my kids had grown a little older without me—and pride—not having the prospect of another flight soon, not feeling as useful or essential once Pete Conrad took over the Skylab group.

Deciding to leave was the first step. Once that decision was made, I gave plenty of thought to how I could make use of all those years as an astronaut. I mean that in the sense of taking advantage of one's education and other life experiences. Of course, to best enjoy the fallout one needed to follow the Bill Anders Principle: be the only astronaut in town! As Anders once put it, "If the governor wants to invite an astronaut to the ball, you don't want to be in a situation where his press secretary says, 'Which astronaut?'"

Even in putting that life behind, it was plain that the competition never really ceases. Just as we kept a jealous eye on the crew rotations, we followed each other's fortunes in private life: books, jobs, business ventures, second marriages. It was the kind of checking one does between class reunions. We would not become old men, living on past victories and regretting old defeats, even though some are still fresh in my mind. The years at NASA of watching a new flight crew come onto the scene, move to center stage, and then fly in a few months sometimes hurt. There went another mission you'd never fly. As someone once said, "Every time a friend succeeds, I die a little."

As each of us faced the dismal prospect of no more flights, or when we concluded that the prize was no longer worth the game, we were faced with several options. One might retire in place, staying in the Astronaut Office, retaining the astronaut label but performing little of what had earned it. It was a shell, a sham, akin to the "partynaut" we often joked about. It would mean attending many design meetings and making an occasional speech. Your astronaut career, as a practical matter, would simply have died without benefit of burial.

A few of the astros tolerated such an existence because they had reservations about making it on the outside. Many of the military astros used it as a holding pattern to complete their twenty years before retirement. Some settled into that role because they liked it and were content to soak up the suds of their celebrity status, like the old boxing champ who allows the hangers-on at the bar to buy him drinks.

Still others chose to remain in the public sector, either in another capacity at NASA or with a different agency of the government. The most successful at pursuing this path were Jim McDivitt, the Apollo program manager for most of the lunar landings, and Bill Anders, who went on to become the first administrator of the Nuclear Regulatory Agency and United States ambassador to Norway. Mike Collins was named director of the National Air and Space Museum, and Dave Scott became director of the NASA Flight Research Center. Others—such as Al Worden, Gene Cernan, Rusty Schweickart, Jack Schmitt, and Jack Swigert—found desirable government jobs with some status and still within the smell of the greasepaint. Following the Challenger accident, in 1986, the opportunities for non-flying astros expanded, with some becoming directors of NASA Centers and Dick Truly even being appointed Administrator of NASA.

A third alternative was to move into the private sector. This was sometimes encouraged by office politics or the lack of an available government job, but for most it was the challenge of an entirely new career and the desire to make some money. When we went out to sell our services it was, as in any commercial enterprise, a case of *caveat emptor*.

Far too often, unfortunately, a potential employer saw us, collectively, as neon signs that said A-S-T-R-O-N-A-U-T in flashing lights, not as unique individuals. That group image carried with it a blanket assumption of certain skills that was not always warranted. Not only did our abilities and technical knowledge vary greatly, but in many cases so did the willingness to dig in and work, to slug it out in the trenches of management with such details as monthly reports and personnel problems. In some cases there was a plainly detectable attitude of "I went to the moon, and now the world owes me a living."

It is a fair assumption that most astronauts are well equipped technically, that we have a certain credibility with the public, and that the name alone will open many doors. If we were all run through a computer— which many seemed to think we were—the printout would probably describe us as highly motivated, goal-oriented, quick-study types, with a high need for achievement. Many had fairly strong leadership qualities, although most lacked specific management skills. Most of us fit somewhere between a professional manager and an entrepreneur, with a reliance on technology but even more on ourselves and our ability to solve problems.

None of this was yet worked out in my mind that day, in March 1971, a few days after my thirty-ninth birthday, when I stopped by Deke Slayton's office. After considering my resignation for several months, I had finally made my decision. I was leaving the program and asked to be relieved of my operational, administrative and technical responsibilities. It would let someone else gain experience by picking up my projects and leave me freer to explore the job market. I had already done some investigating around the country, and it would only have been a matter of weeks before Deke heard it from someone else. Deke thanked me for letting him know and said it was somewhat unusual for him to be told in advance that someone was leaving the program, especially if they had yet to decide where they were headed.

I did not agonize over the decision when I was through playing space. From that moment on, it was only a question of when and where.

When asked, "What's it like to be an astronaut?" I sometimes answer facetiously, "Everyone has to do something for a living." I made a serious effort to be as little changed by the experience as possible. It's impossible to be completely unaffected, but I like to think that my basic personality and character remained pretty much as before.

The job exposed me to things I would never have experienced otherwise. And it happened at the right time in my life. Retiring from NASA three years later, the world outside would not have offered the same opportunities to Walter Cunningham. That was part of the consideration in deciding *when* to leave. Being an astronaut in the 1960s was one of the world's best jobs, but it was not the be all to end all. It had taken five years to reach a position (in the Skylab program) where I could materially influence the destiny of a multi-billion-dollar program.

I came to Houston with few preconceptions about the astronauts. It was encouraging to find out, in many ways, they were no better or no worse than anyone else, full of the same human foibles, and that my credentials were not out of place. We had ass-draggers in the program along with workaholics like Slayton, McDivitt, and Scott.

The economy wasn't exactly roaring along at peak efficiency in 1971, but that concerned me little. It had never been my plan to fly rockets the rest of my life. The decision to leave fit the general plan I had laid out for my life years before: to spend my twenties in education, my thirties in space flight, my forties in the commercial world making a secure future for my family, and in my fifties to consider public service once more. I hoped that, by then, I could afford that luxury, and with the children grown I would feel less guilty about asking my wife to repeat the trials of living with someone whose life would not be completely his own.

I talked with companies in insurance, oil, and microelectronics, and even considered opening my own consulting firm. There was no shortage of opportunities, but many lacked the kind of substance my life demanded, being of the marketing or door-opening variety. It was the operating end of a business that interested me. Sure, it would have been an advantage to land in a high-technology spot, but as matters developed, I went into an entirely new field right there in Houston.

The space corps had been a tremendous finishing school. I joined it with a science education (an essential qualification) and elected to use that training as a tool in my space career. After eight years with NASA there were new tools and a new confidence to use them in a new career.

No career lasts forever, but it should always provide new tools that can be used in the next. Being a part of "man's greatest adventure" was but one of many stimulating challenges, and it could have passed me by through any number of circumstances. Sure, a certain amount of good fortune—luck—enters into it. But without the right preparation one can never take advantage of good fortune. Good luck occurs a lot more frequently for the man who is prepared.

Once my connections to NASA were severed, it was complete. Except for occasional calls to old friends now in senior management, my view in the intervening years has been from the grandstand. Many people assume a former astronaut continues to act as a kind of unpaid consultant, that his vast knowledge is available to the government when needed, that the tremendous investment in his training and education is just waiting to be tapped, again and again. To my knowledge, no former astronaut has ever been called upon by NASA to assist in some critical hour of need or even to express an opinion about any internal matter once he had left the fold—certainly not in that small corner of the NASA universe called the Astro-

naut Office. Occasionally, former astronauts may be appointed to a panel
to study some particular problem that will take the heat off NASA management.

It will be interesting to look back twenty-five years later at what happened to those thirty men who formed the corps of space pilots bridging
the transition from jet aviation to the end of the Apollo program. That was
the Time of Apollo—the golden age of manned space flight, a period
when the astronauts were kings of the mountain. They were heroes without blemish or equal, a condition that will not exist again anytime soon.
When historians make their judgments, the glory of the beginnings of
manned spaceflight will be found among those first thirty.

By 1963, when my group was selected, the character of the candidates
was beginning to change. In order to insure an adequate number of motivated and qualified applicants, and still remain highly selective, the
flight-time experience was broadened to where it could be met by operational fighter pilots. As a result, half of the fourteen Apollo selectees
were operational fighter pilots (myself among them) and half had test flying experience. And while our group had logged more jet time, on average, than the original seven astronauts, it was still less than the experience
of the second generation, the men of Gemini. There has never been much
doubt in my mind that those nine—the second group—had the best overall mix of qualifications for the job. That was in 1962, and Young, McDivitt, White, Conrad, Stafford, Borman, Lovell, and Armstrong (the last in
his group to fly) formed the heart of the Gemini project and filled most
of the key slots for Apollo. (The ninth member and the weakest of the
group, Elliot See, was killed before he could fly in space.) It just might be
that eight people more capable of performing a difficult task well, under
pressure, had never before been assembled.

Time served to wipe out most distinctions between the groups, but in the
beginning the Original Seven were just what the times and the stakes
demanded. They were highly competitive and attracted by the glamour
and renown of being involved in a first-of-a-kind venture. In 1959, the
man-in-space program needed pilots who recognized the mission for
what it was and who understood the challenge. At the time many better-
known test pilots wanted no part of the action.

Of the first three groups of astronauts, twenty-three lived to fly in
space, and between them they were involved in all the firsts the manned

space program has experienced. On the other hand, the most dedicated during my tenure had to be the last three of the six groups—the last of seventy-three astros chosen from 4,000 applicants—for whom the rewards were largely uncertain and the glory pretty much used up. The public was beginning to grow bored with our space achievements. White House visits, world tours, and personal story contracts were no longer among the fringe benefits. Scientist-astronauts like Joe Kerwin and Ed Gibson trained for eight years before Skylab offered them a chance to fly. The siren call of adventure had to be loud and clear for them.

From Buzz Aldrin's nervous breakdown and alcoholism, to Ed Mitchell's experiments in ESP and John Glenn's election to the Senate, the public's interest in the astronauts continued beyond their tour of duty. As some floundered in business, it became evident we were human just like everyone else. Without the stimulus of space and the challenge of new frontiers, some lost the self-discipline that accounted for their success as astronauts.

It is, I suppose, much like being a college football hero. But you can't go on replaying old games forever. As for myself, I left without regrets, secure that the time was right to move on, to find another direction. During one year I had been away from home 255 days and my family was in danger of becoming a matriarchy. Some of the slick magazines depicted the astronauts as the new sex symbols, but I doubt that many of the wives thought of their husbands as sexual athletes. More often than not we came home from travel on Friday night bushed, carrying our work and our laundry, and probably needing to stop by the office on Saturday and Sunday to straighten out the mess that had collected while we were gone. Our children grew up in the space program and took it for granted, but suddenly they were eight and ten years old and celebrity fathers wondered if it was already too late to reclaim them.

Finally, we ask ourselves, "Was it worth it?"

I only asked that question once, the day I made up my mind to leave, and the answer was a resounding "YES!" I achieved a goal that had consumed my life for eight years. The square was filled; I had compromised with myself less than most, generally said what was on my mind, and yet still felt constrained by the organizational straight jacket and maintaining the image. I can only imagine how those who slavishly conformed must have felt. Even a free spirit like Scott Carpenter once had to appear at a supermarket opening in St. Louis to accommodate a Missouri senator.

While actively training, there was little desire and even less time to speak out on controversial subjects. We were so isolated in our individual careers and consumed by our own goals, that reading about the great events that rearranged the country in the 1960s was like reading about the problems of some Latin American government. But for the *ex*-astronaut, there were no good reasons to remain quiet. To the contrary, there was motivation to speak out, especially for those who could use the exposure (to run for office, raise money for a cause—or publicize a book).

Leaving in the spring of 1971, I had the feeling I was beating the crowd. There was another factor. With the cards falling the way they were, the only way I could get another space flight before I was fifty, would be through some calamity to a prime crewman. After eight years, the thought of waiting around like a vulture for something terrible to happen to a friend wasn't very, appealing.

So the break was made. Yet in a very real sense it still goes on. It's as if we had belonged to some kind of church, and though we no longer attend services, we are still considered part of the flock. In one way or another, each of us continues to exploit the fact that we were astronauts and to share in the benefits in one way or another. Sometimes it is for personal gain, which isn't necessarily wrong, and sometimes for personal causes, charities, and so on, in a way that is both tasteful and altruistic.

Rusty Schweickart, for example, involved himself in a program called Crisis Hotline, an agency that tried to help troubled youngsters with their problems. He would have manned the phones and raised money for the organization regardless of who or what he was, but being Rusty Schweickart, *astronaut,* didn't hurt. Rusty and I, also organized an environmental concern organization called the Earth Awareness Foundation, and many a local and national charity drive has been headed by an astronaut. Their contribution is almost invariably limited to their name and their time, because astros aren't rich in spite of what the public may believe.

In an age when movie stars and athletes can sell cologne and electric razors and floor wax and panty hose, it may have been inevitable that many of the fellows would cut a television commercial or two. Ours is a cynical era. Remember the immortal words of Lenny Bruce: "It's time to grow up and sell out." The first commercials were by Scott Carpenter for Chevron gasoline, and Wally Schirra for the railroads. They were followed by a number of others—Jim Lovell and Buzz Aldrin, and even Neil Armstrong for General Time. Each in his turn was criticized by those still in the Astronaut Office, purist and hypocrite alike. Some of those critics went on to commercial efforts of their own: Pete Conrad, for example, for American Express. And that was just the tip of the iceberg.

It isn't difficult to figure out why. It's for the money, ladies and gentlemen, for the money. Astronauts, as a rule, don't get rich, but they do become accustomed to a relatively high standard of living. All commercials exploit the notoriety of the endorser's personality, and in the interest of full disclosure, let me say that I did several public service spots for the Houston Police Department and a commercial extolling the virtues of Houston. Astronauts know this as well as anyone, but we aren't without scruples, or standards of taste. It was years before anyone picked up the rumored $100,000 for making a Tang commercial, and several of us turned down a potential $150,000 deal to advertise a cold remedy. Then there were the space-age, charcoal-impregnated, odor-absorbing socks. Most of us have our price, but we also remain concerned about what our peers may think.

Buzz Aldrin was concerned enough, before he agreed to do his infamous Volkswagen commercial, to ask then deputy administrator of NASA, George Low, for an opinion. George answered him very simply, with a long, slow look, "Well, Buzz, it depends on who you want to be like, Jimmy Doolittle or Wally Schirra." Buzz has gone on to be a prolific advertiser, partly because he is more in demand than the rest of us.

Of course, there are no indispensable men in the space program. One by one we leave, and the flights and the projects go on just as efficiently. For all it matters, we could be living on the moon. But for those of us who actually stood there, or were in the thick of things, the lunar dust is on our sleeves and will always affect our perspective.

I am frequently asked what is the most apparent difference between my experience at NASA and what I saw moving into the private sector. That's easy. In the outside, nine-to-five world of business, people seldom take the same pride in their work—it's no doubt easier to get inspired over sending someone to the moon than over the daily order of widgets. Within NASA in the 1960s everyone took pride in their job, you could count on them—from the top managers to the guy who fastened the last snap on our flight suits.

Pride and teamwork and quality were more than words, and that's the message I took with me. It will still be there after the mistakes and phony sentiments of an earlier time are forgotten, when the scientists have replaced the hotshot pilots and women routinely ride the fire into space.

Dot and I in our last picture with Wally Schirra shortly before his death in 2007.

16

The Russians are coming!
The Russians are coming!

IN THE SIXTIES, the U.S. goal was easily understood; put a man on the moon before the end of the decade. The space race was on and the rallying cry was simple. The Russians are coming! The Russians are coming!

Little did we know that the Russians were using the same message to sell their program—and for the same reason—to justify their spending.

The Sixties began with U.S. getting beat at its own game. America and the rest of the world were shocked in 1957, with the launch of Sputnik, the first artificial satellite placed in orbit. Americans have always regarded themselves as technologically superior. Now, suddenly, we were faced with the fact we were not only *not* the best at everything in the world, we weren't even as good as some people at some things.

Reacting in a typically American fashion, we gave chase. We thought we were catching up when, on 12 April 1961, a day that passes without notice in America, the manned space program lifted off. That was the day the Soviet Union launched Yuri Gagarin into space for a single orbit of the earth. With that brief 108-minute trip around the earth, Yuri Gagarin entered the pages of history. Gagarin was celebrated, venerated—even worshiped in the old Soviet Union. Under the communist system, he was the equivalent of a saint.

Why Gagarin? He was young, good looking, and had the proper peasant background. He projected the politically correct image of the Soviet space program. His qualifications by our standards were minimal, with very little flight time or other experience. But that was adequate. He did not touch a single control—like the space-dogs that flew before him.

But, now, the world began to look upon the Soviets differently.

This was the second time America had been amazed by the Soviet

Union. The first had been in learning how quickly following World War II they exploded their first nuclear weapon and began to develop nuclear power. That was accomplished with a lot of spying and stolen technology. This time, the Soviets were leading the way and setting the standard.

Only three generations passed between man's first heavier-than-air flight and man's first flight around the world in orbit. Yet, today, there are two generations for whom man's first flight into space was only read about in the history books.

From the beginning, the Russians and Americans took two different approaches—as different as their respective philosophies of government and the natural choice for each country. The cold war was engaged again—this time on a political and more peaceful battlefield. Russia and the U.S. launched into this new battlefield on two different trajectories. Both would enjoy success. But, in the end, the American victory could be attributed, in large measure, to our design and operating philosophies. It was only natural. In the American democracy, the individual is paramount; in the Soviet collectivist society, the individual was the tool of the communist system of centralized planning and control. Without our thinking about it at the time, we had just naturally turned the space race into precisely what the Soviet Union advertised it to be—a test of two systems of government.

So, what were the differences?

In the Soviet Union, cosmonauts were subjects to be studied, directed, and totally responsive to trainers, doctors and (during a mission) to ground control. Taking the initiative was not only discouraged, it was unacceptable. Onboard cosmonauts executed instructions transmitted to them from control center in Moscow, called TsUP (pronounced t'soop). They followed, religiously, those instructions passed up from the ground. This master-slave relationship with respect to the ground continues even today with a significant portion of their individual flight bonuses dependent on how well they follow orders.

All Soviet manned spacecraft have performed at least several unmanned flights before cosmonauts were included as "passengers." This is not to say they didn't have important responsibilities during a mission—especially in the event of an emergency. But all normal flight plan events were almost exclusively scheduled by ground controllers. Crew input was discouraged in planning or working out conflicts in that planning. Cosmonauts were perceived as a sometimes troublesome substitute for an onboard sequencer. (Sequencers are computers that control events on unmanned missions.) Many of the shortcomings of the Soviet space program can be attributed to their failure to fully exploit the inherent capabilities of man. Not surprisingly, they never fully trusted the individual as opposed to the "collective" on the ground.

We never fully appreciated the limitations of the Russian program until we worked with them on Apollo/Soyuz. It was brought home to an even greater degree, when American astronauts participated in the Russian Mir space station program.

The Russians have always had a requirement that their manned spacecraft, including the Shuttle look-alike, Buran, be capable of returning with an incapacitated crew. In retrospect, it is difficult to say whether this incapacitated crew requirement led to the pecking order of ground over crew, or the philosophy of central control resulted in the incapacitated crew requirement. I suspect the latter, since it was consistent with prevailing communist doctrine.

This also partially explains the most obvious visible difference between the two programs—the Soviets returned from space on land, while we splashed down in the sea.

As a result, the Soviets developed relatively simple hardware and flew relatively simple missions. In the Astronaut Office, where we had long since formed our opinion about the substance of those early missions, it was a real eye-opener when we learned that so many Soviet "firsts" had been accomplished and they had gained such worldwide prestige with such simple hardware. It was one of the few areas where we could learn from them.

They have been most successful at extending the life of their early rockets, saving money and gaining reliability. The same Proton booster has been in use since 1965.

NASA was a firmly committed to the philosophy of "man in the loop"—the control loop, that is. With man playing an essential role, his infinitely re-programmable brain could be properly exploited. If an occasional engineer wavered from the faith, one of the flight crew was always there to remind him of our essential role. Unlike the Soviets, we believed in decentralized control and distributed management. Astronauts were integral and sometimes critical members of most hardware design and mission planning teams. I know of no place where we were excluded. During a mission we were independent thinkers and decision makers, working closely with mission control to shape flight plans and accomplish mission objectives. It was the American way of life carried into one more challenging environment. Space was the latest of the last frontiers and we set out to conquer it the way we had conquered the West—utilizing individuals with initiative, self-confidence, and bravery.

We maximized the role of the human in the face of a great many unknowns. We also over-planned, over-designed, over-tested, and over-trained throughout the program. We utilized the most sophisticated hardware—sometimes more sophisticated than necessary—to fly very complex missions. Without intending it to be, this excess of caution became the secret weapon that enabled America to beat the Russians in an important political battle of the cold war.

In March 1968, Yuri Gagarin's death shocked the world. Gagarin died while on a routine jet training flight with a flight instructor and the Soviet government and news media never explained the crash. There were dozens of rumors. Gagarin was "drunk," or "flat-hatting," or attempting to shoot a moose from an open cockpit. In 1987, when the accident investigation files were unsealed, the cause was determined to be pilot error— the same finding as for 75 percent of all U.S. aircraft accidents!

In addition to several fatal accidents in their space history, the Russians have experienced a number of exciting near misses. From the beginning, stories had leaked out of cosmonauts returning to earth in Siberia and holding off marauding wolves. And there was the world's first manned launch abort in April 1975 with Soyuz 18. The story of most of these adventures usually slipped out several years after, a little bit at a time. In January 1969, Soyuz 5 returned to earth with the descent module still attached to the equipment module—the worst possible configuration. It reentered the atmosphere wrong end first without a heatshield and the cosmonaut, Boris Volynov, survived. The information was kept under wraps until 1997.

My favorite story is another Russian near catastrophe with Cosmonaut Nikolay Rukavishnikov. In the Eighties, Rukavishnikov (Nicky to everyone he met). was the assigned Soyuz rescue pilot. Nicky's job was to launch, solo, on 48 hours notice, to rescue any cosmonauts unfortunate enough to be stuck in orbit. This rescue capability is an operational nicety we have been unable to incorporate into our program, even today.

I originally met Nicky in 1973 when he was training as a backup crewman for the Apollo/Soyuz Test Project. But my first chance to engage him in a real conversation came in Bulgaria in 1988.

Nicky enjoyed a special reputation with the Bulgarians. In April 1979, he had been the pilot of Soyuz 33, a re-supply mission to the Salyut space station. The objective of the mission was to exchange his fresh spacecraft for the older Soyuz, which had been docked at the station for several months. The procedure, which prevails even today, is to insure that space station crews always have a reasonably "fresh" spacecraft available in the event they have to make a hasty exit and reentry.

Nicky was the first non-pilot to command a Soviet space mission. But what made him special in Bulgaria was the fact he had with him the first Bulgarian cosmonaut, Georgi Ivanov. Ivanov was part of the Soviet guest cosmonaut program, aimed at getting at least one citizen from each of the Soviet block countries into space. Guest cosmonauts were rather poorly trained and were, essentially, along for the ride. It was rumored there had been problems on the flight. Ivanov's pleasant little ride turned out to be one of the hairiest space flights yet flown.

When I ran into Nicky at a party at the American Ambassador's house in Sophia, Bulgaria, I asked him for the real story.

"The Soyuz main engine exploded two miles short of docking with the Salyut. We tried all backup schemes and when we could not get ignition, the mission was ordered aborted. Docking would have been futile. There was no way the damaged Soyuz could have been left at the Salyut. The best course was a quick return to earth."

Unfortunately, the inoperative main engine was essential for de-orbit but there was not enough electric power to ignite it. After many unsuccessful attempts, they were in real danger of being trapped in space until their oxygen ran out—a few days at most.

It was about that time that Nicky remembered Ivanov was carrying a bottle of very special cognac from the Premier of Bulgaria to the crew of the Salyut, a destination they would never reach. As Nicky tells it: "I suggested we not waste the cognac." Ivanov was hard to convince but he finally gave in. Nicky recalled, "I had little drink and Georgi took a good, long drink."

Throughout the ordeal, Ivanov seemed oblivious to the danger of their situation. While Nicky worked the problem, trying to find some way to return to earth, Ivanov had worries of his own. Ivanov wanted to know: "Since we will be going home early, will I have time to develop my films in Moscow before returning to Bulgaria?"

On the second day, they turned off everything except the engine, including the timer. With no way to measure a de-orbit, burn and maintaining attitude visually, they fired the engine—chug—chug—chug—until they were out of fuel. Soyuz 33 returned along a very high-G path—well over 10 Gs and very hot. Since it was a cloudless night with a full moon, the still glowing heat shield of the capsule was spotted by the pilot of a recovery plane for a quick pick-up.

Nicky said, "It was only two days, but it seemed like a month."

By the early Seventies, during a brief thaw in the cold war, the U.S. and the Soviet Union began to permit occasional official visits between astronauts and cosmonauts. In due time, these exchanges led to the first joint space project between the two space powers. Given the relative prestige in the eyes of the world with respect to our two programs, that first mission together seemed to fit a well known cynical definition of a joint venture.

In Texas, where real estate deals and oil syndications are as popular as fried pies, they are often structured as "joint ventures." According to one definition, a joint venture is a deal in which one party has the money and the other has the experience. When the deal is completed, their positions are exactly reversed.

That first joint venture between the United States and the Soviet Union—the Apollo-Soyuz Test Project (ASTP)—that celebrated 1975 "handshake in space" was a good example. Let me say this as fairly and gently and diplomatically as I can: in terms of who gained what from the Apollo-Soyuz mission, we were had! The political shenanigans on ASTP set the pattern for subsequent cooperative efforts on the Shuttle-Mir and the International Space Station programs.

That first joint mission was an artistic success, even a political and show business success. Don't knock that. In view of what else we could have been doing to each other, those were not bad successes. Photographs of the two crews working together looked terrific on front pages around the world, and it must have sounded, well, different, when Tom Stafford spoke Russian with an Oklahoma accent. That alone was almost worth the price of the trip.

It was only in the "secondary" objectives, such as flying the mission, setting technical goals and scientific accomplishment that we may have failed. In theory, both sides gave and benefited equally from this space odyssey that became the very symbol of detente. (Funny thing. Six months after the ASTP, our foreign policy with Russia had grown so cloudy that detente had become a non-word.)

What exactly did either of us gain for the billions the two world powers spent to penetrate this new frontier? Was there really anything we stood to learn from the Russians? And, if there were, would they have allowed us to learn it, given the world situation in the Seventies?

Although the two programs were similar in many respects during those early days, the Russians got off the pad earlier because of the big boosters they had confiscated from the Germans. Like us, by the Seventies, they had flown three generations of manned spacecraft. They began with Yuri Gagarin flying the first of the six orbital missions in the Vostok one-man spacecraft. This was almost a month before Alan Shepard rode his Mercury 7 into space for a fifteen-minute sub-orbital flight and a full year before John Glenn circled the globe three times. Yet in this country, we frequently refer to Glenn as "the first man to orbit the earth."

For years, the Russians rang up firsts like nobody's business: the first satellite, the first man and the first woman in orbit, the first two-manned spacecraft, the first three-manned spacecraft, and the first extravehicular activity. These accomplishments had a political impact even though, in hindsight, they were frequently lacking in technical significance. We tried to rationalize their accomplishments by telling ourselves that our greater concern for human life caused us to move more deliberately.

So consider this. When John Glenn flew his first manned orbital mission, our experience consisted of three orbits on the Mercury spacecraft, one unmanned and automatic and two by monkeys. Before Yuri Gagarin's flight, the Russians had logged approximately one hundred orbits in their Vostok spacecraft, including several missions with dogs.

They, too, had their catastrophes followed by interruptions in their program. In early 1967, when Vladimir Komarov, flying Soyuz 1, died during reentry due to a parachute problem, it was a year and a half before their next flight. In July 1971, their program was interrupted for another two years by the Soyuz 11 accident. After a record twenty-three days in orbit, the three-man crew of was killed on reentry. The spacecraft lost pressurization when the crew separated the descent module from the orbital module of the spacecraft. It was a crushing blow when they opened the hatch to find three dead cosmonauts after an otherwise successful mission.

The Russians always seemed to encounter their greatest difficulties when returning their vehicles to earth. We heard many stories of cosmonauts landing in snow-covered wilds and not being recovered for more than twenty-four hours. These are believable—and not too surprising—when you consider they had no on-board computers and only an extremely limited maneuvering capability to hit a designated touchdown site.

The Russians always recovered their manned spacecraft on land, a solution ideally suited to their unique requirements. Among them: basic hardware design, a great landmass within their national boundaries, and the Soviet fixation on secret, unobserved operations. Aborts during launch from a secret base in the middle of their country would necessitate a land landing, so why not utilize the same technique on normal reentry? We applied similar logic to U.S. launches over the Atlantic Ocean. It was only the operational constraints of the planned Russian lunar landings that would have required them to develop a water recovery capability.

Why didn't the United States make land landings? Any spacecraft landing system must be thoroughly tested prior to its actual use. It must be able to consistently touch down on the hardest surface in the recovery zone and still protect the crew. Since water covers approximately eighty percent of the earth's surface, our craft had to be capable of withstanding an emergency landing in the ocean. And since testing in the sea lends itself to repetition better than a land surface, it was an easy choice for us to design around a water landing. The Apollo spacecraft was capable of safely flying to and landing on a plowed field roughly the size of a large municipal airport—but what if it missed?

How did the Russians overcome our perceived difficulties of landing on land? During the early missions, the cosmonauts would abandon their vehicle around 10,000 feet and land by personal parachute. However, the third generation Soyuz spacecraft incorporated a landing rocket system to reduce the rate of descent to a safe level, eliminating the need to carry personal parachutes. The landing rocket is fired at eight to ten feet above the ground, slowing the vehicle for a soft touchdown. This system has worked very well with a few exceptions, including one failed rocket that subjected the crew to more than 30 Gs on landing.

The Apollo spacecraft utilized three huge parachutes for its water landing. I am neither the first nor the only astronaut to express reservations about a landing rocket system that requires waiting until the last split-second of your life to find out if you will be around for the next second.

It was generally assumed that, being astronauts, we had inside information on the Russian space program. Unfortunately, we did not and frequently turned to such publications as *Aviation Week* as a reliable source. In truth, we spent precious little time worrying about what the Russians were doing. We were too wrapped up in our own work to show more than a passing, professional interest in that other space program. It involved us only to the extent that NASA, as a Pavlovian reflex, would pitch for more public support as a result of anything the Russians attempted. In retrospect, a more fundamental belief in what we were doing, and greater confidence in our own approach, would have led to a more objective assessment of our competition.

We saw only what the Russians wanted us to and judged their capabilities accordingly. Looking at their program through this keyhole, it was easy to see them as larger than life. NASA, along with the American public watched their accomplishments jealously and listened to periodic rumors of program setbacks and cosmonauts dying in orbit. I have never seen a single piece of evidence to support claims of Russian deaths in space (although there were incidents which could have turned deadly), other than those that have been discussed publicly. In retrospect these rumors were little more than wishful thinking. We looked anxiously for signs of their mortality in this contest and breathed a little sigh of relief in the mid-Sixties, when we seemed to be holding our own.

Their hardware was simple, as were their early missions. We judged the technical excellence of their program by the firsts they were racking up and the growing capability that we assumed it represented. After all, weren't we in a race with them to land a man on the moon?

The Soviet Union initiated their moon program sometime in the Sixties. They saw it as a political contest and one they intended to win. They assigned flight crews and flight control teams and began building hardware. Aleksey Leonov, history's first spacewalker, headed the select group of cosmonauts charged with accomplishing the landing on the Moon.

The most difficult challenge of the Soviet program was developing a huge rocket, the N1, capable of landing cosmonauts on the Moon. Between 1969 and 1972, the N1 was launched four times and blew up on each occasion. The last flight was the longest, exploding 107 seconds after launch.

Leonov's cosmonaut team quit training to fly to the moon in 1969, after several N1 rocket failures and when they could see our first lunar landing was inevitable. The program was highly secret and never mentioned in the Soviet media. It was not formally canceled until 1974. The newspaper *Izvestia* first told the story of the moon program in August of 1989, when the Soviet Union began to ease up on censorship.

The effort was not a complete loss, however. The N1 rocket, the most powerful ever built, produced 10 million pounds of thrust. When the program was shut down, Nikolay Kuznestsov, the designer of the N1's very powerful RD-170 engines, was able to save his creations from destruction. A Russian company, Energomash, now sells improved versions of the RD-170 to American launch companies in the largest contract the Russian defense industry has with the West.

The Russian shuttle look-alike, the Buran spacecraft, suffered a similar early cancellation.

Soviet space exploration failures were early indications of the economic weakness of the country. According to unofficial information, the USSR spent only four-and-a-half billion rubles (about $4.5 billion) on their Moon program, while we spent $25 billion on the Apollo project.

Another Soviet weakness was management of such complex undertakings. The USSR had no state agency equivalent to NASA in the United States. All too frequently in the old USSR, political issues, personal views, and imaginary values instead of real ones determined the direction of science. Every Soviet chief designer found it necessary to obtain the patronage of a communist party official in order for his ideas to gain any serious consideration.

In the late Sixties, Apollo was proceeding more smoothly than we had ever expected. Our systems and operational techniques, which may have been overly complex in the beginning, were beginning to pay off. The Russians, too, were reaping the harvest of their early programs. Their simplified missions and hardware were adequate for propaganda victories, but as the game became more technically challenging they proved woefully inadequate.

The early Soviet space "firsts" may have been dubious technical achievements when compared to those of our own program but they were certainly propaganda and public relations victories. The Apollo-Soyuz Test Project (ASTP) of 1975 fit that model perfectly and the Soviets were well prepared to exploit it.

It is useful to review ASTP in some detail because, in many ways, it set the pattern for all future cooperation between the two countries. Some of the precedents established with ASTP became problems in working together in both the Russian Mir space station and the International Space Station.

My conclusions about ASTP were less influenced by politics than by my experience as an astronaut. The Russians space establishment had never been candid and forthcoming about their program, especially the failures. That behavior has carried through to the present day. I was less concerned with the ten-year-old American technology we gave away during Apollo-Soyuz than I was with the risks it might portend in any continuing relationship. (By the late Nineties, western commercial interests were supporting the Russian space program to the tune of $800 million annually.)

At a time when the U.S. space budget never exceeded $6 billion a year the Russians were regularly spending that much on their space program. With a gross national product much less than ours, this was equivalent to three to four times the commitment NASA was receiving. The Russians were outspending us in space, and what they could not buy we seemed hell-bent on giving them for free.

To the Soviets, it seemed an opportune time to hedge their bet. They had always viewed achievement in space as a measure of scientific, military, and even cultural strength. By that yardstick, the United States was riding high. Now we were offering them a chance to regain lost prestige with a minimum of risk. The Apollo-Soyuz mission in mid-1975 seemed like the answer to a prayer—if they only prayed.

Planning for the mission pushed ahead relentlessly in spite of the fact that our growing familiarity with their program convinced us the Russians were well behind the United States in both hardware and attitude. While we expected their equipment to be a Salyut space station, we settled for a Soyuz. When we asked for higher orbits and a longer flight time, we settled for a lower and shorter mission because their Soyuz lacked the capability. And while the long-closed doors of the Russian space program opened a crack, our training in Russia never approached what we made available to them in the U.S.

NASA selected a crew of real old-timers (average age at the time, forty-six years) although only one had ever flown in space. Slayton, at fifty-one, had been director of Flight Crew Operations for ten years, one of a handful of deputies reporting directly to Dr. Robert Gilruth, the director of the Johnson Space Center. Deke's career had suffered a bitter setback in 1962, when he failed a physical two months before he was to lift off as the second of the Mercury astronauts to go into earth orbit. A squiggle in his electrocardiogram was enough to ground him for ten years. Deke was serious about physical fitness and he ran two miles a day. Not that physical condition ever seemed a factor in crew selection, but it would certainly be a topic for discussion if anyone ever questioned the implications of Deke's age.

It must have eaten at Deke's insides that he needed another qualified aviator along whenever he flew. I sat in the other seat on some of those flights, and though Deke was never able to log as much stick time as the rest of us, he remained a superb aviator.

For ten years he operated in a lonely role, sharing his thoughts with very few. We could be working regularly with Deke and worrying daily about crew assignments while he kept them confidential for months after they were settled in his mind.

Deke never let up in his efforts to return to flight status, even as it turned into a question of time. Could he beat the clock? Could he get ungrounded while there was still a flight left, or before he started collecting Social Security?

Over the years he frequently sat in on our training sessions and most of us got the impression he expected to use it all some day. At times it seemed a little sad, like watching an old actor hanging around Central Casting, hoping for a call. We admired him for it, but in a corner of our hearts we hurt for him, too. It seemed so pointless.

Slayton, with fifteen years at NASA, was clearly not your typical rookie. Ungrounded in 1972, he recommended himself for assignment to the next flight crew available (which was the ASTP), resigned as deputy director of the Johnson Space Center (JSC) to devote all his time to training, and began to lobby aggressively for the mission. One might ask, "If Deke was qualified, why shouldn't he get the mission?" The point is, if the assignment was made on the basis of his qualifications, or if there were so many missions that it made no difference, then there was no reason why Deke should not make the flight. What the hell, past crew assignments had not always been made on the basis of qualifications, either. Deke had never claimed they were made objectively or on the basis of measurable abilities.

Sentimentally, it was a winner, but in reality, it was another raw power play accomplished in complete disregard of any objective reasons for doing it differently. There was precedence for playing it the way he did. In 1963 the Mercury astronauts sat down and divided up the Gemini missions such that Shepard got the first one (although he was grounded before it could be flown), Schirra staked out the first rendezvous, Cooper was left with the first "long-duration mission," and Carpenter was frozen out entirely. A more egregious example was Shepard's move from restricted flying status directly to the Apollo 14 lunar landing mission in 1970.

Slayton actually waged two campaigns and he ended up with a 50 percent batting average. Being the senior person on the crew, naturally, he wanted to be in command as well. That put Slayton and Stafford at odds with each other. Stafford let it be known that he considered himself, by virtue of his flight experience, the only one on the crew qualified for the command responsibility. That had to create some tension between them since Deke was responsible for Stafford gaining that experience. Somehow the case was sold and Deke agreed to take a back seat to Tom.

Stafford was Deke's assistant at the time he decided he wanted to fly "the Russian mission." Because he had paid attention to his politics over the years, it really wasn't much of a problem to tie down the crew assignment, but it took a little more work to command it. From Tom's point of view, it must have seemed perfect. Technically the mission was a breeze. The training grind would be long but familiar, and Tom could take that in stride. It would be heavy on the social aspects, with a lot of overseas travel and international notoriety and acclaim far beyond the demands of the mission. It was certain to receive massive news coverage. It had, in fact, everything except a real reason for being.

Stafford and Slayton were joined on the ASTP crew by Vance Brand. Third spot had opened up when Jack Swigert was ruled out in the aftermath of the stamp signing scandal. Vance was a former marine pilot with a boyishly innocent face. For years he slogged away in the trenches backing up several Apollo crews and Skylab before getting his chance. Stafford had been through the training grind so many times he had it memorized and, besides, he was more interested in the peripheral aspects—the travel, diplomacy, new social and business contacts. Deke's spirit was undoubtedly willing but, let's face it, that kind of training is a younger man's game. Anyway it worked out fine. At least one person on the crew has to stay on top of everything and a motivated, dedicated rookie, willing to overkill, feels compelled to do just that. Accordingly, Vance Brand was trained to a sharper peak on the technical aspects than his two older crewmates.

The Soviets threw in a first-class team for their half of this international space spectacular. Both were veterans of earlier space missions. Valery Kubasov, the forty-year-old flight engineer, had been a cosmonaut since 1966. He was shy but a brilliant engineer. He seldom spoke during the joint training sessions. In the shadow of his more flamboyant fellow crewman and mission commander, Aleksey Leonov, it was often hard to detect when Kubasov was around.

Aleksey Leonov was a bona fide Soviet hero. He was one of the original Soviet cosmonauts selected in 1960, and he made an indelible impression on the world in 1965 when he became the first man to "walk in space." Leonov wrote in June 1965, "Return into the ship did not present any particular difficulties. Pulse rate during the extravehicular activity coincided to a great degree with the data obtained during the ground studies in the spacecraft mock-up." The real story was much more harrowing.

Aleksey's orders had been to simply get out and get back in. After only a few minutes floating in space, he tried to get back into the airlock, but he was unable to bend the suit enough at the waist to get through the opening. A spacesuit pressurized to 6 psi is stiff as a board.

In a smart but potentially dangerous procedure, Aleksey reduced the suit pressure to below 4 psi, the only way he could get the flexibility he needed to get back into the airlock.

It worked. The airlock was depressurized for only twelve minutes but Aleksey was soaked in sweat and exhausted—and safe.

Ten years later, during training for ASTP, he gave a more candid appraisal of the experience, admitting, "It did not go at all like the way we prepared."

We might have been less ambitious on Gemini 9, in June 1966, if we had known the true story when Gene Cernan was preparing for our first grand EVA. Gene found himself in a very similar predicament: exhausted, soaked in sweat, and helmet fogged over as he struggled to get back into the spacecraft.

Friendly and outgoing, Leonov's behavior contradicted our preconceptions about the Communist party "organization man." A skilled artist, he made numerous sketches during his mission—including some with religious themes. He has the quick wit and the roly-poly look of a fellow you expect to find emceeing a Rotary Club banquet.

The U.S. crew was training at Star City, which was on a Soviet Army base just outside of Moscow, when President Nixon paid his historic visit there in June 1974. Naturally, Nixon and Premier Leonid Brezhnev dropped by to shake a few hands. A fascinated Alan Bean, our backup crew commander, watched Leonov in action. "On that occasion," said Bean, "Leonov was one of the first to shake hands with the two heads of state, at which time he engaged them in animated conversation. Standing between the two, he turned around to become a part of the receiving line, and proceeded to direct the remainder of the ceremony."

The son of a miner who had risen to the rank of colonel, Leonov was an excellent politician. He was impressed with our technology, but always diplomatically refused to compare the Soviet and U.S. systems.

These five men came together to perform one of the most ballyhooed missions of all time. Part history and part science fiction, it was a showcase for several activities which were commonplace in our program but breakthroughs for the Soviets. Given the usual Russian passion for secrecy, it did have the effect of letting in some light. For the first time, the Soviet Union announced the names of the flight crew prior to a mission, as well as the date of the flight. For the first time, U.S. observers were permitted an inside look at parts of the Russian space program and the American ambassador was allowed to watch the Soyuz lift-off from the once-secret launch site at Tyuratam (really, Baikonur, in Kazakhstan), 1,800 miles Southeast of Moscow.

Perhaps even more noteworthy, for the first time Soviet citizens were able to watch, along with the rest of the world, a live television broadcast of the lift-off and landing, scenes Americans have always taken for granted.

Amidst all that international fellowship, and the growing excitement of a space spectacular that both joined and pitted national pride, it became more and more difficult to pin down exactly what the objectives of the mission were, but along the way these points were emphasized:

The ASTP mission was described as essential for testing the technical solutions for compatible docking systems between United States and Soviet spacecraft. That should have been a high priority for the USSR. Historically, docking has given the Russians more trouble than any other phase of their operations with the possible exception of re-entry. Many of their missions had been judged failures by U.S. experts because of unsuccessful dockings, while we had a near-perfect record in that essential phase of space operations.

They had experienced docking hardware problems, but on this mission both sides were utilizing the same design, one that evolved from a concept proposed by Rockwell for the Apollo Command Module in the early Sixties. The system was put on the shelf at that time because it was much heavier than the probe and drogue concept we eventually employed. Now we handed it over to the Soviets *carte blanche*.

From its conception, the Apollo-Soyuz mission was touted as a "demonstration of space rescue capability." Who could argue with that? Anyone with the ability to think logically! The Space Shuttle, which we would be flying for the next 30 years, would never have the quick response necessary for this critical role. And the Soviets, with their 48-hour response capability from their launch site at Baikonur, were unable to rendezvous with one of our orbiting spacecraft in our *usual* orbits. In any event, for a period of six years following ASTP, there would be no American crews in orbit to be rescued and no American spacecraft on the pad to provide rescue for the Russians.

In the last sixty days before the launch, knowledgeable Americans were facing up to the fact that we were buying an enormously expensive public relations stunt. In an effort to nudge along detente, the United States government encouraged the three major television networks to pool their resources to bring the country a record total of more than thirty hours of live coverage. It was, in short, much more international politics and public relations than a scientific mission.

Science on the ASTP was not only secondary, but second rate. Some experiments were little more than a reclassification of earlier, routine data collection, some trivial and some ridiculous. Special consideration was given to experiments that would take advantage of the presence of two manned vehicles in orbit together. This led to such gems as "exchange of microbial growth," which involved trading objects from one spacecraft to the other.

The Soviets, true to their colors, could not resist a bit of last-minute gamesmanship. Their press kit described six experiments our planners hadn't even heard about!

It was definitely a mission looking for a reason to happen. Operationally, it amounted to little more than a rerun of our 1966 Gemini 8 docking mission. But ASTP did have one redeeming feature—our first inside look at the Soviet space program. It took a while, but our scientists, technicians, and astronauts gradually and cautiously gained some trust. We had seen shadows on the wall and imagined monsters and knowing the swift start they had made and the huge lead they once had, we were shocked when we finally saw their equipment. We had overrated the Russian hardware, their operations and, really, their whole program. Our reluctant conclusions were incompatible with the giant that NASA, the western world, and most Americans pictured as the Russian program of the Sixties. It was almost easier to let our imaginations run wild than to believe the evidence before our eyes.

The Russians deserve great credit for what they accomplished in those early years. They made the most of a limited capability and converted it into excellent press in the world media, and they accomplished it with hardware that was archaic by our standards.

During the joint training phase the Soviet and American crews alternated three-week sessions every three months at each other's facilities. At the Russian end, most of the time was spent in Star City, a Moscow suburb roughly equivalent to the Johnson Space Center at Clear Lake, a suburb of Houston. At Star City the days were spent in loosely structured briefing sessions on the Soyuz spacecraft and the mission. Evenings were frequently occupied by semi-official social gatherings.

It was those "group gropes" on the vodka circuit with the cosmonauts that really took their toll. At dinner and drinking parties vodka flowed like mineral water. At the risk of losing their macho image, our guys freely admitted that the cosmonauts buried them in the vodka consumption. Astronaut Bob Overmyer reported he was worried about getting a bill for dead potted plants, because of the great quantities of the stuff he dumped in the nearest receptacle.

Our lads awoke each morning with a new awareness of what Dr. Schweitzer once called "the fellowship of pain." Their Russian hosts took it in stride. Our guys finally met the challenge by appointing a "duty drunk" for every official or semi-official party. His job was to keep up glass for glass with the cosmonauts and leave the others free to circulate and survive.

On one of the training trips, a couple of the astronauts were joined by their wives in a rare chance to mix business with a vacation. While the flight crews were training during the day, the wives enjoyed the hospitality of the cosmonaut wives, Svetlana Leonov and Ludmilla Kubasov, and others. Some of the American wives were introduced to the modest touches of status available in a classless society when they were taken on shopping trips in Moscow in their hosts' chauffeured limousines. By itself that was impressive, but when it was invariably accompanied by screaming sirens and motorists pulling off to the side of the road to let them pass, it began to seem a bit ridiculous. The cosmonaut wives seemed to take it all in stride.

The American portion of the training took place at the Johnson Space Center. From there, the group branched out around the country on technical and, just as frequently, social missions. These side excursions ranged from Disneyland in Anaheim, California, to the launch control center at Kennedy Space Center.

Compared to past missions, the joint training sessions in the United States for this one were nothing less than bizarre. Since one of the principal objectives was to pump up diplomatic relations, a major portion of each three-week visit was taken up with tourism and public relations activities. For astronauts, accustomed to eighteen-hour training days, it was a much more relaxed pace than they had known before. Social activities were usually high visibility, serving to generate good political coverage. It may have been a legitimate way to "train," but it made a mockery of the preparation for earlier missions.

To be fair, training was both appropriate and adequate because the technical interaction between the crews—as well as the vehicles in orbit—was trivial. The real objective, even during the mission, was social—that handshake in the sky. The theme song for the training period should have been "Getting to Know You."

A good deal of just that took place during a September 1974 visit. The Russian party included their prime crew, *three* backup crews, General Shatalov, their chief cosmonaut, and interpreters. Prior to their departure for home, the ASTP crews held a dinner for the other astronauts and their wives. After Stafford provided a few words of friendship on behalf of the astronauts, he turned the show over to Leonov, who speaks fluent but slightly broken English. He has a real gift for turning a phrase. When asked by a newsman about the merits of Soviet and American space food, his reply was, "It is not what you eat but with whom you eat that is important." (During the flight, however, Stafford bolted down three tubes of soggy borscht and required three Lomotil pills later to settle his stomach.) Leonov delivered a humorous, impromptu speech that ranged from the progress of their joint training to jokes about his success at a recent antelope hunt in Wyoming. He was impressive without seeming to try.

The other cosmonauts were less at ease with English, but all appeared to be politically savvy. It was generally accepted by us that each of the Russians had extra-curricular "obligations" on their visits to the United States. As Al Bean put it, "The Soviet Union does not have so many human resources that it can afford to send such capable individuals to this country without asking each to do some additional reconnaissance."

Leonov's personality and his success at charming his American hosts, pointed up one more area in which the Russians may have outfoxed us. In Stafford, Slayton, and Brand we had selected technicians to do a technical job. All were attractive men and skilled professionals, but no one would describe them as first team in the tea-and-crumpets league. Their Russian counterparts had either been sent to a finishing school or selected on the basis of their charm, proficiency with the English language, and political astuteness. They did a splendid job. For us to match them in congeniality and social footwork, we would have had to send our first team in that category: Wally Schirra, Jim Lovell, and Gene Cernan. Historically, cosmonauts have primarily been subjects riding in an otherwise automated spacecraft. This alone accounted for their ability to send passengers into space with only minimal pilot qualifications. Dogs, non-pilot engineers, and Valentina Tereshkova all survived nicely in the same model spacecraft. As test subjects, you would expect their doctors to have great control over their training—and they do. In addition to the usual flight preparations, Russian medical scientists were given control over the cosmonauts for one week in every quarter plus two additional weeks during the year for controlled medical and physical conditioning. That same authority enforced a six-week vacation leave each year. That meant that each cosmonaut was unavailable for three months out of every twelve, a totally unacceptable reduction of training time in the U.S. program.

What the astronauts had suspected on their first visit to the Soviet Union was confirmed on repeated training sessions over the next three years. In the Soviet program, "man in the loop"—meaning man with an essential job to perform—was more theory than practice. Their own requirement to launch and recover manned spacecraft with an incapacitated crew resulted in a very specific design of control functions; a design in which the cosmonaut was little more than a short circuit for a telemetry signal from the control center. This operational concept has been an integral part of the Soviet program since Gagarin was sent along for the ride. Some aspects remain even today. A crewman was able to perform only a limited number of control functions. Man and his infinitely variable computer were not fully exploited in the Soviet program. This short-sightedness severely limited the accomplishments of their manned program and, I believe, was responsible for turning their lead of the early Sixties into an also-ran by the end of the decade.

Even the Soviets' nominal use of man enabled them to exploit one of his more important advantages: on-the-spot presence for critical operations. In their early manned shots, before they began deploying tracking ships to the Indian Ocean, ground control was in contact with their spacecraft only while it was over the Soviet land mass. This generally limited contact to portions of the first six orbits and no further contact until the sixteenth or seventeenth orbit. They had to rely on the cosmonaut to perform essential functions when the spacecraft was out of contact with the ground, a very significant portion of the time.

Russian manned spacecraft were grossly deficient in many areas. There were no on-board displays for continuous monitoring of many essential systems, such as a good attitude reference display. Russian spacecraft of the seventies had no computer. The pilot could not inject himself into or improvise unscheduled operations. Since they had no re-entry guidance system, a landing spot could only be targeted within tens of miles. They made the most of it, however, and developed efficient recovery operations following the spacecraft landing. I would have to characterize the Russian criteria for a man-machine relationship was *simplicity,* while the United States has always emphasized *capability* and *flexibility.*

The Russian interpretation of fail-safe was considerably different from our own. Their reliance on ground-controlled systems demanded that onboard failures leave them in the automatic mode of operation. This may have been significant in the fatal Soyuz 11 depressurization during reentry. The pressure relief system included a manual and an automatic valve in series. Procedures called for opening the manual valve in orbit, prior to separation to insure that the automatic system would be able to equalize pressure on re-entry. The automatic valve cracked open at separation, evacuating the spacecraft and killing the three-man crew.

For the same system in an American spacecraft, manual valves would be opened only as a backup to an automatic valve failure, which would have failed to a closed position. More importantly, an American spacecraft would not have been allowed to fly when a *single* failure in such a critical system could kill the crew. Equipment and procedures such as these led me to assess their technical level for the 1975 ASTP as between our Mercury and Gemini programs, circa 1965.

A logical explanation for their reluctance to enter a free exchange of information was embarrassment at their own state-of-the-art. Unfortunately, the predominately one-way technical exchange could more accurately be attributed to the Soviet system itself. Even the simplest technical details were treated as state secrets. One day, Bob Overmyer spent forty-five minutes trying to get a Russian engineer to explain how their TV camera mounting bracket worked. On the other hand, U.S. engineers and technicians would launch into the minutest detail of our most sophisticated equipment at the drop of a hat.

The most essential requirement of managing a program as complex as the space business is good communications. Here again the Russians were handicapped by their penchant for secrecy, and not just keeping information away from foreign nationals. There was minimal exchange between their managers on a horizontal level across systems and only a small amount up-and-down. Only at the very top levels of management was it possible to encounter anyone with knowledge of more than one system of the spacecraft. Information provided to one working group of their experts was rarely passed on to the engineers attending the next joint working meeting. Data provided to one engineer in an organization would seldom be made available to another engineer in that same organization. This was consistent with their trust-no-one syndrome and provided increased job security. To give an example, Deke related what happened on one cosmonaut visit to Houston. After some discussion with Leonov and Shatalov, it was agreed that the cosmonaut team would fly to the West Coast at the end of the week. Late on the night before the trip, Deke learned that the travelers had not yet been informed that early the following morning they would leave for the Rockwell Plant 1,500 miles away.

Even the Soviet leaders were not made aware of (or did not understand) the relative strengths and weaknesses in their own space program. This lack of understanding at least contributed to the Soyuz 11 deaths in 1971. The story we heard was that in the 1963-64 time frame, Soviet leaders, aware that the United States would soon be flying a three-man spacecraft, ordered the spacecraft constructor to launch three men in their own Vostok vehicle. It was explained by their scientists that there was neither room nor weight capability to launch three men into orbit. However, in order to accomplish the directive, they eventually did design three launch couches into the vehicle with the third man relegated to a center seat that could best be described as sitting on the shoulders of the other two. In order to place the heavier spacecraft into orbit, the space suits were left out leaving no backup in the event of a cabin depressurization—which did occur on Soyuz 11.

During the ASTP mission, flight controllers in direct contact with the spacecraft from TsUP, the Moscow control center, worked with data that was several minutes old. Data relayed from their tracking ships are two to three hours old before it is available for display. By contrast, the Russians were in the embarrassing position of displaying NASA-relayed data from an American spacecraft flying over the Soviet Union several minutes *prior* to receiving it from their own spacecraft directly overhead.

The conclusion is obvious. After learning of their capabilities we continued to push ahead with a joint venture in which we had nothing to gain technically and everything to lose. The exercise was justified on the basis of political benefits, which were tenuous and highly controversial. Detente might have offered relief in some areas, but in space it translated to wishful thinking and a give-away policy.

We could derive some satisfaction from learning how much we had overestimated Russian capabilities for fifteen years. This awareness could be applied to our estimate of the Russian military capability as well. Our new knowledge of Russian hardware and techniques also convinced me that many of the challenges in space in the early Sixties could have been met with simpler systems than we actually built.

The average age of the ASTP crew briefly made the *Guinness Book of Records,* which also taught us something. Flying a spacecraft is really not all that difficult or physically demanding. There was certainly no obvious reason why a healthy, well-trained, pilot over fifty could not safely handle it. The training grind is a different story! It is a hectic, physically and mentally demanding pace for anyone, and especially trying on older astronauts.

That represented our thinking in the Seventies. How could we know that 20 years later, Grandfather John Glenn, America's first man to orbit the Earth, would return to space at the age of 77? The ostensible reason was to collect data on a geriatric space subject. For John, it was a great trip and he apparently did his job quite well. Most former astronauts were happy for John, especially those who knew President Kennedy had kept him from flying again following his 1962 flight in Friendship 7. But I know of none who approved of the way the flight came about.

I began to hear stories about John campaigning for a shuttle flight as early as the summer of 1996. The campaign didn't get all that far until Senator Glenn was made the Ranking Member of a Senate committee investigating an issue involving then president Bill Clinton. We didn't understand why John did such a good job of defending the president's rather indefensible position. It shocked his friends. We all speculated why, until it was announced that John would fly again. We immediately understood—it was the political payoff for John's efforts on the president's behalf. The medical experiments were dreamed up afterwards to legitimize the assignment.

It was not surprising to learn that Deke had his problems during training. Technically, ASTP was one of our easiest missions ever and, therefore, a good way for him to get into the lineup. Three years to get ready was a far cry from having twelve months to train for a lunar landing.

Stafford? Well, he certainly qualified as an old pro, but that could also lead to a casual approach to the job. You can bet he did not have an all-consuming desire to go into space for the fourth time. It was the glamour and notoriety that brought the fire horse back to the fire. We had two of the three crewmen taking less than a full measure from the training routine.

The load fell on Brand's shoulders. He was a forty-four-year-old rookie, but motivated as we all were on that first flight. For whatever reasons, the crew did far less training *together* than usual, even for those phases of the mission that required close coordination. Given the heavy social schedule, the great emphasis placed on public relations and the political objectives of the mission, NASA may have launched this last Apollo spacecraft crew with a minimum proficiency.

The docking of Apollo and Soyuz went smoothly 140 miles above the earth, and they remained joined for forty-four hours. The crews exchanged handshakes and gifts, ate together, spoke each other's language, and smiled into the television camera. When it ended, the only major mistake—a nearly fatal one—was ours, and most of the benefits accrued to the Russians.

The mission was an artistic and political success, but technically the performance was no better than the training. While the handshake in space and speeches on cooperation, brotherhood, and peace were carried out almost flawlessly, *"secondary"* objectives—such as flying the spacecraft and reentry—were beset with their share of problems. No flights get by without an occasional cockpit error, but the higher incidence of them on this mission, including forgetting the two most critical switches in the cockpit during reentry, could well be a consequence of the crew's casual approach and limited training as a team.

For their debut on international television the Russians came through like champs; the landing was perfect. Soyuz touched down on a dusty plain in Kazakhstan, ending a flight that for them—in Leonov's words—had been as "smooth as a peeled egg."

Our guys had their problems. The crew had no idea the danger they were in when a "brownish-yellow gas" began to fill the cockpit as the spacecraft descended below about 20,000 feet. For the next five minutes they found themselves choking, gagging, and fighting for air. After splashdown, they struggled for another five minutes trying to reach the oxygen masks behind their couches. Vance Brand passed out cold but quickly revived when Slayton and Stafford clapped the mask over his face. As the Navy frogmen swam toward the capsule, only weak radio contact kept everyone from hearing Stafford yell into his microphone, "Get this f…ing hatch open."

They had failed to throw two redundant switches, the ELS (Earth Landing Systems) switches, which precluded automatically dumping the excess fuel and oxidizer from the attitude-control rocket engines and deploying the chutes. These are the last two switches you want to overlook if you are serious about staying alive. Stafford was apparently distracted and neglected to call for them at 30,000 feet, the usual spot. That callout was my responsibility on Apollo 7 but if I had dropped dead at 30,000 feet, Wally would not have missed those two beauties. In any case, Brand, flying the reentry, did miss them. When they discovered their error down much lower, they activated the manual backup switches. In the resulting chain of events, some of the rocket fuel—a highly corrosive nitrogen oxide gas—was sucked in through the cabin vent valve and ingested. If the gas had rendered them unconscious, they would have been unable to deploy the parachutes manually and we would have had our first inflight fatalities.

After recovery the three of them were deposited aboard the carrier and rushed below deck to be examined. It wasn't until seven hours later that any word was released about the seriousness of their difficulty. The effect of such a toxic mixture on the lungs could be permanent and lethal.

As the rookie in the crew, and the Command Module pilot flying the re-entry, Brand made a point of shouldering the blame for the failure to throw the switches. Stafford, glossing over the confusion at 30,000 feet, took some of the pressure off by declaring, "As the commander, I am responsible for whatever goes wrong in the spacecraft." The claim wasn't made too strenuously and it was still Brand who had to field the questions and explain the goof wherever he went in the weeks that followed.

Operationally, it left a lot to be desired. Coupled with some of the Skylab experiences, it triggered a NASA review of crew functions and NASA even considered adopting a higher degree of automation.

From my vantage point outside the agency in the mid-Seventies, there were some disturbing signs: a more casual approach to training, less reliance on the crew, and a great deal of artificial emphasis on ASTP when NASA should have been generating real interest in the Space Shuttle. It didn't help to see a half billion dollars thrown away on a space technology give-away while the Shuttle budget was shrinking monthly.

We did seem to develop one new national consensus: In the Sixties, the U.S. held a much higher opinion of Russian technology than was warranted. The Soviets had made the most of a limited capability. It didn't help to know their new international prestige was achieved with space hardware that was archaic by our standards.

17

Old Competitors, New Partners

FOR THE LAST HALF of the decade of the Seventies, manned space activities were left to the Soviet Union. There would be no American manned flight between ASTP in 1975 and the first Shuttle mission in 1981. It was a decade when NASA's budget was committed to developing a reusable spacecraft—the Space Shuttle Orbiter.

Shuttle design meetings were kicked off in 1969, before Apollo 11 had even landed on the moon. The original cost figure of $17 to $18 billion included both a recoverable spacecraft *and* a flyback, winged booster. Repeated direction of "back to the drawing boards" made it obvious the crucial factor was cost and the reusable booster quickly fell by the wayside. Believing the end justified the means, the Shuttle Program was sold to the OMB and Congress in whatever manner would assure its funding. It went on the books as a $5.5 billion project, scheduled to fly in 1977.

NASA was no longer looking at space as "a place to go to," but as "something to do with"—using space to achieve other objectives. The Shuttle's sixty-by-fifteen-foot cargo bay was designed to accommodate most of the payloads formerly launched on expendable launch vehicles— everything from unmanned satellites to the European Space Agency's Space Laboratory. It would be our "space truck" until at least 2012.

The goal of reducing the cost of putting a pound in orbit from $1,000 to $150 was based on a transportation model of 100 flights per vehicle, 60 to 75 launches a year, and a program life of approximately 600-700 flights. With payloads up to thirty tons, that amounted to millions of pounds a year. Without a backlog of commercial customers, NASA began to propose the construction of fantastic new structures in space such as manufacturing facilities, solar power plants, or space colonies in order to justify this economic model. If Congress would not step up to the $6 billion cost of a recoverable booster, how could anyone think it would appropriate the hundreds of billions of dollars these visionary concepts would cost.

Of course, it never was $1,000 for Apollo to put a pound in orbit. $10,000 was more like it. With twenty years of history behind it, Orbiter payloads still cost about 30 percent more than Apollo did. Deke Slayton once told me, "If we loaded the 15 by 60 foot cargo bay with gravel, flew it into orbit and magically changed it into gold at no cost, it would still not pay for the trip."

The Space Shuttle faced the usual technical risks and, in the end, it further eroded NASA's credibility with Congress. Apparently, even truly outstanding technical programs cannot be sold to the public, the Office of Management and Budget (OMB) or Congress based solely on the facts.

In the 1960s NASA could not, or perhaps chose not to, sell the Apollo program on the basis of fundamental research, or the development of a new frontier for America, or even on the basis of technological parity with the Soviet Union. Instead national support and funding was tied to the slogan "A man on the moon in this decade." This public relations catch phrase actually understated our achievements and their eventual applications. Our manned landings on the moon were really a comprehensive demonstration of the equipment and operational techniques we had developed in the preceding ten years. Predictably, everything was anticlimactic after Apollo 11, and support dwindled when that man actually walked on the moon in 1969.

The Shuttle Orbiter was a vast improvement over Apollo in a number of ways. For our first 25 spaceflights, we had always splashed down in the sea to be recovered by helicopter like a bag of cats saved from a watery grave. The Orbiter makes a smooth landing at the destination airport and the flight crew steps down from the spacecraft in front of a waiting throng in a dignified and properly heroic manner.

Reinforced carbon-carbon tiles on the nose cap and leading edges and reusable ceramic insulating tiles on other surfaces replaced the ablative heat shield used by earlier spacecraft to survive the heat of reentry. Some comparisons with the Mercury spacecraft:

Electrical power for the Mercury capsule came from three batteries producing 9,000 amp-hours, while the Shuttle's three fuel cells produce a total of 21 kilowatts of continuous power.

The Mercury capsule environmentally controlled 36 cubic feet of volume. The Shuttle has 1,300 cubic feet of crew compartment space, 187 cubic feet for each of seven crewmembers. The Mercury environment was 100 percent oxygen, while Shuttle astronauts breath an earth-like mixture of oxygen and nitrogen that can be adjusted for varying pressures.

Mercury had 143 cockpit displays to the Shuttle's 2,312.

Mercury used three solid-fuel rockets for retrofire maneuvers, drag braking, and a main and drogue-stabilization parachute system for ocean splashdowns. Shuttles use a traditional aircraft tricycle landing gear to land on a runway. Mercury had a 63-foot-diameter main parachute, while the Shuttle has only a 39-foot drag chute.

Throughout the Seventies, NASA presented the program as if the technical aspects were well in hand and showed little concern at being able to meet both technical and schedule milestones. That was also the official position of the contractor, Rockwell, although it was not widely shared by the engineers and other working troops.

Through this high inflation decade, Congress held the NASA budget at starvation levels while salary and overhead costs spiraled upwards. What little money was left for hardware paid for less than optimum designs. Systems, hardware, and tests, which could be classified as non-critical, were pushed as far into the future as possible. The prevailing theory was that the huge initial commitment would make it impossible not to fund the postponed essentials to avoid an unsuccessful and embarrassing program. The reality was the funds for later changes were not there either.

Experienced contractor personnel were aware of the technical compromises being made under ever-tighter budget constraints. Under the pressure of reduced funding, design decisions are frequently made which are contrary to operational needs. I had been to this movie! The most graphic demonstration of the impact of such forces (with the added pressure of maintaining a schedule) was the disastrous Apollo 1 fire in January 1967. In that instance, management placed their emphasis on cost and schedule in the face of tremendous technical challenges. It doesn't seem possible the disastrous experience could have been forgotten in such a few short years and that NASA would try to develop a reusable spacecraft with fewer and fewer dollars.

Congressional officials, of course, deny that budget restraints can endanger astronauts, saying they always insisted that NASA officials not compromise safety. But you cannot make draconian cuts in spending, year after year, and maintain acceptable mission safety. Because NASA had to consider other programmatic factors such as costs and schedule, some safety upgrades were not done. But no one can ever know for sure when safety margins have been eroded too far.

In a well-funded and well-engineered Shuttle Program, the astronauts I know would have expressed their enthusiasm to fly the first Orbiter as, "This is the greatest flying machine since the Wright Brothers, and I'm lucky as hell to be flying it." Instead, some of the astronauts I spoke with in the late Seventies approached it with resignation. "If this is the machine I have to fly to become an Astronaut, then that's what I'll fly." It all sounded familiar. They were not unlike the feelings of resignation with which we approached the first flights of the original Apollo spacecraft—the spacecraft as it was before the fire. We, too, knew there were problems, and shortcomings, and that corners had been cut. The awakening which placed our "go fever" in its proper perspective was rude and costly: the fire on Pad 34.

The Shuttle astronauts came by their attitude honestly—it was born out of frustration. Astronauts were first assigned to the Shuttle Program in 1970, but the few "old timers" still in the Astronaut Office gave it little attention until 1974. Their effectiveness was limited by the attitudes of the Program Manager and other managers up the line. Those without a prior space flight under their belt were likely to encounter the "What does he know, he hasn't been in space" syndrome, while those with the magic goofus dust of spaceflight on their shoulders were told it was too late. ("We finalized that six months ago.") They had run up against the dollar barrier and fallen victim to management's condescending "We know what's best for you" attitude.

Engineers with their feet firmly anchored to the ground, who insist they know what is best for the flight crew in the face of requests to the contrary, are not always the best judges. Sometimes they weren't even the best judgment that NASA had to offer. This was a consequence of the system in which the on-going program at NASA absorbs the best people available in all the disciplines. The remaining engineers pick up the next generation program in the design stage, which may be suffering neglect from top management for the same reason.

As I look back, there were some parallels between the first several years of the Shuttle and Skylab programs, on which I worked the last two years of my NASA career. In 1968, the Skylab management team (at JSC) was headed by Bob Thompson, a NASA survivor since Project Mercury days. It was Thompson's first full program responsibility. He was faced with the usual tight budget because the program was being funded on the leftovers from Apollo. The Skylab Program Office "knew" what was best for us and every operational system change initiated by the Astronaut Office came grudgingly. That program had real problems and flight crew input fell on deaf ears *until* Thompson was replaced by Kenny Kleinknecht in late 1969.

Thompson found a new home as head of the Shuttle Program office. The Shuttle Program was not competing with any other major programs but it, too, was running on left over dollars—left over from the funds necessary to maintain the NASA organization and housekeeping chores. Thompson was no more receptive to flight crew input in his new assignment than he had been in his last.

It is tough to assess the impact of another factor. When Skylab was getting started, Dr. Robert Gilruth was still center director, and he was always considered "on the astronaut team." By the Seventies he had retired and been replaced by Chris Kraft. While the Astronaut Office and Kraft's former flight operations directorate always looked to each other for support on operational requirements, we frequently found ourselves at odds when it came to implementation. Couple this with Kraft's longtime resentment of the hero worship accorded the astronauts, and you can appreciate that the line of appeal above Bob Thompson was not particularly helpful.

From the program manager's perspective, a change can frequently be summed up in the weight, schedule, and cost impacts. Astronauts are guided almost exclusively by two factors: crew safety and operational capability. Program management does not ignore these critical items, but their performance is measured against many other criteria as well. For the man who puts his tail in the trap it is a much simpler process. Unfortunately, in the final design and planning phase, when the program office weighed the factors, many decisions went against the flight crew. For example, Shuttle crews would have no abort capability for the first part of boost; the drag chute, used for high-speed landings, was deleted (only to be added back following the Challenger accident.) And, at one point, the ejection seats planned for the early test flights were scheduled for deletion without even discussing it with the flight crew.

The impact of such decisions went beyond the obvious ones of compromised hardware and operating limitations. After seeing compromise after compromise, one of the pilots scheduled to fly one of the first Orbiters told me in 1977, "You know, Walt, for the first time in my career I look at the most advanced new flying machine and I'm just not sure whether I want to fly it or not."

What a sorry state of affairs!

Only a couple of years before flight, the program was in poor shape. It was way over budget and years behind schedule. Some Shuttle costs could be permanently allocated to less identifiable budget categories. Certain other costs were temporarily eliminated, knowing full well they would have to be added back later. The tactic was virtually forced upon the agency by a Congress with its focus on voter appeal—the projection of a minimal cost program until sufficient funds had been committed to make cancellation more costly than continuing.

Why is it that legitimate programs must be oversold in order to get support? How much does one promise in order to secure the political support to accomplish your objectives? There is no precise answer but that's what leaders are for—to render judgments on what is necessary and to know how much to oversell. In my judgment, the OMB was overzealous in squeezing the Shuttle program budget down to a level where there was no realistic chance of achieving program objectives. NASA trapped themselves in the same scenario to sell the space station.

Congressmen welcome the publicity when Monday morning quarterbacking as these projects inevitably go over budget but how many of them are willing to stand up and fight for adequate funding in the beginning? You can't go into space on the cheap—not safely, anyway.

In selling the Shuttle concept to Congress on the basis of low estimates, NASA lost more of its credibility and taxed its management ability when actual costs soared to three times the original budget. The $400 million meaningless indulgence in the ASTP technology transfer to the Russians could have come in handy on the Shuttle program.

Under the pressure of schedule and dollars, operational needs and hardware capability suffer. In the case of the Orbiter, the correct engineering choice had to be made the first time; there was neither money nor time to test several alternatives and there were no unmanned launches. The first Shuttle flight was a full-up manned launch. It was four years late and some important systems had marginal capability; the braking system was poor, the solid rocket booster casings were segmented, and so-on. It was a program that suffered from the unfair advantage in the hands of those who answer to the budget over those whose responsibility it was to bring home the vehicle.

It probably seemed to NASA management, at the time, like a series of small compromises, with no single budget blow severe enough for someone to stand up and say, "We can't do it for so little money." With an agency like NASA, the Administrator must be willing to stand up to the politicians and, if necessary, even the president to maintain the integrity of NASA's mission.

The Clinton administration had targeted NASA for massive budget cuts. As early as 1995 the General Accounting Office (GAO) had begun to issue warnings that cuts in NASA's shuttle workforce budget could pose risks by overworking those who maintain, repair and fly the shuttle fleet. The GAO also noted a serious shortage of NASA shuttle professionals in avionics, mechanical engineering and computer systems.

Between 1993 and 1997, NASA administrator, Dan Goldin, proudly reduced the annual operating budget for Shuttle by $1 billion—25 percent. According to NASA figures, he also slashed spending on safety and performance upgrades by 50 percent. At the same time, he kept pressure on the organization to maintain six to eight launches a year, all the while claiming that safety was being improved. According to Goldin, "Between 1992 and 1999, the risk of catastrophic loss on ascent was lowered by 82 percent."

In these circumstances, the first casualties are usually spare parts and facilities maintenance. Among the NASA programs deferred for lack of funds was an $800 million maintenance overhaul on the Shuttle's ground facilities.

You cannot get away with such concessions indefinitely. We didn't for the ill-fated Apollo 1, where a serious accident and the deaths of three good friends bought the delay necessary for the eventual success of Apollo. As you get closer to liftoff, the men who will ride the rocket carry more and more influence.

The Space Shuttle was the most important and innovative development to come along since Alan Shepard's fifteen-minute ride down-range but flight crew influence was a mere shadow of what it once was. Management was not receptive to what little astronaut input did get through. As Apollo 15 astronaut Dave Scott put it at the time, "The contractor thinks he has a spacecraft that can be built like an airplane, when it is really an airplane that needs to be built like a spacecraft."

A NASA Press Briefing booklet published in January 1977 contained the following entry:

"March 1979—OV-102—First manned orbital flight, Space Shuttle."

The schedule slipped year after year for a variety of technical reasons. In 1979, veteran Apollo astronauts Charlie Duke, Al Worden, and Dick Gordon held a press conference in Cocoa, Florida. The three agreed that the space Shuttle, still two years away from flight, was not as safe as the Mercury, Gemini and Apollo spacecraft. Some of their comments:

"I don't have confidence in the Shuttle program ... the test program just isn't being carried out properly."

"I haven't had confidence in the Shuttle program for some time. . . . . their safety margin is very low and that really concerns me."

". . . Congress isn't ready to give NASA the money it needs to make the program run smoothly."

Once more, we had an opportunity to do it right the first time and we chose to place our priority on cost. The schedule, operational capability and, let's face it, safety paid the price. Astronauts are dedicated to moving us into space with a fully operational spacecraft and maximum safety. But did anyone at NASA care any more? It was as if the Shuttle astronauts had been yelling into an empty warehouse. Not everything was corrected, but most of the essentials were, and the Space Shuttle finally went into orbit on 12 April 1981.

A fair amount of credit for the operational success and the safety records of the Mercury, Gemini, and Apollo Programs was due to the astronauts and their contributions to systems design and operational planning—the historic test pilot's role. All of the early astronauts were tough-minded test pilots and fighter pilots who refused to fly a vehicle that didn't reflect their operational viewpoint. NASA management, acknowledging the experimental nature of the programs, was quite receptive to astronauts' views for the Mercury and Gemini Programs and, to a lesser degree, for the Apollo Program. During the Seventies, an exodus of flight-experienced astronauts accompanied by a rapid increase in the size of the astronaut corps had a net effect of diluting the operational experience in the Astronaut Office. The Astronaut Office had little chance of achieving the operational influence on the space Shuttle that we enjoyed during the Mercury, Gemini and Apollo Programs.

In retrospect, Apollo was the first program to veer off in a slightly different direction. NASA, expanding tremendously, brought in many new managers. With the selection of my group, the astronaut corps doubled in size to thirty but the average test-pilot experience was reduced. Rockwell, the spacecraft contractor was also a brand-new face starting from scratch. These three factors all contributed to the rocky start of a program that was eventually very successful. Apollo achieved its goals, but not as smoothly as Mercury or Gemini, and the flight crew was partly responsible. My most disturbing personal recrimination is that we (the astronauts) did not do enough to prevent the fire on Pad 34. We completed a program in which three crewmembers lost their lives and some missions were less than 100 percent successful.

The Shuttle got off to a late but good start with three Shuttle Orbiters flying 24 highly successful missions in the first six years. In the process, it revolutionized our ideas of what a manned space operation should look like. The only persistent problem was an inability to hold to launch schedules. The program was and is plagued by launch delays. But every time an Orbiter returns from space to touch down on the runway markers, I am thrilled and impressed. And, yes, I am also envious as hell. The task of returning from space in a 200,000-pound glider, with only one chance to land on a pre-designated runway is quite a challenge and yet every Shuttle commander makes it look easy.

To the public-at-large, it probably looked like things were going smoothly. And, yes, NASA believed their press clippings. Wasn't this their fourth generation spacecraft? In spite of the technological compromises forced upon them by under funding, wasn't the program off to a great start? It even seemed like a good idea to go along with the media clamor and fly a "civilian" in space. And the first that NASA selected was a schoolteacher, Christa McAuliffe.

Christa and her backup, Barbara Morgan, reported to JSC for some rudimentary training for a flight on the Challenger. Six weeks before launch, the mission was being described as, "the first flight of an average person on the Space Shuttle." In one interview, a reporter told her, "You'll be thrust into the spotlight. You have met with government leaders, astronauts and celebrities. You've even been described as a viable candidate for state or national office from New Hampshire!" Can you imagine? Just from the notoriety!

Christa, herself, described it as "the ultimate field trip."

NASA managers were anxious to launch the Challenger for several reasons, including economic considerations, political pressures, and scheduling backlogs. On a freezing 28 January 1986 morning, after numerous delays, the 25th flight of the Space Shuttle, STS-51L, was given a "Go" for launch. Onboard for what would be the final flight of Challenger was Christa McAuliffe, civilian passenger, mother of two small children, and now a celebrated schoolteacher.

The fate of the Challenger was sealed from the moment the solid rocket boosters ignited on a freezing cold morning. The mission ended 73 seconds later at an altitude of 46,000 feet with Challenger traveling at nearly twice the speed of sound. An explosive burn, seen by millions on live television, destroyed the vehicle and killed the entire crew. The forces on the Orbiter at breakup were probably too low to cause death or serious injury to the crew. Two minutes and forty-five seconds after breakup the Orbiter struck the water at 207 miles per hour. There was no escape system and most of those on board were probably well aware of their fate seconds after the explosion.

The nation was stunned. The Challenger accident was a personal tragedy for the families of those onboard. For the space program and the Astronaut Office, it was a disaster. Five experienced astronauts, along with two passengers, were lost in the first American space accident off the earth. The media, of course, characterized the last flight of the Challenger as "the civilian teacher's flight" to the exclusion of the more significant mission objectives.

These persons aware of the Shuttle program's history of grandiose promises, funding shortfalls, political handicaps, and technical compromises were not as surprised by the accident.

The space program entered another period of introspection and internal investigations along with outside, independent investigative panels. In an impressive job of forensic analysis, investigators quickly came to a consensus on the accident. Among the morbid findings:

The forces to which the crew was exposed during Orbiter breakup were probably not sufficient to cause death or serious injury;

The crew may or may not have lost consciousness in the seconds following Orbiter breakup. . . . Each crewmember's helmet was connected to an emergency supply of breathing air, which had to be manually activated to be available. There was evidence that at least three crewmembers had activated their emergency breathing air;

The crew seats and restraint harnesses showed patterns of failure which demonstrates that all the seats were in place and occupied at water impact with all harnesses locked. This would likely be the case had rapid loss of consciousness occurred, but it does not constitute proof; and

The cause of explosion was determined to be an O-ring failure in the right solid rocket booster. Cold weather was a contributing factor.

That last finding could just as easily have been "design deficiencies"—cost had dictated that booster casings be segmented—and "poor judgment" to launch with icicles hanging on the launch tower.

The Presidential Commission on the Challenger accident issued a slamming indictment of NASA's flawed management style and said that the accident should never have happened. The commission made a large number of recommendations, the most important of which was redesign of the joints and seals between segments of the solid fuel boosters. NASA was also directed to improve landing safety (Remember the drag chute?) and to establish an Office of Safety, Reliability and Quality Assurance. The responsibilities of this office were to include all safety, reliability and quality assurance functions as they relate to NASA activities and programs. (Where were they when the Shuttle-Mir program came up?)

NASA was also ordered to develop a bailout capability, which included an "escape pole." It was one of those "improvements" that gave everyone but the crew great comfort. Unfortunately, this system has extremely limited usefulness, requiring that the shuttle be in controlled, low-speed flight below about 30,000 feet.

In the aftermath of the Challenger accident, many asked, "Should 'civilians' be flying into space?" Under the circumstances, it seemed like a reasonable question.

When Neil Armstrong landed on the moon, no one questioned flying a civilian in space, although Neil was a civilian throughout his NASA career. I was the second American civilian to fly in space and there have been dozens of civilian astronauts flying four generations of manned spacecraft. Many astronauts joined the program as military pilots and eventually changed their status to civilian employees of the space agency. Space has obviously not been the exclusive province of either military or civilian astronauts.

The movement toward non-pilot, private-citizen passengers was going strong by the late Seventies. Since the space Shuttle would place greater flying demands on astronauts, NASA began recruiting specialists for non-piloting activities. This was a luxury available only because of the size, comfort and convenience of the Orbiter vehicle. With the introduction of Mission Specialists and Payload Specialists into flight crews, the two pilots on the flight deck were freed from a myriad of engineering and technical responsibilities that formerly overloaded their daily schedules. The workload evened out as mission specialists assumed the science and some engineering responsibilities.

The real debate following the Challenger accident and one that continues today, is the role of so-called private-citizen space travelers: politicians, schoolteachers, journalists and others, along with the so-called "guest astronauts" from foreign countries. In the world of manned space flight, is there a place for the "amateur" space traveler? By "amateur" I do not include any crewmember placed in this dangerous environment to accomplish essential mission objectives.

Guest astronauts are the result of a political or diplomatic decision but foreign guests may be the best-qualified candidates their country can offer. Opinions on these guest astronauts probably depend on your view of such politics.

It is more difficult for me to rationalize the private-citizen space passengers on a brief sabbatical from their regular careers. Carrying politicians and teachers into space was not a sensible move in the Eighties and it is not reasonable today—but for different reasons. The contribution to society of these passengers is not dependent on traveling into space and the space program is no better off for their having flown. A policy of taking along private-citizen travelers tends to trivialize the commitment and contributions of those professional astronauts who literally dedicate their lives to opening up this new frontier.

And what have we done for these non-essential, private citizen passengers, other than broadening their life experience? We have placed them in harm's way without their full knowledge and awareness of the risks involved.

They are, to some degree, victims of NASA's amazing success—until the Challenger accident, a perfect flying safety record stretching back 24 years and 56 manned missions. Most missions accomplish a great deal but post-flight press conferences frequently focus on the fun and the enjoyment of the experience. Talk of the long training, the hard work, the challenge, the high-pressure demands or the unique technical aspects is usually received like a business conversation at a cocktail party.

Media coverage of missions tends to focus on the visual images, or what the television or print reporter feels comfortable with, or what the public can relate to. This usually guarantees that coverage emphasizes the trivial.

A NASA policy of encouraging non-governmental use makes it necessary that space flight be characterized as "routine." NASA has created the Shuttle Orbiter, in which any reasonably healthy grandparent can safely make the trip into and out of space.

Astronauts take their demanding job profoundly serious. Only because of their dedication and training, do they make it look easy. In postflight discussions at NASA or the Department of Defense, you can bet there is little time devoted to discussing "the fun of it all." Astronauts do not fly these missions for the fun of it, nor for the thrill of it. The flights represent a pinnacle of achievement and a demonstration of their proficiency in a career to which they have devoted their lives. These professionals and their families sacrifice a great deal for the privilege of contributing to worthwhile national goals.

The case is precisely the opposite with the space flight "passengers" I have observed. These passengers are permitted to dabble in the real work of space flight for a couple of months, enjoy the thrill of a unique vacation and then carry away that experience as if it were a prize for an athletic or academic achievement. These amateurs, who are just along for the ride, take from the program a thrill and the pleasure of being touched by the glamorous aspects of it all.

NASA maintains these shuttle passengers do understand the risk involved. But can they, given the way the experience is characterized by the media and their own preparation for the mission? They may know you can die from the experience but that is not the same as understanding the risk.

Here is how Christa McAuliffe described her preparation a few weeks before flight:

"People think our training is grueling. We are no more tired than we would be teaching in a classroom. I find teaching more tiring.... I never sit down when I teach. I am always moving around the classroom. And you have a lot of deadlines. The kids have to get those papers back."

And I am certain that the families of passengers are much less prepared than the families of astronauts for the kind of tragedy that occurred on the last flight of the Challenger.

Christa McAuliffe was in the same circumstance as a spectator shot while watching a police shoot out. Her death was avoidable; Dick Scobee's and the other Challenger crewmembers' deaths were not.

In the case of Christa, the news media seemed not to realize that carrying a passenger was really nothing more than public relations—a little frosting on an otherwise important mission. Who recalls that the Challenger's principal mission objective was to launch one of the most sophisticated, expensive, and important communication satellites in history (TDRS-2), an essential element of the manned space flight communication system? The media were left to cover in suffocating detail the tragic fallout of a private citizen being placed, mostly unknowingly, in harm's way.

The Challenger accident was a graphic reminder that space is the most hostile environment into which man has ever ventured; it requires systems that are the most complex in history. The professionals addressing this challenge are dedicated to the task, understand the risks and are better prepared than others to pay the ultimate price that is sometimes exacted. Only when the true nature of this environment and the systems with which we tame it are well understood can one fairly evaluate the risks and rewards of riding a rocket into space.

The absence of specific quotas to carry certain categories of passengers into space does not mean they are being excluded. No one is being discriminated against. As we continue to both explore and exploit our last frontier let us always select the very best people for the tasks at hand. When we need a teacher or a butcher or a baker in space, let us take the best we can find—whoever they are and wherever we find them. Until we need those people, let's leave it to the professionals.

When the time is right for passengers or tourists, let's make sure the risk is minimal, there is a real reason for them to be exposed to the dangers, that they truly understand the risk and their consent is truly informed, that the media is able to keep their role in perspective, and then, call them what they are—passengers.

Following the Challenger accident, a local television reporter looked me up. He took issue with an opinion piece I had written for the *Houston Chronicle* about flying passengers on the Shuttle. He was a finalist for the "Journalist in Space" program, rumored to be next on the agenda and he told me, quite indignantly, "We have a right to risk our ass just as much as you do." He just didn't get it! I tried to explain to him that we did not go into space to "risk our ass," as he put it. We did it because it was a natural thing for us and, given our experience and skills, it was much less of a risk than it was for him. It was a fruitless discussion.

Following the Challenger accident, the "Teacher in Space" program was put on the shelf for 12 years. The disaster did make people realize that space travel is risky and may not be appropriate for civilians who aren't full-fledged astronauts. NASA's solution was to make the teachers full-fledged astronauts. In 1998, the program was reincarnated as the Educator Astronaut program and Barbara Morgan, Christa McAuliffe's backup, was brought back to train as a full-time astronaut. Barbara was designated the first educator astronaut and assigned to a November 2003 shuttle mission to re-supply the international space station.

Barbara is a career teacher and probably a great one. But, if this is the appropriate pool from which to select mission specialists, why haven't we been recruiting from there for the last 25 years?

In January 2003, NASA announced a national call for applications to add up to six more educator astronauts into its 2004 astronaut class at the Johnson Space Center. It looks like an affirmative action program for teachers of kindergarten through 12th grade with a bachelor's degree in education, math, science or a science-related discipline, and who have taught for at least three of the past four years. Upon graduation, they will be eligible for a Space Shuttle flight assignment as a fully trained mission specialist. According to a NASA spokesman, "This is not a one-shot opportunity, where you go home after one mission. Educator astronauts are professional astronauts."

What a politically correct but misguided effort to regain lost relevance. The ultimate objective, of course, is broader support on Capitol Hill and an easier time at the annual budget battle. Space missions are too difficult, expensive, important, and risky an undertaking for NASA to experiment with turning teachers into mission specialists. Mission specialists should be selected from the best pool of qualified candidates for the position.

For what profession will we establish the next quota? Artists? Journalists?

A science teacher at a Middle School and an applicant for the Educator Astronaut Program, after hearing of the Columbia disaster in February 2003, said it had shaken her but not her resolve to fly into space. "Am I apprehensive? Oh yeah," she said. "A part of me is scared out of my mind, and a part of me wants to make a very positive difference in the way space is perceived." She still has an eye exam and three essays to submit to NASA.

Three essays? That's a new one for "the brotherhood of the right stuff?"

Appearances not withstanding, things had not really been going that well before the Challenger accident. I had begun to hear from more and more astros who were leaving the program—after their Shuttle mission, of course. The Orbiter wasn't the problem, or the missions. That was their job; that was the thrill for which they had signed up. It was the changing management style at NASA, the dysfunctional organization in the Astronaut Office, and the insidious politics in the Flight Operations Directorate at JSC. In two words, it was George Abbey.

Back in 1969, when Chris Kraft became JSC Center Director, he appointed George as his technical assistant. In that capacity, George exercised the authority of the center director and, apparently, quite effectively.

The appointment of Abbey as Deputy Director for Flight Operations in 1976 was the beginning of 12 years of politics and misery for most of those in the Astronaut Office. George had a Machiavellian talent for achieving the outcomes he wanted without ever leaving his fingerprints at the scene of the crime. Theoretically, all flight crew assignments were made by the Chief Astronaut and approved by Abbey for forwarding to NASA Headquarters. In actual practice, during Abbey's tenure, crew assignments were regularly returned to the Chief Astronaut as "not quite right." When the Chief Astronaut figured out just exactly which astronauts George wanted to see on the crew, they would be approved. It was a stifling political environment that none of the astros liked, even those who benefited from it.

It created a whole coterie of astronauts who came to be known as "friends of George." They ate with George; they partied with George; and they tucked George in after parties when George was unable to do it himself. As the other half of this Faustian bargain, George took care of those who agreed with George and took care of George.

When I spoke with Bob Overmyer, a fellow Marine, in October 1986, following the Challenger disaster, we discussed why he had recently resigned rather than waiting for another flight. He said, "It boiled down to feeling that my role in the Challenger investigation placed me permanently on George Abbey's shit list." Consequently, he would never fly again.

When I commented that Abbey would be gone sometime, his response was, "Don't count on it." He felt Abbey had been very successful at getting his loyalists (astronauts who would feel obligated due to past favorable treatment) into key positions where they could protect him. Two astronauts Bob singled out as being helped by Abbey and who occupied positions to protect him, if necessary, were Bob Crippen and Dick Truly. Crippen flew the first Shuttle mission and had four flights in three and one-half years; Truly flew the second mission and one other.

Bob claimed to have been present during a telephone conversation in which Abbey unsuccessfully proposed Truly for Administrator of NASA, Director of the Johnson Space Center and finally Associate Administrator for Manned Space Flight. Truly was eventually appointed Administrator of NASA, while Crippen became the Director of the Kennedy Space Center.

In Overmyer's opinion, the Challenger investigation did not delve deep enough into the role Abbey played in preventing the flight crews' memos and long standing concerns from getting properly aired before NASA management. Bob felt that Abbey had been sheltered from aggressive questioning by the various investigating boards by Tom Tate, a Naval Academy classmate and Administrative Assistant to Don Fuqua, the Chairman of the House Science and Technology Committee.

Bob was not the first to tell me that flight crew assignments were based, to a great degree, on a relationship with George Abbey. That opinion was shared by every astronaut with whom I ever discussed the subject: the personal favoritism of George Abbey was the biggest determinant of flight crew assignments. That automatically made it a major consideration in the why and when an astronaut resigned from NASA or left the Astronaut Office.

A counter example, or maybe it is the exception that proves the rule, was Story Musgrave. Story had an exceptional career, flying six Shuttle missions, in spite of never enjoying a good relationship with George Abbey. I suspect, it was a case of Story's skills overriding Abbey's prejudice even though many of those infamous crew lists with Story's name on them were sent back to the Astronaut Office for reconsideration. When Abbey returned to JSC in the Nineties, Story's career stalled and, in the end, George got him. According to Story, one of the best-trained astronauts ever, when he was finally accepted for the STS-80 crew, he was told. "You are being assigned to STS-80 and it will be your last flight."

According to Story, "The total disempowerment {sic} of the astronauts and the destruction of the esprit de corps of the astronaut office so traditional of flying units, was affected or approved by the highest levels of management at JSC during the mid-Seventies.

"There was absolutely no functioning organizational structure within the astronaut office. Communication was generally handled one-on-one from George Abbey to separate individuals in the Astronaut Office. John Young (Chief Astronaut, at the time) wrote memos but the information never get beyond George's office. George managed to select his favorites, reward them with crew assignments and place them in supporting administrative positions. The pilots allowed the crew assignment carrot to dominate all facets of their activities; operations, management, social activities, etc. Flight crew assignments were totally controlled by George Abbey and subject to his personal favoritism. The result was to effectively stifle informed dissent and constructive criticism from the Astronaut Office."

A number of people, including some former astronauts, knew conditions weren't as good as they had been at the beginning of earlier programs but management was attempting to compensate for them with hard work, dedication, and launch delays. In the Astronaut Office, they were making the same mistake we had made before Apollo 1, thinking, "We can fly the crates they ship them in."

Bob Overmyer was wrong about one thing. Following the Challenger investigation, a 1988 JSC internal assessment concluded that Flight Operations, which included the Astronaut Office, was deficient in all areas of management and Abbey was literally "kicked" upstairs to a headquarters position. The astronauts thought, or maybe hoped, he was gone forever.

Wishful thinking is what it was.

It took 33 months to implement the recommendations of the Presidential Commission and make the Orbiter a safer vehicle. Astronauts carried more influence in the redesign—just as we had following the Apollo 1 fire. The modified post-Challenger Orbiter was supposed to be the safest spacecraft ever to fly.

The probabilistic risk assessment for the Orbiter before the Challenger accident (the 25th mission) was supposed to be one in 78 flights. That is, there was a 50/50 chance of the loss of an Orbiter (or worse) in 78 flights. However, this number only took into consideration launch risks, the most dangerous phase of a space mission, and accounted for about half of the risk. After nearly 1,000 safety improvements following Challenger, this figure was raised to about one in 250 flights, but this figure also encompassed orbital and reentry risks. Further improvements were supposed to have slowly raised the figure for catastrophic loss to the range of one in 500-600 flights. NASA would soon learn that theory doesn't necessarily match reality.

I can only guess that the probabilistic risk assessment during the Apollo program would have been in the range of 15-20. We beat the odds, partially, by flying only 11 missions and quitting while we were ahead.

To put these figures in perspective, the risk of catastrophe loss for a commercial jetliner is one in 2 million; for a fighter jet, it is one in 20,000.

The Space Shuttle returned to flight a little more cautiously, with some higher standards and many changes in management ranks, but it never really shook the risk factor.

Funding for NASA in 2003 was at almost exactly the level it was in 1993, despite a decade of inflation. Tight budgets always have an impact. Some safety upgrades that had once been considered critical, like one on the shuttle's electric auxiliary power units, were canceled because of delays, technical problems and a tripling of the costs. An OMB study making a cold assessment of the value of future safety upgrades, noted that funding future improvements would reduce the odds of catastrophic failure only 10 percent—from one in every 556 missions to one in 620 missions.

NASA began a string of 88 difficult and very successful missions, the most impressive of which have been the launch and maintenance of the Hubble Space Telescope and construction of the International Space Station. The loss of a second Space Shuttle, the Columbia, on 1 February 2003, after another 88 flights, showed how misleading failure calculations could be.

STS-107 was a 16-day science mission—one of the rare missions between 1998 and 2006 not committed to construction of the International Space Station (ISS). It was the 113th space shuttle mission and the 28th flight of the Space Shuttle Columbia. Columbia was the oldest and heaviest vehicle in the fleet—having flown the first five shuttle missions beginning in 1981.

It had taken years to get the STS-107 mission planned, trained, and launched. It had not always been scheduled to do science. Initially, Dan Goldin, to show his commitment to equal opportunity and political correctness, had considered it as a mission for an all-female crew. NASA officials insisted it would provide an opportunity to learn more about how women adapt to weightlessness and gain some dubious (and temporary) public relations benefit.

It was abandoned when even female astronauts scorned the idea of an all women crew as a publicity stunt. An independent panel of medical experts agreed that, while more research was needed on women, it did not require an exclusively female crew.

Then it was proposed as a carrier for the Earth-observing spacecraft dreamed up by Vice President Al Gore when he was the obvious Democratic presidential candidate. In 1998, Gore "challenged" NASA to build a satellite, called Triana, to beam back continuous, live images of our home planet from an orbit one million miles out in space "by the year 2000." With no legitimate scientific purpose, this $200 million boondoggle, was characterized as a "way to inspire young minds."

Instead of pointing out that Triana was a foolish and wasteful scheme, Goldin, acting as if NASA had been challenged to put a human on Mars instead of simply deploying a dumb camera in a very high Earth orbit, stated publicly, "We're up to the challenge." At Congress' behest, the unfinished Triana was pulled off the mission in 2001 and ended up in NASA storage.

After Triana fizzled out, NASA decided to share the mission with the Israel Space Agency, which had a commitment from President Clinton to place an Israeli astronaut on a space mission.

Eli Ramon was part of a wonderfully successful, 16-day science mission. On 1 February 2003, at an altitude of 37 miles and just 16 minutes from landing, the Columbia disintegrated. I believe the crew suspected nothing until a few seconds before their vehicle came apart; the Commander and the Pilot probably watched the situation deteriorate for, possibly, tens of seconds; and all seven of them died very shortly after Columbia began to break apart. There was absolutely nothing anyone in the air or on the ground could have done to save them, even had they known of the failure beforehand.

STS-107 was a near perfect mission until it ended in a manner faintly reminiscent of the Soyuz 11 tragedy in July 1971. After a record 23 days in orbit, the three-man crew was minutes from landing when radio contact was lost. When the hatch was opened on the ground they found three dead cosmonauts.

Our crew did not make it back to the ground but they were all aware that you do not always survive this hostile environment. That's the nature of the business.

On the ground, in mission control, it was a different story. Some of those waiting, watching, and listening had to be keeping their fingers crossed or saying a prayer, depending on what they believed in. At the time of breakup, no one could know for sure what caused the disintegration, but a knowledgeable few had been aware of at least one potential cause for several days. A team of NASA and contractor engineers spent a week following launch studying the consequences of a piece of external fuel tank foam insulation, weighing 2.5 pounds, striking the underside of the left wing of Columbia 81 seconds after lift-off.

They were conscientious, experienced, professional engineers and no one was better qualified to perform the analysis. The group concluded that the insulating foam, even if it had impacted the underside of Columbia's wing, would probably not be a factor on reentry. There are so many uncertainties and assumptions associated with such an analysis that a number of those engineers had to be sweating out that reentry, hoping or wishing they were right. After the disaster, it was painfully apparent they were not right. And no one probably felt it any more than those who performed the analysis.

It was possible more than one piece impacted the wing to trigger a critical heat leak. What if the other piece was not foam, but ice that weighs 25 times as much?

It was always possible that some other failure had caused the loss of Columbia. There are some 2,000 possible system failures on the Orbiter that could lead to catastrophic failure and not all of them are covered by redundancies in design. If the investigating board could positively identify another failure as the cause, there still might be the nagging doubt that the foam impact might have been the triggering event.

In one respect, knowing the foam had caused critical damage would have been academic. There was absolutely nothing anyone could have done to save the crew. Columbia had to reenter with or without a critical failure, and they would have attempted it even with advance knowledge of the failure. However, it might have changed the timing in some way.

I believe most Shuttle commanders would have wanted the flight director to advise them if it was known the thermal protection system had been compromised during launch. Certainly, we would have insisted on it with Apollo 7. That is a big burden on the flight director, but an even bigger one for the Shuttle commander. Imagine having the responsibility of informing the rest of the crew what would be facing them on reentry.

After a disaster of this kind there is always talk of how heroic they were and who should get what kind of medals. Compared to what passes for heroism in today's society, yes, they were heroes, but not because they died at the end of their mission. They were heroes because of the job

they and the other 140 astronauts in training do every single day. They
don't have to be there but they are. They have a choice.

I don't know if the Columbia astronauts were heroes. They were
doing something challenging that was quite dangerous but the end came
so fast they had no opportunity to respond. They died doing their duty.
I agree with Buzz Aldrin's comment following the accident, "A hero is
someone who is faced with a decision, and the choice he makes is ultimately what makes that person into a hero. But these men and women
had no chance to choose. They were just doing their duty."

I have similar feelings about medals and what they mean today. In the
late Nineties, there was a brief flurry of excitement when Shannon Lucid
was awarded the Congressional Space Medal of Honor for a long-duration flight on the Russian space station Mir. Shannon is brave and spunky
and did a great job during her six-month mission but the lavish attention
her feat attracted says much about the diminished state of our space program.

Endurance records are fine. But the Congressional Space Medal of
Honor? It used to be given to the likes of Alan Shepard and John Glenn,
who had the insane courage to park themselves atop an unstable, largely untested eight-story bomb not knowing whether it would blow up
under them; or Neil Armstrong for setting foot on another body in the
universe for the first time. Now we give it for spending six months in an
orbiting camper with a couple of Russians. Sign of the times, I guess.

Investigations and findings are for the living; for the survivors; for
those who must climb back into the vehicle and hang their backsides out
over the yawning chasm the next time.

NASA looks at tragedies as a problem to be solved. They fix the
things they can, as they did for us following the Apollo 1 fire. They examine engineering design, operations, procedures and management for
ways to prevent a repetition. Sometimes we learn the details of *what* happened without ever learning exactly *how* it was triggered. But we were
already aware of some factors that *could have* contributed to Columbia's
disintegration.

Was money a factor? That's difficult to say, but money can be a
major factor in establishing a work environment and shaping the attitudes of a workforce. NASA personnel (and I include among them, con-

tractor personnel working exclusively for NASA) were presented with conflicting mandates. They were told that neither schedule nor cost should ever be allowed to compromise safety at the same time emphasis was being placed on achieving cost and staff reductions, while increasing the flight rate.

NASA's annual budget has been flat for a decade, while Congress has "earmarked" hundreds of millions of dollars of the agency's annual appropriation for pork barrel projects in their home districts in return for support. NASA's budget as a percentage of government spending has been cut by 84 percent since 1966. During the Nineties, the agency's percentage of federal spending was cut by 30 percent.

Billions of dollars have been transferred to the Russian space agency and their space contractors to pay for Russia's "contribution" to the ISS. Once the space station was linked to American foreign aid policy, Dan Goldin lost some of his spending prerogatives. When the Russians missed their ISS commitments, NASA transferred $200 million from a Shuttle reserve fund into the space station program. The following year, Goldin diverted more funds to help keep the Russian program afloat. No matter how many times the Russians failed to deliver, broke their promises or made excuses, Goldin continued to be a "true believer"—their staunchest supporter.

At one time, in 1996, NASA froze the Shuttle design so it could divert funds to the development of a single-stage-to-orbit (SSTO) launch vehicle, a project with little chance of success. The freeze was lifted one year later, but NASA still did not commit to major Shuttle upgrades until the SSTO vehicle was cancelled at the end of the decade. Only $100 million a year was authorized for shuttle improvements, including safety measures.

The House and Senate have been responsible for many of the budget cuts, despite repeated warnings from their own members and outside experts. Senator Bill Nelson, himself a Shuttle astronaut, described the cultural change that has come over NASA as it turned into a management exercise: "We've got accountants making life-and-death technical decisions for our astronauts and our ground crews, instead of the engineers and program managers."

To rebut criticism that Congressional tightfistedness impacted Space Shuttle safety, the House Appropriations Committee released figures showing that the agency's funding closely mirrored its requests to Congress. In denying it was their fault, Congress was pointing the finger at the budget requests of Administrator Goldin and his boss, President Clinton.

Then there is the matter of the loss of foam insulation from the external fuel tank. The external tank shed insulation on more than one launch *since* switching to a new, lighter version of spray-on foam insulation in the mid-1990s. The decision to change seemed based more on politics than technical improvements. It was done to reduce ozone-depleting chemicals. The original foam was aerated with Freon, containing CFCs. NASA could have obtained a waiver to stick with this well understood product but, in a bow to political correctness, they elected to change to an environmentally friendly, non-CFC bearing material. This modification changed the performance characteristics of the foam and, possibly, the bonding properties as well.

If the classical pattern holds, there will be a brief honeymoon of pulling together and analysis, followed by a partisan blame game. Even though space exploration is one of those rare issues that tends to cut across party lines, there will be major disagreement between Democrats and Republicans over whether safety was compromised by the Clinton administration's restricted funding for the Shuttle.

There is a real risk of committees, engineers, managers, and don't forget Congress, concluding they must take all risk out of the operation. That is neither possible nor cost effective. When the benefit exceeds the perceived risk, we should get on with the mission.

Considering what the Shuttle Orbiter has accomplished in the past 22 years of opening up a new frontier, it has been a marvelously safe machine. How many died opening up the American West in the nineteenth century? How many aviation pioneers lost their lives in the 30 years before commercial aviation took off in the 1930s?

Even when spaceflights appear routine, astronauts know it is still quite dangerous. They understand there is only so much that can be done to reduce the inherent risk in every space mission. The thermal protection system has always been the weak underbelly of the Orbiter—its Achilles' heel. It is a weakness we must live with until the next generation of manned vehicles. NASA should improve the thermal protection if possible but it might be easier to eliminate any possibility of damage from other parts of the launch system—that includes the foam insulation on the external tank.

To be truly operational, a space vehicle should be robust; able to take occasional abuse and still function satisfactorily. The Orbiter's exterior is covered with a thermal protection system that is quite delicate. It needs to be coddled.

Everything practical should be done to improve the system but we can never remove all the uncertainty. The only way to make spaceflight completely safe is to not fly!

Shuttle crews strap themselves to 3.5 million pounds of explosives, the energy equivalent of a small nuclear blast, and then light it on fire. The trick is to burn those explosives in such a way as to precisely control the release of energy.

The chemical energy of the fuel is transformed into potential and kinetic energy, lifting a quarter million pound spacecraft 240 miles into the air and accelerating it to 17,500 miles per hour in eight-and-one-half minutes. At that point, the engines are shut down and the shuttle coasts around the earth at 17,500 mph until it is time to reenter and land.

Reentry entails dissipating the energy in such a way as to bring the Shuttle back to earth, dead-stopped on a runway, with no energy remaining. It begins by firing a rocket to slow down, causing the vehicle to "fall" out of orbit. The potential and kinetic energy of the orbiting Shuttle is converted to thermal energy as the vehicle encounters the atmosphere. In the Apollo command module, the thermal energy was dissipated in a process called ablation. The heat of reentry was used to turn the solid material of the heat shield into a gas.

The Shuttle Orbiter re-enters the atmosphere gradually but still heats up tremendously. The heat is radiated into space and the atmosphere.

The conversion of huge amounts of energy from one form into another is a difficult and dangerous activity. Utilizing the energy stored in the rocket on the pad is rather obvious. It is more difficult to visualize the energy management problem of returning to earth from orbit, but it is just as big a challenge.

NASA had little choice. They returned the Space Shuttle fleet to flight status as soon as possible. Too much investment and too many people were dependent on it. Since the Orbiter is absolutely dependent on the tiles for thermal control, they should reemphasize quality control on installation and maintenance of this critical system—and go fly. While the engineers are at it, they should insure the external tank insulation is the best technical solution we have and not the most politically correct one.

18

Parked In Earth Orbit

AS WONDERFUL A MACHINE as it is, the Shuttle Orbiter has always had its inherent safety concerns, particularly the main engines, the solid rocket boosters and the thermal protection system. It is my opinion, however, that our astronauts have faced even greater risks in programs not under our control. Probably the most controversial and riskiest operation for American astronauts was the Shuttle-Mir Program, not due to the Orbiter, but to the Russian Space Station Mir.

The Mir was launched in 1986 with a planned six-year lifetime. After a couple of years, the Russians began lobbying the U.S. for a visit by the Space Shuttle. A NASA committee studied the possibilities and in 1993 concluded: "Mir is an aging space structure prone to breakdowns, noise, and vibration, starved for power and totally inadequate to host any visits by U.S. spacecraft." The committee recommended *against* any U.S. use of Mir!

The Mir was designed to accommodate a crew of two more or less indefinitely, or four people for a few days, primarily during crew changeovers and exchanging the Soyuz "lifeboat." All the records for duration in space were established during Mir's amazing 14 years in orbit. Sergei Avdeyev accumulated 749 total days during three stays on Mir while Valery Polyakov "enjoyed" a single, 437-day visit.

By the early Nineties, Mir was a middle-aged space station, experiencing a growing number of breakdowns, in the possession of a country and a political system in the last throws of its existence. The Soviet Union was breaking apart and going bankrupt. (Or was it going bankrupt and breaking apart?) Russia, successor to the USSR, retained control over the space program, of course, but they had precious little money to fund an aging space station.

Mir was saved from the scrap heap by help from a surprising direction. America rode in on a white horse to prolong its life for a few years. A new era of "cooperation in space" was born purely out of politics. Nothing else! The Russians absolutely needed the U.S., although they were reluctant to admit it. Their space program was in the toilet and they were broke. Our only need was to satisfy internal politics.

Some would say NASA was always politically driven and, in a sense, it has been. But the motivation for both the Mercury and the Apollo programs was external politics. It was the cold war and our leaders believed it was important to show the rest of the world that American technology and our way of life were superior to the communist alternative. With ASTP, it was a political decision to reduce international tensions by staging a cooperative mission with the Soviet Union. The International Space Station (ISS), eventually designated Station Alpha, triggered politics of the more venial kind—the Democrat and Republican kind. It was an attempt by one political party to gain an advantage over the other—internal, domestic politics played out in a foreign arena.

In 1993, William Jefferson Clinton came into the presidency with no foreign policy credentials and no foreign policy initiatives. He also had no real affection for either the military establishment or the space program, and was more than willing to pay for his domestic programs out of their budgets. But he was an opportunist. The Berlin Wall had come down and the Soviet Union had come apart at the seams. When someone suggested to the president that working with the Russians in space would offer him an opportunity to move cooperation with Russia to a new level, he practically jumped at it. NASA was directed to explore bringing Russia into the ISS consortium as a full partner.

Unfortunately, the ISS was very late and way over budget, due to both grandiose design and Congressional re-direction. The political meddling may have looked like a life preserver to NASA. Dan Goldin, the NASA administrator, had been appointed in the last year of the George H. W. Bush administration after a frustrating search to find someone who would take the job. Goldin was supposed to bring private industry techniques, such as decentralization and rigorous performance targets, to the top-heavy and sluggish NASA bureaucracy.

Goldin had a great deal of experience with unmanned, military, reconnaissance satellites—the so-called "black" programs—but absolutely no experience with the manned space program. To fill this little void, in 1992,

George Abbey was resurrected as Goldin's right hand man. Typical of George, he (along with Tom Stafford) had a hand in selecting his own boss and then going to work for the man he had helped select. The joke at the time was to the effect that when something difficult came up, Goldin would solicit Abbey's advice. Abbey would say, "Let Stafford's firm study it." It seemed to work out pretty well for all three of them.

Goldin may have been the front man but George Abbey was the architect of the love affair with the Russians for Shuttle-Mir and the ISS program. With Abbey's return for a second run at NASA politics, some astronauts with long memories began referring to George's 1976 to 1988 tenure as the era of George the First.

While in exile following the Challenger disaster, Abbey spent a short while at the National Space Council where he was instrumental in plotting the replacement of NASA Administrator Richard Truly with Dan Goldin. He returned to NASA as Goldin's accomplice and by 1994, George was back directing the affairs of the Johnson Space Center. This includes the two years when Carolyn Huntoon, one of Dan Goldin's many politically correct, diversity appointments was nominally the Center Director. George was Carolyn's deputy, but political correctness and quotas will only carry you so far and everyone knew who was calling the shots. Abbey's brand of politics and Machiavellian manipulation through the Nineties was accurately described in Bryan Burrough's book, *Dragonfly*. The reign of George II would last until 2001 but it could take another five or six years after that to repair the damage to the management culture at JSC.

After the damning 1993 evaluation of Mir, it was a bit of a surprise when Clinton announced the Shuttle-Mir program later that year. It was officially called Phase 1 of the Russian participation in the International Space Station. The announced purpose: to find out how well Americans and Russians could work together in space. Unfortunately, the decision had been made politically not logically. The administration had already decided to include the Russians as full partners in the ISS; Shuttle-Mir was merely a way to justify the initial transfer of $400 million to the Russian Aviation and Space Agency (Rosaviakosmos), the Russian space manufacturing Corporation (RSC Energia) and other parts of the Russian space industry. This down payment would eventually grow to billions of dollars.

Between late '95 and June '98, we had an American astronaut continuously onboard the aging relic known as the Mir space station. Seven
astronauts spent as long as six months each on the station exposed to the
dangers associated with broken down hardware, a shortage of spares,
fires, and mid-air collisions. Visits with most of them following their
return confirmed my suspicion that it was one of the riskiest periods for
astronauts in the short history of manned space flight.

It was an adventure for our guys to learn Russian, move to Russia,
train on Russian hardware, and fly in Russian spacecraft. We always
believed our equipment was better and this would be a good opportunity to compare the two. Cosmonauts training in Houston probably felt the
same about their equipment.

The experience was invariably described as, "interesting, challenging
and rewarding." Our Mir astronauts had anticipated some culture shock
but they also faced other big adjustments—especially in their training
routine. Astronauts and cosmonauts go at their training from opposite
ends of the spectrum. At NASA, we learned all the spacecraft and booster systems, developed procedures and worked on mission planning; and
all mission phases and objectives were rehearsed in simulators, frequently integrated with mission control. Repetitive training was carried to the
point where the mission seemed second nature; we participated in the
checkout and testing of the spacecraft. We were an integral part of nearly all phases of the program. It works!

Cosmonaut training unchanged since the days of Yuri Gagarin relies
on lectures, classroom training and oral and written examinations. And
it works! I should say it works for the Russian cosmonauts!

They do not conduct integrated simulations. It is hard to say whether
the Russian philosophy of training was dictated by poor computer technology, the high cost of good simulators, or simply the cultural patterns
of the closed Soviet society. We have always known the role of the cosmonauts in their program was different from ours but it took thirty years to
confirm just how different. In the beginning, cosmonauts were, and generally still are, study subjects. They are components to be "plugged in"
when and where management sees fit.

The Russians have always made less special tooling and other accom-
modations for their activities in orbit. They take greater advantage of
"residing" in space and adjusting to that environment as appropriate. For

example, they will send a box of parts up to their crewmen with instructions inside. The cosmonauts put the equipment together according to the instructions and begin operating the experiment. We were quite pleased and impressed during one Shuttle mission when the crew improvised a three astronaut EVA to retrieve an Intelsat satellite by hand. That kind of improvisation is part of the day-to-day activities of the cosmonauts—at the direction of ground control, of course.

When our guys began showing up to train for Mir at Star City, outside of Moscow, they were treated like the "Guest Cosmonauts" from the former Eastern Bloc countries the Russians had been taking up with them. Our astronaut may have been a veteran of two, three or four missions on the Shuttle but he was still given the dumb-ass treatment as a Mir crewmember. The first three months of Russian language instruction was to top off the twelve months they had completed at home. The year of simple-minded Technical Training that followed was particularly galling. It consisted of, for example, 20 hours of lectures on simple space toilets and two hours on complex guidance and control systems.

It wasn't much better when our astronauts reached Mir. The Russians gave Shannon Lucid a work program so light she had days off and time to read and watch movies. Our people spent most of their days repairing the station and exercising to prevent as much bone density and muscle volume loss as possible with a small amount of time thrown in for experiments. John Blaha, an experienced Shuttle commander, was busy with these tasks from early morning to midnight, seven days a week, including holidays. Because of the poor humidity control, Dave Wolf sometimes spent 10-12 hours of the day collecting condensate from the cool walls of the station. The cosmonauts were sometimes so concerned about their onboard "guests" that they put tape over some of the switches.

Nineteen-ninety-seven was a particularly bad year for Mir. Two of the worst life-threatening incidents were a fire on 23 February and a mid-air collision with a Progress freighter on 25 June.

The Mir space station consisted of a half-dozen interconnected modules. Distributed throughout the station are the principal elements of the crew life support system, the oxygen, thermal control, CO_2 removal, humidity control and waste management systems, all of which were dependent on the electrical power system.

Two "Elektron" oxygen generating units employed electricity to break waste water into oxygen and hydrogen, a process called electrolysis. For backup, Mir had three canisters that burn lithium perchlorate elements referred to as "candles." Each "candle" generated enough oxygen to support one man for one day.

Life support for the station itself was no less critical, but the systems were somewhat simpler than those required to keep the human crew alive. Principal needs were thermal control, electrical power, and attitude control, a system whose gyrodynes generate a great deal of heat and consume a great deal of power.

Mir could maintain attitude control only so long as the thermal control system could carry the heat away from the gyrodynes; thermal control was maintained so long as the electrical power system supplied current to the coolant pumps; and the electrical power system only worked so long as the attitude control system was able to keep the solar arrays pointed toward the sun. This circular dependency meant a total failure in one of these systems was a precursor to failure in all three unless corrective action was taken very quickly. In the event of a total shutdown, startup was a "bootstrap" operation that could take weeks.

While our astronauts were onboard, the thermal control system was greatly degraded and was being controlled manually. The station was plagued with high temperatures, high humidity, and bad condensation problems.

In February 1997, Korzun, Linenger and Kaleri were joined on Mir by a change-over crew of Vasily Tsibliyev, the commander, Aleksandr Lazutkin and the German, Reinhold Ewald. With a complement of six, it was necessary to regularly burn candles to have enough oxygen to breathe—one per person per day. As Lazutkin activated a new candle in its container, he could smell the fresh oxygen and feel the small amount of heat the device gave off. The next instant, the candle erupted into flames like a blowtorch. The ensuing fire lasted a shorter time but was every bit as critical an emergency as the Apollo 13 oxygen tank explosion. The entire emergency took place while Mir was out of contact with the ground and, depending on whom you choose to believe, Linenger or Korzun, the fire burned for "14 minutes" or just "a couple of minutes."

There is no disagreement that the fire blocked the route to one of the Soyuz spacecraft, expected to function as a lifeboat in just such emergencies. The smoke was so thick you couldn't see your fingers in front of your face and the intensity of the fire made a burn through of the hull of the station a real possibility. The fire extinguishers were not capable of putting out the fire but they were effective enough to cool the walls until the fire burned itself out. The first breathing mask Linenger put on didn't work and the first fire extinguisher he grabbed from the wall was still bolted down from launch eleven years before.

The Russians waited half a day before informing NASA about the fire. And when they did report, they claimed it was "the first failure of an oxygen candle in 10,000 uses." Back in 1994, these same "partners" had certified there had *never, ever* been any fires aboard Russian manned space vehicles. NASA's own investigation of the fire would uncover the fact that Mir had suffered at least four fires while in orbit!

Perhaps the most disturbing comment I heard following the fire was a statement out of the Mission Control Center in Moscow, TsUP, intended to provide reassurance: "Not to worry, they (the crew) have enough fire extinguishers for at least one more fire."

Details of the fire and the crew's subsequent recovery were thoroughly covered in Linenger's book, *Off the Planet*. But what of other failures of the Russian manned program and our futile efforts to learn of them? The Russians, obviously, thought we should personally experience the failures of their space hardware before we could assess the real risk of flying on their equipment. It was rare that anything negative was volunteered until we, independently, first uncovered a problem. The Mir fire, once more, exposed the deceit, which marks the Russian attitude in their dealings with NASA and the U.S. government. In a fair partnership, each partner carries his own weight and is honest with the other. The Shuttle-Mir program was another one of those Texas joint ventures; they took our money and we came home with a great deal more experience.

By June 1997 Jerry Linenger had been replaced by Mike Foale on Tsibliyev's crew—a crew that would face their own trial—not by fire but by mid-air collision.

On June 25, Tsibliyev was asked to perform a manual docking experiment, remotely flying the unmanned Progress re-supply ship to a docking with Mir. Without going into details, the ground was testing a hare-brained scheme of estimating the range and velocity from a laser range finder and a stopwatch. Tsibliyev was plainly nervous about the test, having nearly flown the Progress into Mir during an earlier March attempt. Now, he was expected to succeed with his confidence still shaken from that earlier failure.

It is also possible that Tsibliev's poor state of mind was due to the possible loss of a bonus if he did not succeed. Cosmonauts receive relatively low pay but with a significant bonus incentive system. For example, they are paid "flight allowances" of $300 per day for every day in orbit. They have a sliding scale of bonuses for spacewalks, depending on the time spent outside the station and starting at $1,000. The bonus for performing a manual docking is twice that of the one for supervising an automatic docking.

Not surprisingly, the second manual docking attempt was a total failure, probably due more to a flawed procedure than to Tsibliev's technique and proficiency. The resulting collision damaged the solar arrays, knocked out half of the station's electrical power and cracked the hull of the Spektr module, causing it to leak. The crew briefly considered abandoning the station before getting the situation under control. However, they could not keep Mir from going into free drift and experiencing a complete loss of power. It was a month before they fully recovered.

Mike Foale apparently earned a bit more respect during 30 hours in the dark following the collision. He was the only one onboard able to conceptualize and implement recovery from the total power loss using the thrusters on the Soyuz to regain attitude control on the station.

An investigation was made into several 1997 incidences of attitude control loss, which would rapidly lead to complete loss of power. The report noted that the Soyuz lifeboat concept was flawed, since the Soyuz spacecraft could NOT undock from Mir unless there was power on the Mir station. What the report did not say is that the new manual technique was necessary because a Belarus supplier had ceased making spare parts for the automatic system following the breakup of the Soviet Union.

Why were American astronauts placed in harm's way on such dilapidated equipment? Why would NASA compromise a reputation for safety established over the preceding 35 years?

A little digging uncovered that when NASA initiated the Shuttle-Mir program, they had not performed their usual rigorous risk assessment analysis on the Mir space station. Our risk assessment process includes analyzing possible failures and then considering the probability of that failure occurring. Since senior NASA managers "understood" Mir to have a history of safe operations, they elected to forego this process in favor of evaluating *the methods* used by the Russians when they performed their original safety analysis. If the Russian process was judged to be adequate, NASA would then accept the safety record as presented by the Russians. The Russian method was quite different from our own. They first determined if a potential failure was "credible" and, if so, would then perform a formal analysis; if not, it wouldn't even be analyzed.

While this subjective review by NASA was faster and cheaper, it was far less than the systematic safety and reliability analytical techniques utilized for all prior U.S. human spaceflight. The decision was made at the highest levels of NASA that any formal safety analysis for the Shuttle-Mir Program would apply only to *new* joint operations activities, *new* experiments, and *new* procedures.

The Russian process was judged adequate but, unfortunately (and not surprisingly), the Russians were less than candid about their historical systems failures and other problems. NASA's acceptance of the existing Mir safety record meant there was no formal, documented risk baseline for the start of the program. It also seemed in total contradiction to the recommendations on safety made by the Presidential Commission following the Challenger accident.

When we began the Shuttle-Mir program, most of the dangers unique to Mir facing our astronauts were unknown. Either Russia withheld relevant information, or nobody had bothered to check up on key features of Mir. As the flying program progressed, the risk level for our guys on the Station only got worse. NASA, in compromising their safety policies, guaranteed higher risk levels for human safety.

Without that risk assessment baseline, it was a bit disingenuous for NASA to minimize public concern for crew safety, as they did during this period. NASA began to characterize life-threatening situations on Mir as "opportunities to learn." If that really was their philosophy, all that was necessary to learn more was to take a few more chances. Hopefully, we did learn from the crises, but to consider survival emergencies, as "opportunities" was a bit bizarre. In Apollo, we relied on planning, training and simulations to avoid such crises. Emergencies are a failure of planning, training or equipment.

It is plain that a different attitude about safety was in style at NASA during the Nineties.

As James Oberg, author of *Star-Crossed Orbits,* a history of the U.S.-Russian space alliance, puts it, "NASA's safety evaluators, . . . influenced by the political pressures to perform U.S.-Russian joint space projects, approached their evaluation of Mir from the frame of mind that the existence of dangers had to be proven. This was opposite the proper approach in which danger is assumed and safety must be demonstrated by verified checks and precautions."

Did NASA really believe that absence of proof of danger was equivalent to proof of safety?

Oberg hit it right on the head when he wrote: "The mishaps plaguing the Russian space program (Shuttle-Mir) have been excused as only being typical of any bold space exploration. This is not true! Russia's current problems come not from trying NEW projects, but from simply struggling to stay afloat, performing hitherto routine operations, ones that used to be easy for them. These mishaps are not the price of progress (there is none) but are the predictable consequences of decaying hardware, aging personnel, and fitful financing within the Russian space infrastructure.

"NASA's claim, 'We've learned so much from the breakdowns,' has been a self-serving, exculpatory mantra for bunglers throughout the history of engineering. Most of what we learned was obvious or could have been learned in simulations."

Following the fire, the mid-air collision and other major problems, a number of former astronauts and other NASA alumnae questioned sending any more astronauts to the decrepit space station. Before launching Dave Wolf to Mir, NASA felt compelled set up a special "task force" to take the heat off the decision to continue with the program. The task force, under the leadership of former astronaut Tom Stafford, was charged with assessing the hazards and making recommendations about manning the remaining two missions. After one look at the makeup of the task force, which included eight people with past or current NASA ties, I felt certain they would ratify a decision that had already been made to continue manning the station.

NASA's Inspector General must have been concerned as well. In February 1998, he issued a report citing the presence of task force members who "are so closely aligned with NASA and the Space Station program as to "negate the appearance" of impartiality." Some members had contracts and financial dealings with both the American and the Russian aerospace industries.

The report also faulted the presence on Stafford's group of active astronauts who may feel constrained in their advice for fear of losing scarce flight assignments, and of NASA engineers and scientists directly involved in the Station program. It also suggested that JSC Director George Abbey may have played too large a role in selecting the membership of the task force to preserve impartiality in advising a program under Abbey's direct supervision.

Sure enough! Right after Dave Wolf replaced Mike Foale on the MIR resident crew, they found two leaks in the structure of the Spektr module.

There is a difference between risky activity, such as the Apollo missions or a Shuttle launch, and reckless activity, as when we kept sending astronauts to Mir. In a *risky* activity, you can quantify the payoff or benefits, compare it to other known and estimated risks, and determine the cost/benefit ratio. In *reckless* activity, risks are unmeasured and unknown, and payoffs are ill defined and ephemeral.

Space is inherently dangerous—the most hostile environment ever explored by man. But there are benefits to be derived from our exploration and utilization of space. NASA's job is to reduce the risks to where the benefits to be derived are judged to exceed the risks and then get on with the job. The astronauts will accept whatever risks are necessary to accomplish objectives in which they believe.

I breathed a small sigh of relief when our last astronaut departed Mir for home without our having lost anyone.

When NASA got around to writing their official history of Shuttle-Mir, it was self-laudatory, glossing over the dangers in many events and ignoring the concerns about the safety of the program expressed by current and former astronauts. For a full and accurate view of this episode in space history, please refer to authors James Oberg and Bryan Burrough.

Mir lasted a couple of years after our last astronaut departed without ever recovering full operational capability, in spite of the nine Shuttle loads of spare parts we delivered to keep the station running. The Shuttle special delivery service was responsible for Mir's recovery from one crisis after another. Because of the Russians' lack of candor, we probably expected too much from this aging piece of space hardware. Mir became a luxury the new Russian government could not afford and I am convinced our participation prolonged the station's life by several years.

All of our astros made it back alive and, hopefully, we learned something about dealing with the Russians that would help us in working with them on the International Space Station. But, of course, that was the same hope we had following Apollo/Soyuz.

Here's what Blaine Hammond, the Astronaut Safety Officer during the Shuttle-Mir program had to say, "The main lesson of Mir is we can't rely on the Russians."

While I agree with Blaine on the main lesson, there are a number of other things we learned about cosmonauts. Among them:
Cosmonauts don't engage in independent thinking or take independent action;
Cosmonauts are good at the execution of planned events;
They don't really want to know what happened after an emergency, anomaly, or accident;
Cosmonauts are excellent "shade tree mechanics;"
Cosmonauts don't take the initiative;
Their communications are poor, both internal and external;
Their training does not include esoteric academics (such as orbital mechanics and the coriolis force effect on rendezvous & docking of two vehicles); and
The Russian Chiefs accept cosmonaut input *only* when they ask for it.

These very significant differences in operating philosophies could be the source of problems for the Russian-American crews operating the International Space Station.

As this was written, the Expedition 6 crew, comprised of two Americans and one Russian, was living comfortably onboard the International Space Station. They were advised of the breakup of Space Shuttle Columbia during reentry on 1 February 2003, resulting in the deaths of their seven colleagues. The plan had been to replace the trio with the Expedition 7 crew brought up on a Space Shuttle in May. Now, faced with an unexplained catastrophe and with the Shuttle fleet grounded indefinitely, no one knew for sure when they would return to earth.

The public at large was deeply concerned. NASA was concentrating on the accident investigation and reviewing their famous "contingency plans" for the Station; but with the Station crew, it was probably "business as usual." In the near-term, they were no worse off for the STS-107 accident. The Soyuz lifeboat was there to be used whenever needed, or at their discretion.

The near-term programmatic considerations were, no doubt, immediately apparent to the crew. Until the Space Shuttle returned to flight, we were completely dependent on Russia's under funded space program. Russian Progress cargo vehicles are essential for re-supplying the Station and re-boosting it to a safe altitude. Most importantly, with the Shuttle grounded, the only way to ferry crews back and forth to the Station was with the Russian Soyuz capsule.

Just two months prior to the Columbia disaster, Rosaviakosmos, the Russian space agency, announced they would not be able to deliver the four to six Progress cargo vehicles and two to three piloted Soyuz crew rescue spacecraft the Station requires each year. At the time, it presented a problem to be worked out but, with the STS-107 disaster, it was transformed into a full-blown crisis.

To understand how the proud American space program became so totally dependent on the international welfare case that was Russia at the turn of the millennium we have to go back 20 years.

In 1984, President Reagan envisioned Space Station Freedom as a 10-year program at an expected cost of $8 billion. Freedom was supposed to boost American prestige and counter the Russian Mir Space Station program. Within four years, Europe, Canada and Japan had been enlisted in the program as full partners.

From the beginning, the program was beset with cost, engineering and political problems. Design standards for crew safety and mission success established by the Mercury, Gemini, and Apollo programs and first compromised for the Space Shuttle, became a faded memory. In the absence of an authoritative vision, the kind that sets firm priorities, the advocates of Space Station Freedom tried to cover their bets by promising everything to everybody.

Maybe too many senior people had already left NASA, or perhaps the best engineers remaining were tied up on the Space Shuttle.

When the Shuttle fleet, down to three following the 1986 Challenger

accident, was grounded for nearly three years, a number of astronauts
went to work on space station design teams. By mid-1986, the Astronaut
Office was expressing the concerns you would expect from operational
and test pilots. A major issue was the omission of a crew escape vehicle,
or space lifeboat, other than the shuttle fleet. Keeping one-third of a three
spacecraft fleet available for emergency crew return would impose severe
operating constraints and would become totally unacceptable if a problem grounded the shuttle.

The Astronaut Office believed the requirements placed on the Shuttle, itself, for assembly of the station were "unreasonable." Eighteen Shuttle missions would be required for assembly and four a year thereafter to
re-supply and staff the facility. They also maintained the space station was
too dependent on extra-vehicular activity (EVA), requiring 450 hours to
construct.

NASA headquarters dismissed these concerns, characterizing them as
merely "expressions of individual concerns."

Was NASA overly optimistic or was it simply a case of wanting to "get
the nose of the camel under the edge of the tent?" There was no question
that NASA had misrepresented to Congress and the public what could be
accomplished for $8 billion.

Over a period of eight years, the station underwent five major
redesigns, four of them at the direction of the Congress or the White
House. At first briefing for former astronauts on Space Station Freedom
in 1991, our consensus was: "too grandiose" and "the wrong station at the
wrong time." It was our opinion you should be able to do much more
with a smaller and less costly space station. We were all supporters of a
space station but just not fans of the Space Station Freedom concept.

By 1993, the estimated cost had grown to well over $30 billion, *includ-
ing the Shuttle launches to assemble it.* Freedom was terminated by the Clinton administration after the expenditure of $11.2 billion with precious
little hardware to show for it.

Dan Goldin, the NASA Administrator, arrived on the scene in 1992
with a mandate to tighten up an agency perceived in Washington to be
slow, bloated and outdated. He had nothing to do with the Freedom mess
and could, therefore, afford to walk away from it. In fact, it was an excellent opportunity to put his stamp on the agency. Goldin, bypassing his
engineering and program managers as well as his Center directors, set up

a redesign team headed by astronauts Bryan O'Connor and Bill Shepherd. The two were admired as astronauts but many old NASA hands at JSC felt this team was weak in those disciplines most essential for such a huge task: program management, design requirements, systems and operations integration, cost assessment, and leadership. The team produced a space station design that would become the source of most of NASA's problems in the Nineties.

Boeing was awarded a sole-source contract to build the new and, supposedly, less expensive International Space Station. The contracted amount, two billion dollars below NASA's best estimate, was achieved by eliminating integrated testing, fit checks, redundancy, habitability provisions, and other such frivolous "luxuries." The total cost of the station was also capped at $17.4 billion.

The International Space Station was no sooner announced than it was saddled with what would become very expensive baggage. President Clinton had arrived in Washington in 1992 with sparse foreign policy credentials and no foreign policy initiatives. When his advisors pointed out that including the Russians in the International Space Station would be looked upon as a symbol of new cooperation between East and West, the administration jumped on the idea. At the insistence of the administration, the Russians were brought into the Space Station project as full partners. The relatively pure arena of exploration and technical achievement was infected by the politics of foreign aid and Russian "perestroika."

In the early 1990s, with the Cold War over, a large number of Soviet-era missile scientists were going unpaid or were out of jobs. U.S. officials viewed U.S.–Russian cooperation as a way to deny aggressor and terrorist nations advanced rocket technology. They believed it would be cheaper to keep those rocket scientists employed in Russia than it would be to pick up the pieces if they wandered off to work for the Iranians, Pakistanis, Indians, or North Koreans.

Whether that was just a speech or they truly believed it, things didn't work out that way.

In the Nineties, Russian space scientists helped India develop a 200-mile-range submarine launched ballistic missile that could carry a nuclear warhead. This assistance is continuing today, despite Russian assurances that its scientists are not contributing restricted technology to Indian missile programs.

In the mid-Nineties, Russian space scientists and engineers also began to work with Iran to increase the range of their intermediate range ballistic missiles even after signing specific agreements with the U.S. to the contrary. They contracted to construct the Bushehr Nuclear Power Plant in spite of objections by the U.S. and Israel that the plant could help Iran to develop nuclear weapons. Only a few years later, U.S. intelligence officials confirmed Russia had, indeed, supplied Iran with much of the equipment and expertise used to build *two* new nuclear facilities. According to the intelligence officials, the plants were part of a weapons program and "the Russians were involved in all aspects of the Iranian nuclear program."

When the partnership with Russia was signed in 1995, Goldin promised Congress that Russia would not be in the critical path of space station development. Russia, supposedly, was going to spend an estimated $4 billion to build some of the principal components. Ignoring his own testimony, Goldin eventually assigned Russia responsibilities for some of the station's most crucial components: attitude control, refueling, solar panels, and lifeboats. He did it with little concern for the political and technical difficulties or the cost and schedule risks. Russia remains solidly entrenched in the critical path and the station is more dependent on them than ever.

Goldin embraced Clinton's initiative and worked zealously to establish Russia as a full partner in the ISS. By ignoring the technical problems and disregarding the economic consequences, he saved his job in the new administration.

The deal was sold to Congress on such dubious claims as saving American taxpayers more than $2 billion (some claimed $4 billion), expanding the space station's capabilities, and enabling the station to be deployed two years sooner.

The Clinton administration also initiated a policy permitting a limited number of U.S. commercial satellites to be launched on Russian rockets. However, their commercial launch costs were set artificially high, not by the Russians but at American insistence. Russian rocket firms could undercut Western rocket prices by 50 percent and still make handsome profits. The U.S. Commerce Department, spurred on by U.S. rocket makers, decreed these low prices were unacceptable. In the end, they allowed Russia to sell a set number of rockets but only at prices that did not "undercut world market prices for launch services by more than 15 percent."

The Russians began raking in money. They happily doubled their asking prices and a flood of Western overpayments began pouring into the Russian space industry and to their Western industrial partners. Tens of millions of dollars of commercial launch funds have rebuilt Russian payload processing and fueling facilities, as well as the equipment at launch pads and control bunkers. These were convenient improvements for Western customers but the upgrades were even more important to Russian military space programs, which use the very same facilities.

In 1994, the General Accounting Office (GAO) placed the total cost of the International Space Station at $94 billion, including the $33 billion cost of Space Shuttle missions required to support the station during the decade of operations following assembly. The GAO had also figured out that our partnership with Russia would not be a savings but would cost us at least $1.8 billion.

Senator William Cohen called the space station a "financial black hole." In Congressional testimony, Administrator Goldin fired back, "Russian participation will not cost the U.S. taxpayer one penny more."

By 1998, the Agency's internal estimate of station costs through completion of assembly was $58 billion, which included $10.2 billion for the aborted Space Station Freedom and $6.4 billion for cooperative activities with the Russians. Europe, Canada and Japan were to contribute $9.4 billion, while the Russian contribution was valued at a minimum of $3.5 billion.

It is virtually impossible to get a handle on the real costs of the ISS, especially those costs attributable to our partnership with the Russians. Adding Russia to the team increased costs to the station itself but there were also costs to outfit an Orbiter to dock with the Russian station Mir. Other NASA programs supporting the Space Station would cost more, science programs were reduced, and Shuttle science missions were eliminated. But the largest increase in cost of all came from changing the station's orbital inclination from 28.5 degrees to 51.6 degrees. This is a cost that has still not been appropriately discussed in Congress or the media or, perhaps, even within NASA, even though it dwarfs all other additions.

Other than the decision to build it in the first place, inviting the Russians to join was the single costliest decision of the program. The moment we decided to rely on Russian Soyuz capsules and Progress launch vehicles, we were committed to changing the orbital inclination if the station from 28.5 degrees, which the Russians could not reach, Northward to 51.6 degrees, because the Russians' launch facilities were there. Flying to this higher orbit requires more fuel, for which the Shuttle pays a 30 percent payload penalty. The projected 120 Shuttle missions to the ISS during the 20-year life is almost a third more than would have been necessary flying to the original orbit. At $500 million per launch, this orbital change alone adds about $18 billion to the program cost—a figure that shows up nowhere in the official budget.

Russia's orbital requirements also caused NASA to spend hundreds of millions on Shuttle upgrades and to cancel as many as nine Shuttle science flights to carry additional supplies to Mir during phase 1.

In testimony before the House Science Committee in 1997, all pretenses that the partnership would save money were dropped. Joe Rothenberg, NASA's Associate Administrator for Human Spaceflight, conceded that Russian participation in the ISS was responsible for $1 billion of added costs. At the Johnson Space Center, the estimate of added costs was running as high as $5 billion.

The program may not have been working out exactly as we had planned but the Russians, some of them at least, were also having second thoughts. However, they seemed to draw their conclusions from a totally different reading of the facts.

The Russians believed their knowledge and experience exceeded ours and it was only our money that put us in the leadership role. Yuri Koptev, head of Rosaviakosmos, had this to say: "In 1993, after $12 billion dollars was spent on Freedom, the Americans and all the other partners had to admit that such an ambitious project was not feasible and that it could only be accomplished with the participation of Russia, which has immense expertise and experience that no other country in the world has."

The fate of Mir at the completion of the Shuttle-Mir program was another sore spot. There was much animosity created when Russia wanted to continue supporting their own decrepit Mir Space Station but were unable to meet their hardware commitments to the ISS. Historically, RSC Energia, the Soyuz and Progress manufacturer, has been able to produce four to six Progress cargo vehicles and two to three piloted Soyuz crew rescue spacecraft a year. There was no way this production rate could support both the Mir and the ISS even though Mir was Russia's only remaining human space program and one of their few remaining sources of national pride following the collapse of the old Soviet Union.

On occasion, cosmonauts have had to stay in orbit longer than planned due to a shortage of Soyuz boosters to launch a replacement crew. American astronaut Shannon Lucid experienced this manufacturing delay prior to her visit to the Mir Space Station. At one time, Rosaviakosmos admitted they could produce only five expendable launch vehicles a year, be they Progress or Soyuz. That was it!

Following Perestroika, the Russian space program had quickly collapsed and for several years, Rosaviakosmos annual budget hovered around $100 million, about one-fifth the cost of a single Shuttle launch. In 2000, when NASA funding was $14.5 billion, Rosaviakosmos received only $165 million for space programs. That was about a third of what India was spending on space programs and one-fourteenth of what France was spending. For 2003, Rosaviakosmos budget was only $260 million, an embarrassingly small amount even allowing for the difference in purchasing power,

Rosaviakosmos was frequently in even worse straits than its budget implied. For example, it actually received only 78 percent of its 1996 budget authorization. In 1997 it was only 57 percent. The 1999 budget for space programs was only $131 million—far less than the minimum needed to service all Rosaviakosmos projects. The difference was made up by NASA and payments from Western countries for launch services.

By the time of the first Russian commercial satellite launching in April of 1996, the cash flow from abroad already accounted for about 40 percent of the actual funds received by the Russian Space Agency. And by 1997, the Russians were annually raking in more than $600 million in Western commercial contracts, accounting for two thirds of the entire cash flow into the space industry. Russian officials expected that flow to reach a billion dollars per year by the turn of the millennium. According to Koptev, state funding accounts for five to fifteen percent of total income for aerospace industry enterprises, although RSC Energia, prime contractor for some station components, gets 30 percent of its budget from state contracts.

Russia had initially proposed that the ISS be based on the Mir station with some new modules docked to it. The Russians felt this would solve many problems from financing to servicing the station. They weren't stupid. It would have been a near perfect solution from their perspective—their hardware paid for by American money. Come to think of it, that's pretty much the way it has worked out.

We rejected their proposal and Russia, unable to provide financial and physical support for two stations, made the difficult decision to deorbit Mir.

"The decision to deorbit the Mir station in March 2001 was only made under pressure from the Americans," Russian cosmonaut Anatoly Solovyev claimed. He was right about that. Solovyev flatly denied any allegation that the station had fully exhausted its service life.

Many Russians believe that NASA contemplated cutting Russia out of the project and that the only reason we did not is because Russian know-how was crucial for the construction of the station.

Russia also has their opponents of any involvement in a costly space station project. Professor Konstantin Feoktistov, a spacecraft designer and former cosmonaut from the Sixties, thinks that Russia is too poor to continue its manned space flight program. His arguments sound a lot like those made by some Americans about our space program in the Sixties.

According to Professor Feoktistov, "We can't throw money on manned flight programs when we need so many things for the army, for culture, for science, for social needs. Russia is to build 12 out of the station's 36 modules and, accordingly, will have to bear just under a third of total construction costs, estimated at between $35 and $40 billion. The U.S. will make the biggest contribution to the building of the station and will enjoy overall control over its operation. NASA is paying Russia $400 million for the construction of the cargo module and some other elements, but analysts say this sum does not cover the cost of Russian unique know-how."

Poor Konstantin. He is getting old and should be forgiven for getting his numbers so muddled but his opinion is shared by many of his countrymen.

A journalist for the Russian daily, *Trud*, thought he had it figured out when he wrote, "The core elements of the international space station were designed on the basis of the Mir-2 project, developed in Russia to replace the current Mir Station but abandoned for lack of financing. Russian know-how will save Americans at least $10 billion and three years, but the U.S. will actually pay Russia only $400 million. Is it fair?'

Other opponents of Russian involvement in the ISS argue that the costs involved would heavily outweigh any possible spin-off for Russian space science and industry. They point out that the station's orbital inclination allows it to observe only five per cent of Russian territory. This is a fair criticism but it ignores the fact that the orbit was dictated by Russian launch capability and it was the same one used for virtually all their manned missions.

Other critics say the Russian space industry is working solely for American benefit. "We earn money by launching American satellites and spend it on the international space station, which will be run by Americans. Meanwhile our space industry infrastructure and communications are crumbling. It is time we realized that manned space flights are too costly for us and abandon them."

This criticism peaked at a time when the White House had just transferred $700 million of NASA's budget to Russia for various goods and services, including flying our astronauts on Mir, and we were expending approximately $4 BILLION in Space Shuttle launch and operations costs to carry out "Phase 1" of the program on Mir. All of this effort was expended to make viable a Russian partnership that would purportedly save the U.S. $2 billion dollars in space station costs.

None of these costs were offset by any payment for the twenty or more Russian cosmonauts we have flown on the Space Shuttle since the early Nineties. American scientific research equipment was dumped off more than one Shuttle flight in order to make room for last minutes Russian repair tools and emergency supplies for Mir—all at no cost to our partner.

The joint venture relationship with Russia has turned out to be more costly and less valuable to us than originally envisioned. Since the start of the station program, NASA has spent billions of dollars propping up the Russian Space Agency and their contractors. American payments were based not on any serious cost-benefit analysis, but on considerations of foreign policy and foreign aid.

The simple fact is that the Russians always wanted to be treated as full partners in the project while insisting on being paid as contractors.

It is not that the Russian space industry does not have money to pay for promised modules and services. It does have money, but the officials who control it want to keep it. The huge influx of dollars flowing into the Russian space industry has had the same corrupting influence that Western money had elsewhere in the post-Soviet Russian economy. After a massive transfer of dollars, the Russian space program was still as bankrupt as ever. Tens of millions of dollars went missing at a time when space industry higher-ups, including some cosmonauts, were building million-dollar mansions on thousand-dollar salaries. NASA ignored or downplayed persistent reports of top-level corruption, apparently ignoring that it could have an impact on flight safety.

There is plenty of money flowing into the Russian space industry, in addition to several hundred million dollars from the Russian government each year. According to Rosaviakosmos, they received $40 million from international space projects in 1993. By 2000, foreign sales alone were worth $800 million, with the main sources being the ISS project and commercial launch services. Foreign sales are as much as two thirds pure profit due to their cost structure and the agreement on pricing. Delivering the goods and services requires only a fraction of the dollars to be spent inside Russia. Much of the money has gone to dachas, yachts and offshore bank accounts of crooked Russian politicians, rather than to the engineers to build space hardware. That may explain why some of them still sold missile guidance systems to Iran.

What is NASA's official position on the corruption and the mansions? "What Russia does with their own money is none of our business."

With foreign sales contributing so much to their annual space budget, Russia will never opt out of the ISS. That would immediately cut off nearly a billion dollars a year of Western cash.

Because the station's control systems were Russian designed, these American financed modules can only be maintained by TsUP, the Mission Control Center in Moscow. When the TsUP communications system with their spacecraft was falling apart, NASA spent money to provide them communications through our own tracking network. We also spent money to hold together the staff of the Control Center, which would have a crucial role in controlling the ISS during its assembly phase.

Through one schedule delay and cost increase after another, Administrator Goldin "stayed the course." He argued that the American and Russian programs were linked so intimately that the Russian effort must be preserved lest the American space program suffer. He said, "Without the Russians, the ISS construction would be delayed by years and add as much as $2 billion in costs."

Schedule problems have a way of turning into money problems. While money can't always solve schedule problems, it can usually alleviate them. ISS schedule problems were huge. A 1996 NASA press booklet showed Zarya, the first of ten space station modules, being launched in 1997. Subsequent launch dates were, well, "flexible,"—principally due to uncertainties in Russian manufactured hardware.

As we neared launch of the first Space Station components, NASA went to Congress for approval to spend an additional $660 million to bail out its partner. In another attempt to make it look like we were getting something for the money he wanted to transfer, Goldin told Congress the agency would buy, for $60 million, "up to 100 percent of the research time previously allocated to Russia." Including the new money for the Russians and $540 million to modify shuttle orbiters to do more station lifting, the 1999 bailout of the Russians was projected to cost about $1.3 billion.

A Congressional opponent said NASA might as well have proposed a leveraged buyout of the Russian Space Agency. The latest proposed rescue would have all but made Rosaviakosmos a subsidiary of NASA.

When Congress forbade NASA to "bail out" the Russians, Goldin, as usual, put the best face he could on his disappointment with the statement, "After conferring with the administration and Congress, we have decided we are going to put zero dollars beyond 1999 because it disincentives the Russian government to fund the Russian Space Agency."

What is that expression? "So long dumb, so quick smart." Even without transferring more money, we were dependent on Russia. The Clinton administration had insisted on their inclusion in the partnership and then refused to rethink that decision, leaving the future of American manned space flight twisting in the zero gravity of incompetent (or simply corrupt) Russian officials and naïve American administrators.

The Russians disappointed Dan Goldin over and over but still he remained a "true believer." With an open mind, NASA would not have been blind-sided on so many issues. Goldin's view of the Russian program did not match the reality.

Goldin said NASA's budget in 2001, his last year, was actually less than his first budget nine years before. Not known for his modesty, he claimed, "For what NASA does now on $14.3 billion a year, they would have spent $25 billion a year under earlier leadership."

Since the ISS work packages were awarded to make it impossible to proceed without Russian support, NASA will now have to live with the consequences.

In November 1998, Russia launched the Zarya control module, followed a month later by a NASA launch of the Unity Node. ("Node" is a fancy word to describe a central module to which other modules will be attached. It becomes the intersection of various pathways through the station.)

Many of us believed it was unnecessarily risky to launch Zarya and Unity so many months before the station could be manned, which required the Russian built Zvezda service module. But NASA had other concerns with the station, including the annual threat of cancellation by Congress. Now, with Zvezda running so many months late, NASA felt if they could just get some space station hardware—any hardware—into orbit, there would be less pressure from Congress to abandon the program.

Joe Rothenberg justified the premature launches with, "We're going to get these first two ISS launches off so we can gain the experience of trouble shooting the modules."

Joe, in the "good old days" we would do our trouble shooting on the ground and then aim for error-free operation in orbit.

The Zvezda service module was finally launched in July 2000, 19 months late. The Clinton administration tried to justify the long delays and added costs as an effort to prevent a "brain drain" of Russian experts in rocketry and missile development to nuclear wannabe countries. That was difficult, since the Russian government had proved more than willing to provide its missile and rocket expertise to other countries—sometimes without the scientists even leaving Russian research institutes.

In November, the Expedition 1 crew, consisting of American Commander Bill Shepherd and two Russian cosmonauts, manned the International Space Station. The budding station had gone unmanned for 24 months. Shepherd promptly dubbed it "Space Station Alpha" and they settled in for a 140-day stay. It has been manned ever since.

Shepherd's crew was representative of a mutually agreed to plan for the first four expeditions. The crews would alternate between American and Russian commanders with the other two crewmembers provided by the other country. This command structure was referred to as "minority commander." Cosmonaut Anatoly Solovyev had resigned from the original crew when he learned he would not be the commander. It was his contention that he was much more qualified by experience and he should not have to work for Shepherd. That sounded a lot like some of the arguments used by the Mercury Astronauts back in the Sixties.

Cosmonauts commanded Expeditions two and four and it seemed to work out just fine. Regardless, beginning with Expedition 5, they went to a "majority commander," where one crewman was from the same country as the commander.

A fully integrated test of space station hardware prior to the first launch had never been in NASA's plan. It wasn't in the 1995 Boeing contract award. The newest generation of NASA management seemed to believe if contractors faithfully followed their specifications, each part could be assembled in space with minimum testing and risk. According to one former NASA senior manager, Joe Rothenberg was heard say, "If we design it right and we build it right, then why should we have to do all this testing?"

The Russian components were running very late and NASA had 12,000 people working on the station program. Each month of delay was costing a fortune but they could not afford to release personnel and lose their expertise.

In January 1997, when the Russian program delay on Zvezda grew to 19 months, NASA assigned a team of engineers to perform an integrated test on the first six mission components, except for the Unity Node. During late ninety-eight and early ninety-nine, engineers and technicians at Kennedy Space Center's huge Space Station Processing Facility, operated an accurate facsimile of Space Station Alpha. The flight hardware was connected mechanically, electrically and hydraulically and turned on before it was launched and assembled in space.

During the testing, they found more than 1,000 software problems and uncovered at least one "black box" problem that, if found in orbit, would have required the Shuttle to return home with a truss assembly for repair. The cost of repairing the box on the ground was insignificant. Had

NASA skipped the test as initially planned, the failure in orbit would have delayed the program for several months while the Shuttle returned with the truss. The bill for the round trip, encompassing two shuttle missions, would have been nearly $1 billion.

Weighed against this, the $100 million cost of the test program looked like a bargain.

As this is written, NASA is operating under a 2001 directive from the White House not to exceed the $26 billion spending cap set by Congress the year before. The cap applied to costs incurred since the "final" redesign of the ISS in 1993, the year Russia was invited to join the global lineup of Europe, Japan, Canada and the United States.

To compensate for wildly spiraling costs, NASA scaled back the scope of the station on several occasions. In 2001, the spending cap became limiting when development costs were projected to exceed the cap by $4.8 billion. The White House directive left NASA little choice but to cancel plans for the habitability module and a propulsion module immediately and the seven-man X-38 space lifeboat the following year. The habitability module, with its crew living quarters and life support equipment, and the lifeboat were essential pieces of hardware if the station was to ever go from a three to a seven person crew. The directive also restricted the number of Shuttle visits to the ISS to four annually.

The projected overrun was due, principally, to the lengthy delay in launching of the crucial Russian-furnished service module. Another contributor to the ever-escalating cost was NASA's constantly changing hardware and software and design requirements.

NASA had spent $515 million designing and building part of the habitability module, before canceling the whole project when costs for the station began to soar. And they were facing another $425 million in spending they couldn't afford after underestimating the cost of the propulsion module.

One can't help but wonder, given the history of the project, if Congress did appropriate another $5 billion, would it be enough to complete the three cancelled modules?

Cancellation of the habitability module and lifeboat had an immediate consequence. With a 3-man crew, 20 hours per week could be scheduled for science experiments; with a 7-man crew, that number would go up to 180 hours.

With five Shuttle visits a year and a crew of seven, triple the amount of scientific gear could be delivered to the ISS and the station's crew could devote nine times as many hours to research.

Four flights a year will allow the station to be furnished with about 2,000 pounds of scientific gear. With five flights, the deliverable scientific cargo rises to 7,000 pounds.

Currently, the station's tenants manage about 20 hours of research a week in the Destiny laboratory module. But as the station is expanded, maintenance requirements will increase. By 2004, they will have less than 10 hours available for research each week. And after European and Japanese laboratory modules join the American lab facility, the time available for research will drop to about 6 hours per week. With a crew of seven, the hours available for scientific duties climbs back to 55 a week.

These are official projections and they paint a rather bleak picture of the future, especially when science was the advertised reason for the station's construction in the first place. The available time now is hardly adequate to perform NASA's own research projects and leaves our European and Asian partners nothing but scientific crumbs on which to feed.

The ISS is far too important and we have far too much invested to stop at the current limited configuration. We are in the position of having paid 90 percent of the total cost of the station but can only realize only 10 percent of what was originally planned. The expenditure of the last 10 percent would allow us to perform at least 100 percent of what was intended.

A reasonable approach at this point would be to raise the $26 billion cap in conjunction with rigorous budgetary discipline and finish the job. It is the only responsible way to justify the $37 billion already invested.

If reason does not prevail and we find ourselves living with a partially complete station, it should be possible to improve on the grim picture just presented. The 20 hours of science is based on official planning and operational guidelines. These guidelines are overly conservative and they are not adhered to by expedition crewmembers in real time.

As you would expect, all time, every day, on the ISS is strictly scheduled. After setting aside 8.5 hours for sleep time, approximately 6.5 hours per day are reserved for "assembly, systems maintenance, and utilization;" utilization being a code word for science activities. One-and-one-half hours per day are blocked out for planning and scheduling. The balance of the day is consumed by exercise, meals, etc. This results in approximately 20 man-hours per week being scheduled for science activities.

The crew also maintains a job list, kind of like a "to do" jar at home. Tasks, which the ground would like to see accomplished but cannot work into the schedule, go on the list. They get worked off by the crew when they are caught up or on their "off time."

Weekends are occupied with housekeeping chores and some relaxing.

In real time, Expedition crews spend a lot more time on science than officially scheduled.

Three-man Expedition crews perform non-scheduled science on their own time. For the EXP-2 crew, non-scheduled science activities on their own time averaged 4.5 hours per day or 22 hours per week. For the EXP-3 crew it averaged 7 hours per day. For the EXP-4 crew it averaged 1.5 hours per day. For the EXP-5 crew it was 2 hours per day. Overall, there is an average of 1.2 hours per crewmember per day that could be scheduled. That is approximately 20 hours per week.

Each Expedition crew has had their stay extended an average of 21 days per increment, creating more unplanned time for science activities. The first five Expedition crews spent, on average, about twice the amount of time on science as in the daily schedule, an amount that could increase as construction tasks wind down.

If the ISS continues as an incomplete outpost with a crew of three, it is nice to know what could be accomplished in the way of productive science. Of course, the scientific equipment must be there to fully utilize the crew's time, and scientific experiments must be launched long before they can be used. Through the first five years, we have been unable to get enough science gear onboard to utilize the available time. There has not been enough cargo capacity for both construction and science equipment and construction necessities, for obvious reasons, have been priority payloads.

After Mir was deorbited, NASA had assumed Rosaviakosmos could furnish all the Soyuz "lifeboats" and Progress re-supply vehicles necessary for ISS assembly. The program required dozens of Progresses to re-boost and re-supply ISS. Thirty-three Progress supply ships were originally promised to haul up cargo and propellant. When the number available dwindled to 17, we resigned ourselves to making up the difference with Space Shuttles.

In spite of being in financial crisis since 1993, Russia had always found ways to launch two piloted Soyuzes and three or four Progress cargo vehicles to the International Space Station each year. However, the effort drained their dwindling space budget and the production of Soyuz "lifeboats" to assure ISS crews a way home stopped and the construction of Progress spacecraft ground to a near halt.

In December 2002, Yury Koptev claimed Russia would have to reduce its involvement in the ISS *unless* its partners helped finance the production of Soyuz spacecraft and Progress resupply vehicles. He added, "Why should Russia set aside the same amount or more for space when its partners (referring primarily to the U.S.) had cut their Space Station budgets?" He said Russia would announce delays—and perhaps cancellations—in the production of Soyuz spacecraft if they did not get help. It sure sounded like a ploy to get more funding from NASA for the Russian space industry.

For its part, NASA is phasing out funding for experiments in evolutionary biology, environmental health and materials processing. And NASA began to study a contingency plan for "de-manning" the ISS—leaving it without a permanent crew for up to a year. De-manning could become a necessity rather than an option if Russia does not provide the manned Soyuz and unmanned Progress supply vehicles. In the "worst case," if Russia can only launch two vehicles a year to a de-manned station, it would make sense for them to be Progress vehicles for re-boosting.

Even without a permanent crew, Station assembly flights could continue every three or four months but it would entail more work during each of the 10-12 day visits. And, of course, ongoing science activities would be reduced by more than 80 percent.

There would also be significantly increased risk to the station without a permanent crew to make any urgent repair space walks. Such outside maintenance can become necessary in the normal course of equipment breakdown. The NASA study did conclude that they could continue station assembly during de-manned operations.

Only a month later, Koptev reversed himself and announced Russia would continue to provide ISS crew rescue capability and furnish three Progress tanker spacecraft annually until 2010. Crew rescue will require four Soyuz spacecraft a year between 2007 and 2010 to accommodate additional crewmembers. He also announced space station support spending was now a line item in the federal space program budget and that the Russian Space Agency was also examining evacuating the station.

Koptev had the temerity to engage in some partnership sniping with one more announcement: "Since NASA was stopping work on a seven-man crew return vehicle and the habitation module, if the Space Station program survives, the lead role should go to Russia."

He probably missed the irony of it all. If Russia had simply met their obligations to the partnership, the project would not have been over budget and it would not have been necessary to make the cancellations.

The station's current problems and cost overruns are less a failure of NASA technical management than a failure of political leadership. Even in its incomplete state, NASA and its partners have accomplished an engineering feat unrivaled in human history—the most complex project ever devised by man, either on or off the planet Earth. Space Station Alpha is 146 feet long, weighs in at nearly 400,000 pounds and is about the size of a three-bedroom house with solar power arrays longer than the wingspan of a Boeing 747.

The original estimate of $8 billion had soared to $19.4 billion by 1993, was $23.3 billion in 2000, and reached $30 billion in 2002. The involvement of Russia has cost NASA an estimated $3-4 billion and we have funded the reconstruction and expansion of the entire Russian space infrastructure. According to the General Accounting Office, the total price tag for the ISS will now exceed $100 billion when development, shuttle and research costs are included.

The country that has made the best of it so far is Russia, for whom space station funding is a critical component of an otherwise seriously under-financed space program. Besides the Shuttle Orbiter, Russia's Soyuz and Progress vehicles have been the primary ferries to the station, a role that will grow anytime the Shuttle fleet is grounded. The Russians are expecting the U.S. to pay for their increased role despite a 2000 law that bars U.S. government agencies from financing Russia's portion of the station. The law does contain an exception that allows NASA to provide funding if the Russians are conducting work aimed at preventing "imminent loss of life" or "grievous injury" to astronauts aboard the station.

In the aftermath of the Columbia disaster, NASA had to consider its options for maintaining a human presence on the ISS. Discussions focused on the obvious: Russia's role had become critical.

So long as the Orbiter was grounded, the three-person Soyuz capsule was the only means of transporting replacement crews or returning the station's crew to Earth. Scenarios under consideration for the ISS ranged from de-manning the Station to continuing operations with a crew of two.

Consideration of de-manning was brought about, at least partially, by the inability of Energia to produce the necessary Soyuz and Progress vehicles. De-manning may have been a viable alternative when the Shuttle could continue construction of the Station with three or four visits a year. If the Shuttle fleet were grounded, it is hard to imagine an acceptable de-manning operation, supported solely by the Soyuz and Progress.

Following the Columbia disaster, we continued to operate the ISS, transitioning to a two-man crew in order to reduce the logistical requirements. That strategy required several changes for Russia and the U.S.

It required increasing the production of Soyuz and Progress vehicles. This could only be done with outside financing and that's where we come in. Over the next few years, the U.S. will have to transfer additional hundreds of millions of dollars to Rosaviakosmos and Energia for Russian space hardware. And we won't be in a position to negotiate the best price.

Here at home, before we could send funds to Russia, we needed a waiver of the Iran Non-Proliferation Act of 1999. That Act prohibits NASA from purchasing Russian space hardware until the U.S. President certifies to Congress that Russian aerospace organizations have not supplied missile-related technology to Iran within the preceding 12 months. That was plainly not true, so we relied on a permitted exception "to safeguard the health and well being of the crew and the safety of the station itself."

It was the strategy adopted, since none of the steps were unreasonable or too difficult. Operations were still tenuous for the 12 to 18 months it took Energia to increase production but the station did survive until the Shuttle Orbiter was once more cleared for flight.

When the Shuttle fleet returned to flight, the net effect of the Columbia disaster was a much stronger Russian aerospace industry. The biggest change was the greatly increased leverage of Russia within the International Space Station partnership.

Cooperation in space has been an infatuation of every administration since President Nixon. It is a high-profile activity that, ostensibly, promotes cooperation on other levels and promotes world peace in general.

It is always defended on the grounds it saves money and makes projects more affordable.

In the case of the space station, international cooperation was strongly pushed by the bureaucrats at the State Department. It offered a means of providing foreign aid to Russia, without it counting against the foreign aid budget—it came from NASA.

If our goal is to make serious progress in conquering space then cooperative efforts are usually counterproductive. International cooperation certainly does not make space activities more affordable; it increases costs due to the management inefficiencies of such programs and the increased influence of politics on program decisions. Certainly the many delays caused by failure of the Russians to deliver hardware on schedule in the Nineties were a significant contributor to the billions of dollars in overruns currently plaguing the ISS program.

Even if it actually did save us money to join with other countries, it is silly to think we can't afford it on our own. The NASA budget is less than one percent of the federal budget, about as much as we spend on pet food. We can easily afford it—we simply choose not to.

Moreover, cooperation inherently reduces or eliminates the prospect of actual competition. We made more progress in space during the eight years that we were racing the Russians to the moon than we have in the two decades in which we have been engaged in a cooperative venture to build the International Space Station.

When we compete, we all are motivated to do our best. It works in every other sphere of life, and it's the most promising route for progress in space as well.

As Americans, we operate in a very straightforward manner. When we develop a "party line" on something, it is the result of a considered opinion. Not only do we get behind it as a team, we actually "buy" into it. It is consistent and predictable behavior.

When the Russians adopt a "party line," it frequently is a political decision. Even though they may get behind it, they never lose sight of why it was made and, therefore, they are not constrained by it. The Russians have always been six months to a year ahead of us on the politics of the ISS. They study where we are going in the future and then figure out how they can make money out of the situation.

The ISS is another major step into the unknown and, except for costs, the construction plan has been largely successful. It remains America's cornerstone project for human space exploration into the foreseeable future. For better or worse, the American manned space program is joined at the hip with the Russians, so it behooves us to make the best of it.

19

What Our Past Tells Us About the Future

AS THIS IS WRITTEN in 2003, the skeptics, the doubters and those who absolutely reject the idea of putting a man in space have reopened debate on whether the U.S. should even have a manned space program. They are asking the same question as others have been asking since the Sixties. "Why do we waste money on space when there are so many unmet needs right here on earth? Social spending continues to consume a growing percentage of our gross domestic product, while NASA's share keeps shrinking. Neither trend will be interrupted for the foreseeable future.

Must our resources be used only to feed our existence and never for dreaming and reaching? The Apollo program to land a man on the moon was a big dream and a long reach.

What did we get after 12 years, 24 billion tax dollars, and eight deaths other than a thousand pounds of rocks to prove we had been to the moon? Once you wade past the stock answers, what was accomplished? These are legitimate questions. And the public deserves better answers than the need for earlier weather warnings or Teflon coated frying pans or knowing the mineral composition of the moon to three decimal places.

That question couldn't really be answered in 1975 or 1985 or, perhaps, even today. But the intervening thirty years have given us time to consolidate the gains made in those first fifteen years and to reflect on whether it was worth the investment. As for myself, I never put a price tag on romance and adventure. The question of whether it was necessary, whether we needed to explore a world beyond our own, can't be answered simply.

The space program represents different things to different people. The U.S. program was the one with the high profile, the one that made the giant leaps. We are the ones who started behind and quickly reached a point where our technology and operations were years ahead of Russia. The U.S. program was the one the world was able to watch in broad daylight and the rest of the world has been most affected by our early efforts. But the tribesman in Africa is bound to have a different reaction than middle-class America. Each must judge the impact on their own life. I don't presume to be impartial in my own judgment, but I have tried to be honest about what I learned, saw, and felt in the years when the United States poked a hole in the fabric of the future.

By any yardstick, my eight years with NASA were rewarding and fulfilling. They were also frustrating and confining. Many of the astronauts would have known great achievement without a manned space program. But most of us would also have experienced greater difficulty reaching the same level of achievement or gaining the same recognition in any other career. I can't imagine a better opportunity to attract attention to your ability than that offered by NASA in the 1960s. But we were all educated and motivated self-starters, so none of us would have wound up on a street corner selling apples.

Regardless of what might have been had we not become astronauts, whatever we have accomplished since that hallmark will somehow be related in all men's minds to that experience. We should accept that. For me it was an opportunity to get my candle out from under the proverbial bushel basket. However, I do strongly identify with Phyllis George, a former CBS sportscaster, who said, "One of my goals is to reach a point where nobody introduces me as a former Miss America."

When I reported to NASA in 1963, the entire nation was moonstruck. By the mid-seventies the American public had grown bored with manned space flight. But that is part of our national character; as technology accelerates, so does our capacity to become bored with its accomplishments. Compare the current media stance with that of the late Fifties when scientists could, and did, constantly warn of space dangers: meteoroids, cosmic radiations, severe temperature changes, unfiltered sunlight, and so on. There was a feeling that a mechanical spaceship might survive—but could man?

The science editor for *Life* magazine reported in 1953 the opinions of air force doctors: "If humans want to work in the vacuum outside their spaceships they must do it in solid walled cylinders—if they want to walk on the surface of the moon they will have to do so by means of mechanical or leg-like appendages."

A *Business Week* editor wrote in 1957, "There is a long theoretical gap between making an unmanned satellite circle the earth, and building a spaceship in which man can travel through outer space with a reasonable expectation of living to tell about it."

Just as the Oregon Trail became a highway, the hostile environment of space has been transformed into another byway of man's travels with relative ease. Equipment failures and inflight crises, have been overcome quickly and routinely by the astronauts and technicians on the ground. By 1972 a rocket trip to the moon had become almost commonplace to the American public.

So what if the public takes it for granted. It wasn't until we began taking airplanes, television, and computers for granted that we began to exploit them for man's needs. It was essential that space flight be removed from the mystery and awe that once surrounded it and placed in the realm of public understanding and acceptance, if we were ever to get the full measure of return from our investment. So, while NASA may be crying over the public's reaction to their current accomplishments, I'm not.

We can only put things into perspective if we take the long-range view. In a burst of enthusiasm, then President Richard Nixon called the first lunar landing "the greatest achievement since the Creation." That does seem to cover a rather broad sweep. There is no question it was the challenge of the sixties. Today, most would acknowledge it as the premier accomplishment of the twentieth century. And so it was, that only 194 years after we first unfurled it on our planet, the American flag was planted on a foreign body in the universe. We had the courage to look around the moon and reach for the stars.

With all the concerns of the 20th century—two world wars, environmental scares, new diseases and medical break-throughs, the cold war, the collapse of the Soviet Union, the computer revolution, etc.—only one thing stands the test of time—man on the moon!

In the 25th century, the one thing for which the twentieth century will be remembered is the first time man left this planet and landed on another body in the universe.

What is the legacy of the Apollo program to land a man on the moon?

It has to be more than fireproof material, smaller computers, and powdered energy drinks. When the Russians launched that little electronic ball, we found ourselves playing catch-up, and it triggered a near-revolution in education. The space program provided first a challenge to, and then a tremendous catalyst for education. In the decade of Sputnik, U.S. spending on education doubled; science, math, and foreign languages were upgraded; and the number of high school graduates doubled. Two generations have been educated since Sputnik. For them, the first lunar landing is not a memory but a few passages read from a history book. They take for granted what those of us over fifty recognize as a giant leap forward in education.

When Neil Armstrong and Buzz Aldrin planted their boots on the lunar surface they stood, literally, on a new plateau for all mankind. From that plateau each of us now looks out on new and more distant horizons. I sometimes picture knowledge as a huge, spherical balloon, with each new generation having a responsibility to inflate that balloon a little bit more, to expand man's knowledge. Most of the time, knowledge grows in little spurts here and there, now and again. In the Sixties, this nation blew a huge breath into that balloon and expanded man's knowledge tremendously in many directions all at once.

Many people, including astronauts, have compared that first trip to the moon with Columbus' voyage to the new world. In that analogy, Columbus has now returned to Spain; some have been convinced that the world is not flat but Magellan has yet to set sail for other, uncharted ports—just as we will set sail for the planets.

History will ultimately conclude that Columbus' voyage was insignificant when compared to man's first trip to the moon. It was only 60 years between man's first flight at Kitty Hawk, North Carolina, and man's first orbit of the earth and a landing on the moon. Now, 40 years later, man has not moved one step farther into space. Until our voyage to the moon, escaping our own gravitational pull, we had not really freed ourselves from good old Mother Earth. Yet we freed ourselves from the sea millions of years ago. Perhaps the most apt comparison to leaving the earth and reaching a foreign body in the universe is that time, millions of years ago, when the first single-celled animals moved from the sea to dry land.

Three months prior to Apollo 11, I addressed an audience consisting, for the most part, of people older than myself. I was describing in detail the upcoming mission—just how we were going to land on the moon. Every two or three minutes two elderly ladies seated just in front of me would shake their heads, incredulously. They were not alone in that reaction. Even after the event, many people were convinced that it was a hoax and that the rocket had actually touched down in some remote part of the New Mexico desert. By the end of the millennium, there were television "documentaries" describing how the landings had been faked.

I have yet to address an audience of young people with heads shaking in disbelief. Anyone under thirty-five grew up with the idea and takes it for granted. As we grow older, things that seem impossible to accomplish are nothing more than challenges to be overcome by the young. When whole generations grow up taking for granted something as fantastic as flying to another planet, think what their minds can imagine and the contributions they will make to the next generation. Man's vision is limited not by what his eyes can see but by what his mind can imagine. The Apollo Program freed the imaginations of new generations.

It took little time back in private industry to notice the differences between that environment and my years at NASA. The most notable is that I rarely see the same pride and motivation in the business world as everyone displayed at NASA. Look around. How many of your co-workers and the people around you would you describe as truly dedicated individuals who absolutely believe in what they are doing? At NASA, during the Gemini and Apollo programs, there was a sense of every job counting, of being an important part of a movement. It was akin to religious zeal. What did that enthusiasm and motivation create? Only the most remarkable piece of equipment ever built by man to be operated by man—the Apollo spacecraft. The Apollo spacecraft was an example of New World craftsmanship at its best. With the entire world looking on, the Apollo Program added a new dimension to that phrase so prominent on the sides of World War II crates and seen again on the hull of Apollo: *Made in USA.*

Some benefits were so unlikely they could never have been anticipated. With the race to the Moon, we had challenged the Soviet Union to a technological fight to the finish.

The Soviets poured everything they could into the race but their efforts failed, even as Apollo triumphed. We cannot over-estimate the profound effects of that victory. Apparently, the Soviet Union became convinced that, in programs of vast technical scope, particularly those requiring the practical application of high technology to very complex problems, America could accomplish anything. They viewed us as having achieved an extremely difficult technological goal. *And they never forgot it!*

In 1986, in Reykjavik, Iceland, president Ronald Reagan announced to Soviet leader Mikhail Gorbachev we were going to "render nuclear missiles impotent and obsolete" with the Strategic Defense Initiative (SDI). The Soviets thought SDI would succeed and were adamantly opposed to Reagan's plan. They were convinced that we would do what we set out to do and achieve this new technological goal. The ensuing competition eventually bankrupted their system, rendered their huge military machine obsolete and hastened the end of the cold war in our favor. How do you put a price tag on that?

That was the Soviet perception of Apollo: any technological challenge America undertakes, it can accomplish. We had attempted and successfully achieved a goal so difficult and demanding, that it made virtually any similar goal seem equally achievable. The success of the Apollo program had given America the highest technical credibility.

There was still another benefit—complex, difficult to analyze, and to me at least, beyond value—it kept alive the spirit of adventure for one more generation. It was especially important in the chaotic sixties to be reminded that there will always be new horizons. Where we came from is no more a miracle than where we are headed.

As much as anything else, astronauts were attracted to their calling by the opportunity to use their knowledge. Mankind, like the individual, needs an arena in which to test its muscles. The Apollo program provided an arena so large as to be unique in the world we knew. When such arenas are no longer available, those men who feel compelled to explore them will become as extinct as dinosaurs, and the spirit of adventure will also be dead.

That thought was eloquently expressed in a message from Prime Minister John Gorton of Australia, left on the moon (along with messages from the leaders of the other free nations) by the crew of Apollo 11. The last sentence touched a chord:

"... May the high courage and technical genius which made this achievement possible be so used in the future that mankind will live in a universe in which peace, self expression, *and the chance of dangerous adventure are available to all.*" [Italics added].

The peak annual funding for NASA in the sixties was $5.9 billion at a time when the Department of Health, Education, and Welfare was spending that amount every eight days. But comparisons are pointless and I am not, at least directly, trying to justify that commitment. All I want to do is to describe what happened during those years that saw Americans first travel beyond the pull of gravity and to tell how it affected me and others—and how it changed our world, if at all.

How simple our world looks when we are hundreds of miles above it—or thousands, even hundreds of thousands—observing great problems as though looking through the wrong end of a telescope. Seeing the earth as a small dot in the universe, fragile, beautiful, innocent, and pure, is a very subjective experience. Reactions to that vision are personal, often abstract, and frequently political.

A better interpretation might be, not how tiny and fragile the earth is, but how it sets in the vastness of space. It is a lovely vision to look down on our planet and see unity and serenity because one is so far away, seeing no borders and no conflicts. But is that the real world?

While a student at UCLA, I had a friend who was student teaching. One morning he blurted out that he was thinking about giving up on becoming a teacher.

That was a shock and I asked him why?

It developed that he had been student teaching all week in a high school art class with uniformly disappointing results, even when each student was asked to sketch whatever he could draw best.

"So I discussed it with the regular teacher," he said. Her solution was quick and simple. "Ask them to draw smaller pictures; then you won't see so many mistakes."

That was part of the beauty of looking at the earth in miniature from outer space. You couldn't see the mistakes or the boundaries that kept one person's France from becoming the next man's Germany.

Many astronauts use that small, fragile world description on audiences to create a warm mood but it does not necessarily mean they experienced a revelation in orbit. I know of no astronaut who set out deliberately to discover what was in his soul, but there were some who claimed a new consciousness from looking back at the earth. There were others who "found God on the moon." And some found six-figure salaries as captains of industry. None of us got into the program for very complicated reasons. We wanted to fly and NASA was the best game going. Most of us thought of ourselves as test pilots in a new branch of aviation. Whatever we did, whatever was accomplished, however we behaved, was related more to that view of ourselves than any duty or calling we might have felt.

Someone once said, "A man is never so much alive as when he is close to death." And Winston Churchill added, "There is no more exhilarating moment than to be shot at and missed." That was part of it! Race-car drivers, mountain climbers, bullfighters, ski racers, and others feel it. Their exhilaration comes not from being reckless, but from taking calculated risks requiring great skill and confidence. To the astronaut, test flying or space flight is his sport—his risk exercise.

Astronauts are proficient and confident. Many take his strong ego, as egotism and it can be intimidating to others unless they themselves have great self-confidence. In certain situations he is not above feeling almost omnipotent—knowing he is not invincible, but enjoying the experience anyway. Astros have a high need to achieve, to accomplish tasks requiring great skill and effort.

To understand the early astronauts, it is important to remember they were first fighter pilots and test pilots. Flying is the hallmark of those who do it. Whatever else they are, they are fighter pilots. Among other fighter pilots they always find themselves at home, however little they may otherwise have in common. The aviator's experience acts upon them like a narcotic upon an addict. Whatever it is, it is a profound experience that reaches back into the recesses of the soul.

Flight is a symbol of human ambition and daring, applying skill and intelligence to problems that seem to defy solution.

Fighter pilots are not so much clever as they are fortunate and they have a real appreciation for their good fortune. It's what keeps them going despite poverty, divorce, and bad horoscopes. Sometimes it keeps them going despite bad weather as well, and that is the dangerous side of the matter. The most difficult of the pilot's arts is knowing when *not* to fly. It is also the last test of the real pilot, for if flying is proficiency and mastery, it is good sense and self-mastery as well. That limit is different for each pilot. The best legitimately recognize almost no limit.

Flying can transform a life from just existing to really living. The "danger" associated with flying is of little concern. A fighter pilot needs little approval or support from others, but he can't bear to find himself lacking in his chosen pursuit. It is a painful thing. Anything which even temporarily challenges belief in himself merely spurs him on to more concentration and a better effort—an uncommon response.

Take the time in 1954 when, as a Marine second lieutenant two months out of flight school, I was being trained as an all-weather fighter pilot in one of the first jet night-fighter aircraft. In those days, flying fighter aircraft at night and bad weather was considered the exclusive province of senior officers. A night-fighter pilot was expected to have excellent judgment and, most of all, experience.

I was fortunate to be in that vanguard of young pilots breaking into this so-called "old man's game." We were greeted with some skepticism, and I did little to change that reaction one morning around 2:00 A.M.

With about twenty-five hours logged in the airplane and a grizzled old master sergeant named Dan George as my radar observer, I was returning to El Toro Marine Air Station from a night patrol. I had that world-by-the-tail feeling. In command of the Marine Corps' most expensive fighter airplane and with my two-man crew performing like a well oiled watch, I let down for the final approach and landing on runway 34 right. The field was fogged in, not unusual for that time of year, and I was set up for a GCA (ground-controlled approach). I must have been born with a perverse streak in my character because I was pleased at the lousy weather. I was proud of my new proficiency and welcomed the opportunity to impress the old top kick at my side. As we started down the glide slope, with the ground controller calling out headings and altitudes, I was mentally applauding myself for one of the best instrument approaches in my brief career.

Within seconds it nearly became my last. At about 300 feet and glued to the glide slope, the airplane picked up a rapid right drift, a fact which completely escaped me. The frequent heading corrections fired at me by the GCA controller finally brought my peril slamming into my brain: "Turn left to a heading of three-three-zero degrees, you have developed a rapid right drift. Turn left to three-two-zero! You're drifting way off to the right and passing through minimums (200 feet and a half mile visibility). Take a wave off! Take a wave off! When you have leveled off straight ahead, give me your intentions."

As the controller's voice moved a half octave higher there at the end, I came to my senses and got a good instrument scan going once again. Between 300 and 200 feet I had stopped my instrument scan pattern and developed a bad case of vertigo, the instrument pilot's nemesis. It wasn't my first nor my worst case of vertigo but it was one of the few times I would experience it without realizing it was happening. The result was an inadvertent 30-degree right bank.

It didn't take a genius to realize that at 200 feet, coming down at 150 mph, in a 30-degree bank, we were seconds away from becoming a big bonfire in the housing development to our right.

As I leveled my wings and began a climb out straight ahead, three thoughts immediately came flooding into my brain, one upon the other:

"Whew! The best instrument approach I ever made and it wasn't good enough to get us in."

"At GCA minimums, two hundred feet, there was no sign of the runway or even a light on the ground."

"I'll have to do better to make it in on my next pass."

I told the controller I wanted to make another approach. Needless to say, that next approach was a hell of a lot harder on the old psyche. I still had a touch of vertigo and was fighting it all the way. Two planes attempting to land behind me diverted from El Toro to land at El Centro, 120 miles away.

This time, as we settled down on the glide slope, it dawned on me that Dan George, sitting next to me, was probably not enjoying this challenge as much as I was. He was probably not enjoying it at all! Like me, he wanted to spend the night in his own bed but no doubt wished his getting there didn't depend on the performance of a brash young 2nd lieutenant flying an airplane through the murk.

I assumed it would be necessary to descend below the minimum altitude to make it in but in those days that was what I thought all-weather fighter pilots did. I was concentrating so intently on the glide slope and heading control down low that it came as somewhat of a shock to feel Dan tapping on my right knee, indicating he could see the runway lights, at about the same time my wheels were touching down.

Only after we taxied off the runway did the adrenalin begin to kick up a bit. As I listened to the next couple of airplanes execute missed approaches and head out to El Centro, I dared not ask Dan what he thought. That would have violated "the code." My feelings at the time were of a challenge accepted and met, not of a risk stupidly taken. I was even a little proud.

That emotion lasted right up to the moment I climbed out of my cockpit to be met by our Operations Duty Officer. He quickly informed me that I was the only pilot stupid enough to land in the preceding half-hour, and that I should consider myself unofficially grounded until the commanding officer decided whether or not to make it official.

In the end, it all blew over and I was left with a little proud satisfaction, but it still stands as one of the dumber moves I made in my flying career. Yet, that kind of reaction to adverse circumstances has carried me through a career. On one's mind at such a time is not fear of the task, but the fear of failing, of not measuring up to self-imposed standards. Why be apprehensive about getting hurt or even killed when you may be facing a rare opportunity to meet those standards? In this business, it isn't uncommon to be less concerned about getting killed than about making an ass of yourself—especially in front of your peers.

The Gemini abort situation was a good example. Two pilots sat side by side in the Gemini cockpit, very close, each with an ejection handle between his knees. Either pilot could initiate an ejection, firing both seats simultaneously to avoid the rocket exhaust from one side burning the pilot on the other. During launch, especially the early phases, conditions could go to hell so rapidly that the difference between a successful and an unsuccessful abort, the difference between life and death, was measured in milliseconds. The reaction to a typical abort condition was a race against the clock.

Under those circumstances, you can picture each crewmember with his hands on the handle, poised for instant action during lift-off. They were alert all right, but most of their attention was directed at *not aborting*. It wasn't unusual for both pilots to place their hands in their laps to reduce the possibility of an unnecessary and embarrassing abort.

I don't recall any Gemini crew ever expressing concern about their safety during that extremely time-critical launch phase but nearly all of them, at one time or another, mentioned the "nightmare" of an unnecessary or premature abort and an empty spacecraft being placed successfully in orbit. The risk to their lives was of no great concern when compared to the "nightmare" of performing badly.

Not surprisingly, astronauts are frequently asked about fear, and just as frequently described as "courageous." The question never comes from the fighter pilot, the race driver, or the man engaged in his own risk behavior. To someone sitting at a desk, it may seem dangerous and foolhardy, or even stupid, to fly into space. To the fighter pilot, physically, mentally, and psychologically prepared to make such a trip, it is but a slight extension of his prior experience.

Space exploration is a risky business, but astronauts are carefully trained volunteers who knowingly accept the risks. Despite disastrous setbacks, NASA's overall safety record in the face of daunting challenges is testimony to an agency that places high regard on the lives and health of its flight crews. Any shortcomings with respect to safety are, in my opinion, honest mistakes.

It's no secret, astronauts are not attracted to the job because of its comfort and safety. Being an astronaut is a job where danger is a basic assumption. If the truth be known, that is part of the appeal along with the opportunity to demonstrate skills, daring and "the right stuff." The scale is balanced by the Space agency's obligation to take reasonable precautions to minimize the risk.

We now have a breed of space travelers, for whom the trip into space is a totally foreign experience. This new breed—the space tourist—was introduced to us in 2001. The opportunity arose from the need to replace the Soyuz lifeboat at the International Space Station every six months. Only two men are required to fly the Soyuz, leaving the third seat for a passenger. In the Eighties, a "guest cosmonaut" from one of the Soviet satellite states frequently filled this seat. In the Nineties, to gain a new source of hard currency, Russia resorted to carrying passengers for hire. The going rate for a 7-10 day trip into space is in the neighborhood of $20 million. The first "tourist" in space was an American, Dennis Tito. The second was Mark Shuttleworth, a South African Internet entrepreneur.

Russia can hardly be blamed for exploiting this source of hard curren-

cy. What each passenger pays is equivalent to 15-20 percent of the budget appropriated by the Russian government at the turn of the Millennium. To the Russians, it is found money. If they launched, orbited and
returned in Russian craft, I would have no quarrel with them. Unfortunately, that would probably not cover the cost of the trip. But the ISS program pays for the Soyuz and the trip, which makes the "extra" seat
available—and it is nearly all profit.

And I have nothing against adventurers graced with big bank
accounts and good health paying good money for the trip of their lives.
It is a perfectly symbiotic relationship; the Russian Space Agency needs
the money and the tourists want to pay. When the Russians expect their
revenue passengers to be hosted and baby-sat by the ISS crew, then I have
a problem.

The first two space tourists are, apparently, pretty good guys. Tito,
however, attempts to elevate his joy ride to something more by claiming
the world gains from flights made by people like himself and Shuttle-
worth. Average citizens tell him, "They wish they could fly, so it's inspi-
rational to all human beings, and that's valuable," Tito says.

He also claims, "People who fly in space understand the risk. They
know the benefit of developing human exploration far outweighs the
risks." Tito said his eight months of training made him well aware of the
risk, but he wasn't afraid.

That's nice, but simply knowing you can die is a far cry from understanding the nature and range of the risks involved in the exploration of
space. He also seems unaware of the added burden and responsibility his
presence placed on real astronauts and cosmonauts wherever he went.

Talgut Musabaev was the Soyuz pilot of the flight to and from the ISS
with Tito. Talgut is very bright and has a good sense of humor. He
laughed heartily when I asked about his experience with Tito. His attitude
was one of having put up with a great deal. He described himself as,
"Number one pilot, number one baby sitter and number one nurse."

When asked if eight days with Tito was enough, Talgut reared back
his head and laughed, while nodding his head "Yes." When I asked
would he do it again? His eyes got really big and he howled with laughter. Talgut said, "Tito was very sick most of the time, and I was almost a
full-time nurse. But I was assigned the job before launch of taking care of
Tito."

In late 2002, the Commission on the Future of the U.S. Aerospace Industry recommended that NASA follow the lead of the cash-starved Russian program and begin to carry tourists into space on the Shuttle. The study said that tourism could turn into a helpful subsidy for NASA *if* future generations of craft were designed for pleasure, as well as performing the shuttle's present tasks. Supposedly, NASA, once hostile to the idea of selling seats on its spacecraft, is coming round to the idea.

That would be a big mistake. The price of the ticket would not come close to covering the cost of the undertaking. It is difficult enough to sell NASA's annual budget to a skeptical Congress without them having to explain why they are subsidizing flights on the Space Shuttle for rich tourists. Besides, with the construction schedule to complete the ISS, it will be years before there are any unfilled seats on a Shuttle mission.

Space tourism should be the business of private sector space companies, not NASA. We are a long way away from passenger space travel becoming a true business. A 2001 report concluded that, by the year 2021, 60 passengers a year would be willing to pay $5 million each to orbit the earth. That is not a big market. For space tourism to be commercially viable, it will require the next generation of reusable space vehicle designed for high sortie rates, a turnaround in hours rather than months, a shirtsleeves cabin environment, and a host of other operational requirements. For passenger spacecraft operations to be economically viable they must be capable of making hundreds of flights annually with reliabilities that compare favorably to commercial aircraft.

Accidents like Columbia's disintegration are not likely to affect what demand there is for spaceflight adventures but it could inject some common sense into the equation. What Columbia emphasized again are the realities of the hazards that are present. In the wake of the Columbia disaster, we won't see any American tourist trips of a lifetime for quite a while.

It has become quite fashionable for people to say they want to travel in space. They are usually romantics without an awareness of what the task entails. For them, it is a foolhardy, not a calculated risk. Those who perform well in dangerous professions are quite comfortable about what they are doing. They are not romantics, but cold, hard realists about their professions. While I have never discussed fear with another astronaut or another fighter pilot, I know fear is a minimal consideration in their lives just as it has been in mine.

An astronaut derives his love of the job from three fundamental challenges, which the job entails. The first and easiest is man against machine. The Apollo spacecraft had neither heart nor soul but, in its time, was perhaps the most complex piece of machinery to be operated by man ever constructed. The astronaut masters this mechanical creation of man. The better the pilot, the more he is able to get out of the machine.

The second, man against man, is a more challenging contest. To reach the enviable position of riding a rocket, we had faced tough and lifelong screening and 10-15 years survival in a challenging and dangerous profession. After being selected for our knowledge, skill, and competitive drive, a space mission becomes the place to vindicate that judgment. I suppose in a sense we were saying, "I'm a winner; watch my victory lap." Winners become stronger and go on to prevail over other men in even more trying circumstances.

At the top of this hierarchy of competition is man competing against himself. It is that pursuit which provides the satisfaction of being "the master of my fate, the captain of my soul."

As a student pilot, at the age of twenty, Charles Lindbergh concluded, "If I could fly for ten years before being killed in a crash, I would be willing to trade an ordinary lifetime for that experience." I have shared that feeling and know that experience.

Any idiot can get an airplane off the ground, but I believe an aviator earns his keep by bringing that plane back safely anytime, anywhere, under any circumstances that man and God can dream up. A pilot's only real obstacles are the elements and the problems he creates for himself in his mind. Bringing a single-place fighter aircraft home at night with a low ceiling, in fog, rain, or ice increases the stakes considerably. If you are apprehensive about your ability to handle the elements, it can create a crisis regardless of piloting skill. For twenty years my greatest personal satisfaction came from flying anywhere, anytime, in any kind of weather. What some might consider poor judgment was to me a way of life.

Flying into a strange airport, with marginal weather and barely adequate fuel, is one of the most exciting and satisfying experiences in life. When the radio crackles with the news the weather is deteriorating and threatening to close the field, it can create an anxious moment. In the next instant, my nervous system responds appropriately: my heart picks up the pace a bit and adrenalin is pumped into my system. This is followed by the thrill of a challenge accepted and, sometimes, a self-conscious smile. The heavens have thrown down the gauntlet and I am already anticipating the warm glow, even a smug feeling, after landing. Do your damndest, elements. An intelligent man surely must recognize he may not win someday and, yet, that has always been my reaction.

It worked. I survived.

My astronaut peer group was one of the most competitive ever assembled. For some, selection into this group and flying in space seemed to satisfy their highest ambitions. For most of us, it was both acceptance into an elite fraternity and a stepping-stone from which to accomplish many of the other things we still wanted out of life. But for all of us, from the minute we were accepted, it triggered a renewed effort to rise to the new peak among the best in our chosen profession.

An astronaut cannot afford to be awed by his job. Only when he has developed the confidence, born of proficiency, that he is bigger and better than any aspect of the task ahead, is he capable of performing at his best. The definition of courage I like best is "the capacity to overcome fear." No fear—no courage required. The astronaut who arrives at that special challenge in his life, and feels in complete control of those moments where fear might intrude, does not require courage to fly his mission.

I was certainly not courageous. My approach has always been to understand all I can of whatever may affect me, and to reduce the unknown elements to a bare minimum. Identifying those moments during the mission when my neck was sticking out, and then knowing when they were passed, made it easy to tolerate the brief moments of exposure to physical danger. We worked for years to minimize those periods when we had no control over the outcome.

At launch, theoretically, the spacecraft has an abort capability while sitting on the pad. But all crews realized if a pad abort was necessary, the circumstances were conducive to getting killed. Therefore, from some point late in the count until sometime shortly after lift-off, our life is hanging out over the edge. As the spacecraft gains altitude, we gradually gain more control over the situation and pull back from the edge. A small weight was lifted from my shoulders at lift-off plus one minute when we disabled the automatic abort circuits. And when we jettisoned the launch escape tower after two and a half minutes, it turned into a picnic.

Sure, if the landing parachutes don't open, it's a bad day. But we did-
n't spend an eleven-day mission worrying about the chutes? There was
no cause for concern until they had a real and immediate influence on our
destiny.

No one should be surprised that those first steps into space were
taken by a bunch of brash young fighter pilots who approached every
mission with anticipation. A good fighter pilot lives every day (only a little self-consciously) thinking he is "the best fighter pilot in the world." It
may not be rational, but it is certainly real. For such a man, it is only a
short step into space.

The fighter-pilot image of wine, women, and song is one all of us cultivated. That may be nothing but image because flying is truly our mis-
tress. It is unfair competition for a wife and family at times. When I strap
on a high-performance airplane, I feel more relaxed, more alive, more
filled with self-esteem and confidence than I do at any other time or place
in my life. Doing what a fighter pilot does—alone—requires great matu-
rity, but at the same time the fighter pilot is the child that lives in all of us.
Airplanes are his toys, and it's tough to give them up. Lets face it, after
all the high-blown reasons are dissected, we remain fighter pilots because
it's fun. That lifelong fascination with airplanes can easily become an
obsession. Giving them up, cold turkey, is a tough decision that some just
will not face.

Bill Anders became a fighter pilot in the early Fifties and has never
even thought about taking the cure. After flying the Apollo 8 mission in
1969, Anders became Executive Secretary to the National Space Council,
then head of the Nuclear Regulatory Agency—government jobs in the
Washington D.C. area.

During his six years in Washington, Bill did his usual thing: applying
himself to his job from dawn until well after dark, which left him little
time for flying. Most would have given it up, but Bill worked out his own
accommodation. He accepted the Washington appointments on the condition that he remain eligible to fly NASA airplanes. He then used his
influence to get a ruling that former astronauts in government jobs were
permitted to fly NASA aircraft left in the Washington area while their
pilots were visiting on official business. If Alan Shepard flew a T-38 into
a local airport for two days of meetings, it wasn't unusual for two or three

former astronauts in the area to fly it before it was returned to Houston. Broken airplanes from this activity eventually caused their share of arguments.

On many a morning, Bill would rise at 3:00 A.M., drive to Andrews AFB, fly a T-38 to some distant field, refuel, return, and walk into his office at 8:00 A.M., ready for work. By late 1976, Ambassador Bill Anders was stationed in Oslo, Norway, and still flying helicopters off of visiting U.S. Navy ships and returning to Houston every couple of months for his jet flying.

After retiring as Chairman of General Dynamics, Bill got his own hangar and bought his own little air force. Why is Bill still flying everything from helicopters to jet airplanes? Why, for the fun of it, of course.

That kind of passion for flying, that joy (or craziness), partly explains why a fellow will hang around NASA for ten or fifteen years, waiting for a space flight that might never come. Is there anything better in life than cutting through the sky in something new and wild and exploring the unknown?

Why we became astronauts, and how we survived that experience, is a complex question. Not the least of the reasons is that our instincts are those of a fighter pilot. Yes, I was fortunate to take part in "man's greatest adventure," but most of the things I am or ever can be have their roots in an airplane cockpit. I can't imagine what life would have been like had I not become a Marine Corps fighter pilot.

As we began the 21st century, flight into space is almost routine. Routine is not what inspires. It is time to do something magnificent and awe inspiring, something history will call a Great Thing.

The Apollo program galvanized the world because it went somewhere that man had never gone before: the moon. Hundreds of millions of viewers watched the Mars Pathfinder rover because it went somewhere, too. It is time for humans to go somewhere again—this time, to Mars.

The purpose of a civilization is not to simply survive, but to move society forward and pursue achievable dreams. We will be remembered a thousand years from now less for the disasters we avoided than for the quests we had the courage to commence.

Achieving the goal of landing an American on the moon was one of our finest hours and one of the greatest technological achievements in history. It was a national commitment of the highest order, beginning with vision and leadership and followed by the political will and determination to accomplish a seemingly impossible task. It took understanding the enormous risks involved, as well as the human sacrifice required. The Apollo program represented a huge investment of our national treasure and, tragically, cost the lives of some of our best and brightest.

When will we find the political will to accept another impossible challenge? What should NASA be doing to inspire the same kind of commitment?

First, a few words about what NASA should not be doing—most of which are being advocated by the Moon Society; establishing a private lunar base for commerce and tourism, placing cremated remains or etched words and images on the lunar surface, or squeezing oxygen to breathe from out of the rocks. I also do not believe in building plants on the Moon, probably at the poles, "to manufacture the hardware or fuel we will use to go to Mars." I can think of a hundred, more cost effective ways to get to Mars. Many of these silly ideas may eventually be pursued by entrepreneurs.

There are two uses for the Moon I could support, neither of which will come to fruition in our children's lifetimes: a radio-telescope facility on the backside of the Moon, and mining Helium-3, an isotope of Helium, from the surface material. Helium-3 would be an ideal fuel for fusion reactors, the ultimate answer to our energy problem. But fusion reactors will not be practical until the end of the 21st century.

The question of what NASA should be doing is not all that difficult to answer. Planet Earth is a port on the seashore of the universe. From this homeport, we must venture out to explore this pristine ocean of space. Arthur Clarke said it best, "We have set sail on an ocean whose farthest shores we can never reach."

NASA should announce, after approval by Congress and the White House, that its new mission is to study the universe and explore the solar system. Within this charge, the Agency should select goals that fit comfortably within this mission statement. It would not require selling a brand new start each time an intermediate goal, such as landing on the Moon or Mars, is accomplished.

There are three things NASA should be doing right now, since we have already lost 10-20 years in our effort to conquer space. Yes, I mean conquer. There is no reason why space should not come under our control and exploitation just as all other geographic and environmental boundaries here on earth have surrendered to our exploration.

These objectives should be pursued simultaneously as, more or less, equal priorities. None of the three are easy or inexpensive or, for that matter, safe.

First and foremost, NASA must keep the Shuttle Orbiter flying as regularly as possible. It is the key to success of the ISS and our ability to launch large scientific satellites. Yes, it will still be a risky operation. Launch, with the shuttle main engines and the solid rocket boosters, will continue to be the riskiest part of the operation. But the Achilles' heel will remain the TPS, the thermal protection system of ceramic tiles and reinforced carbon-carbon. Given that we have good, even urgent, reasons to be flying, we are wedded to this system. NASA is obligated to minimize risk within other requirements but it is neither necessary nor possible to eliminate risk altogether. Don't saddle Shuttle operations with "fixes" and procedures that, themselves, will be risky. There have been improvements in the past that have caused more harm than good, allowing the "law of unintended consequences" to come into play.

And, please, no cosmetic changes to make management and Congress feel good but provide no increase in safety for the crew.

The age and recent history of the shuttle program means a replacement of that system is certainly in order. The program is experiencing rising costs to maintain an aging fleet, partly because each vehicle requires a small army of engineers and technicians to disassemble it, check out the parts and rebuild it for the next flight. Every flight is a first flight, and no flight will ever be routine.

While we have to live with the Orbiter for at least the next ten years, we must find the funds to develop a sensible replacement for it if manned flight is to continue for long. One of NASA's ill-advised attempts to do just that was VentureStar, a single-stage-to-orbit (SSTO) vehicle, where the launch vehicle and spacecraft were one and the same. VentureStar was expected to carry its entire launch mass (minus the expended fuel) into orbit and out. NASA wasted a number of years on this flawed concept— one of the most stupid ideas to ever come out of the agency.

NASA, in partnership with Lockheed Martin, sank $900 million into the X-33 project, a one-third-scale version of VentureStar. Lockheed Martin spent another $350 million of its own money. There are good reasons why all our successful launch vehicles have been staged to avoid carrying dead weight into orbit. In addition, VentureStar had to be manufactured where it would be launched and launched from where it landed. It was too large to be ferried back to its launch site, a huge operating limitation. The X-33 was cancelled in 2001, when the contractor could not manufacture the huge liquid oxygen tanks from composite materials and switched to aluminum, which proved too heavy.

What does make sense for the next generation is a launch vehicle that takes off horizontally, like a huge transport aircraft, and flies to 170-190,000 feet and Mach 7 or 8. There, at the edge of space, it would release a rocket vehicle to carry the payload into orbit or it might go another 100,000 feet higher on rocket power before releasing the second stage. The launch vehicle would return to a landing for another launch in two or three days. The technology developed in NASA's work on a so-called aerospace plane could be applicable to this new launch vehicle, if it can be scaled up.

My candidate for this new horizontal take-off launch vehicle utilizes rocket-based combined cycle (RBCC) ramjet engines capable of operating at zero velocity. Such a "booster" would weigh in the neighborhood of 1.3 million pounds at take-off (lift-off), about the same as the huge Russian Antonov 225 transport or the new Airbus A380. It would use oxygen drawn from the atmosphere as the oxidizer. There are a number of unanswered questions about the technology and scaling it up but they are not nearly as daunting as the technical challenges we faced before Apollo.

We have flown thousands of engines using this RBCC technology but never of the size needed for this launch vehicle. NASA's single most important priority is developing low-cost, reliable access to space, and this is the only technology of which I am aware that has a prayer of reducing the cost of putting a pound in orbit by a factor of ten.

That brings us to what should be NASA's third objective—the Holy Grail of manned spaceflight, a manned mission to Mars—the nearest planet on which human explorers could safely land. Mars has plentiful supplies of water ice and gaseous carbon dioxide, the raw materials for oxygen, hydrogen, and hydrocarbon fuels. The planet is a storehouse of scientific information—important in its own right but also for what it may tell us about the origins of life or on safeguarding the environment of our own planet. Mars once had abundant liquid water, with seas and rivers. What happened to it? How did a once Earthlike world become so parched, frigid and comparatively airless? Is there something important on Mars that we need to know about our own fragile world?

When the first president Bush called for a mission to Mars in 1989, representatives of the various NASA centers apparently got together, listed all of the dream projects they had always wanted to do, and all agreed to scratch each other's backs. The effort never got off the ground when NASA told an indifferent Congress that the program could cost as much as $500 billion and would take decades. In the past dozen years, NASA has taken a more sensible approach and now claims a more realistic estimate would be in the neighborhood of $100 billion.

Why should we be going? How do we justify spending the more realistic $200 billion a manned mission to Mars would cost? For just about every argument one can make in support there is a good counter-argument. If you want to go for Science, it's arguably cheaper using robots. Spin-offs? What might come about from the advanced propulsion systems and the closed life-support systems that will have to be developed? To many, they are not a compelling argument any more than Teflon frying pans, fireproof cloth, and new materials were in the Sixties. We can claim we do it for Education but educators and politicians would much rather spend the money directly. It can't even be sold as a place for humanity to expand. No one has even dreamed of launching into space the world's daily incremental population increase of 250,000 people at any time even in the distant future. If no single reason can justify a manned mission to Mars, perhaps their combined weight will provide a legitimate justification. Failing that, the trip must be justified on religious (in the broadest sense) grounds. That is: *faith*. You either believe in the value of exploration for the human race or you do not. It is a matter of faith!

No major new technological advances are required. The step from today to the first landing of humans on Mars is a smaller technological leap than the step from President John F. Kennedy's announcement of the Apollo program on May 25, 1961 to the first landing of humans on the Moon on July 20, 1969. Mars is also more affordable today as a percentage of GDP than Apollo was in the 1960s.

Not surprisingly, a manned mission to Mars gets the same criticism about social priorities that Apollo faced: Why are we spending all this money on space when there is so much poverty, disease and suffering at home? It is a maddening question because it entirely misses the point. Poverty and disease will always be with us. The government is not very good at solving social problems. We have spent more than $5 trillion in the war on poverty and the poor remain as big a segment of our population as ever. On the other hand, government can be extremely good at solving technical problems, such as the Panama Canal, the Manhattan Project and the Apollo Program.

A trip to Mars would require assembling in earth orbit, a vehicle weighing in the neighborhood of 1.2 million pounds. As Earth and Mars circle the Sun, they repeat the proper relative "starting positions" for realistic travel between planets about every 26 months. For each of these conjunctions, we have, approximately, a 30-day launch window. The full mission would take close to three years, including a stay on the Martian surface of more than a year. The exposure to medical hazards, such as long-term weightlessness and cosmic rays (gamma radiation), would be a hundred times higher for Mars missions than it was for the lunar missions. For this reason, NASA wants to limit radiation exposure outside of the Van Allen radiation belt to less than one year.

Missions shorter than three years are possible if the spacecraft carries more fuel (requires a bigger Mars vehicle), or improved propulsion systems are used, or if highly specialized trajectories are employed. But even under the most optimistic designs, mission durations are still 18 months or more.

Some say we should not go to Mars until we can do it in a spacecraft with artificial gravity. Nonsense! Artificial gravity would require a rotating space station, either a wagon wheel shaped vehicle or two vehicles connected by a long, strong tether. The jury is still out on the amount of gravity that could be generated by centrifugal force in space but it could be as much as a third of a G. Subjects in a rotating room get nauseous if the room rotates above a couple of degrees a second. For a space station to create a third of a G, while holding the angular rotation to less than a couple of degrees per second, would require a wagon wheel about half a mile across—hardly a practical solution. And, it would sacrifice most of the very significant advantages of zero G.

Landing on Mars will not be easy; of twelve attempts with unmanned

Landers, three have made it. The Russians lost all six of their Mars landers.

John Young, America's most experienced (and oldest) astronaut, says, "Send old men to Mars because they're going to die anyway." I think John was just lobbying for the mission.

NASA should put a priority on designing and testing the "enabling technologies" that will reduce the risk for human exploration of Mars. One priority should be nuclear power for future missions of exploration—a "nuclear rocket." Spaceships powered by such propulsion systems could get us to Mars in three weeks rather than eight months. Propulsion is the key to shrinking the universe and putting it within our reach.

Another priority should be closed life-support systems. Long-term survival in space will require that we recycle every drop of water, every breath of air, and every molecule of food, if we are to survive.

Some experienced planners and economists believe our technology has reached levels that would enable Mars missions at costs equal to or even less than those of the Apollo program. In today's dollars, the Apollo program cost about $125 billion. Since Mars is a much more remote destination than the moon, common sense tells us that the price tag for a manned mission to the planet should be higher. Since much of the required space infrastructure, such as launch pads, ground equipment, and communications and control facilities has already been developed and paid for (unlike in the days of Apollo), the add-on costs of the Mars mission seem a little less imposing. NASA analysts have long argued that a human Mars landing would be equal to the cost of Apollo—or less. They have also concluded that the required spending rate would be approximately twice what the International Space Station is costing, or about $5-6 billion dollars per year.

The usual considerations when we contemplate a major new program, like a mission to Mars, are our technical ability to accomplish it and our financial ability to pay for it. Another major consideration should be our ability to manage such a program during both development and subsequent operations. NASA seems to have a better record in development than in operations. Or, it may just seem that way because development is less dramatic and a less risky activity. People get killed in operations.

The Columbia disaster was the third (of three) space disasters, in which management and administrative decisions were a contributing factor—sometimes a major factor. As management of our space program has evolved and changed (deteriorated, actually) over the last 30 years, the individual astronaut's role as well as that of the Astronaut Office has evolved, too.

The most exciting and glamorous aspect of an astro's life is flying the space shuttle into and out of orbit. And, of course, it is the most visible part. Perhaps more valuable in the long run, however, is the technical and operational contributions astronauts make to the development of flight hardware. It was certainly my major contribution during my time with NASA.

Early NASA was an organization of entrepreneurs. They were individualists, creative people, and risk takers. It was a time when technical challenges and risks were more readily accepted. As Gene Kranz, one of NASA's first flight controllers put it, "Often we had no alternative but to accept risk because we did not have the many proven options in design, materials, and computer technology that we have today. Sometimes we accepted risk because it was the most direct path to our objective.

"Mercury, Gemini, and Apollo were playing to a nation, a Congress, and a media who accepted risk and accepted the fact that we, as engineers, mathematicians, technologists, and managers were not perfect. We wanted to be perfect; we just failed at times. We were in a tough business and sometimes things just do not go right; that was the nature of our business. It was flight test."

We would never have made it into orbit had we not been willing to take carefully calculated risks—something Congress and NASA management seem afraid to do these days. Legislators are not noted for being risk-takers. The current congress has very few members with any experience in the military services, one place where many members of society gain the experience of exposure to risk.

Through the Sixties and early Seventies, with the Mercury, Gemini, and Apollo programs, economy and simplicity were important goals of spacecraft design. Tried and true, reliable hardware was favored over cutting edge technology whenever we had a choice. With missions that were pushing the limits of human and technical achievement—doing the impossible, so to speak—no one wanted to introduce any more uncertainty than necessary.

The Russians also worshipped the god of simplicity. The motto of the Soviet Academy of Science was borrowed from Voltaire: "The better is the enemy of the good."

Forty years later, NASA has become a mature bureaucracy. Since developing the Space Shuttle, it has seemed more intent on perpetuating itself than on pursuing ambitious new programs. As NASA grew, so did the paperwork. Committees proliferated. "Oversight" and "political ram-ifications" became the new watchwords. Engineering design moved in the direction of new materials and what engineers call state-of-the-art technology—the newer the better.

NASA is still an impressive organization at the technical level in spite of engineers and managers spending more of their time defending their own turf. It not only takes longer to get things done, but it can take months to get a *bad* idea out of the system, while it continues to consume money and human resources. Projects, such as the ISS, are split up between many more contractors with oversight by many more NASA centers. The Agency has made a transition to slower and more expensive programs and that is what is choking NASA today.

Any large or growing enterprise requires organization. In the begin-ning, NASA was good at that. Their forte, an area where they established an enviable reputation, was in project management. The Apollo program efficiently organized the efforts of 400,000 people and thousands of com-panies to land a man on the moon, on schedule and pretty much within cost. The organizational structure for the Apollo program was excellent, well documented with authority appropriately matched to responsibili-ty. In the NASA matrix organization, (program management cutting across the line authority of functional managers) we, in the astronaut office, had a limited amount of program management responsibility or authority. Occasionally, but rarely, an astro would be pulled out of our office to assume a program management responsibility.

The informal organization was quite a different picture. But, on occa-sion, the admiration and respect that accrued to an astronaut could blind engineers and planners, especially at the contractors' plants. In meetings at every level, participants had a tendency to defer to the opinion of the man who would strap a rocket to his backside and ride it into what was then unknown. We carried an implied authority that went far beyond our position in the organization table. This authority could (and did) lead to abuses. A well intended but uninformed remark by an astronaut could discourage or override more qualified and experienced engineering judgment when the celebrity of crew status entered into the equation. This bred resentment, especially when the most informed judgment did not prevail.

The troika of NASA engineers, flight controllers and astronauts has co-existed in a symbiotic relationship since the formation of the original Space Task Group. It was like a three-legged stool with each leg essential for the system to work. There has always been tension in this triangle: between flight controllers and astronauts, between astronauts and engineers and, to a lesser degree, between engineers and flight controllers. Most of the time it was constructive tension.

Many NASA engineers believed their lives would be much simpler if astronauts were never involved in design meetings and were content to "play" with their airplanes and fly the spacecraft. Astros were supposed to be just another piece of interchangeable equipment, pulled off the shelf when needed and dropped into the next empty spacecraft seat. One old Mercury hand once told me, "Chris Kraft would like to just reach up and pull one Mark IV, Mod 3 astronaut off the shelf and plug him into the spacecraft."

For NASA's first engineers, accommodating a human cargo added complexities to an already difficult task. It probably started with the original, windowless, Mercury capsule design. When the Mercury astronauts arrived on the scene, not surprisingly, they fought to get a window installed. The window argument became part of a larger disagreement about the extent to which astronaut pilots would actually control the spacecraft; something our guys insisted upon and the engineers opposed. Outstanding engineers like Max Faget, Guy Thibodaux, and Caldwell Johnson argued that the capsule would be flying so fast that it would be better to control it automatically, in which case the astronauts would not need to see much of anything.

It was Guy Thibodaux who said, "To be quite honest, I don't think we need human pilots, … Of course, human beings ought to be able to go into space. And if the astronauts want to pretend they're flying, that's O.K. But they can't react fast enough if a problem arises, and they shouldn't tell us how to design spacecraft. From our point of view, the best thing that any of the Mercury astronauts could have done during reentry was to pass out and let the automatic controls bring the craft to a splashdown."

A window was added in time for John Glenn's mission.

Since at least the 1940s, test pilots have played a critical role in the design of new flying machines, a role that has paid for itself a thousand times over. The test pilot contributes much more to his company's goals than test flying the aircraft. He is involved in the early engineering design to insure, as much as possible, that there are no nasty surprises when the project reaches flight-testing. Of course, it behooves him to deliver his messages with diplomacy. It's no secret that some early astronaut superstars and prima donnas contributed to the bad attitude displayed by some NASA engineers and managers.

Today the aerospace business is so specialized and so cost sensitive to design deficiencies that it is irresponsible to proceed with any project without scrutinizing it at all stages with the best professional eyes available.

In the beginning, the Astronaut Office was headed by Alan Shepard, who reported to Deke Slayton, Deputy Director of the Johnson Space Center, who reported to Dr. Robert Gilruth, the Center Director. Shepard and Slayton enjoyed the respect of their peers and Dr. Gilruth was the astronauts' friend, guaranteeing a sympathetic ear at the highest levels of the agency. That insured astros were well represented in any forum and our counsel was usually well received.

In the early Seventies, the old guard in the Astronaut Office began leaving and the future began to take shape along different lines. Dr. Gilruth retired and Deke Slayton abandoned his management responsibilities to join the ASTP crew, creating the opportunity for George Abbey to impose his will on the Astronaut Office.

In the early eighties, when Max Faget, Chris Kraft, and several other original Space Task Group members retired within six months of each other, it insured that it would be Abbey's shadow that dominated the Astronaut Office, the Johnson Space Center and, to only a slightly lesser degree, NASA headquarters, for the next two decades.

In the "good old days," NASA was an engineer driven organization. Technical people are concerned with technology and safety. They not only solved some of the toughest technical problems in history, they understood that solutions to problems often create other problems. Their key to success was a culture where workers knew they wouldn't lose their heads if they told the boss bad news.

At NASA, the Nineties belonged to Dan Goldin, the longest serving administrator in the history of the agency, and his "faster, better, cheaper" philosophy of space missions. Nobody was ever quite sure what that philosophy meant when it came to implementation, but it was not the same as our consideration of the cost, schedule, and weight impacts in the days of Apollo. We considered those factors when evaluating changes in design or compared changes. That was toward the end of the process.

The application of faster, better, cheaper, to aerospace products seemed to encompass a lean development team, minimal systems redundancy and the use of software simulation in place of hardware testing. And the principal was applied at the beginning of the process.

Any experienced engineer will tell you that the *best* you can ever do is two out of three of these otherwise laudable goals. It can lead to reduced performance goals and mission success on less ambitious mission objectives. Checks and controls are replaced by "consensus management," where no single person is actually in charge and ultimately responsible.

The Goldin administration discouraged bringing bad news forward and was famous for its "kill the messenger" management style. Goldin's faster, better, cheaper philosophy can lead to quality-control problems, and it may have contributed to an attitude that allowed a Shuttle Columbia disaster to take place.

Managers pride themselves on "looking at the big picture, and base their assessments of safety partly on the prior number of safe flights flown. Following the Columbia liftoff, managers admitted they discounted the possible damage done by a piece of foam to the underside of Columbia's wing because such incidents had occurred a number of times before and those shuttles had all returned safely.

Their confidence was based on past success, thinking they could get away with the risk because they had been fortunate with prior incidents, but mid-level engineers were as cautious as ever and continued to explore the problem.

Since the Seventies, the influence of the Astronaut Office and individual astronauts on operations and design has experienced its ups and downs, but generally down from what it was in the time of Apollo, for a variety of reasons:

The great increase in the number of astronauts; a majority with little or no operational flying experience and many from scientific and academic environments not noted for management skills. Beginning in the mid-Seventies, NASA began selecting not the best man for the job but the best "persons," with special emphasis on women and minority candidates. The impact was felt beyond just the gender and ethnicity makeup of the astronaut office.

The importance of getting assigned to a flight crew and training for a mission; this dominant factor in the career of an astronaut leaves little time and, for many, little interest in administrative or engineering activities. The astronaut reward system—flight crew assignment—is heavily weighted toward operational (i.e. stick and rudder) activities over engineering abilities and administrative duties. In the days of Apollo, it was infinitely more valuable to be working on the spacecraft hand-controller than the latest technology fuel cells for the electric power system.

The military background of many astronauts and active duty status of most; a byproduct was commitment to the seniority system (rank) for organizational structure rather than individual ability or experience.

Leadership is best exercised by influencing others. A less satisfactory alternative is authority. With its influence reduced, it would be nice if the astronaut office had the authority to get things done. Perhaps this can be offset by a fairly recent trend to move more astronauts into management positions.

The Columbia disaster of February 2003 will probably trigger a cycle of increased astronaut influence as it did following the Apollo 1 fire and the Challenger accident.

The siren song of flying in space is so strong that some of the world's most capable military pilots have been willing to get along by going along, even if it meant submitting to the arrogance of program managers pursuing a variety of priorities other than operational.

I am confident the subjective flight crew selection, process based on personal favoritism, that prevailed during George Abbey's reign will be replaced with a more objective one. One improvement might be to uncouple flight crew assignments as much as possible from an individual astronaut's management and/or technical responsibilities. The withholding of a flight crew assignment would no longer be an effective tool to discourage candid communication.

Flight crew assignments should be made out of the Astronaut Office with the onus on top management to make the case if they believe a particular crewman is not acceptable. The selection criteria should be heavily weighted toward ability to get the job done. There is no place for personal favoritism and ass-kissing in undertakings as critical as manned space flight.

The Astronaut Office should be organized to implement such a policy.

Our choices for the future are constrained less by technology than by economics, politics, and our willingness to accept some failures as the price of success. In practical terms, this means that decisions will be dictated more by what we feel we can afford to do and by how important we believe space is to the human future.

Decisions made in the coming years will determine the timing and character of our exploration of the Solar System. Will we assume a leading role? Or will we sit back and let other countries take the lead? Can the United States ignore this challenge and remain a major force in the twenty-first century? What will be the verdict of history if the United States has the ability and does not pursue the opportunity to go for Mars?

The society that does not utilize its knowledge and capabilities to push back boundaries begins to decline and is replaced by those societies that do utilize their capabilities. The frequently cited example is that of China during the Ming dynasty.

Sixty years prior to 1492, Chinese explorers had traveled to India, Arabia and as far as Africa. They returned a wealth of scientific data but a new emperor considered such journeys a wasteful extravagance. His successors burned the boats and banned all Chinese from leaving the country under threat of execution. Their technological edge was lost and China has been a net importer of technology ever since.

The consequences of that 15th century decision to *not* explore are still felt in China today. For a country with the most people on Earth, China still looks inward—its culture hardly the dominant force in the world that it could be.

Columbus, too, had great difficulty finding financing for his project to find a new way to India. One rejection after another was based on the excuse of too many problems at home. Only Spain's Isabella was willing to look beyond the many problems on her own shores, and see the potential reward for her investment in the future. Spanish explorers, following the example of Columbus, turned Spain into a great world power. They carried the language and culture of Spain throughout the new world where it still prevails in most of Latin America.

If we consciously decide *not* to go to Mars, our generation will truly achieve a first in human history. We will be the first to stop at a frontier, to draw a line and say to our children, "This far, and no farther."

In the end, we will surely go. As I heard Dan Goldin say more than once, "Is there life on Mars? Maybe not now; but there will be!"

Man's real limitation in the foreseeable future is the boundary of our solar system. That remains the next barrier to be broken, just as we broke the sound barrier and the earth's gravitational pull. Someday, we will have an engine that's fast enough to allow us to travel to distant planets within a single lifetime but if we are to travel into deep space; we will need tremendous advances in propulsion systems. It will take a quantum leap forward in science and physics.

There are destinations beyond Mars that beckon us, such as Europa, an icy moon of Jupiter. And, in due time, we will travel to Beta Centauri, our nearest neighbor in the galaxy—4.2 light years away. That means we could get there in 4.2 years *if* we could travel at the speed of light, 186,000 miles per second. With today's chemically propelled spacecraft that trip would take about 70,000 years, longer than all of recorded human history. The need for better methods of propulsion and more advanced communications systems is obvious if we are ever to travel beyond our solar system.

Will man tolerate even a 40-50 year trip using nuclear propulsion? Probably not! But I do believe that what the mind of man can imagine, he will eventually accomplish. It is only a matter of time before man will find a better means of propulsion and further expand his operating universe.

When I was an active astronaut, I expected to see unmanned probes to all the planets in our solar system by 2000, and maybe even a manned visit to Mars. These accomplishments were well within our grasp. What happened?

It has been 30 years since we last visited the moon, leaving tracks, boot prints and equipment all over Taurus-Littrow and Hadley Rille. Much can happen in 30 years. 30 years after Columbus found the new world, Magellan's expedition circled the earth. Thirty years after the first successful American locomotive, there were railroad tracks all over the eastern United States.

Exploring our solar system and beyond requires more than just technology, which we have; it requires will, which we don't seem to have. National will is expressed in funding. Where is the national will to explore? Since the glory days of Apollo, we have regularly held down funds for space exploration year after year. Funding for NASA today is one fifth what it was in 1965, less than 0.8 percent of the federal budget.

It takes a sustained national commitment for a government to carry out a program of space exploration—a commitment in which we are currently deficient. It requires leadership—not only from the President and the politicians, but the media and other organizations as well.

Our bold successes in the past elevated America in the eyes of the world. However, a faint-hearted reluctance to lead in the 21st century will change that impression. Technically sophisticated nations of the world are committed to catching up—which we should expect. While America's "cutting edge" technology is envied and exploited by other nations, the U.S. Congress subjects our commitment to one agonizing re-appraisal after another. It is hard to understand how some Congressmen are perfectly willing to throw away technological achievements for which other nations would give anything to have. I can only conclude the space program is poorly understood by political and economic leaders as well as the general public.

In the booster-for-hire business, Arianespace, a French company, has captured 50 percent of the commercial world market in 2001. Russia can undercut American launch system prices by millions of dollars and still make a huge profit. China, the world's newest space power, seems intent on re-creating the glory days of Apollo. They are pursuing multibillion-dollar programs to construct a space station and explore the moon. Their annual spending on space is estimated at $1.3 to $3 billion, many times what Russia spends on its much-depleted space program. As a Chinese scientist said, recently, "In science there is only a Number 1, no Number 2."

China hopes to exploit the moon's abundant supply of helium-3, a rare isotope on earth that some scientists believe may prove to be a clean fuel of choice when used in nuclear fusion reactors. Chinese scientists are talking of a colony on Mars.

Necessity is truly the mother of invention. Challenging the unknown creates new problems. New problems require new solutions and these new developments generate "fallout" or "spinoffs" for humanity. Over the last forty years, there is not a man, woman or child in America who has not been favorably impacted by the space program.

Whether it is advances in fire fighting technology, sewage recycling, communications, medical technology and instrumentation, manufacturing, agriculture, drought and hurricane forecasting or educational technologies, what NASA initially developed for astronauts in space has found its way into our daily commerce. Space spin-offs have led to the development of new products and new markets that strengthen our economy and improve our quality of life on Earth — today as well as in the future. Space technology works for you, for me, and for all Americans in ways that are transparent or unknown to most people. What an incredible record of accomplishment it has enjoyed and such a significant return on investment over the last 40 years.

Trying to justify a manned-space program based on economics, science, etcetera, is almost certain to fail. Who justified building the great cathedrals in Europe in the Middle Ages as a percentage of their gross national product? Some of them represented an investment over centuries.

Economic problems and social progress were serious issues in 1961— much as they are today. So was the budget. But President Kennedy showed that even in hard times you cannot take your eye off the future. While responding to the needs of today, we must also invest in tomorrow.

As a result of the vision of our leaders in the early sixties, America manifested its technological leadership and gained the upper hand in the Cold War. Great challenges, such as the ISS or going to Mars, represent more than our sustained commitment to technological leadership. Developing and deploying the Space Station is as important to our children's generation as the successful implementation of the Apollo program was to America in the Sixties. As James Michener once said so eloquently at a hearing in the U.S. House of Representatives, "We risk great peril if we kill off this spirit of adventure, for we cannot predict how and in what seemingly unrelated field it will manifest itself. A Nation which loses its forward thrust is in danger, and one of the most effective ways to retain that thrust is to keep exploring the possibilities."

The world leadership the United States has enjoyed since World War II stems from many factors. One of the most crucial sources of American leadership over the last half of the 20th century has been our technological superiority. The aerospace sector provided the key area of struggle between the United States and the Soviet Union through the height of the Cold War. Technological leadership is absolutely central to American economic, political, military, and diplomatic power.

The engineering prowess developed in space initiatives is employed in a variety of activities across the economy. The space enterprise is a research and development engine that benefits sectors far removed from initial contact with outer space exploration. Without the research and development necessary to maintain that edge, our position as the world's leading power will be in grave jeopardy.

A passion for discovery and a sense of adventure has always driven America forward. These deeply rooted qualities spur our determination to explore new scientific frontiers and spark our can-do spirit of technological innovation. Continued leadership depends on our enduring commitment to science, to technology, to research, to learning. Such a commitment, in conjunction with accelerating technology gains, will trigger a renaissance of exploration and, in the end; it will do what exploration always does—*it feeds the human spirit.*

After two decades without a clear goal that excites Americans, NASA, for the most part, has slipped from the public consciousness except when disaster strikes. The people employed by NASA want to go somewhere. They look back at the journeys of Apollo with nostalgia and hope for the day when the country allows NASA to, once again, go somewhere.

Tasks that can be relegated safely and efficiently to robots, automated equipment, and unmanned launch vehicles should be performed in that manner. But the heart and spirit of the American space enterprise lies in the manned spaceflight program and we must use people for those activities where they have an advantage.

While space might seem to be an entirely technical domain, the most important byproducts of the space program are actually emotional ones.

The program was, in fact, conceived in emotion—first for national security and then for the need to feel the thrill of beating a rival society to the moon. We have experienced many other emotions since then: joy; pride; awe; and occasionally, horror.

That's why it's hard to imagine a space program without people. We could fill up untold gigabytes with the data streams of probes, monitors and robots soaring through the heavens. But an unmanned mission, with its data collection, could never put a spring into your step or fill your heart with pride the same way John Glenn did when he returned to space, this time as a wise old man.

America is at a crossroads. Will history record that we took one step into the void, then turned and, for the longest time, retreated to home and hearth? Or that we retained our nerve, our hunger for horizons, and embraced our destiny?

Are we to maintain our technological leadership and invest in our future or do we want to mire ourselves solely in the problems of the day and squander our future? The choice is ours. We can build an International Space Station, go to Mars and invest in our future and that of our children or we can forgo our leadership in space. To me, that is no choice—let's get on with going to Mars. The future waits! It is time for another "giant leap for mankind!"

Epilogue

AT THE AGE OF FIFTY, NASA has its hands full. The Space Shuttle Orbiter returned to flight in July 2005, but the impact of the Columbia disaster is reverberating far beyond a two-year hiatus in manned space flights. While unmanned programs are enjoying major accomplishments, the human space program is reeling from a combination of four factors: 1) the Columbia disaster, 2) the Columbia Accident Investigation Board (C.A.I.B.) Report, 3) NASA's overreaction to that report, and 4) President Bush's "Moon, Mars and Beyond" space initiative. Many things are changing at the agency, but it is hard to say what is improving.

Only days after the Columbia disaster, a statement was first leaked and then released, to the effect, "NASA could have staged a rescue mission had *managers recognized that fatal damage had been done.*" There were two caveats. 1) Management had to have been aware of "mortal danger," and 2) they would have to have learned of the lethal wound "almost immediately." Both of these requirements were physical impossibilities.

The media seemed to buy the far out rescue scenarios emanating from both inside and outside of NASA; scenarios that may have been technically possible but were absolutely impractical in the real world.

It is little more than wishful thinking to claim the loss of the crew of Columbia was preventable following the insulation strike. Only one thing could have saved the crew: proper risk assessment of the foam insulation failures on earlier missions, followed by aggressive corrective measures. Failures like those with the insulation would have been handled quite differently by the NASA of the Sixties and Seventies.

You are on the side of the angels to argue that the crew of Columbia could have been saved if NASA had only correctly analyzed the insulation strike on the orbiter. That might be comforting but would serve no one well; wishing won't make it so. In holding out false hope, even after the fact, NASA further compromises their credibility, something the agency can ill afford. The fact is, no one can be absolutely certain one way or the other, but it makes sense to consider only realistic scenarios when considering the possibility.

The Columbia disaster has frequently been compared to the Apollo 13 oxygen tank explosion. The thinking goes: since NASA saved Apollo 13, they should have been able to save Columbia. But Apollo 13 is not a good analogy for Columbia.

Apollo 13 experienced what I characterize as an *objective* emergency; it was quantitative in nature. Saving the lives of the crew was a case of measuring consumables and developing procedures to conserve them for four days. The consumables would either be sufficient or they would not. All the critical decisions were made *after* the triggering event and became part of the solution.

The Columbia disaster should be thought of as a *subjective* emergency—dependent on opinions and judgment calls for critical decisions—not objective measurements. All the critical decisions were made before the event and, thereby, were part of the problem.

The Monday morning quarterbacks seemed blissfully unaware that after-the-fact analysis, made with full knowledge the crew was doomed without outside intervention, is decidedly different from any analysis conducted in real time. In real time, with death only a potential consequence, emphasis is on mitigating the problem. To put it bluntly, reckless schemes are a luxury for second-guessers.

NASA's rescue scenario assumed that information to justify a decision to prepare Atlantis for a rescue mission was "miraculously" obtained five days after the January 16 launch of Columbia. Implicit in their scenario was the sacrifice of the Columbia to a watery grave. It also assumed Columbia's consumables could be stretched to 30 days—until 15 February. That might have been possible if NASA were willing to compromise some long-standing safety standards here and there. It would have required immediate cessation of crew activities, which would seem to rule out the EVA essential for confirmation of damage to the thermal protection system (TPS).

A spacewalk by a Columbia astronaut faced obvious problems. Columbia had two spacesuits but no maneuvering units and no robotic arm. NASA would have had to conclude the severity of the damage within a few days, in order to develop and check out procedures for an emergency spacewalk inspection and possible repair. Engineers would have had to conclude precisely the opposite of their real time conclusions. Not likely!

An EVA inspection by the crew of Columbia would have been difficult and risky, but justified by the gravity of the situation.

Successfully repairing any breach in the Thermal Protection System
(TPS) would have been much more difficult than the inspection, and it
would have a vanishingly small chance of success. The wing repair NASA
considered ex-post-facto would have been woefully inadequate to survive the 3,000-degree heat of reentry. It was confirmed, early on, that no
modification of the reentry attitude or trajectory would have reduced the
heat load enough to change the outcome.

Since a repair was relatively easy to rule out, the investigation focused
on staging a rescue operation. It would not be as easy, morally, to justify
imposing unusual risks on the crew of the Atlantis rescue vehicle—
though the Atlantis crew would surely have volunteered.

In order to be met by a live crew, Atlantis, which was six weeks away
from launch, would have had to complete all critical pre-launch safety
checks and launch no later than February 12th. That required compress-
ing the Atlantis pre-launch prep down to less than three weeks. In doing
so, NASA would have had to violate a great many procedural rules established specifically to insure crew safety. Still, it wouldn't be impossible *if*
they encountered no glitches in checkout or countdown.

Along the way, NASA would have designated a crew of four for the
mission. They would probably have wanted to send the most experienced
and best qualified astronauts in the office, and they had seven experienced commanders and eleven EVAers available. One commander was
Eileen Collins, who was already training for Atlantis' next mission. To
replace her may have created a problem in that it would have violated the
political correctness to which NASA has been dedicated for more than a
decade.

In this scenario, it is necessary to assume that NASA would commit
to launching the $3 billion Atlantis and exposing it to the same unknown,
potential damage that would prove fatal to Columbia, before fully understanding the cause. That could be considered a reckless decision and
NASA is not noted for making reckless decisions—knowingly, that is.
However, such a decision could be justified if there was a reasonable
chance of a successful rescue.

If a rescue mission proved to be unsuccessful, it would be considered one more bad management decision.

This entire scenario of launching Atlantis to rescue Columbia would have required enough evidence to justify the biggest decision in human spaceflight history—dumping Columbia into the ocean.

In the opinion of the Chairman of the Columbia Accident Investigation Board, Admiral Harold Gehman, "The mission would be very, very risky, but not impossible."

In the real world we have to deal with real facts. The foam insulation strike was noted on day two. It would (and did) take a couple of days for analysts to conclude the strike *could have* dealt a mortal blow to Columbia. Only then would NASA have moved to obtain confirmation by high-resolution earth or satellite based cameras.

It would take at least several days to position a satellite and obtain pictures. At this point NASA would still be trying to *confirm or disprove* a suspicion of danger, not to document a disaster. For many reasons, the satellite pictures could also prove to be non-conclusive.

I believe an EVA, probably with pictures, is the only observation that could support a decision to launch Atlantis and abandon the Columbia. They would also want to rehearse procedures in the water tank to safely perform an unscheduled, emergency EVA, eating up a couple of more days. It is possible even EVA pictures could be non-conclusive, costing a few more days.

Instead of five days, Columbia would have been 7-10 days into its mission before NASA could have gathered enough information to decide whether to:

A) Attempt a reentry, or attempt a repair and then reenter. In either case, we now know Columbia would be lost! Or,

B) Launch Atlantis prior to 12 February, a very difficult if not impossible task, and certainly risky; perform several risky EVAs; and dump the $3 billion Columbia into the ocean, something the Shuttle was not capable of doing autonomously.

NASA and the public would feel better for having tried a rescue and the media would love the story, but the odds against pulling it off are greater than winning the lottery.

It is interesting to note that shortly after the Columbia was lost and Atlantis was 41 days away from launch, NASA gave the impression they could have launched a rescue mission in three weeks. Yet, a year later, in defending a decision to cancel the Hubble servicing mission (SM4), a senior NASA official had this to say: "One of the many lessons we took from the Columbia accident is that, for the Shuttle, we need rescue capability in space. That's where a Hubble servicing mission gets more complex. For a rescue on a Hubble mission, we would need a second Shuttle positioned for launch, which would require an unprecedented double workload, for ground crews. A Hubble rescue would involve a Shuttle-to-Shuttle crew transfer, which is something we've never attempted. All this would have to be done under extreme schedule pressure because Space Shuttle life support, food and water are extremely limited."

In July 2004, a NASA internal presentation admitted that 60 days was possibly less than the time required to prepare a second Shuttle mission to rescue a crew that had reached a "safe haven" at the ISS.

What a difference a year makes!

Regardless of the criticism of NASA's performance during Columbia's last mission, the job they did in reconstructing events during that fateful reentry measured up to their best of the past. A painstaking search by 30,000 workers over thousands of square miles of East Texas and Louisiana recovered some 84,000 pounds of debris from the Columbia breakup, approximately 38 percent of the spacecraft. They did an amazing job of reconstructing the spacecraft from the pieces.

It was an eerie feeling walking into the hangar where this painstaking work was going on—an experience not to be forgotten. For the hundreds of NASAites working on this special, but gruesome assignment, it was an honor. The faces in the hangar were somber, but they went about their work lovingly, displaying nothing but caring and pride. It was evident they were engaged in more than just piecing together broken pieces of cold metal. Not one would rest until the job was done, but there was neither complaining nor bragging about what they were doing. They spoke of their work with such emotion you would have thought the crewmembers were family. These men and women were on a very personal mission, and they were the best in the world at what they were doing.

The hangar maintained a near clean room atmosphere. Big trucks delivered the debris in large containers. Each piece was handled with white gloves and given a bar code noting what it was and where in Texas or Louisiana it had been found. Everything was meticulously tagged and displayed for easy assessment. It was then sent to the discipline from which it originated: hydraulics, fuel, boosters, communication, etc.

A grid work and an outline of the Shuttle were drawn to 110 percent scale on the hangar floor. As each piece was identified and labeled, it was placed on the grid in the precise location where it belonged on Columbia. Positively identified pieces were tagged in a unique color to distinguish them from those awaiting identification. Along the outer walls of the hangar, stacked floor to ceiling, were metal bins holding pieces yet to be identified. Plans, charts and shop drawings for the Orbiter were laid out on large tables. These documents were used to show exactly where each identified piece belonged.

It was impressive to watch an engineer look at a small piece of torn, jagged, scorched metal and know immediately where to place it on the grid. The average time for identification was about two hours. When an especially critical piece of structure was identified, a team would sometimes be sent to the impact site to search for other pieces of the puzzle. The team was frequently successful.

The "black box" data recording system was a wonderful find. Data from the onboard sensors continued to function well into the breakup of the Columbia and provided the earliest indications of heat building up in the left wing. It furnished clues that could be used to improve the survivability of future space vehicles and possibly the three remaining Orbiters.

A special jig for the leading edge of the left wing was built in clear acrylic, permitting engineers to see inside the wing even as pieces of Reinforced Carbon Carbon were identified and overlaid on the acrylic. The fact that the least amount of material was recovered from an area around wing panel 8 was telling. The forensic evidence from the wreckage, correlated with telemetry, sensor data, eyewitness accounts and other analysis pointed convincingly to the foam strike Columbia suffered during launch as the cause of the accident.

While some news reports immediately after the accident suggested that the crew died as soon as the Shuttle broke apart, the space agency and the Columbia Accident Investigation Board withheld comment about such details. The crew module proved to be a pretty good container, and it was the last part of the vehicle to come apart. It appears the Columbia astronauts could have lived for nearly a minute after their final communication with mission control and well after the first signs that the Orbiter was in serious trouble.

With Columbia, as with every other space disaster, the faint-hearted came out of the woodwork to save us from the risks of exploring this ultimate frontier. Detractors were concerned age and corrosion had taken its toll, or the Shuttle was too fragile, or space was too dangerous an environment, or the wear and tear of going in and out of space was greater than anticipated. Reason usually prevails, and NASA gets back to the business of flying in space relatively quickly. With Columbia, NASA managers seemed ill prepared to fend off these modern day Luddites, and unwilling to resist or offer alternatives to recommendations in the C.A.I.B. Report.

The truth is, Columbia will not be the last space tragedy! It may not even be the last attributable to the factors common to all three of our space disasters—overconfidence, complacency, and bad management decisions.

In responding to the C.A.I.B. Report and public criticism, NASA could add so many constraints on the Shuttle in the name of safety, it could lose its operational flexibility or no longer be capable of performing the missions for which it was designed. It wouldn't be the first time engineers, managers, and Congressional Committees took the position it was their "duty" to rid the program of all human risk. In the past, when appropriate, these overreacting do-gooders were politely but firmly resisted by the NASA team.

Historically, deficiencies in the Shuttle system have been less culpable than failures in the management decision process. If management's track record was as good as the Orbiter reliability for the last 20 years, NASA would still be in good shape.

The Space Shuttle was developed to carry large, heavy payloads and crews into near earth orbit on a routine basis, *not* to be 100 percent fool-proof and absolutely safe. No country can afford such a luxury. President Kennedy did not say, "We will make spaceflight absolutely safe in this decade, and when we have achieved that, we will go to the moon."

According to the Columbia Accident Investigation Board, "The physical cause of the loss of Columbia and its crew was a breach in the Thermal Protection System on the leading edge of the left wing, caused by a piece of insulating foam which separated from the bipod ramp section of the External Tank at 81.7 seconds after launch, and struck the wing. During reentry, this breach in the Thermal Protection System allowed super-heated air to penetrate through the leading edge insulation and progressively melt the aluminum structure of the left wing, resulting in a loss of control, failure of the wing, and break-up of the Orbiter."

The report made a number of recommendations, mandating some "to be accomplished before returning to flight." The greatest operational impact will come from the requirement for complete on-orbit inspection of the Thermal Protection System. Even with a new boom extension, it is unlikely an EVA crewman will be able to reach all of the tiles. Repairing TPS damage when it is found will always be a marginal procedure, and no one can guarantee that more damage won't be done by the repair than was there in the first place.

NASA administrator, Sean O'Keefe, announced he would do *everything* recommended by the C.A.I.B. even *before* their report was finished. But recommendations are just that, recommendations, not something which management must blindly accept. Leadership demands that intelligence, common sense and operational factors be applied in considering which recommendations to follow, when, and by how much. Even in their wounded state, NASA knows more about what went wrong and what needs fixing on the shuttle than any committee of instant experts. They know where the Shuttle's original development was under-funded and which Shuttle upgrades or enhancements they have been reluctant to fund over the years.

When O'Keefe says, "We've got to focus beyond [Columbia] to correct everything we think might stand in the way of flying *as safely as humanly possible,*" he sounds like the most devout convert, willing to adopt any and all recommendations or suggestions coming from the power on high—the Columbia Accident Investigation Board. Following Columbia, NASA made pronouncements about launching Shuttle missions only during daylight hours to improve video monitoring; proposed landing all Shuttles at Edwards AFB in California to minimize the danger to people on the ground should another shuttle breakup on reentry; and reducing crew size—an alternative that doesn't improve the odds of survival but does reduce the number of people exposed to the risk. I can't imagine these nice sounding but fruitless restrictions ever being implemented.

O'Keefe's response to the Report? "Recommendations on deficiencies will be not only met, but exceeded. If it applies to the Shuttle, it ought to apply to every program at NASA."

What nonsense! It misses the point completely! Human spaceflight has always lived with trade-offs. All programs do not carry equal risk nor do they offer the same benefits. The acceptable risk for any particular program or operation should be commensurate with the potential benefits. The goal of management should be a system that puts safety first, but not safety at any price.

The most costly proposal to improve crew survivability, in terms of operational flexibility, is restricting Shuttle missions to the same orbit as the Space Station. (The station would be occupying a Shuttle compatible orbit today if President Clinton had not insisted that Russia be included as a full partner in the project.) A Shuttle constrained to fly only to station compatible orbits will lose billions of dollars in lost payload capability, but that is less important than the lost mission opportunities.

NASA should at least explore alternatives to some of the Accident Board proposals that make spaceflight in the future more expensive, less useful and not necessarily safer. Does NASA not believe in a thing they have been doing with the most amazing flying machine ever built? Considering what it is called upon to do, the Space Shuttle is the safest manned space vehicle the U.S. has ever developed. Its record of two failures in 113 missions translates into reliability greater than 98 percent—and good management decisions could have avoided both failures.

The hardware, operational, procedural, and training "fixes" made to the Shuttle will add cost, weight, and additional complexity, but will improve its reliability relatively little. In the process, some dubious improvements will be funded and some of the so-called "fixes" will introduce new risks to the program.

Human spaceflight is not an endeavor that can be "perfected," in the sense that all risk can be eliminated. Since risk is inherent, operating the Shuttle will always be risky, never routine and, even after years of flying, will require careful attention and tender loving care. Flight safety should always be a high priority, but the key to a successful program is living with those risks that are commensurate with the expected gains.

NASA Management was strongly criticized following the Challenger disaster, but little changed and management culture remained a problem. The Columbia Accident Investigation Board also cited management culture as a principal cause of the Columbia disaster, decrying management's apparent unwillingness to hear bad news and the lack of upward communications.

NASA's response to the Columbia crisis was to transfer personnel, establish new committees, and reorganize. They also hired a behavioral science consultant to assess NASA's organizational problems. Among other things, the consultant found that, more than a year after the Columbia disaster, space agency workers were still afraid to speak up about safety. This led to a three-year contract to provide intensive, one-on-one coaching ("sensitivity training") to the agency's top managers. That is a 21st century solution that would have been neither needed nor attempted in the age of Apollo.

Internal communications and organizational concern about safety are consequences of the organization's culture. They are symptoms. Treating these symptoms is essential, but does not necessarily address the disease.

During Apollo, we concerned ourselves with safety but not NASA's attitude about safety. That flowed from the culture and was one of our strengths. Insiders today wonder whether the agency's safety culture can be improved without compromising the agency's other strengths.

Hardware and operational changes cannot protect flight crews from poor decisions spawned by the organization's culture. Culture is not a problem that can be fixed with a bigger budget or higher pay for NASA engineers, or more inspectors. There may be good reasons to reorganize the space agency and change key managers, but that won't solve the culture problem, either.

Culture is difficult to define because, in many ways, it is in the eyes of the beholder. Culture reflects the basic values and practices of an organization. It underlies how the employees do their work; it is usually ingrained in the early days of an organization; and in ongoing bureaucracies it takes years to change. The culture problem that permeates the agency will not be fixed overnight. It took a couple of decades to deteriorate, and it will take many years to get it back to what worked—if it can even be done. It is virtually impossible to reinvent bureaucratic government agencies as corporate entities regularly do, usually in response to competitive market forces.

Two prerequisites to "fixing" this critical problem are 1) management must acknowledge the problem, and 2) they must have a good understanding of what it is that has been lost. The accident board got it exactly backwards when they characterized the cultural status quo that existed prior to Columbia. To paraphrase the C.A.I.B. Report, the board said the problem arose from NASA trying to hold on to the Apollo culture instead of changing with the times. Some individual managers have added, "The culture of Apollo has outlived its usefulness."

That sounds a lot like "not invented here," especially when those expressing this opinion were not there in the Sixties and Seventies.

Overconfidence, particularly by the flight crews, was a factor in the deaths of three friends in the Apollo 1 fire. With a strong culture of individual responsibility, the program recovered in time to fly five missions and land a man on the moon two-and-a-half years later.

In the early years of NASA, spaceflight programs were driven by managers and leaders who came out of the X-plane test flight culture. It was a culture that accepted risk and failure as inevitable aspects of operating in space. Accordingly, they placed great emphasis on reducing the chance of failure by attention to detail. Those people are gone today and they took with them much of the corporate memory. Today is a new world with a risk-averse management culture. Given their different life experience, I can understand their different perspective on risk/benefit.

Astronauts in those early years had a pure test pilot mentality. We had the invaluable experience of living with the birthing of our spacecraft and growing up with the vehicles we were going to fly. The design compromises and the changes *not* made became an important part of our common history. As the program grew and could afford the luxury of specialists, the astronaut office became less homogeneous. For more than 20 years, new astronauts have reported and been presented with a fait accompli in the Orbiter vehicle. It is much like reporting to a new squadron to be checked out in a new flying machine, with little awareness of the tradeoffs and compromises made during design and testing.

Drawing a contrast with "the good old days" is not meant to disparage the many fine engineers and managers who are doing the best they can in the current environment. No one believes for a minute that any of them knowingly or intentionally compromises safety.

Complacency and overconfidence, in spite of numerous instances of exhaust gas leakage through a solid rocket booster seal, were factors in the Challenger disaster during launch.

After twenty years of living with foam insulation shedding from the Shuttle's external tank, NASA management became complacent and failed to fix it even as the problem grew more dangerous. It was eventually treated as an acceptable flight risk and a chronic maintenance problem that culminated in the 2003 breakup of Columbia during reentry.

If NASA management could become complacent about launch and reentry, the two most dangerous phases of any mission, might not this same attitude infect other aspects of Shuttle operations?

There is no room for complacency or overconfidence in human spaceflight. The current attitude, stated or implied by Administrator Sean O'Keefe and other key managers, is that good intentions, or lack of malice, or trying their best are acceptable substitutes for good judgment and satisfactory results. They are not! In manned spaceflight, only results count, not efforts.

Those who were there know that NASA began to depart from the so-called Apollo culture by the late seventies. The problem is that NASA was unable to preserve the culture of Apollo as the agency grew and became more bureaucratic. They allowed it to slip away or even hastened its demise.

An organization's culture starts at the top. Former NASA Administrator Dan Goldin's era of "faster, better, cheaper" was not better, was less safe, and delivered only on the promise of cheaper. During his decade, focus switched to avoiding individual blame or accountability and a "shoot the messenger" mentality. Risk avoidance became part of the new culture, even as mission operations became more risky.

With funding for NASA down to less than 0.7 percent of the federal budget, research spending in the NASA safety office and the personnel level have been cut almost in half, wiping away much of the corporate memory, an important ingredient of management culture. NASA's answer is to add committees and boards in the decision-making hierarchy.

In response to the C.A.I.B. Report, NASA established a new, "independent" Engineering and Safety Center staffed by 250 engineers. NASA should absolutely have an engineering capability, but the Center could easily become one more layer of bureaucracy, diluting responsibility and insulating management even further from critical decisions, such as "launch commit." In the "good old days," we depended on the quality of the decisions not the number of people involved.

Admiration for the ethos of Apollo as something to be emulated is not universal. Some have gone so far as to say that the organization for accomplishing Apollo was inefficient and poor. That is beyond my comprehension! Even if they wanted to, it would be a real challenge for any Administrator today to regain NASA's founding culture without ever personally experiencing what it was.

Many of us have been saying for a number of years that NASA lacked focus. In January 2004, for the first time in a decade, an American President made an attempt to address this deficiency. President George W. Bush chose to identify himself with NASA when he announced a new charter and a grand vision for the agency. The basic elements of this new vision were clear, but it appeared to have very little input from engineers and the operations specialists. How the plan would be accomplished and how it would be paid for was less clear.

The first goal was really an old one: finish construction of the International Space Station (ISS) by 2010. What constituted "completion" was a bit hazy. Is the ISS to accommodate a crew of three? Six? Seven?

When ISS construction is "complete" in 2010, the Space Shuttle is to be retired. In the meantime, NASA is developing a new Crew Exploration Vehicle that will be used to return to the Moon before 2020. All of this will lead to a manned mission to Mars "sometime after 2030."

This grand vision for NASA, characterized as "The Moon, Mars and Beyond," represents a major redirection of space policy. It specifically omits discussion of funding replacements for the heavy-lift and on-orbit servicing capability of the shuttle Orbiter. The Orbiter's large payload bay, its dexterous manipulator, and the ability to project a human presence and return 100 percent of the weight it carries into space have been at the core of U.S. space policy since the Seventies. These capabilities were considered essential to construct large space structures, to lift and deploy large spacecraft, or to service satellites.

Implicit in the president's new vision and mission for NASA is a decision to abandon these capabilities. Crew and cargo will now be separated and reusable heavy lift for humans eliminated.

Using the Moon as a testing ground for a mission to Mars is, at best, a controversial rationale. We did not have the luxury of, or feel the need for such a diversion of resources for the Apollo landings on the Moon. What has changed? Only our will to do it! If Congress and the public are unwilling to step up to the risk and the cost of setting out for Mars, then a base on the Moon is probably the next best objective. And it may be the only way to eventually get a mission to Mars funded.

A mission to Mars is an ideal goal for our country. A passion for discovery and a sense of adventure has always driven America forward. These deeply rooted qualities spur our determination to explore new scientific frontiers and spark our can-do spirit of technological innovation. Our continued leadership of our world is dependent on an enduring commitment to science, technology, research, and learning.

Space technology improves the quality of life on Earth in ways that are transparent or unknown to most people. Research and development associated with space exploration is an "engine of change" that benefits sectors far removed from the space industry. What is initially developed by NASA for astronauts in space, eventually finds its way into our daily commerce. The engineering capability developed in space initiatives is applied to a variety of activities across the economy. Without the research and development necessary to maintain an edge, America's position as the world's leading economic power will be in jeopardy.

President Bush's commitment to a new exploration initiative was risky in the same ways that President Kennedy's was in 1961. There were political, technical, human, and economic risks. The *political risk* sits squarely on the shoulders of the President because there is no huge constituency clamoring to send humans to Mars. According to the polls, most Americans would rather spend money on domestic needs.

The *technical risk* should be well in hand. We first went to the Moon in 1969 and, given our current technology, only the high cost and the willingness to try have stood in the way of an active Mars program for the last quarter century. We may be able to go to Mars faster, and possibly even safer, if we put off this monumental voyage of exploration long enough. But it is not likely to get cheaper, and we may run out of the will to do it at all. A human mission to Mars is much more feasible today than was a manned landing on the Moon when President Kennedy announced the intention in 1961. Eight-and-one-half years later, "man on the Moon" was history. President Kennedy enunciated a simple vision, and then stepped back and allowed the engineers and scientists to determine how to do it right.

The huge *human risk* in any mission to Mars may seem overwhelming to our increasingly risk averse society. For many, human space flight will always seem extravagant and illogical. We have always had to coexist with those who opposed fording the next river, crossing the next sea, or traveling beyond the next ocean. Most successes are preceded by many failures. No one remembers those who tried to fly the Atlantic before Charles Lindbergh, but they went. We celebrate successes after the fact, and very conveniently forget the failures, even though they contribute to the accomplishment.

A society with the capability really has no choice but to continue. To quote George Cecil, "On the plains of hesitation lie the bones of countless millions, who, at the dawn of victory, sat down to rest and, resting, died."

The potential cost of establishing a Moon base and going to Mars was conveniently ignored in the new vision for NASA. Money, one measure of the *economic risk,* is the real obstacle. To support new exploration activities, President Bush proposed funding of $1 billion in new money, spread over five years. To augment this pittance, NASA was challenged to divert $11 billion out of their five-year projected funding to support the new initiative. Even if that amount could be freed up without decimating worthwhile projects, it would be woefully inadequate. No one and no country can send humans into space on the cheap.

There are several truisms about space exploration. One of them is that space exploration will always be risky. Another is that space exploration will always be expensive. Without an honest assessment of the cost of the program and a commitment to fund it, NASA's new vision is little more than an unfunded mandate. Without adequate funding, a vision is nothing more than a hallucination.

It is not difficult to estimate the cost of the lunar portion of this grand adventure. The Apollo Moon landing program cost about $25 billion, equivalent to $100-125 billion today. Returning to the Moon now will be at least as difficult and no less costly than it was in the Sixties. We have already paid for some of the infrastructure, and NASA is more experienced today and armed with better technology. But NASA is also more bureaucratic with less efficient management. Optimistically, we could return to the Moon for $90-100 billion. That is 75-80 percent of what it cost in the Sixties. It is also only slightly more than what Americans spend on alcohol each year.

The Mars portion of the dream should cost another $100-150 billion.

Surely, we can afford to spend what we do on alcohol each year for such a grand and rewarding voyage of exploration. It should not be done at the expense of current programs.

Historically, NASA has enjoyed a symbiotic relationship with Congress whereby NASA over-promises on results and low-balls the cost of new programs. This seduces Congress into funding the program. When the under-funded program is, inevitably, late and over budget, NASA is criticized mercilessly by Congress and the public. It would be nice, just once, to see Congress endorse a program based on realistic expectations and honest cost estimates from NASA.

Two days after President Bush delivered his "Moon, Mars and Beyond" speech, NASA announced the first casualty of the new initiative. They were canceling the last Space Shuttle mission to repair and upgrade the Hubble Space Telescope (SM4), originally scheduled for 2005. The public outcry over the cancellation drowned out support for the new initiative. No doubt NASA was thinking about the time that would be saved and the $500 million to $1 billion they believed could be diverted to the new initiative if Hubble was abandoned.

SM4 was to have been the only remaining Shuttle mission not dedicated to completion of the ISS. Hubble's contribution to scientific knowledge has been more valuable than the ISS. Since the first human servicing mission fixed its original blurry vision, the Hubble Space Telescope has been one of the most remarkable facilities in the history of science. It has rewritten the astronomy books and our understanding of the universe. With the now-cancelled equipment upgrades, Hubble could continue its breakthrough scientific observations into the next decade.

NASA claims the Webb Telescope will replace the Hubble in 2011, but no observatory seriously planned for launch anytime in the next 10 years can replace the optical and ultraviolet capabilities of Hubble. The Webb should be a wonderful instrument if its highly experimental design works, but it is not a proven observatory, and its infrared capability would be complementary to the Hubble's visible and ultraviolet range, not a replacement for it. It took 18 years to take the Hubble from design stage to launch in 1990, and today the Webb is in its design stage.

NASA would not abandon Hubble just for the money that would be saved. I believe the cancellation was due to NASA's reaction to the *Columbia* disaster. Administrator O'Keefe, citing the safety recommendations of the C.A.I.B. Report, had this to say about his decision: "It was one based on risk exclusively." He described a Shuttle flight to Hubble as "a one-of-a-kind, unique, very different and riskier mission...that's not a risk that I could deem to be an acceptable one." Presumably, this was because the Shuttle Orbiter would be unable to reach a safe haven" at the ISS from the Hubble orbit.

The NASA Administrator was expressing no confidence in what is arguably the world's greatest flying machine, after spending two years and $700 million to make the system even safer! The Hubble orbit, now considered too risky, has been the destination for two-thirds of all Shuttle missions. On 90 occasions since 1962, manned spacecraft have been launched into orbits from which they could not reach the ISS. Was Mr. O'Keefe suggesting those 90 missions were not worth the risk?

Those ninety missions were not only worth the risk, they paved the way for everything we are now accomplishing in space. In the process, they built the agency Mr. O'Keefe was heading. The current attitude on risk adds fuel to the fire for those critics who say the ISS is there to serve as a destination for the Shuttle, while the Shuttle exists only to service the ISS.

Is an agency, unwilling to accept the risk of flying a truly great spacecraft in familiar Earth orbits the right one to deal with the inherent risks of landing humans on the Moon, let alone sending them to Mars? Then again, NASA's attitude is consistent with society's growing desire for a risk-free existence. NASA was established to explore the unknown, evaluate the risks versus gains, and then take calculated risks to move our society forward. With today's attitude about risk, we would never have reached the Moon or become preeminent in human space flight.

We should continue to improve the safety of both missions and spacecraft, but we cannot allow failures to paralyze our ability to move ahead. NASA management should take a more pragmatic approach to the technical, political and emotional issues of spaceflight. Yes, we have lost flight crews, but it wasn't the end of the world. If NASA insists on avoiding risk at all costs, they could be sounding the death knell of manned space activity.

Nothing in the C.A.I.B. Report precluded the Shuttle from flying missions that could not reach the ISS, the only destination on Mr. O'Keefe's shuttle itinerary. Harold Gehman, the C.A.I.B. Chairman, showed more flexibility than the Administrator, saying, "Only a deep and rich study of the entire gain vs. risk equation can answer the question of whether [a Hubble servicing mission] was worth the risks involved."

While O'Keefe talked incessantly about reducing risk, he rarely mentioned the tradeoff between risk and reward, even though NASA is the most qualified agency to carry out such analysis. Gehman at least acknowledges that each mission is a balance between perceived risk and the benefits to be gained.

Most astronauts disagreed with cancelling the Hubble servicing mission, believing if we fail at something, it should be because we are unable to do it, not because we are unwilling to try it in the first place. In the golden age of flying to the Moon, we each had a commitment: "If this mission fails, it won't fail because of me!" Today, the motto at NASA seems to be, "If anyone dies in space, it won't be because of a decision I made."

At least a few of the former Air Force pilots now at NASA headquarters should be able to recall the counsel of Boots Blesse, an Air Force double Ace from the Korean War. When Boots returned, he documented the lessons of air-to-air combat in a manual titled, *No Guts, No Glory*, which served for three decades as the authoritative guidance on how to train for and fly in combat. A good dose of Boots Blesse's philosophy is needed at NASA and with our national leadership.

In truth, some missions are marginally more risky than others. But NASA would not have returned the Shuttle to flight unless they believed the problem that destroyed Columbia had been fixed, which reduced any need for an orbital safe haven. This also tends to further equalize any difference in risk profiles between a Hubble mission and an ISS mission.

Even with sophisticated risk assessment techniques and decades of experience, we still cannot calculate an absolute value for the risk on a particular mission. However, the techniques are quite useful for comparing the relative risk between different missions. A case could be made that a mission to the Hubble Telescope orbit has *less* risk exposure than one to the ISS.

Over half the contribution to total mission risk comes during the launch phase, with the Shuttle main engines the major culprit. The next largest contribution comes from reentry, and the balance from orbital operations. A Hubble mission should fare somewhat better during launch phase, while all other risks are more or less comparable. A Hubble-bound mission, carrying a lighter payload than most missions to the ISS, requires less thrust to reach orbit, lowering the risk of engine failure and improving the abort capability.

For a station-bound mission to execute an abort-to-orbit, where the shuttle parks in orbit while a safe landing plan is worked out, all three main engines must fire for 282 seconds. For a Hubble bound mission abort to orbit, the engines have to fire for only 188 seconds, providing 94 more seconds of safety.

For a return-to-launch-site abort, Hubble missions fare even better. Regardless of destination, the Shuttle's main engines must fire for no more than 232 seconds if it is to glide back to Cape Canaveral. If the engines failed between 232 and 282 seconds, a station-bound flight could not execute abort to orbit or to Florida. (A trans-Atlantic abort capability would have been available.) On the other hand, a Hubble bound mission will have a window from 188 to 232 seconds in which it could abort to either Florida or to orbit (or a trans-Atlantic abort).

In response to the public outcry over cancellation of SM4, NASA began to scramble. O'Keefe agreed to have his decision reviewed by the National Academy of Sciences. But on that same day he told reporters that no matter what the study found, he considered a Shuttle mission to Hubble out of the question. "Somebody else would have to make that decision—not me, because I'm not doing it," he said.

At the time, NASA embarked on a campaign to sell the public and Congress on a robotic servicing mission as the answer to extending Hubble's life. In the process, they could demonstrate new technologies to advance its broader space exploration agenda. Everyone would like to see a robotic servicing mission that worked, but in attempting one, NASA would have been risking science, exploration, taxpayer dollars, and possibly even human lives—all to adhere to an artificial "safe haven" requirement for human missions.

The Hubble was designed to be serviced by Shuttle astronauts, not robots. Prior to the Columbia tragedy, the Shuttle flight manifest listed SM4, the planned Hubble servicing mission, for 2004 or 2005, and another Shuttle mission in 2011 to retrieve the telescope or attach a propulsion stage that would enable a controlled deorbit.

After Columbia, SM4 was pushed back to 2006, and the 2011 Hubble retrieval/deorbit flight was changed to a robotic deorbit mission. This was predicated on the crew of SM4 attaching devices to Hubble that would make the subsequent robotic end-of-life mission easier to accomplish. This would have allowed NASA time to develop and demonstrate currently unproven robotic rendezvous and servicing techniques before they were needed in 2011.

In January 2004, when NASA cancelled SM4, citing safety concerns for Shuttle astronauts, they moved up the Hubble robotic mission to 2007. This "faster, smarter, sooner" robot would have been required to perform the servicing tasks originally scheduled for SM4. That is, doing twice as much with half the time to prepare, and a predictable impact on cost.

NASA officials asserted "it is possible a robot will work." Of course, it is also possible the robot will fail, in which case it could cost more than a Shuttle flight. The priorities for a robotic mission were:

1. Attach a deorbit motor that would permit a future, controlled descent into the sea;
2. "Don't break the Hubble," (assuming it was operating when the robot arrived);
3. Replace the batteries; and
4. Replace the gyroscopes (a close fourth).

If successfully executed, this plan could buy Hubble an additional four to six years of service. It didn't even mention upgrading the scientific capability, which was an integral part of SM4. Based on past history, even a less-challenging robotic servicing mission would have a good chance of failure. And no one brought up the possible unintended consequences of such an outcome.

Robotic rendezvous and docking is an absolute requirement for a robotic servicing mission. The Russians have performed this routinely for 25 years, but NASA has no spacecraft capable of doing the same, and it is debatable if we had the time or the funding to develop one.

Robots are unproven and risky. Our experience suggests that a rushed robotic servicing mission, using unproven technology, would have been expensive and likely to fail, as with these past attempts at automated operations:

> NASA's Orbital Maneuvering Vehicle was cancelled in 1989, after three years, when the estimated cost exceeded $1.3 Billion. Europe's Automated Transfer Vehicle originally scheduled for completion in 2002, is three years late and will cost over $1 Billion.
>
> Japan's Hope Transfer Vehicle is running six years behind its original completion date.
>
> NASA's program to demonstrate automated rendezvous, with both spacecraft designed specifically to rendezvous and dock with each other, is running six months late.
>
> A number of NASA's past attempts at robotic or partially automated approaches resulted in satellites being incapacitated or left in a useless orbits. Intelsat VI, Syncom IV, Palapa-B, and Solar Max satellites would all have been failures if not for direct, "hands-on" intervention of humans in space. In each of these cases, the ingenuity of humans in space, sometimes resorting to extraordinary means, overcame unanticipated problems that could not be resolved robotically.

A robotic servicing mission would have had increased risk exposure for innocent bystanders on the ground.

According to NASA policy, "safety is prioritized to protect: (1) the public, (2) astronauts and pilots, (3) the NASA workforce, and (4) high-value equipment and property." An uncontrolled reentry of the Hubble telescope would have a 1 in 700 risk of casualty to persons on the ground, when the established historical standard for such casualty risk is 1 in 10,000. Since a rushed and complex robotic servicing mission was *less* likely than a manned mission to successfully install a deorbit rocket on the Hubble, it was *more* likely to lead to an uncontrolled reentry, thereby increasing the possibility of loss of life on the ground. Whether a robotic servicing mission would have been reliable enough to meet the accepted standard, or whether NASA is still committed to meeting this standard, is unknown.

The Hubble was never designed to be robotically docked with a robot, let alone to be serviced by robots. And since robotic on-orbit servicing has not been demonstrated, any such servicing mission is clearly a risky program. Therefore, NASA must have a backup plan for a failed Hubble robotic servicing mission. Without an announced backup plan, we could have a repeat of the 1979 public fear over the death plunge of Skylab, followed by a public outcry for a Shuttle servicing mission to Hubble. At that point, public policy makers would have faced a Hobson's choice among three painful alternatives:

Attempt another robotic de-orbit mission, with improved or different hardware and software than the first failed attempt. Whether this could be accomplished before Hubble begins to tumble, making a robotic approach impossible, is not clear.

Ignore the risk of a ground fatality and allow Hubble to make an uncontrolled re-entry into the Earth's atmosphere. This would not only risk lives on the ground, but exposes the government to potential claims for property damage from whatever nation on which debris may fall.

Conduct a rushed Shuttle flight—with the same risks as SM4—but producing only a safe de-orbit and none of the scientific benefits of SM4.

The unintended, but predictable result of attempting to reduce risk to human life by robotically servicing Hubble would have been a further risk to human life, either on the ground or in space, or both, at a greater cost to taxpayers than the manned servicing mission. NASA's January 2004 cancellation of SM4 had these negative impacts on the Hubble end-of-life mission:

The challenging robotic de-orbit mission, originally planned for 2011-12, would have to be carried out 3-4 years earlier, because once Hubble's batteries or gyroscopes fail, the telescope will tumble and be much harder, if not impossible, to capture robotically.

Because SM4 did not prepare Hubble for a robotic rendezvous and capture (e.g., installation of optical targets and other aids), the robotic mission is more difficult to accomplish even if it stayed on the original schedule.

A new Spectrograph and Wide field Camera, already built at a cost of $250 million would be effectively dead, since they would have to be placed deep inside the telescope after the removal of existing instruments. This is considerably more difficult and risky than bolting new gyros and batteries to the outside of the observatory and connecting a few cables.

In the absence of good logic to support O'Keefe's cancellation of SM4, it had to be a political decision. He could hardly be blamed for believing he had little to gain by using the Shuttle to repair the Hubble, but a lot to lose if there was a Shuttle failure. But when logic was not used to reach a decision, logic will not be effective in changing that decision—something engineers have a hard time accepting.

With the odds so high against its success, the robotic servicing mission would eventually be cancelled. NASA could claim they gave it the old college try, but it would still raise questions about whether the robotic servicing mission was intended to save Hubble or to save NASA management from more public criticism.

(In 2006, the Hubble Servicing Mission 4 was reinstated in NASA's mission planning.)

NASA took the position that they had so much work to do just getting the Shuttle back in the air that they couldn't afford to be distracted by a Shuttle mission to Hubble. The hurdle for returning the Shuttle to flight was set so high by the administrator that it was very difficult to get off the ground. But the requirements for "return to flight" were a self-inflicted overkill. When you insist on a 100 percent chance of survival, at every phase of a program, it gets extremely difficult to accomplish anything. The ultimate refuge in their safety net was a so-called "safe haven" on the ISS, an unproven concept that introduced new questions and further delays.

O'Keefe said, "Each mission to the station will afford Shuttle crewmembers up to 45 days of safe haven aboard the station, which would give NASA—or possibly the Russians—time to launch a rescue mission." In this scenario, the ISS, which could not yet support a crew of six without augmenting the life support systems, would be expected to accommodate as many as ten (3 from the ISS and 7 from the Orbiter) for

45 days, and possibly longer.

Someone once said, "Be careful what you wish for, you may get it." The prospect of docking a Shuttle at the ISS that proves to be incapable of reentry, forces NASA to make additional changes before the Shuttle flies again. Suppose the shuttle reaches the station, docks, and transfers the crew successfully, but is damaged beyond repair; e.g., an attempted tile repair that is not 100 percent effective. The Columbia TPS damage would probably have fallen into this category.

What would NASA do with the Shuttle? It could not be left permanently attached to the station because of the problems it would create for station control systems; it could not be separated and left in orbit, because the orbit would eventually decay and endanger thousands of square miles of area during an uncontrolled reentry. And NASA has neither designed nor tested an automatic undocking and deorbit of the Shuttle. If NASA gains that capability, would they risk landing the vehicle? Or, would they just dump it into the ocean?

Many functions on the Orbiter are controllable from the ground but there are a number of critical actions that can only be performed manually; e.g., starting auxiliary power units; deploying the air data probes, landing gear, and drag chute; and braking on landing rollout. Most of these functions could be automated, but would that be the best use of NASA's limited resources for a low probability event in a limited program that was being phased out in 2010? Such changes would guarantee further delays in getting the Shuttle back in the air.

The ISS safe haven, along with complete on orbit inspection, repair, and rescue capability are unreasonable requirements that can cause the Shuttle to become too costly, too encumbered, and too restricted to fly productively.

If the Space Shuttle really is "retired" in 2010, long before NASA has any replacement, it will be another great loss. The Shuttle Orbiter is the only vehicle capable of carrying to and from the ISS the biological and engineering equipment necessary to perform the research needed to accomplish our future goals in space. Some station systems are broken, while others are in frequent need of repair. Ground crews and station residents can usually come up with innovative techniques to conserve fuel, water, clothing and other supplies. But some systems can't be fixed without Shuttle visits because new parts are too big to fit aboard Russian re-supply vehicles. If things go according to plan, NASA will have no capability to capture, repair, or return satellites, or to fly laboratory type missions in low earth orbit after 2010.

Enthusiasm for the ISS seems to be fading. The consensus among "ancient astronauts" is: too grandiose; too expensive; and in the wrong orbit to support operations beyond low earth orbit.

Ferrying people and cargo and constructing a space station is extremely difficult, but it has not captured the public's fancy. The ISS is the most complex project ever devised by man, on or off the planet, and was intended to be the cornerstone project for human space exploration into the foreseeable future. Even though it is over budget, it is largely successful. It was another giant step into the unknown—an engineering feat unrivaled in human history, right up there with the Pyramids and the Panama Canal.

Alas! The pyramids have lasted for 6,000 years, while the ISS seems headed for the junk heap of history in the middle of the next decade, only a few years after its "completion."

Will NASA's new vision get the agency back on track and rekindle enthusiasm for the space program? Probably not—at least not for a long time! It will take men in space doing spectacular things, like the Hubble Telescope repair missions, or the Moon landings. The public wants Buck Rogers operating at the edge of the envelope and the boundaries of our knowledge, not educator astronauts and the occasional civilian tourist. Americans want bragging rights inherent in a national program, not the watered down satisfaction of sharing in an international consortium. Without truly challenging goals at the cutting edge of the envelope, public enthusiasm and Congressional support will stay pretty flat. Put another way, "No Buck Rogers, no bucks."

Exploration is part of the American character. It is in the genes of humanity, and outer space remains "the final frontier." We are compelled to search for life elsewhere in the universe, and Mars is the next destination because it offers the nearest and best chance of finding that life.

Human history has been written by explorers, and the benefits of exploration are clear. The argument against society's expenditures on exploration has changed little since the time of Alexander the Great. Can't opponents come up with something better than, "If you gave me the money, I'd do something different."

Before the President's new charter for NASA, Mr. O'Keefe said, "We are not going to be destination-driven." He went on to explain how we could develop the hardware and overcome the problems and then get on with a national dialogue about where to go and how to use our new capability. He couldn't have had it more wrong!

It is the challenging goals that generate the needs that drive inventions, not the other way around. We cannot decide to sit out the next generation of exploration and catch up later when we have the tools. No one, especially Congress, is looking for neat, new technology; they are looking for missions to match our imaginations. If that mission does not include humans, it will not sustain interest and will quickly lose public support. And without a clear destination, human spaceflight cannot be sustained politically.

President Bush's vision statement at least gave us the Moon and Mars as destinations.

There were no "hard" targets in the vision statement except the 2010 date for completing the ISS and grounding the Space Shuttle. If the date for the next Moon landing is "before 2020," and we don't go to Mars until "sometime after 2030," there is obviously no sense of urgency on the more grandiose objectives. Why not relax the 2010 deadline as well?

Since we are not in a hurry, why not keep flying the Shuttle until the new Crew Exploration Vehicle (CEV) is in hand? Orbiter retirement should be tied to first flights of the CEV, not the arbitrary date of 2010. There doesn't necessarily need to be an overlap of the two vehicles, but there should not be a long hiatus, either.

When the Orbiter was certified for flight following the Columbia disaster, it should have been cleared for all missions in its performance envelope, not just to the ISS.

Many of the stringent safety requirements NASA imposed on the Shuttle as prerequisites to its "return to flight," will become unacceptable constraints on future vehicles and operations. The requirements for rescue capability, in-flight inspection and repair, and safe havens for all phases of flight exceed the safety provisions for all earlier NASA programs. These will prove unrealistic and insurmountable constraints on missions to the Moon or Mars. It will put NASA in the position of telling astronauts on those missions that they cannot be provided the same level of safety as present day Shuttle and ISS crew members.

When the ISS is supposedly out of NASA hands or out of orbit by 2016, how will they rationalize operating in low earth orbit without a rescue capability or a safe haven?

If a low earth orbit safe haven is a necessity for the Shuttle, which has flown 113 times, how will NASA rationalize launching out of low earth orbit to the Moon on a new, unproven system?

If this kind of flawed logic is used in this instance in the name of safety, where else might it be applied in the future to rule out some real or perceived danger?

Many of the current generation of scientists say, "Only send robots because it costs too much to send people and it's too dangerous." But when asked what stimulated their interest in science, 80 percent of those same scientists say it was the manned space program of the 1960s.

It will ultimately require a human presence on Mars to examine the details of the ancient past of the planet. Scientists agree that robots are a valuable tool for exploration, but they are inferior to humans in terms of speed and in grasping what's been observed and judging what to do next. NASA's Spirit rover on Mars, over the course of its 2-3 year lifetime, will accomplish what an astronaut could do in a day or two. The science return for putting a person on Mars is exponentially better than for a robot.

There are any number of technical, psychological, and physiological challenges to be overcome before attempting a mission to Mars (and returning, of course). The technical problems will be the easiest to overcome, and there is no reason why we should not begin to develop the hardware for the journey.

A big problem may be simply overcoming boredom on the two plus years trip. Apollo 7 was only an 11-day mission, but we flirted with boredom during the last several days. A highly motivated male crew should be able to adjust to the group dynamics and close quarters for the long round trip. I am not convinced it is a mission on which to send a mixed gender or an all female crew.

The human body can probably overcome all the physiological obstacles except one, and that one is a possible showstopper. We have no solution to the radiation exposure to humans when traversing deep space.

During the Apollo missions to the Moon, the direction of the principal radiation flowing out from the Sun was known and, to some degree, predictable, and the spacecraft could be oriented for maximum shielding effect.

That is not the case in interplanetary space. Enroute to Mars, the crew will be well beyond the protection of the Earth's magnetic field and the Van Allen Radiation Belt, and radiation will bombard them from *all* directions for more than two years. We will need a breakthrough in either protection or immunity to make the trip feasible for humans. Humans will only experience a telepresence on other planets unless one of three things is developed: 1) lighter weight shielding, probably some form of electromagnetic diversion of the various sources of radiation, or some as yet undiscovered technique; 2) medicine to reduce the effects of or to ward off radiation sickness; or 3) means to get to Mars so quickly that the reduced exposure to radiation makes it less hazardous. This could be achieved by nuclear propulsion, if environmental fanatics can be kept at bay.

When we reach Mars, we will have to deal with the problem of radiation reaching the surface of the planet. With a density of only one percent of that on Earth, the Martian atmosphere provides little protection from radiation.

No matter how much we would like to go to Mars, it takes three things to undertake such a complex project: the resources, the technology, and the will to do it. Driven by the cold war, those three elements all came together in the Sixties, and we went to the Moon. It was an anomaly in time. Without some similar unique circumstance forcing us to action, neither the Congress nor any President will have the "will to do it." In the aftermath of Columbia our will seems to have been reduced even farther, if that is possible.

In the brave, new world of NASA, the "right stuff" may be going out of style.

For sales, editorial information, subsidiary rights information
or a catalog, please write or phone or e-mail

IPICTUREBOOKS
1230 Park Avenue
New York, New York 10128, US
Sales: 1-800-68-BRICK
Tel: 212-427-7139 Fax: 212-860-8852
www.ibooksinc.com
email: bricktower@aol.com

www.ingram.com

For sales in the UK and Europe please contact our distributor,
Gazelle Book Services
Falcon House, Queens Square
Lancaster, LA1 1RN, UK
Tel: (01524) 68765 Fax: (01524) 63232
stef@gazellebooks.co.uk

CPSIA information can be obtained
at www.ICGtesting.com
Printed in the USA
BVHW07s0825200618
519524BV00001B/28/P